THE LICE

THE LIBRARY AS PLACE

History, Community, and Culture

Edited by John E. Buschman
and Gloria J. Leckie

Foreword by
Wayne A. Wiegand and John Carlo Bertot

LIBRARIES UNLIMITED

A Member of the Greenwood Publishing Group

Westport, Connecticut • London

Library of Congress Cataloging-in-Publication Data

The library as place : history, community, and culture / edited by John E. Buschman and Gloria J. Leckie ; foreword by Wayne A. Wiegand and John Carlo Bertot.
    p. cm.
  Includes bibliographical references and index.
   ISBN 1-59158-382-9 (pbk : alk. paper)
    1. Libraries–Social aspects.   2. Libraries and community.   3. Library architecture.
   I. Buschman, John. II. Leckie, Gloria J.
  Z716.4.L485   2006
   021.2–dc22   2006033743

British Library Cataloguing in Publication Data is available.

Library of Congress Catalog Card Number: 2006033743
ISBN: 1-59158-382-9

First published in 2007

Libraries Unlimited, 88 Post Road West, Westport, CT 06881
A Member of Greenwood Publishing Group, Inc.
www.lu.com

Printed in the United States of America

The paper used in this book complies with the Permanent Paper Standard issued by the National Information Standards Organization (Z39.48–1984).

10 9 8 7 6 5 4 3 2 1

Contents

Foreword *by Wayne A. Wiegand and John Carlo Bertot*   vii

Introduction

1. Space, Place, and Libraries: An Introduction   3
    Gloria J. Leckie and John E. Buschman

Section I: The Library's Place in the Past

2. Beneficial Spaces: The Rise of Military Libraries in the British Empire   29
    Ronald Tetreault

3. Libraries in Public before the Age of Public Libraries: Interpreting the
    Furnishings and Design of Athenaeums and Other "Social Libraries,"
    1800–1860   41
    Adam Arenson

4. A Grand Old Sandstone Lady: Vancouver's Carnegie Library   61
    Ann Curry

Section II: Libraries as Places of Community

5. The Fruit and Root of the Community: The Greensboro Carnegie Negro
    Library, 1904–1964   79
    Julia A. Hersberger, Lou Sua, and Adam L. Murray

6.   Locating the Library as Place among Lesbian, Gay, Bisexual,
      and Queer Patrons   101
        Paulette Rothbauer

7.   Behind the Program-Room Door: The Creation of Parochial and Private
      Women's Realms in a Canadian Public Library   117
        Pamela J. McKenzie, Elena M. Prigoda, Kirsten Clement, and
        Lynne (E.F.) McKechnie

8.   Seattle Public Library as Place: Reconceptualizing Space, Community,
      and Information at the Central Library   135
        Karen E. Fisher, Matthew L. Saxton, Phillip M. Edwards, and
        Jens-Erik Mai

Section III: Research Libraries as Places of Learning and Scholarship

9.   Stimulating Space, Serendipitous Space: Library as Place in the Life of
      the Scholar   163
        Karen Antell and Debra Engel

10.   Setting the Stage for Undergraduates' Information Behaviors: Faculty
      and Librarians' Perspectives on Academic Space   177
        Lisa M. Given

11.   The Research Library as Place: On the Essential Importance of
      Collections of Books Shelved in Subject-Classified Arrangements   191
        Thomas Mann

Section IV: Libraries, Place, and Culture

12.   On the Myths of Libraries   209
        Bonnie Mak

13.   Managing Pleasure: Library Architecture and the Erotics of Reading 221
        Abigail Van Slyck

14.   Going to Hell: Placing the Library in *Buffy the Vampire Slayer*   235
        Adriana Estill

Index   251

About the Editors and Contributors   257

Foreword

"Libraries are more than resources," writes media critic and cultural historian Siva Vaidhyanathan in a December 2, 2005, *Chronicle of Higher Education* article, in which he seeks to provide an alternative perspective on the Google Library Project to make available online the full text of millions of public-domain books. "They are both places and functions," he continues. "They are people and institutions, budgets and books, conversations and collections. They are greater than the sum of their books."

When we took over as coeditors of *Library Quarterly* in July 2003, we determined to publish several special issues during our tenure on topics that demonstrated how libraries were "more than resources." Our plan was to find qualified scholars on each of those topics who would agree to function as special issue editors, solicit manuscripts that spoke to the topic, and select from among those submitted five or six of the best of the lot to fit into a single issue of the *Quarterly*. Among the topics we selected in 2003 was "library as place."

To edit this special issue, two people immediately came to mind: Gloria J. Leckie of the University of Western Ontario's Faculty of Information and Media Studies, who had written with colleague Jeffrey Hopkins an outstanding article published in the July 2002 issue of the *Quarterly*, entitled "The Public Place of Central Libraries: Findings from Toronto and Vancouver," and Rider University library faculty John Buschman, whose brilliant *Dismantling the Public Sphere: Situating and Sustaining Librarianship in the Age of the New Public Philosophy* (2003) was the centerpiece of his American Library Association's Elizabeth Futas Award. When we asked both if they would agree to become a team to put together the special issue, they quickly accepted, and shortly thereafter issued a general call for papers.

What followed, however, surprised us all. While we were hoping for six good papers, submissions soon numbered over thirty. Obviously, "library as place" was on the research agenda of more LIS scholars than we anticipated. Gloria and John spent considerable time carefully screening the essays, and ultimately came back to us with their conclusion: they had so many good papers, they did not want to limit themselves to six. Would we instead agree to allow them to publish the essays as a collection in a separately issued monograph? Of course, we replied, convinced it was much more important to our profession to introduce librarianship to the best work on "library as place" than to fill *Quarterly* pages.

So before you are the results of Gloria and John's editing efforts, a series of quality research essays on "library as place" that we recommend highly. Taken together, they can help broaden our professional vision, expand our research discourse, and perhaps enable us to see opportunities to further connect our libraries even more closely to our host communities. They all demonstrate convincingly that for their users libraries are indeed important places to be, and they also suggest that libraries are important as places for many more reasons than we currently realize. It is the hope that this book will encourage others to research the "library as place" so we can discover even more of those reasons.

Wayne A. Wiegand and John Carlo Bertot
Coeditors, *Library Quarterly*

Introduction

I

Space, Place, and Libraries: An Introduction

Gloria J. Leckie

Faculty of Information and Media Studies,
University of Western Ontario, London, Ontario, Canada

John E. Buschman

Department Chair of Moore Library,
Rider University, Lawrenceville, New Jersey

Libraries as spaces, libraries as places—such phrases are frequently used, but what do they really mean? We recognize libraries as physical entities where a complex mix of activities, processes, actions, and performances occur on a daily basis. We know that they acquire and house an ever-changing array of cultural resources for public use. We also know libraries are a type of social and cultural institution, fitting within a larger context of other institutions, agencies, and corporate interests, such as schools, governments, public services, businesses, and other socially created entities. Accordingly, a wide variety of people (both users and staff) visit libraries, bringing their individual values, beliefs, expectations, assumptions, daily practices, and cultural awareness. How does this complicated set of characteristics, including elements from the personal, the private, the public, the physical, the intellectual, and the cultural, coalesce into the space or place that we call the library? What is the difference between the library as a space and the library as a place? Does it matter if libraries are spaces, or places? If so, what ultimately makes the library a place?

Our purpose here is to present an array of answers to those questions. Libraries, as a component of cultural space, are ubiquitous to almost every society during almost every time period. However, as places of cultural, symbolic, and intellectual meaning, libraries have varied greatly. From the royal library serving the elite of ancient Mesopotamia to the cross-cultural scholarly library of Alexandria, the private libraries of the Greek philosophers, the Cathedral libraries of historical Britain, the university libraries of colonial America, and the contemporary public library, all have played a role in the development, collection, and spread of knowledge during their respective eras. All have represented a particular kind of place at a particular period in time to a particular culture and community.

To capture both the ubiquitous nature of libraries and their particular place-based character, this volume is dedicated to library spaces old and new, real and imagined, large and small, public and private. As such, the essays contained within provide diverse and wide-ranging perspectives on the role and place of different kinds of libraries as cultural institutions as well as the library as a physical, social, and intellectual place within the hearts and minds of its clientele and the public at large. With such in mind, let us now take a look at some of the thinking/theorizing that has gone on about space and place in general.

SPACE AND PLACE IN SCHOLARLY DISCOURSE

Ideas about space and place have been articulated for centuries and in this respect, what is old is new again. For Greek mathematicians such as Euclides, place was subordinate to the space of geometries, with place being points in a matrix, a location within finite dimensions. Conversely, Greek philosophers such as Plato, Aristotle, and Philoponus saw place as the more prominent concept integrated into their respective ideas about the cosmos, the void, and ontology. Not until the seventeenth century did modern notions of space emerge, such that by the eighteenth century, place "vanished altogether from serious theoretical discourse in physics and philosophy" (Casey 133).

Although there is insufficient room to detail of modern conceptions of space, some of the most long-standing include absolute, extensive, and relative space. Absolute space is associated with Newton (1642–1727), whose ideas extended those of Gassendi (1592–1655). Unbounded and infinite, absolute space precedes the universe and will continue to exist after the universe ceases. It is invisible and it cannot be measured. It subsumes the notion of place "by making it a part of space, that is, a mere portion of that which is always already there. . . . As such, place has no being or identity apart from that of space itself and is determined . . . by whatever attributes are ascribed properly to absolute space." (Casey 144). By way of exception, extensive space (as per Descartes 1596–1650) portrays all space as containing matter of some sort, bodily extensions that are integral to space. "Not only does matter occupy space, but space *is* matter" (Casey 153). Accordingly, for Descartes, there is no void, and place becomes a subordinate characteristic of both space and matter. Rejecting Descartes, Locke (1632–1704) then posited relative space, a concept not unlike some of the early geographical understandings of space and place discussed later in this chapter. For Locke, space incorporated a plurality of places, which sat in relation to one another through distance. Thus "place is what human beings create when . . . they set about determining the distance between the positions of things" (Casey 165). Like Newton, Locke also imagined space as absolute and infinite, but it is not surprising given the complexity of the topic that differing and competing visions of space/place should exist within the work of a single writer.

Within the modern academy, the concepts of space and place have continued to vex philosophers, geographers, sociologists, cultural theorists, and other interested scholars for most of the previous century. Geographers, with their concern over the earth's spatial surfaces and the content of those landscapes, have been theorizing ideas about space and place throughout that time and have built a large body of literature putting forward various conceptual frameworks. Since academic geographical writing extends back into the 1800s, it is possible to see how notions about space and place have evolved by exploring some key works since that time and the thinking about space and place that these works have exemplified.

Early geographical scholars, many of whom were influenced by explorers and voyages of discovery, naturally emphasized the elements of the physical world, which was regarded as the space against which human activities occurred. A good example of such early work is the five-volume *Cosmos*, by Alexander von Humboldt. Writing in the mid-1800s, von Humboldt painstakingly described the physical geography of Central and South America, where he had spent five years traveling. In *Cosmos*, he detailed all of the natural elements of the physical spaces through which he had traveled, including the flora and fauna, altitude and temperature, as well as how variations in the physical environment produced differences in human settlements and agricultural practices. Physical space, basically regarded as the canvas for the development of human society, was therefore seen as more complex and important than the mere physical setting alone.

However, some nineteenth-century theorists believed that place, as a concept, was distinct from space. Foremost among these was Walter Christaller, whose ideas regarding "central place theory" were influential for almost a century. Christaller regarded "places" as villages, towns, and cities existing in a hierarchical relationship to one another, with some places being more central in the hierarchy than others. These central places provided goods and services to a cluster of surrounding smaller places, which in turn could be central places in a network of increasingly smaller towns and villages. The larger the central place, the larger the range of goods and services provided to lower-order places within the hinterland. Within such a theoretical framework, places were regarded as urban areas of human settlement and habitation with a primarily economic function to provide/distribute goods and services.

It is probably fair to say that these two basic approaches to space and place held sway in geographic thinking well into the twentieth century. Space was the established backdrop against which human societies arranged their affairs, whereas places were human creations, generally encompassing the locations where people lived. Agnew (*Space: Place* 82) captures this distinction quite succinctly when he states:

In the simplest sense, space refers to location somewhere and place to the occupation of that location. Space is about having an address and place is about living at that address. . . . Place is specific and space is general.

One of the most controversial results of thinking about space/place in this relatively simplistic way was the rise of environmental determinism, which held sway well into the twentieth century. Environmental determinists believed that human society was shaped by the environment of the earth's surface and that within those constraints, only certain kinds of human development were probable. Some of the most egregious examples were posited by Semple, who made astonishing claims such as

- living in a plains area is "stultifying to national life" (479) because of its extreme monotony;
- those who live in mountain passes tend to be marauders and robbers (586);
- "a cold climate puts a steadying hand on the human heart and brain" as opposed to warmer places where "national life and temperament have the buoyancy and thoughtlessness of childhood, its charm and its weakness" (621).

While environmental determinism was eventually discounted, remnants of it linger in various discourses about certain places to this day.

Even at its zenith, many geographers rejected environmental determinism in favor of other more holistic ways of looking at spaces and places. A strong competing tradition of geographic scholarship known as "arial differentiation" stated that it was the role of geography to examine how smaller places and larger-scale spaces (such as regions) came to be through the integration of a particular set of specific characteristics. Within this tradition, regions became the focus of study and regional analysis the methodology, examining a region's physical features, climate, vegetation, population, industries, socioeconomic organization, and landscape change. Places, then, were cast as sites of habitation within the larger-scale spaces of regions, so by extension would vary according to their regional location. Both regions and the places within them could be systematically described and analyzed, thus facilitating greater understanding of how different spaces and places took on their particular characteristics and how they changed. The regional perspective was prominent well into the latter half of the twentieth century.

CHANGING VIEWS IN THE SPACE–PLACE DISCUSSION

Despite the fact that earlier views of place and space (especially the regional focus) were widely held by many geographers, important and discipline-altering shifts in the thinking about space and place occurred during the post–World War II era. For one thing, through the blending of physical and cultural geography, it became increasingly apparent that macroscale environments (i.e., spaces) and the implications of the human uses made of them (i.e., places) could not be ascertained by simply detailing or describing the contents of certain landscapes. Fraser Hart's monograph *The Look of the Land* is one example of the transition to this mode of thinking and writing within rural geography. Hart demonstrates how the familiar and seemingly natural large-scale spaces of rural landscapes can produce both the natural environment and human activities simultaneously. He comments:

As a general rule, men cannot live where they cannot grow food. . . . Making a living by producing food . . . not only must be considered one of the most fundamental human economic activities, but it also plays a major role in shaping the rural landscape. . . . Any rural landscape is the product of a host of independent decisions made by the multitudes of individuals (including groups behaving as if they were individuals) who control and have controlled the individual pieces of land. If we wish to understand the look of the land, we must identify the individuals who have made the decisions and we must try to learn why they made them as they did. (67)

Although Hart's work is classically descriptive at times, it is nonetheless an early attempt to unpack the wide variety of factors that went into constructing a rural landscape. In this vein, he was in the vanguard of later, more sophisticated studies that explored the ways in which space and place are represented through various culturally constructed landscapes. Because landscape is regarded as symbolic, elements such as social/power relations and labor conditions can be teased out through a close analysis or reading of its features and processes. Landscapes can include extensive parts of the earth's surface (such as the Prairies), particular places (such as a cityscape, neighborhood, or national park) or even the interior spaces of the mind (as revealed through the representations of landscape in paintings, literature, etc.). Current examples include an exploration of "therapeutic" landscapes of health and well-being (Kearns and Gesler), landscapes of tourism and the leisure society (Aitchison, MacLeod, and Shaw), Arriess' work on creating the landscape of a Vietnamese refugee community in New Orleans, and Domosh's examination of nineteenth-century New York's retail district and skyline.

It became apparent during the post–World War II era that places were much more complex than being simply areas or locales of human habitation—they involved human perception and imagination. At the forefront of this more phenomenologically oriented perspective was Yi-Fu Tuan, whose work *Topophilia* set the stage for new ways of looking at places. Tuan defined topophilia as the "affective bond between people and place or setting" (4). He argued that, across cultures, there were many common elements in the ways that people viewed places of personal importance. He commented that "the human mind is disposed to organize entities into antinomic pairs ... (e.g., seaside vs. mountainside, below vs. above) ... and to seek their mediation ... certain colours, particularly red, black, and white, acquire symbolic meanings that overstep cultural boundaries" (246). He also showed how the places that hold meaning for many cultures, such as the garden, the river, the city, and the neighborhood, are also symbolic, offering a complex interplay of physical sensations and contact, aesthetic appreciation, senses of well-being, familiarity, and attachment, and the culturally constructed ideologies of certain landscapes to their inhabitants (e.g., the notion that rural landscapes and the places within them are idyllic). As a result, humanity's

affective ties with the material environment ... differ greatly in intensity, subtlety and mode of expression. The response to environment may be primarily aesthetic: it may then vary from the fleeting pleasure one gets from a view to the equally fleeting but far more intense sense of beauty that is suddenly revealed. The response may be tactile, a delight in the feel of air, water, earth. More permanent and less easy to express are feelings that one has toward a place because it is home, the locus of memories and the means of gaining a livelihood. (93)

Writing at about the same time, David Harvey provided a far different discussion of space and place in his widely influential work *Social Justice and the City*. Harvey believed that space was not just a blank canvas upon which nonspatial things were drawn, but also the creation of social processes. He comments that

there are various ways that we can think about space.... Space is neither absolute, relative or relational in itself, but it can become one or all simultaneously depending on the circumstances. The problem of the proper conceptualization of space is resolved through human practice with respect to it.... The question "What is space" [is] ... replaced by the question "How is it that distinctive human practices create and make use of distinctive conceptualizations of space?" (*Social Justice* 13–14)

Using a Marxian analysis, Harvey demonstrated how the city as we know it is in fact a large resource system that is spatially structured and differentiated through "fixed capital investments" (*Social Justice* 309–310). As capitalism changes, the structuring of urban spaces changes as well. In a related piece, he elaborates further, stating that capitalist development walks a razor's edge

between preserving the values of past capital investments in the built environment and destroying these investments in order to open up fresh room for accumulation. As a consequence, we can expect to witness a perpetual struggle in which capitalism builds a physical landscape appropriate to its own condition at a particular moment in time, only to have to destroy it, usually in the course of a crisis, at a subsequent point in time. (*Spaces* 247)

One has only to look at the abandoned factories and warehouses in the older areas of many North American cities to recognize the truth of that statement. The many permutations of capitalism, along with attendant characteristics and effects, have undoubtedly done more to shape the spaces and places of our world than almost any other formational process.

Furthermore, Harvey continues, the specific characteristics of urban space are simultaneously reflective of, and constitutive of, social relationships and the ideology of ruling groups and institutions. He suggests that "our culture, conceived of as an ethnic domain, emanates from created space more than it succeeds in creating space" (*Social Justice* 310). He concludes that the urban malaise of alienation is really an expression of our fundamental estrangement from created space.

These ideas are a far cry from earlier notions about space as a backdrop and place as habitation. Thus, by the 1960s and the 1970s, the previously more distinct and more simplistic concepts of space and place had been refuted, or at least had begun to blur considerably, leaving many geographers asking uneasy questions about the proper field of study for the discipline. One response to this was the claim that geography was truly a spatial science and should study spatial phenomena (Johnson and Sidaway 111–118, 135–139), which gave rise to an unprecedented quantitative turn in the discipline sometimes referred to as the "spatial revolution." It seemed that the study and understanding of space was to be reduced to locational analyses, matrices, and directional flows, while places as objects of study became devalued, relegated to the realm of the nostalgic and the quaint (*Devaluation* 9).

INTEGRATION OF THEORIZING ABOUT SPACE AND PLACE

Fortunately, the spatial science phase was relatively short-lived and was eventually overtaken by a plethora of other ways of thinking about space and place and of bringing the two concepts together into some theoretical whole. Agnew (*Space: Place* 89) suggests that there were several major ways that this was accomplished, including

- Feminist approaches, which seek to disentangle the particular social and power relations having a direct impact on women's lives and experiences in historically contingent spaces/places, and to reassert that what happens in those places (such as the home) is worthy of study. Patriarchy, as a system of power relations and related ideologies, constrains the role of women in cultural space and changes how lived places within the cultural landscape are experienced. Prominent feminist geographers who have had been at the forefront of analysis of the ways in which patriarchy has shaped the spaces and places of daily life include Gillian Rose, Gill Valentine, and Doreen Massey. Feminist approaches also have opened the door for the analysis of space and place with respect to numerous disadvantaged and marginalized groups (see, e.g., Sibley's *Geographies of Exclusion*, or *Envisioning Human Geographies*, edited by Cloke, Crang, and Goodwin). Patriarchy, however, is not the only system of thought and practice that shapes cultural space. Incorporating a global vision of constraining forces, Doreen Massey contends that "The spatial ... can be seen as constructed out of the multiplicity of social relations across all spatial scales, from the global reach of finance and telecommunications, through the geography of the tentacles of national political power, to the social relations within the town, the settlement, the household and the workplace.... All attempts to institute horizons, to establish boundaries, to secure the identity of places can ... therefore be seen to be attempts to stabilize the meaning of particular envelopes of space-time" (4–5).

- Neo-Marxist perspectives, which explore the ways in which spaces and places are produced, reified and reproduced by the hegemonic practices of capitalism. In particular, neo-Marxist geographic analyses are interested in the spatial characteristics of capitalism, including regimes of production and accumulation, concentration, spatial inequality, capitalistic expansion, and globalization. There are many scholars who write in this vein, most notably David Harvey and Edward Soja. Soja is a particularly good example of neo-Marxian thinking in that while he recognizes the enormous complexities inherent in late stage capitalism, he attempts to provide new ways of looking at the familiar problem of the restructuring of the capitalist order. Drawing upon the work of Henri Lefebvre, Soja (*Thirdspace*) coined the term "thirdspace" to describe "what is actually a constantly shifting and changing milieu of ideas, events, appearances, and meanings" (*Thirdspace* 2). *Thirdspace*, then, is a more open and flexible way of thinking about "the social production of human spatiality" (*Postmetropolis* 11). To Soja, much of the analysis of spatiality has been either from a "Firstspace" perspective, where the materialist conditions and patterns of life dominate, or a "Secondspace" perspective, where ideas and perceptions about spatiality are more prominent. In comparison, *Thirdspace* analyses examine "fully lived space, a simultaneously real-and-imagined, actual-and-virtual, locus of structured individual and collective experience and agency" (*Postmetropolis* 11). For Soja, spatiality is "fundamentally constitutive of social life" and his writings emphasize that critical social theory "needs to take space seriously if it is to make sense of society" (Latham 270).
- Humanist or agency-based approaches, which look at space and place from the perspective of the sensing human being who is experiencing various aspects of both space and place simultaneously. Valentine gives a good overview of the humanist approach in her monograph *Social Geographies: Space & Society*. She begins with the notion of the body as a space and remarks that "Our bodies make a difference to our experience of places: whether we are young or old, able-bodied or disabled, black or white in appearance does, at least partly, determine collective responses to our bodies" (44). Valentine examines how the body physically occupies space, noting that women's bodies are often expected to occupy less space than men's (41). From there, she explores a range of other spaces and places, including the home, the community, institutions, the street, the city, and the nation. In her discussion of the home, she notes that the home can be experienced as a site of fear, resistance, work, or violence, depending on "who has the power to determine how the space of the home and social relations within it are produced" (85).

Along these lines, an accessible contemporary discussion of space and place can be found in the work of Robert Sack. Although Sack is identified with the humanist approach, his work draws upon a wide range of theoretical perspectives beyond geography. For the most part, he claims that space, as most of us perceive and understand it, is Euclidean.

Although its description is a cultural matter, this space is not a cultural artifact; it is not cultural constructed. Space exists, and the natural sciences take these geometric descriptions to be reasonably accurate. The objects and events of the universe and the world have location and extension in this space. Trees, grass, mountains, and soil occur in it and extend through it. (31)

For instance, even while recognizing that a forest extends through space, we still may refer to it as a place. However, it may be a place in name only, as a convenient way of referring to a location within space. Sack considered this very loose application as a designation for "secondary place" (32), wherein any one secondary place can be replaced with another. Sack is more concerned with what he refers to as "primary places," which are those places that have the ability to influence, affect, and control. Primary places are "delimited, they possess rules about the things to be included and excluded, and they have meaning" (32). Primary places, then, are more artifactural or socially constructed and cannot be replaced.

Primary places are affected by three realms, or forces, including nature, social relations, and meaning. When these three realms are combined in particular ways, "place" thus becomes a force in itself, altering the flow of interactions (whether of people, institutions, or cultural processes) within it. Sack notes that "a social or cultural construction of space means creating place and its interactions" (33). Places can be very different from one another because the ways in which the prevailing forces (nature, social relations, and meaning) and their constituent elements (such as physical resources, labor, and belief systems) are combined and the interactions that flow from those combinations are highly variable. So, for instance, cities as places can differ greatly and have varying impacts within a national or international context, just as can communities and neighborhoods on a smaller scale. Similarly, certain institutions as places have particular affects that may be far-reaching, or not. Sack notes that "libraries, museums, schools, and universities share an interest in the truth. This makes them different from other kinds of places, such as advertising agencies, which create meanings for the purpose of influence and control rather than edification and truth" (69).

How do people figure into Sack's conception of place? People are the agents or "geographical beings" who must continually negotiate the interconnections among nature, social relations, and meaning on a daily basis (73). The mix is constantly challenged and revised with, at some points in time, one force more ascendant than another. Since every place contains social relations, the act of maintaining places perpetuates a particular set of social practices. In other words, places both produce and reproduce the distinctions contained within them. Places "constrain and enable our actions and our actions construct and maintain places" (13). At the same time, they "constrain and enable not only our actions but also the content and extent of our awareness" (17).

Although the feminist, neo-Marxist, and humanist approaches to space and place occupy a great deal of the literature, it could be argued that postmodernist and/or poststructuralist perspectives also should be added to Agnew's list. While it may be that all of the approaches noted in this section incorporate at least some elements of a postmodernist take on space and place, it is still useful to examine such thinking as an area of theorizing in its own right. Two of the most prolific, and some would say controversial, scholars relating to postmodernist spaces are Michael Dear and Stephen Flusty who have written extensively on the topic since the 1980s. In the Introduction to their edited volume entitled *The Spaces of Postmodernity*, Dear and Flusty state that "we live in an era of postmodern consciousness" that there has been an "unprecedented increase in quality scholarship devoted to the relationship between space and society" (11), and that the importance and role of space in social theory has been reasserted through this scholarship.

Perhaps their most thought-provoking paper is the 1998 piece entitled "Postmodern Urbanism" (reprinted in *The Spaces of Postmodernity*). In this paper, Dear and Flusty remind us of the important theoretical groundwork laid by Ted Relph, who distinguishes between modernist and postmodernist cityscapes. For example, the space of modernist cityscapes is characterized by megastructural bigness, straight space (such as city center canyons) versus prairie space (such as suburban vistas), rational order and flexibility (resulting in landscapes of boredom), hardness and opacity (from the displacement of nature with endless freeways e.g.), and discontinuous serial vision (from movement in automobiles). Postmodern cityscape spaces, on the other hand, are "more detailed, handcrafted, and intricate. They celebrate difference, polyculturalism, variety, and stylishness" (217). The authors then go on to posit in more detail some of the other postmodern characteristics of contemporary urban space (using Los Angeles as the main example), including

- Privatopia—walled-community private housing developments;
- Hetero architecture—a mixture of architectural styles reflecting diverse cultural communities;
- City as theme park—prepackaged landscapes of suburban fantasies;
- The fortified city—dividing the city between fortified areas of affluence versus unfortified areas of despair and fear;
- Global latifundia—where everyday spaces are affected by globally integrated consumption regimes;
- Keno capitalism—a seemingly haphazard and fragmented urban landscape is in reality a reflection of an international geographic order of flexible capitalism causing indistinguishable monocultural production, evolving much like the randomly generated spaces on a Keno card.

Dear and Flusty conclude that the spatial model of the concentrically ringed city of previous centuries has given way to a much more complex and dynamic urban spatial form, where there is a "non-contiguous collage of parcelized, consumption-oriented landscapes, devoid of conventional centers yet wired into electronic propinquity" (232). Although some of Dear and Flusty's ideas have been criticized as being too reflective of Los Angeles and not necessarily applicable to other urban centers, nonetheless their commentary on the nature of urban spaces and places in the twenty-first century does capture the general direction of change that many urban places of all sizes are experiencing.

While most of the analyses discussed understandably are related to urban areas, there is also a strong tradition within geographical thought of examining nonurban areas. Along these lines, Cloke and Little have provided a close look at the changing spaces and places of rural areas, remarking that the "cultures of nature and rurality are (re)discovered to be transcending the supposed boundaries of rural geographical space" (1–2). In other words, rural spaces are not realms of idealized country lifestyles but are subject to the same instrumental forces as other parts of society. As such, rural spaces and places have a number of "hegemonic and mythical cultures ... which often serve to hide and marginalize a whole host of other identities" (14) including those of women, children, the elderly, various ethnic groups, and those living in poverty. Despite a strong motif of the idyllic rural environment, the current organizational force underpinning much of the rural space in developed countries is actually that of relentlessly advancing postproductivist agriculture, where surplus production has taken previously cultivated areas of rural land out of the agricultural system. This in turn has fostered changes in labor patterns and migration, giving rise to rural spaces of residence rather than production (Halfacree 72). Accordingly, as with urban areas, the organization, content and relations/ideologies embedded within rural spaces and places have changed irrevocably within the last several decades, and often not for the better.

How do the more contemporary views of space and place from a geographic perspective relate to the notion of library as place? Libraries are part of the cultural landscape writ large, at least in the Western, industrialized nations. As such, it is possible to discern how their presence and role within the changing contours of this landscape have been constructed at different times, in different ways. The place, meaning, and role of libraries within the cultural terrain have always been debated and continue to be (Augst and Wiegand; Buschman; Kranich). Through a neo-Marxian lens, it is possible to understand how libraries are placed within the capitalist enterprise and to see, for instance, that the library philanthropy of Andrew Carnegie in the nineteenth century really may not differ so markedly from that of Bill Gates in the twentieth century in terms of its underlying purpose and effects (Stevenson). Using feminist and critical theoretical analyses of the library as a place of work, scholars such as Roma Harris and Suzanne Hildenbrand have shown that gender plays a huge role in how libraries as workplaces are constituted and how librarians are perceived as a professional group, while Dilevko and Gottlieb have demonstrated that the collection spaces of public libraries may be influenced by subtle biases in the purchasing tools used by librarians. A humanistic approach to the library as place enables us to explore questions related to how libraries function as physical places of embodiment in the everyday, how they are understood and used by their clientele, and what symbolic meaning they hold for their community of users (Leckie and Hopkins). Finally, using a postmodern frame, we may examine how libraries function as sites of surveillance, contestation, and resistance, or as places of inclusion versus marginalization (Lees).

Of course, geographers are not the only contemporary scholars who have been concerned with notions relating to space and place and the centrality of those concepts to our lived experience. A variety of academics from a wide array of disciplines have incorporated ideas related to space and place within their work (see volumes edited by Hubbard, Kitchin, and Valentine; and Crang and Thrift), and in turn have been very influential on geographic thinking. Although this chapter is too brief to discuss these other scholars and their space/place related thinking in detail, some of them include,

- Pierre Bourdieu and the notion of *Habitus* (see the edited volume by Hillier and Rooksby);
- Anthony Giddens and the spaces of social reproduction and change (in *The Constitution of Society*);
- Henri Lefebvre's spatial triad (in *The Production of Space*);
- Donna Haraway and the spaces of situated knowledge (in "Situated Knowledges");
- Benedict Anderson and nations as places (in *Imagined Communities*);
- Manuel Castells and the space of flows (in *Rise of the Network Society*);
- Edward Said and the poetics of space (in *Orientalism*);
- Richard Sennett and spaces of authority (in *The Conscience of the Eye*);
- Michel de Certeau and practiced space (in *The Practice of Everyday Life*).

Along with the various conceptions and permutations of space/place just noted, it also must be pointed out that in the social sciences in particular, there is a long tradition of scholarship regarding the notion of community that can be traced back to the work of Ferdinand Tonnies in the late nineteenth century, and later scholars such as Emile Durkheim, Raymond Williams, Robert Moore, and Victor Turner (Delanty 31–48). However, used as a term that is synonymous with place in common parlance, community can be very problematic because it very quickly breaks down into a multiplicity of other concepts: a place of residence, a way of life, a moral code, a symbolic moment, even a set of social relations that may be place-based (such as a local neighborhood association), place-less (from a generic African American community to a particular online community), or simultaneously place-based and place-less (as in a local reading group which meets both face-to-face and for online discussions). While a community has traditionally been thought of as limited and local, today's increasingly heterogeneous world has produced communities of common interest that are global in focus and transcend even large place-based boundaries such as countries. Thus, although there may be considerable overlap and areas of intersection, the concepts of community and place are not truly synonymous.

Nonetheless, the ideas that a community can form around a place, can create a place and/or have strong ties to a place are notions that fit very well with this discussion of libraries. Libraries, as culturally constructed places, have an important role to play in fostering and developing varying senses of community and providing services to different communities. Libraries as space/place and notions of community, therefore, go hand in hand. As the chapters in this book will demonstrate, libraries sometimes succeed in supporting community and sometimes do not. Nor surprisingly, the ideas that community and library may be mutually reinforcing (or not) leads us into thinking about one of the most important analytical concepts related to libraries, and that is the public sphere.

THE PUBLIC SPHERE

As the discussion above demonstrates, there are a multiplicity of ways in which space and place are theorized and analyzed. However, within the larger academic discourses about place and space, one of the most long-standing and vibrant areas of scholarship and discussion is devoted to the analysis and understanding of "public" spaces, both physical and ethereal, real and imagined, local and global, and the related notion of the "public sphere." The fundamental questions here are, of course, whether such a thing as true public space/sphere still exists and if so, what its characteristics and vulnerabilities might be? Closer to our purpose, we might also ask: How do libraries fit into the ongoing discussion of the public sphere?

In this era of political and social turmoil and the technological and cultural imperatives of late-stage capitalism, the very notion of the public sphere is a hotly debated topic. Goheen notes that when it comes to examining questions about the viability of the public sphere, there appear to be two camps. On one side are those who believe that the public sphere is now a meaningless concept and that the continued alteration of the material conditions of existence have diminished the participatory elements of social life. The control of the public domain has been appropriated by corporate, state, ideological, and other interests, leading to the corollary idea that public spaces, as part of the public sphere, are no longer spaces of public engagement and diversity; rather, they are spaces of fear and/or surveillance, which must be controlled to eliminate the dangers of association with others. Under this perspective, streets, parks, promenades, and other public spaces are places of continual threat, with no real connection to the positive aspects of civic life.

In the other camp are those who argue that the public sphere is very much alive and that public space is still an essential component of this sphere, albeit changed from that of previous eras. "Public space for these authors is a vital locus for moulding public opinion and asserting claims" (Goheen 484). While most scholars writing from this perspective recognize that the line between public and private has blurred considerably and that the shifting spaces of what is regarded as "public" are problematic, there is nonetheless a considerable literature about how contemporary public space functions. Two of the most thorough and interesting (though not necessarily the most recent) discussions of public space are by Stephen Carr, Mark Francis, Leanne Rivlin, Andrew Stone; and Sharon Zukin. Carr et al. begin their commentary by stating that

Public space is the stage upon which the drama of communal life unfolds. The streets, squares and parks of a city give form to the ebb and flow of human exchange. These dynamic spaces are an essential counterpart of the more settled places and routines of work and home life, providing the channels for movement, the nodes of communication and the common grounds for play and relaxation. There are pressing needs that public space can help people to satisfy, significant human rights that it can be shaped to define and protect and special cultural meanings that it can best convey. (3)

Carr et al. examine notions related to the changing nature of public life, the balance between publicness and privateness, the differing types of public space such as symbolic, functional, etc., the impact of technological factors and many other related issues. Despite the changing nature of public space, the authors are optimistic about its status and notes that the pressure from the public for cities to provide recreational venues has led to the development of jogging and cycling paths and other outdoor recreational facilities, all of which add to the stock of public space. In some cities, such as Vancouver, British Columbia, a mix of walking streets with high-density housing, public esplanades, public beaches, desirable parks with natural features, and commercial marketplaces suggest a "strong and blossoming public life" (41).

While Zukin also explores the positive aspects of public life and public space as the "points of assembly where strangers mingle" (45), she tempers her comments with the realization that contemporary public spaces are often contested, fragmented, and encroached upon by private interests (e.g., Disneyfied). Zukin regards these forces as part of the changing landscape of urban public culture, where collective views of what is acceptable in terms of publicness and privateness are continually evolving.

More recent work has tended to look at the diversity of public spaces and the challenges inherent in determining or uncovering the publicness of those spaces. For example, in terms of the physicality of public space and its evolving meaning, Hebbert explores the importance of the street as a repository of shared memory using Berlin as his touchstone, and Southworth looks at how the new types of shopping arrangements such as the "townscape" mall function as a type of public space. Other authors examine how certain technological artifacts contribute to the production and reproduction of certain public spaces. In this vein, Beckmann demonstrates how the automobile has constructed and configured "driving spaces" (598) within everyday life while Li, Whalley, and Williams and Crang examine the electronic spaces of the information economy. Finally, in terms of the impacts of neoliberal globalization on public spaces, Conway posits that the World Social Forum is providing a new kind of public space, which she refers to as "placed, but transnational" (367), the purpose of which is to "give rise to a transnational subaltern counterpublic" (367) that fosters an evolving global citizenship.

HABERMASIAN INFLUENCES

The debate over the definition, existence, evolution, and value of various kinds of public spaces will continue. However, no matter on which side of the public sphere question they find themselves, scholars in all disciplines have been greatly influenced by Jürgen Habermas's work on the public sphere. Habermas' work grounds a transition from conceptions of place to the social role of the library as place and as a locus of inquiry. It is Habermas who allows us to make normative and democratic claims about libraries as places.

While only a sketch of Habermas' thesis is possible here, his is an important conceptual framework for this volume. To begin, Habermas asked a basic question neither asked nor answered yet by historians: How and why did a system of individual rights and democratic rule arise from the complete and closed political system of the absolute divine right of kings? His answer was rooted in ancient and shifting distinctions concerning space and place and their various purposes: in other words, between public and private (*Structural Transformation* 1–5), two realms that were formerly fused. For instance "there is no indication European society of the high middle ages possessed a public sphere as a unique realm distinct from the private sphere" (*Public Sphere* 50). Governmentally, there was no essential division between the private *person* of the monarch and the *public* symbols of power and state authority. The public sphere (in contrast) is not the state, nor a crowd, but rather the historically developed "sphere of non-governmental opinion-making" (*Public Sphere* 49). Trade and the society it engendered essentially grew beyond the ability and authority of government in the person of a king to effectively manage and exert authority, and the turning point was the eighteenth-century development of mercantile economies in northern Europe (*Structural Transformation* 12–19).

Habermas locates the shift toward a public in the commercial and political conversations of the day in new urban public spaces like coffee houses, and via the intellectual press of the day. Both the type of conversations and the places where they took place were new and two crucial things happened as a result. First, opinion became something recorded and communicated beyond the home and acquaintances and, as distributed by and in the press, essentially *created* the public sphere (and its requisite space) with opinions separate from formal government policy: "public discussions about the exercise of political power which are both critical in intent and institutionally guaranteed have not always existed" (*Public Sphere* 50). Second, the act of critique, discussion, and explication of the state's actions created the principle of supervision: The principle that for power to be truly legitimate, its proceedings must be made public. Supervision (in the Habermasian sense) transformed the nature of power and its legitimation through rational critique (what has been called "the force of the better argument") in public discussion in both place and print (*Public Sphere*)—constituting a public forum. What we today understand of libraries as a *public* space with democratic undertones is deeply embedded in the historical processes that Habermas identifies.

Habermas never valorizes this achievement. Rather, his analysis focuses on two crucial problems with the bourgeois public sphere. First, while the public sphere arose among a highly educated, cohesive class, democracy became a mass affair during the nineteenth century. Politics became "a field for the competition of interests" and laws did not "aris[e] from the consensus of private individuals engaged in discussion [but rather] the compromise of conflicting private interests" (*Public Sphere* 54). As rational critique and political will formation began to break down, maintaining the legitimacy of the state became a process of stimulating mass loyalty—both to the state and to the economy in the form of consumption (*Problems of Legitimation*). Second, the economic half of the genesis of the public sphere came to dominate. With formal rights established, the press was "relieved of the pressure of its convictions [and free to] take advantage of the earnings possibilities of a commercial undertaking" (*Public Sphere* 53). In a return to "publicity" and "refeudalization," the press became a means to administer the public sphere in service to a highly volatile and unequal economy: "Public relations do not genuinely concern public opinion [and] the public sphere becomes the court before [which] public prestige can be displayed" (*Structural Transformation* 200–201). Substituting for the spectacle of kingly splendor and authority, the refeudalized public sphere provides ample diversion and pseudo-debate (Peters). Instead of focusing on policy or the extent, nature, and legitimacy of authority in a democratic society, we are presented with the unauthorized release of videotaped celebrity bedroom escapades, "wardrobe malfunctions" at Super Bowl halftime shows and the soap operas of the ensuing governmental hearings, and trumped-up "debates" over the patriotism of candidates for office. Politics thus becomes a form of public relations: "Because private enterprises evoke in their customers the idea that in their consumption decisions they act in their capacity as citizens, the state has to 'address' its citizens like consumers" (*Structural Transformation* 201). In sum, the rational, communicative basis of democratic decision making in the public sphere is corrupted by the commercial culture with which it coincided. In Habermas's terms, an integrated public sphere has been crippled by manipulation in the service of consumerist values, the gyrations of a state on the horns of a democratic dilemma, and the consequent evacuation of meaning in politics and public communication.

FROM IDEAS OF PLACE TOWARD A PLACE OF IDEAS

The transition to libraries-as-public-sphere is suggested in a recent article by Gathegi on the legal doctrine of public forums and its relationship to libraries. While public libraries were the focus of *United States v. American Library Association* (and focus of his analysis), the constitutional issue before the Supreme Court was not necessarily limited only to public libraries. First, public school/university libraries certainly share much the same status as public libraries, which in turn frequently cast themselves as supplemental to these educational institutions. Second, there is a strong argument for private libraries (in universities, museums, etc.) that they too are "public" institutions: the vast number hold tax-exempt status (they are thus subsidized in recognition of their general social benefits); laws specifically protect them (public and private) from particular types of vandalism; the courts have recognized professional privileges like intellectual and academic freedom within them. Third, large endowed private university libraries (like Harvard) describe their missions and collections in national (that is, public) terms and participate in interlibrary lending, share cataloguing records, and make access to their collections available—if on a more limited basis. (Buschman 9–10). Gathegi's analysis of libraries and public forums has broader implications.

The whole of Gathegi's argument with the 2003 Supreme Court decision upholding the Children's Internet Protection Act in *United States v. American Library Association* need not be recounted here. Instead, consider his contention that the Court avoided undertaking an analysis of public libraries as a public forum by "merely cit[ing] the supposition that, for purposes of First Amendment analysis, the[y are] a limited public forum." As a result, "such a characterization determines the different levels for review of regulations that constrain speech" (2). In other words, defining the library as a *particular* type of public place/forum powerfully shapes a core issue (intellectual freedom) embedded in the institution and in its professionals' values through available restrictions on and regulations of expression. Gathegi goes to the heart of definitions of public places and their purposes, grounding the transition from general considerations of place to conceptualizing libraries as *specific* types of places with a strong relationship to free and unfettered interchange (as public sphere/public forum).

Traditional public forums—streets, sidewalks, and parks—hold a high degree of First Amendment protection: "content-based speech regulations in a public forum are proscribed. To survive strict scrutiny, [they] must serve a compelling state interest and must be narrowly drawn to achieve that end" (Gathegi 6). In contrast, libraries defined as a limited public forum results in speech and expressive restrictions and regulations: they "must be content neutral, be designed to serve significant government interests, including public health and safety, and leave ample alternative channels for expressive activity" (Gathegi 7). As Gathegi notes (7–11), such definitions are rooted in conceptions of the purpose of private property—regardless of whether the government is the owner. Chief among these restrictions is the requirement for a governmental intent to create a public forum, the range of uses of the facility, and whether the place (forum) is "compatible with expressive activity" (7), the result of which is a lower standard of expressive protection for libraries than is found in traditional public forums. Further, Gathegi notes an aspect of managerial control to government and its relationship to limited public forums: that being oversight which "focuses on the kind of government property at issue and the historical First Amendment treatment of such property, whether or not the exercise of [such] rights is compatible with the nature of the property" (14).

Thus a narrow and anachronistic definition of the traditional public forum effectively freezes it as a place that preceded the Internet or widespread public libraries—or any newer social place or organization that facilitates expression (Gathegi 13)—specifically at odds with prior Court decisions and contradictory of its characterizations of public libraries as the "quintessential locus of the receipt of information," "as designed for free-wheeling inquiry," and a "mighty resource in the free marketplace of ideas." Ironically, the Court even cited core American Library Association documents like the Library Bill of Rights and the Intellectual Freedom Manual in the process of those decisions (in Gathegi 8–9). In contrast Gathegi argues that the *social* role and *purpose* of public places—libraries in this case—means that they should "fall under a category of public property that exists to facilitate the free exchange of ideas. [T]he public library should assume its seat in the quintessential traditional public forums" with its higher level of First Amendment protections (13–14). Even so, he takes care to review the regulations libraries would still be able to retain so that they could continue to operate *as* libraries—for instance the typical limitations on noise, the booking of meeting or gathering rooms, access to processing areas, etc. (9–11).

The crucial question is begged: what will (or can) take the place of the debased democratic public sphere described by Habermas? He maintains that it is still "indispensable" (Hohendal 47) and not merely a dead ideal: "Rational formation of opinion and will, and personal and political self-determination have infused the institutions of the constitutional state to such an extent that, functioning as a utopian potential, they point beyond a constitutional reality that negates them." The public sphere contains the seeds of its own extension—"unrestricted inclusion and equality" and the victories of the "force of the better argument" to extend formal rights and social inclusion to women, labor, and minorities are indications (*Further Reflections* 442, 425–430). He also (*Postscript* 136–137) sees an express link between the self-constitution of the public sphere and the legal system's function as a "safety net for failures to achieve social integration." There continues to be institutional locations (places) for the functioning of public reason: "the public sphere as the space for reasoned communicative exchange," thought of in terms of a "conceptual triad of 'public space,' 'discourse' and 'reason'" (*Public Space* 2004). This is important because the issue of "when and under what conditions the arguments of mixed companies could become authoritative bases for political action [is] crucial—for democratic theory" (Calhoun 1). The democratic public sphere is not merely a histori-cized theoretical category, it has always been tied to *places* and their purposes—a long overlooked aspect. The obverse is Jameson's argument that postmodern design of public space reflects the "unmediated relationship" between architecture and the economic, and the fact that "aesthetic production today has become integrated into commodity production generally" (56). In short, if our public places can reflect and house the frenzy of market activity, then they can also house and support a democratic public sphere.

We thus come full circle from Habermas to Gathegi and back again: the library as a true public forum as well as its collective existence in democracies embody and enact much of Habermas's classical definition of the public sphere. For instance,

Libraries and librarianship preserve and promote rational discourse through the organization of collections coupled with the principle of unfettered information access.

Libraries and librarianship enact the principle of critique and argumentation to rationally arrive at values and conclusions primarily through the commitment to balanced collections, preserving them over time, and making a breadth of resources available, extending and furthering inclusion through active attempts to make collections and resources reflect historical and current intellectual diversity.

By their very existence libraries potentially verify (or refute) authority claims in making current and retrospective organized resources available to check the bases of a thesis, law, book, article, policy etc.—which lies at the heart of the public sphere and democratic process.

Libraries maintain the *potential* to realize, re-create, and ground rational and individual/comm-unity self-actualization and the democratic process. (Buschman 47–48; see also Andersen; Alstad and Curry; Webster, 176–177; and Williamson)

Library practices thus represent elaborations on both the means and results of the historical development of a democratic public sphere. In Fyvbjerg's formulation (213), libraries as institutions (and places) at least partially realize four of the six conditions of validity and truth—seriously blunting his criticism of Habermas's discourse ethics as unrealistic. As Wayne Wiegand (*Structure*) has put it, while it is an incomplete and incompletely realized mission, libraries have for the last fifty years or so supported (sometimes completely alone) a fundamental right of access to information, and though capitalism may not appreciate it, democracy does. The evolved social role and purpose of the public places of libraries have a deep and fundamental connection—however latent— to the needs of a democratic society. There is, in other words, a normative historical framework to our research about libraries as places: when we research libraries as places, we are engaging the idea of the democratic public sphere.

STRUCTURE OF THE BOOK

Not all of the ideas discussed in the previous sections fit comfortably alongside one another. That is perhaps the central point of this volume: the field has too long neglected this avenue of research (Wiegand "Library"), and in entering it, we have little choice but to begin by exploring the avenues of theory and research begun in other fields and their applicability (or not) to libraries. Libraries as places are thus viewed through traditional and novel lenses in this volume.

There are four thematic sections to the book. The first section, The Library's Place in the Past, features chapters by Tetreault, Arenson, and Curry, which provide historical perspectives on an overlooked place of libraries established on the frontiers of empire, libraries-as-place in terms of the historical interactions of people with the physical structures of social libraries, and the evolving place of the library within an urban community. The second section, Libraries as Places of Community, features chapters by Hersberger, Sua, and Murray, Rothbauer, MacKenzie et al., and Fisher et al. Community as enacted within and via libraries is the prominent theme within this section. The third section, Research Libraries as Places of Learning and Scholarship, features chapters by Antell and Engle, Given, and Mann. These three chapters explore different aspects of what libraries provide in the physical structures of the buildings and collections, which support and extend academic learning and research. The concluding section, Libraries, Place and Culture, has chapters by Mak, Van Slyck, and Estill, investigating three very different intersections of the library as a place within broader conceptions of culture, including an examination of the fifteenth-century text *Controversia de Nobilitate*, the architecture and erotics of reading and the library as imagined space in the television series *Buffy the Vampire Slayer*. A summary review of each chapter follows, in the order in which they appear in the book.

The impact of reading and garrison libraries on the evolution of the British military in the first half of the nineteenth century is a neglected subject explored by Ronald Tetreault in the first chapter. While the British army was undergoing a period of reform, improving the education and literacy of its soldiers became a priority and military libraries gradually became an instrument of Imperial policy. Over time, garrison libraries from Gibraltar to Nova Scotia became important places of the military order and offered alternative places of civility and recreation to the men (and women) who used them. These were, however, not merely places of entertainment: officers and men trained to read and write were needed as administrative duties gained prominence over action on the field of battle. British authorities came to see the library as a space devoted to the salutary practice of reading, thereby cultivating the intellectual and moral faculties of those meant to serve in the enterprise of the empire.

Adam Arenson's chapter is both a description and analysis of the furnishings and design of athenaeums and social libraries in the early to mid–nineteenth century. He reviews the elite culture that sponsored library projects and shaped library content by examining the design, decoration, and furnishing of "social libraries." What these material forms tell us about the social function of these libraries in the years of their prominence—from 1800 to 1860—using Barbara Carson's method of analysis along with a variety of sociological, anthropological, art-historical, and historical approaches to illuminate the lost details of these institutions, and to examine the leisure activities of urban workers. Through an understanding of the architecture and furnishing of social libraries in juxtaposed with private forms as well as with other newly created public spaces, a rich picture of what libraries in public meant in the first half of the nineteenth century emerges.

Ann Curry studies Vancouver's Carnegie Library, built in 1903 and which continues to serve as a public library. She analyses historical documents and sources to provide an overview of the roles the building has assumed (scholarly temple, place of refuge and political protest, cultural artifact) and the different user groups who have needed the building's services. In particular, the context of changing Vancouver communities, social issues, municipal politics, and national priorities is highlighted in her history. Focusing on meaning as revealed through the building itself, this chapter draws on information from Board minutes, annual reports, newspaper accounts, and personal correspondence and reminiscences to reveal how Vancouverites have regarded their Carnegie Library during the past century. The Library's services during the First and Second World Wars and during the Depression are examined, and the Library's current role is highlighted. Throughout the years, a thread of grudging respect by citizens is apparent, as the Carnegie Library has survived changes in clientele, community, and economic support. Now serving a neighborhood with Canada's poorest citizens, the Carnegie Library remains a place of importance in the community.

Julie Hersberger, Lou Sua, and Adam Murray examine the segregated South of the early part of the twentieth century in which the Carnegie Negro Library of Greensboro, North Carolina, played a very important role in the African American community. They use historical documents and interviews to examine this unique library's place in the community, tracing the history and role of the library as a place based on membership, local influence, fulfillment of individual and group needs, and providing a touchstone for a shared emotional experience. Forty years after the library had closed, former patrons hold an extremely strong sense of the library as a highly influential physical and symbolic place of opportunity. This chapter documents and explores the meaning of that unique historical experience of place.

Paulette Rothbauer writes on the contexts of lesbian, gay, bisexual, and queer (LGBQ) library patrons. While there are common understandings of the library as place via its physical features and its location within a community, this is only one way the library functions as place in the lives of its users. Library uses can also be analyzed within a framework of spatial practices informed by ideas from recent geographies of sexuality, identity, and place. This chapter argues that space is a practiced place. LGBQ library users are constituted, in part, through interaction with particular spaces and places that either permit or deny the public and private expression of their sexualities. Using a spatial frame for an analysis of LGBQ patrons as reported in studies disrupts the way the public library is commonly understood as a fixed place that supplies or provides information and reading material on the subjects of sexual orientation and sexual identity.

Pamela McKenzie, Elena Prigoda, Kirsten Clement, and Lynne McKechnie explore the creation of women's realms in a Canadian public library via a knitter's group and a young child/caregiver program. Observational and interview data are used to discuss the spatial and appearential ordering available to those participating in the program. Among the findings, they note that there are important processes taking place like the sharing of material resources, simultaneous work and leisure, children learning about the library, informal conversation constituting social support, gender identities, and facilitating a variety of modes of information practice. Each of these has a relationship to how place and space are constituted, used, and in turn, contains important questions for library and information research.

The new Seattle Public Central Library (SPCL), which has been the object of much publicity and scrutiny, is the subject of the chapter by Karen Fisher, Matthew Saxton, Phillip Edwards, and Jens-Erik Mai. Fisher and her coauthors have undertaken a sociocultural study of the loop of influence of the public on the design of the building, and then the public's interpretation and use of the space-as-built. Utilizing two frameworks for understanding libraries as place—Oldenburg's "third place" and Cresswell's five facets of place—this chapter analyzes responses from survey participants regarding the social, political, cultural, and economic meaning of the newly constructed SPCL. Emergent themes of the library as a physical place, a social place, and an informational place are discussed, and while the two frameworks help explain some portions of libraries as "places," neither adequately addresses the concept of information as it figures in the broader notion of place. This study contributes "information" to the research considerations of place by including themes regarding information finding and seeking, lifelong learning, learning resources, and learning environment. This chapter has implications for library buildings and as well as other major (and highly visible) municipal projects.

Karen Antell and Debra Engel look at the academic library as a physical space and identify an interesting question: Does a faculty member's chronological age and scholarly age (i.e., date of the most advanced degree) have an impact upon how much she/he values and uses the university library as a physical (vs. electronic) space? In a survey of all faculty and doctoral students at the University of Oklahoma, the authors found an unexpected affinity for place among younger users of the physical library and its perceived value as a scholarly place. The library as place has a value for scholars that goes far beyond mere access to materials, and not only do they love the convenience of access to electronic resources, but they also value the physical library, often for intangible but nonetheless crucial reasons, like its "conduciveness to scholarship."

Lisa Given's paper takes the perspective that the university campus is an informing space, of which the library is but one. Her study examines the ways in which physical spaces facilitate or hinder students' academic achievements and is drawn from interviews with faculty and librarians. The need for different kinds of spaces for academic work was behind the belief that the library had not moved beyond its traditional role as a quiet space. This study used in-depth, qualitative interviews to explore faculty members' and librarians' perceptions of campus spaces (e.g., libraries, computer labs) that facilitate or hinder undergraduates' academic information behaviors. The findings show that students require comfortable, welcoming spaces that allow for both noisy and quiet activities, and that current spatial design does not facilitate many students' academic information behaviors.

Thomas Mann's chapter represents an explication of the research uses of physical collections organized by intellectual classification systems. Mann dissects much of the language and justifications currently employed to move libraries toward a digital/information science model because, as he argues, the concept of research libraries as physical bricks and-mortar places is under siege. Too many facile assumptions about the "digital library paradigm" and the "transition" from print to electronic sources are being made, and these are coupled with the conviction that subject-classified collections of printed books are no longer required. The chapter fundamentally challenges this notion of an "evolution" to digital forms and the metaphors used to support it. In the process he uncovers the invaluable intellectual access that on-site book collections controlled by traditional cataloging and classification enable.

The cultural status of library spaces is discussed by Bonnie Mak through her examination of the 1428 text *Controversia de Nobilitate*, which describes the form and significance of having a library in the home. The thesis is that, while the library is considered the embodiment of a collective intellectual heritage, its definition and social role have fallen under intense scrutiny since the World Wide Web has laid claim to be the new library of the twenty-first century. By exploring the design of modern and fifteenth-century libraries, and by examining how copies of the *Controversia* have been classified in both settings, broader questions are raised about traditional spaces generated as libraries. As a cultural symbol, the library is more than a space for books or a place in which to read them, and this chapter explores the ways in which the ideal of the library has been embodied from the fifteenth century into the modern period.

Abigail Van Slyck writes about library architecture and how the physical form of libraries is bound up with the erotics of reading. A building's exterior is a formal vocabulary, and it shapes the individual's encounter, in this case with the institution of the library. Gates, steps, and doors suggest the library's approachability (or lack thereof), its scale inspires awe (or not). Interactions with books, with library staff, with other users are possible and impossible based on a building's plan. A building's interior spaces, along with the furnishings and fittings, form a stage set that encourages defined and sanctioned roles, while making others unthinkable. Her thesis is that design has played a central role in shaping the library user's experience of the institution and as a place and her chapter traces the messages (implicit and explicit) in library architecture, concentrating on the arena of women's reading in the nineteenth century and the erotics of reading as an act.

The final paper in the collection is by Adriana Estill, whose analysis of the role of the library in the television series *Buffy the Vampire Slayer* is representative of a media/cultural studies approach to space and the language of images as applied to an archetypal institution. The library in *Buffy* embodies a central meaning of the show playing off common historical and cultural assumptions. The first three seasons of *Buffy* consistently addressed how the high school library's character as place influenced its multiple uses and meanings. How the place of the library is lived and socially produced by the characters that make use of it while in turn acting constitutively to influence their practices is a key finding of this chapter. The library does not act as a simple depository or retrieval space for information but rather, the library's place entails negotiations around the acquisition of knowledge, the relationship between research and power, the drive to create community, and the desire for sanctuary. An understanding of the library's power and relevance depends upon a consideration of how the place of the library is heterogeneous and relational.

While this volume does not seek to define, even in broad terms, the boundaries of inquiry on library-as-place, we believe it does definitively establish that libraries and the discipline of library and information science (LIS) can productively utilize this vein of scholarship and research to further unpack and examine what Wayne Wiegand has long called a seriously underresearched institution (along with its associated phenomena). The papers in this collection clearly do not exhaust the applications of the theoretical ferment around space and place as it applies to libraries, but even a cursory reading of the preceding descriptions indicate that the topic has found a "place" in the literature of LIS. In turn, the LIS literature can—and should—contribute to the historical and theoretical work concerning place and space. This book is a beginning in that ongoing project.

REFERENCES

Agnew, John. "The Devaluation of Place in Social Science." In *The Power of Place*. Ed. John A. Agnew and James. S. Duncan. Boston: Unwin Hyman, 1989, 9–29.

———. "Space: Place." In *Spaces of Geographical Thought*. Ed. Paul Cloke and Ron Johnston. London: Sage, 2005, 81–96.

Aitchison, Cara, Nicola MacLeod, and Stephen Shaw. *Leisure and Tourism Landscapes: Social and Cultural Geographies*. London: Routledge, 2000.

Alstad, Colleen and Ann Curry. "Public Space, Public Discourse, and Public Libraries." *LIBRES: Library and Information Science Research Electronic Journal* 13(1) (March 2003), http//libres.curtin.edu.au/libres/13n1/pub_spaces.htm.

Andersen, Jack. "Information Criticism: Where Is It?" *Progressive Librarian* (25) (2005): 12–22.

Anderson, Benedict. *Imagined Communities: Reflections on the Origins and Spread of Nationalism*. London: Verso, 1983.

Arriess, Christopher A. "Creating Vietnamese Landscapes and Place in New Orleans." In *Geographical Identities of Ethnic America: Race, Space, and Place*. Ed. Kate A. Berry and Martha L. Henderson. Reno: University of Nevada Press, 2002, 228–254.

Augst, Thomas and Wayne Wiegand, Eds. *Libraries as Agencies of Culture*. Madison: University of Wisconsin Press, 2001.

Beckmann, Jorg. "Automobility: A Social Problem and Theoretical Concept." *Environment and Planning D: Society and Space* 19 (2001): 593–607.

Buschman, John E. *Dismantling the Public Sphere: Situating and Sustaining Librarianship in the Age of the New Public Philosophy*. Westport, CT: Libraries Unlimited, 2003.

Calhoun, Craig. "Introduction: Habermas and the Public Sphere." In *Habermas and the Public Sphere*. Ed. Craig Calhoun. Cambridge, MA: MIT Press, 1992, 1–50.

Carr, Stephen, Mark Francis, Leanne Rivlin, and Andrew Stone. *Public Space*. Cambridge, UK: Cambridge University Press, 1992.

Casey, Edward S. *The Fate of Place: A Philosophical History*. Berkeley: University of California Press, 1997.

Castells, Manuel. *The Rise of the Network Society*. Oxford, UK: Blackwell, 1996.

Certeau, Michel de. *The Practice of Everyday Life*. Trans. Steven Rendall. Berkeley: University of California Press, 1984.

Christaller, Walter. *Central Places in Southern Germany*. Trans. C.W. Baskin. Englewood Cliffs, NJ: Prentice-Hall, 1966.

Cloke, Paul, Philip Crang, and Mark Goodwin. *Envisioning Human Geographies*. London: Arnold, 2004.

Cloke, Paul and Jo Little, Eds. *Contested Countryside Cultures: Otherness, Marginalisation, and Rurality*. London: Routledge, 1997.

Conway, Janet. "Citizenship in a Time of Empire: The World Social Forum as a New Public Space." *Citizenship Studies* 8(4) (2004): 367–381.

Crang, Mike. "Public Space, Urban Space, and Electronic Space: Would the Real City Please Stand Up?" *Urban Studies* 37(2) (2000): 301–318.

Crang, Mike and Nigel Thrift, Eds. *Thinking Space*. London: Routledge, 2000.

Dear, Michael J. and Stephen Flusty, Eds. *The Spaces of Postmodernity: Readings in Human Geography*. London: Blackwell, 2002.

Delanty, Gerard. *Community*. London: Routledge, 2003.

Dilevko, Juris and Lisa Gottlieb. "The Politics of Standard Selection Guides: The Case of the Public Library Catalog. *Library Quarterly* 73(3) (2003): 289–337.

Domosh, Mona. *Invented Cities: The Creation of Landscape in Nineteenth-Century New York and Boston*. New Haven, CT: Yale University Press, 1996.

Flyvbjerg, Bent. "Habermas and Foucault: Thinkers for Civil Society?" *British Journal of Sociology* 49(2) (1998): 210–233.

Gathegi, John N. "The Public Library as a Public Forum: The (De)Evolution of a Legal Doctrine." *Library Quarterly* 75(1) (2005): 1–19.

Giddens, Anthony. *The Constitution of Society: Outline of the Theory of Structuration*. Cambridge, UK: Polity Press, 1984.

Goheen, Peter. "Public Space and the Geography of the Modern City." *Progress in Human Geography* 22(4) (1998): 479–496.

Habermas, Jürgen. "The Public Sphere: An Encyclopedia Article (1964)." *New German Critique* 4 (Fall 1974): 49–55.

———. "Problems of Legitimation in Late Capitalism." In *Critical Sociology: Selected Readings*. Ed. Paul Connerton. New York: Penguin, 1976, 263–387.

———. *The Structural Transformation of the Public Sphere: An Inquiry into a Category of Bourgeois Society*. Cambridge, MA: MIT Press, 1989.

———. "Further Reflections on the Public Sphere." In *Habermas and the Public Sphere*. Ed. Craig Calhoun. Cambridge, MA: MIT Press, 1992, 421–461.

———. "Postscript to *Faktizität und Geltung*." *Philosophy and Social Criticism* 20(4) (1994): 135–150.

———. *Public Space and Political Public Sphere—The Biographical Roots of Two Motifs in My Thought*. Kyoto Prize Commemorative Lecture, Kyoto, November 11, 2004, http://homepage.mac.com/gedavis/JH/Kyoto_lecture_Nov_2004.pdf, accessed October 12, 2005.

Halfacree, Keith. "Contrasting Roles for the Post-Productivist Countryside." In *Contested Countryside Cultures: Otherness, Marginalisation and Rurality*. Ed. Paul Cloke and Jo Little. London: Routledge, 1997, 70–93.

Haraway, Donna. "Situated Knowledges: The Science Question in Feminism and the Privilege of Partial Perspective. *Feminist Studies* 14 (1988): 575–599.

Harris, Roma. *Librarianship: The Erosion of a Women's Profession*. Norwood, NJ: Ablex, 1992.

Hart, John Fraser. *The Look of the Land*. Englewood Cliffs, NJ: Prentice-Hall, 1975.

Harvey, David. *Social Justice and the City*. London: Edward Arnold, 1973.

———. *Spaces of Capital: Towards a Critical Geography*. New York: Routledge, 2001.

Hebbert, Michael. "The Street as Locus of Collective Memory." *Environment and Planning D: Society and Space* 23 (2005): 581–596.

Hildenbrand, Suzanne, Ed. *Reclaiming the American Library Past: Writing the Women*. Norwood, NJ: Ablex, 1996.

Hillier, Jean and Emma Rooksby, Eds. *Habitus: A Sense of Place*. Aldershot, UK: Ashgate, 2002.

Hohendahl, Peter. "Jurgen Habermas: 'The Public Sphere' (1964)." *New German Critique* 4(Fall 1974): 45–48.

Hubbard, Phil, Rob Kitchin, and Gill Valentine, Eds. *Key Thinkers on Space and Place*. London: Sage, 2004.

Johnston, R.J. and J.D. Sidaway. *Geography & Geographers: Anglo-American Human Geography Since 1945*, 6th ed. New York: Oxford University Press, 2004.

Kearns, Robin A. and Wilbert M. Gesler, Eds. *Putting Health into Place: Landscape, Identity and Well-Being*. Syracuse, Sicily: Syracuse University Press, 1998.

Kranich, Nancy, Ed. *Libraries & Democracy: The Cornerstones of Liberty*. Chicago: American Library Association, 2001.

Latham, Alan. "Edward Soja." In *Key Thinkers on Space and Place*. Ed. Phil Hubbard, Rob Kitchin, and Gill Valentine. London: Sage, 2004, 269–274.

Leckie, Gloria J., and Jeff Hopkins. "The Public Place of Central Libraries: Findings from Toronto and Vancouver." *Library Quarterly* 72(3) (2002): 326–372.

Lees, Loretta. "Ageographia, Heterotopia and Vancouver's New Public Library." *Environment and Planning D: Society and Space* 15(3) (1997): 321–347.

Lefebvre, Henri. *The Production of Space.* Trans. Donald Nicholson-Smith. Oxford, UK: Blackwell, 1984.

Li, Feng, Jason Whalley, and Howard Williams. "Between Physical and Electronic Spaces: The Implications for Organisations in the Networked Economy." *Environment and Planning A* 33 (2001): 699–716.

Massey, Doreen. *Space, Place, and Gender.* Minneapolis: University of Minnesota Press, 1994.

Peters, John Durham. "Distrust of Representation: Habermas on the Public Sphere." *Media, Culture, and Society* 15 (1993): 541–571.

Sack, Robert David. *Homo Geographicus: A Framework for Action, Awareness and Moral Concern.* Baltimore, MD: Johns Hopkins University Press, 1997.

Said, Edward W. *Orientalism.* New York: Pantheon, 1978.

Semple, Ellen Churchill. *Influences of Geographic Environment, On the Basis of Ratzel's System of Anthropo-Geography.* New York: Holt, 1911.

Sennett, Richard. *The Conscience of the Eye: The Design and Social Life of Cities.* New York: Knopf, 1991.

Sibley, David. *Geographies of Exclusion: Society and Difference in the West.* London: Routledge, 1995.

Soja, Edward. *Thirdspace: Journeys to Los Angeles and Other Real-and-Imagined Places.* Oxford, UK: Blackwell, 1996.

———. *Postmetropolis: Critical Studies of Cities and Regions.* Oxford, UK: Blackwell, 2000.

Southworth, Michael. "Reinventing Main Street: From Mall to Townscape Mall." *Journal of Urban Studies* 10(2) (2005): 151–170.

Stevenson, Siobhan. "The Post-Fordist Library: From Carnegie to Gates." PhD Dissertation. London, Ont.: University of Western Ontario, 2005.

Tuan, Yi-Fu. *Topophilia: A Study of Environmental Perception, Attitudes and Values.* Englewood Cliffs, NJ: Prentice-Hall, 1974.

Valentine, Gill. *Social Geographies: Space & Society.* Harlow, UK: Prentice-Hall, 2001.

Von Humboldt, Alexander. *Cosmos: A Sketch of a Physical Description of the Universe.* Trans. E.C. Otté. New York: Harper, 1851.

Webster, Frank. *Theories of the Information Society*, 2nd ed. New York: Routledge, 2002.

Wiegand, Wayne. "The Structure of Librarianship: Essay on an Information Profession." *Canadian Journal of Information and Library Science* 24(1) (1997): 17–37.

———. "Library as Place." In *North Carolina Library Association Biennial Conference*, Winston-Salem, NC, September 22, 2005.

Williamson, Matthew. "Social Exclusion and the Public Library: A Habermasian Insight." *Journal of Librarianship and Information Science* 32 (December 2000): 178–186.

Zukin, Sharon. *The Cultures of Cities.* Oxford, UK: Blackwell, 1995.

Section I

The Library's Place in the Past

2

Beneficial Spaces:
The Rise of Military Libraries
in the British Empire

Ronald Tetreault

Professor of English, Dalhousie University, Halifax, Nova Scotia, Canada

INTRODUCTION

For more than twenty years before the defeat of Napoleon at the Battle of Waterloo in 1815, Great Britain was almost constantly at war with France and her continental allies. During the so-called long peace that followed, however, the British Army underwent a long period of slow reform. An expanding empire and a diminishing troop force meant that Britain could no longer depend on the sword alone to govern. Serious self-controlled officers and men, trained to read and write, were needed as administrative duties gained prominence over action on the field of battle. An increasing emphasis on literacy in the Army was supported by the establishment of military libraries at bases of strategic defence, from Gibraltar to Nova Scotia to India. These were not intended simply as places of entertainment. The British authorities came to see the library as a space devoted to the salutary practice of reading, which offered the benefit of cultivating the intellectual and moral faculties of those meant to serve in the enterprise of empire.

LITERACY AND THE ARMY

A field commander through and through, the Duke of Wellington was firmly of the opinion that a soldier's role was to fight and not to read. Most of his officers were of course products of the British public schools. Though mostly inclined by their privileged formation to sport and profligacy, they nevertheless acquired a smattering of the classical languages and certainly a degree of literacy adequate to their purposes. The enlisted men, on the other hand, were drawn from the poorest and least educated strata of society; Wellington himself often called the troops he led into battle against the French "the scum of the earth" (Longford 321–22). But while the common soldier may have been valued most for his ferocity on the battlefield, these men were not simply brutal and ignorant. They could behave well when sober, and even during the Napoleonic wars some read, wrote, and occasionally treated noncombatants kindly. There was, for example, the charming story of the way the unknown author of *Journal of a Soldier* taught the children of a Spanish family to read (Laffin 75).

Although training was for battle, the Army did not completely neglect the mental and spiritual development of its troops. Literacy and reading gained support in military circles—as it did in the rest of society—only gradually in the early 1800s, yet by midcentury military libraries had become instruments of policy. As early as 1811, the Duke of York instigated a broad educational program staffed by sergeant schoolmasters, and regimental schools developed where men could gain the qualifications necessary for promotion. It has been estimated that about half of the armed forces under Wellington were illiterate, but that by 1841 that had declined to a third and by 1846 the illiteracy rate fell further to 27 percent (Strachan 89). Looking back on the 1840s, one old soldier was struck by the "very great difference as to education" during his years of service:

When I first entered the Army not one in twenty recruits could read or write, and now fifteen out of twenty can either do one or the other. Now, to be a non-commissioned officer a man requires to be well up in reading, writing, and arithmetic. (Stewart 1: 69–70).

More and more, a rising generation of officers was showing concern about the state of the Army and the condition of the troops.

When a serious-minded young artillery officer named John Henry Lefroy was appointed Inspector General of Army Schools in 1857, he expressed alarm that the literacy rates of British troops still lagged considerably behind that of their counterparts on the continent. In his meticulous 1859 report on Army schools and libraries, he found a 60 percent literacy rate among the troops, with a further 18 percent somewhat functional; it was his view that "adult pupils of average intelligence may be taught to read and write, and made to master the elements of simple arithmetic, in about twelve months, by attending school regularly for four hours a week," though he found such programs in a woeful state of neglect (Lefroy 6–9). Promotion in the ranks could have literacy requirements, he discovered; to become a corporal in one regiment, a soldier had "to read and write well; to take orders from dictation; and to work the first four rules of arithmetic (simple and compound)," while for promotion to sergeant men also needed "to have a fair knowledge of grammar; and to show a general intelligence by their answers in history, geography, or any other subject in which they might have been instructed in the school" (Lefroy 31). Increasingly after Waterloo, the administrative duties and operations of a peacetime army meant that an ability to read and write was the ticket to promotion.

MILITARY LIBRARIES AND EMPIRE

Elite divisions, not surprisingly, always enjoyed a high level of literacy. The Royal Engineers and the Artillery had libraries of scientific books from early days, reflecting their emphasis on the technical skills of their officers. Here and there, reform-minded commanders of fighting regiments established libraries for the edification of their men, but these were difficult to sustain as the regiment moved to each new posting. The first permanent library to serve a British garrison was created at Gibraltar in 1793, and had a storied history. Other libraries were established for officers at bases in the

Mediterranean such as Malta in 1806 and Messina in 1810, the latter being moved to serve the Corfu garrison in 1814. After Waterloo, officers' libraries were founded at important bastions in British North America, such as Quebec in 1816 and Halifax in 1817. Somewhat later, similar libraries were established at St. George's, Bermuda, and at the three main headquarters of the Indian Army, Bengal, Madras, and Bombay. The picture that emerges shows libraries as an essential part of virtually every strategic base of Imperial defense, whether these controlled key trade routes or protected colonists from attack by indigenous peoples or foreign powers like the United States (Tunstall 808). Many of these collections have since been absorbed into others or have vanished without trace. The garrison library at Halifax, Nova Scotia, in Canada, however, survives to this day and is the best documented of these institutions. A look (below) at the records of this great North Atlantic sentinel will give us some insight into the reading practices of soldiers in the early nineteenth century.

The military life these men had known was changing. During the so-called long peace, which ensued after the defeat of French, the British Army found itself adapting to a new social and economic environment. In Parliament, the Whigs advocated shifting the burden of colonial defense to the colonists themselves and urged retrenchment in the Army lists. Army expenditures slumped from £43 m in 1815 to £8 m in 1837; during the same years, troop strength was allowed to decline by almost two-thirds, from 233,952 to 87,993 soldiers by the time Queen Victoria ascended the throne (Burroughs "Defence and Imperial Disunity" 323–24). Meanwhile the British Empire was expanding. The twenty-two colonies that existed in 1793 had grown to thirty-four in the 1820s, and had doubled to forty-five by 1846. Because this burgeoning colonial network had to be governed and policed by an ever-diminishing number of troops, the role of the military changed. No doubt the Empire was based on power, but that power now had to be translated into "systems of authority" that could be conducted by agents through administrative institutions (Burroughs "Imperial Institutions and the Government of Empire" 170). Not only were soldiers with a high degree of literacy required to perform bureaucratic functions, but a new kind of moral authority came to be valued as a justification for the right to govern. Lord Cromer, who enjoyed a long career as a colonial administrator in Egypt, articulated these emerging trends many years later once they had become clearly evident. In an *Edinburgh Review* essay "The Government of Subject Races," he recognized that an Empire could be won by conquest, but was not to be governed merely by force:

The maintenance of Empire depends on the sword; but so little does it depend on the sword alone that if once we have to draw the sword . . . the sword will assuredly be powerless to defend us long, and the days of our Imperial rule will be numbered. . . . Imperialism should rest on a moral basis. . . . Bad government will bring the mightiest empire to ruin. (Cromer 2–3)

Sound and durable government called for new men, intellectually improved and morally aware of the needs of those they ruled. The eighteenth-century type of the rakehell gentleman officer was no longer in demand.

Halifax

Halifax, chosen as a strategic base in 1749 because of its fine harbor and impregnable citadel hill, hosted a good many such rogues. By the 1760s the land and sea forces

outnumbered the civilian population five or six to one, and the town was reputed the
most wicked in North America. In the words of one contemporary observer:

There are 1,000 houses in the town. We have upwards of 100 licensed [drinking] houses and
perhaps as many without license, so the business of one half the town is to sell rum and the other
half to drink it. (Raddall 70)

Brawling and lechery were the other common pursuits of the garrison. The main thor-
oughfare just below the fortress carried the regal name of Brunswick Street, but was
known as Barrack Street and more popularly as "Knock-Him-Down Street." Lined
with taverns and brothels, it was for His Majesty's soldiers and sailors their chief
place of recreational resort. If the men's behavior was bad they were not wholly to
blame, for in the eighteenth century they were housed in squalid conditions, ill-fed and
neglected. Deprived of any healthier amusements or any constructive social life, they
naturally ran riot once relieved of their monotonous daily duties. Furthermore, the only
standard their officers set for them was a life of selfish dissipation. The vivid drama of
their gambling and their duels, their kept women and their marathon drinking bouts,
is laid bare in a diary kept by William Dyott during his five-year stint (1787–1792) in
Halifax as a young lieutenant on his first colonial posting. On one memorable evening in
the mess, the General and the Colonel of the regiment got "as drunk as two drummers,"
after the party of twenty officers managed to consume 63 bottles of "the very best claret"
Dyott had ever tasted (Dyott 45–46).

   Dyott's life of carefree debauchery stands in marked contrast to the more sober
pursuits of an officer of a different generation after the wars. Captain William Scarth
Moorsom regrets his posting to Halifax in the 1820s. He finds himself disconnected from
powerful individuals in London who might further his advancement, and laments "the
odours of rusticity" which pervade this colonial outpost. His mode of self-expression in
his memoirs is restrained and reflective, at once a sign of his seriousness of mind as well
as his sense of aspiration to higher responsibilities. He complains of what he describes as

neglect of all those exercises more peculiarly adapted for enlarging the mental capacity. . . . The
literary *emporia* of the town but too clearly bear evidence to the same fact. A few law and school-
books fill the catalogue . . . of the solitary bookseller of Halifax. In vain do we inquire for some
of those numberless sheets printed for the instruction of the juvenile, or for the standard works
that assist in forming the more advanced mind: none such are to be procured, except by express
commission to England. (Moorsom 99–100)

His emphasis on forming and enlarging the mind may be only a personal predilection,
but it is hard not to hear an echo in his words of the familiar Victorian taste for self-
improvement. He wants to get on in his career despite the diminishment of opportunity
in the peacetime army, but he also craves intellectual stimulation. It is fitting, then, that a
man of such serious interests should find solace in a new place of resort. Moorsom writes:

Although . . . the absolute monotony of the routine of duties affords little scope for acquiring
practical information, a resource (for which this Division of the army is indebted to the patronage
of the Earl of Dalhousie) is provided in a well-assorted military library, which is open on very
liberal terms to all officers of both sea and land service, and of which every officer who regards a

season of peace but as a valuable interval to be seized and maintained, in preparing a foundation for the exigencies of war, will not fail to appreciate the value. (Moorsom 32)

For this young hero-in-waiting, the garrison library is not just a private retreat but a "resource" for others of like mind. The military library thus takes its place alongside grammar schools and the establishment of Mechanics' Institutes as an agent in the intellectual awakening of a colony (Harvey 19).

When George Ramsay, Lord Dalhousie, first arrived in Halifax in 1816, he too was shocked by the lack of books in the colony. Following Sir John Sherbrooke as governor of Nova Scotia, he was part of a generation of military commanders who had served under Wellington in the Napoleonic Wars and had now embarked on careers as colonial administrators. He took advantage of the time of peace following the wars on the continent (as well as the War of 1812 against the United States) to found institutions dedicated to mental cultivation. Using the fruits of conquest garnered by his predecessor, he established Dalhousie University in Halifax and in 1817 endowed a library for officers at the Halifax garrison. He records an outline of his plan in his diary:

At present the young men in garrison are much at a loss to get any reading, there is not a Booksellers shop in Halifax, nor is there an individual possessed of any thing that can be called a Library . . . I lately suggested to the Officers in this command the great comfort, and advantages that might result from the establishment of a Garrison Library, the idea has been discussed and every Officer has entered into it. We propose to follow exactly the plan of the Gibraltar Library as far as circumstances admit—We have already subscribed £400, and I have appropriated £1000 from a public fund at my disposal, the Castine duties, to aid its first attempts—Our half yearly subscription will be about £300, amply sufficient to cover ordinary expenses when our first collection of books is purchased. (Dalhousie, *Personal Journal*)

In a letter to Sherbrooke, who had now gone on to command at Quebec, he reports that he has sent £200 to London "for the purchase of Books of value & character" and £100 "to New York for others of light reading & trifling value" (Dalhousie, *ALS to Sherbrooke*).

The library founded at the Halifax garrison was one of a new type of permanent collection whose existence did not depend on a particular regiment or specialized branch of the service. Previously, regimental libraries had traveled with the troops to each posting, and consequently had often become dispersed or were abandoned as they moved. Here was a library attached to a particular strategic outpost that was intended to be a fixture. According to the *Rules and Catalogue of the Halifax Garrison Library* from 1835 (which is the earliest known to survive), members were "entitled permanently to all the advantages of this Institution" (*Rules* 6), an advantage only if one were reposted several times. Membership was by annual subscription at a cost of "six dollars," though anyone wishing to join the subscribers on shorter terms could do so for a monthly fee. It was governed by a committee of its members, and the 1835 catalogue counts 570 persons on its rolls, mostly officers from various regiments as well as from the Artillery and the Engineers. Of this number, twenty-six were ladies, since wives and widows of garrison officers were admitted under the bye-laws. Among the other special members were four half-pay officers, a company clerk, a hospital assistant, and two others from the medical staff. Officers of the Navy were also served by the garrison library and welcomed as equal members with officers of the Army, since there seems to have been no provision for similar establishments by the Royal Navy. Evidence for seamen's libraries is scant, apart from the mention of Captain Vere's personal collection of books aboard the fictional HMS Bellipotent in Melville's *Billy Budd*.

An analysis of the collection itself is revealing of the reading habits of its mostly officer-class membership. In 1835, the holdings of the Halifax Garrison Library numbered over 1,000 titles, many of which were multivolume works. These were ordered into twelve subject classes, the three largest of which were Novels and Romances; Biographies, Letters and Memoirs; and Voyages, Travels and Geography. Bibles and sermons figure prominently in the Theology and Law category, but this class also contains philosophical works like Adam Smith's *Wealth of Nations* and James Mill's *Political Economy*. A surprising number of liberal writers are included, such as Montesquieu, Voltaire, Rousseau, and Volney, whose *Ruins of Empire* argued for the inevitability of imperial collapse through a critical survey of failed regimes from the past. Almost one quarter of the collection was made up of novels, poems, and drama, which compares very favorably with the popular subscription and commercial circulating libraries of the day, which, studies show, held an average of 20 percent fiction (Hamlyn 218). The most popular contemporary writers such as Lord Byron and Sir Walter Scott are heavily represented, but others who enjoy enduring fame are there too, such as Dryden, Smollett, and Sterne. Of particular interest is the number of works by women authors held in a collection heavily used by men. Jane Austen is completely absent, but her predecessor Fanny Burney is represented by two of her best-known works, *Evelina* and *Cecilia*. Gothic novels are present in the form of Anne Radcliffe's *Mysteries of Udolpho* and William Beckford's *Vathek*. James Fennimore Cooper's *The Last of the Mohicans* also seems to have been a popular work, and figures prominently among soldiers' reading, especially in North America.

Quebec

A library at the Quebec garrison had been founded in the previous year, and differed from its Halifax cousin only in springing somewhat more spontaneously from the will of its officers. At a meeting of the staff and corps of the garrison in the spring of 1816, it was unanimously agreed that a library would be "a source of great advantage, as well as of rational entertainment, to the Officers" of the fortress, and that their library would follow the plan of the Garrison Library at Gibraltar (*Regulations* 4). The library was on a somewhat smaller scale than the one at Halifax, but by 1835 the printed catalogue lists 935 titles, although the membership was less than half the size of its sister library. The collection was strong in history, biography, and travels, but also included the novels of Scott, the poems of Burns and Byron, along with the *Moral Tales* of Maria Edgeworth and Fanny Burney's *Cecilia*.

Gibraltar

The ancestor of all these was the Gibraltar Garrison Library, which was founded by the officers of the garrison in 1793 and became the pattern on which the others were modelled. From its earliest inception, the library was regarded (in the words of the preamble to its catalogue) as "truly beneficial to His Majesty's service," especially as it offered officers an alternative to "having their minds enervated and vitiated by idleness and dissipation" (*Catalogue* vi). Its facilities included reading rooms, billiard tables, and a racquet court (Teall 6), making it the focus of recreational activities for the upper ranks. This emphasis on making the library a space for sociability was repeated at other bases, including Halifax.

The Gibraltar library seems to have been started with 460 volumes donated by its members, to which were added a further 674 ordered from England (Teall 2). According to its rules and bye-laws, membership was open to officers of the Army and the Navy, as well as to the ladies of their families, on payment of an annual subscription of six dollars; fines were imposed on a daily basis for late returns, and bringing a dog into the library was subject to a further one dollar penalty (*Catalogue* xii, xxviii). The catalogue shows that by 1837 the library boasted 2,300 subscribers and its collection had grown to over 7,500 titles, of which about 10 percent were novels. This proportion grew to 16 percent when its generous holdings of poetry and drama were included. In addition to the predictable presence of Scott and Byron, the poetry section included Wordsworth's *Excursion* and an 1800 *Lyrical Ballads*, as well as volumes by Coleridge, Southey, and Shelley. Mary Tighe's *Psyche* is prominent among poetical works by women, along with volumes by Felicia Hemens, Mary Robinson, Anna Laetitia Barbauld, and Charlotte Smith's *Elegiac Sonnets*. Alongside Shakespeare and Ben Jonson stand Joanna Baillie's *Plays on the Passions*, and twenty-five volumes of Elizabeth Inchbald's *British Theatre*. Prose fiction includes (besides Walter Scott) Jane Austen's *Pride and Prejudice*, *Persuasion*, *Emma*, *Mansfield Park*, *Northanger Abbey*, and *Sense and Sensibility*, and Mrs. Edgeworth's *Moral Tales* and *Castle Rackrent*.

The collection was notably strong in history, theology, and politics, but pays little attention to sport, unlike soldiers' libraries elsewhere. These officers' fastidiousness of taste is reflected in the practice at Gibraltar of banning certain books. It is recorded that in 1799 "the 'Memoires of the Chevalier Faublas' being represented to the Committee as an immoral and indecent publication, it was decided that the same should be burnt, as also 'The Child of Nature'" (Teall 7). The latter proves to be a translation of a French play by Mrs. Inchbald, telling the story of an orphan miss brought up in ignorance of love and men, suddenly beset by lovers, one of whom imprisons her and another who stalks her. Matthew Lewis's *The Monk* was similarly consigned to the flames, as being fit reading only for a debauchee.

India

The Indian Army followed in the footsteps of the British forces, and added an important innovation of its own. In 1823, the Bengal Government proposed the first subscription library for European soldiers, firm in the conviction that reading about "the histories of our Commanders and their exploits, and the heroic traits of national character from the Black Prince till Wellington by directing their eyes to national glory will animate [the men's] courage and cement them by a national bond of union" (Baxter 26). Soon after, libraries were established for service men in the two other principal presidencies of Bombay and Madras. A unique feature of these collections was that from their inception "European NCOs and privates were to have first choice of books" (Baxter 27), a significant departure from the practice in the rest of the Empire of maintaining libraries strictly for the use of officers. These libraries were usually in the charge of the chaplain, most often assisted by a "steady NCO" who took responsibility for the care of the books and kept records of their circulation. The men paid a small annual subscription, and they favored works of history, travel, and military memoirs. The novels of Scott seem to have been the most popular works of fiction, along with Maria Edgeworth's *Popular Tales* and *The Arabian Nights*. Far less interest was shown in the moral treatises supplied by the Society for Promoting Christian Knowledge, though the chaplain at Cawnpore took great satisfaction "that a very large proportion of the readers have made a moral advancement" merely through the adoption of more sober habits (Baxter 28).

THE ORDINARY SOLDIER

The British Army was much slower to acknowledge the value of making books available to the ordinary soldier. Wellington distrusted any form of education for soldiers, and for many years books were banned from barracks. "By Jove," he once declared, "if there is a mutiny in the army—and in all probability we shall have one—you'll see that these new-fangled schoolmasters will be at the bottom of it" (James 36). In the 1820s there was a list of twenty-eight titles approved for reading by other ranks, but these were available only in sick bay (Laffin 122). Controlled by the chaplain and consisting of religious and moral tracts, it is little wonder these collections were rarely used by the troops. But because the regimental system gave modernizing officers considerable autonomy, local reforms became the norm. Regimental commanders often spent large sums of their own money on their units. While commanding the 7th Royal Fusiliers, Lord Frederick Fitzclarence, an illegitimate son of William IV, established at his own expense company schools and a regimental library (Strachan 30). By the simple expedient of introducing an evening meal into his soldiers' routine, Fitzclarence cut down on drunkenness; enlightened discipline could also often include awards for good conduct, as was the setting up of savings banks. These younger officers started a trend toward positive incentives that led to reforms on a larger scale.

In 1840, the commander of the Horse Guards, who had authority over the cavalry and the infantry, issued a general order establishing libraries in barracks for NCOs and enlisted men, from which "most beneficial results are expected." The aims of the program are made very clear by the terms of the order:

The object of these Institutions, it will readily be perceived, is to encourage the Soldiery to employ their leisure hours in a manner that shall combine amusement with the attainment of useful knowledge, and teach them the value of sober, regular, and moral habits. (General Order No. 544)

The order mandated the establishment of barracks libraries at twenty-nine key home and foreign stations, including Halifax, Quebec, Bermuda, Gibraltar, and the Cape of Good Hope. The strategic importance of this Atlantic ring of colonial defense is difficult to miss. What is more, these libraries arose as a result of deliberate policy. In 1835, a Commission of Inquiry began an investigation into the system of discipline in the Army. Many officers gave testimony, some defending the traditional punishment of flogging while others advocated solitary confinement or hard labor as means of keeping the troops in line. The Duke of Wellington told the Commission in no uncertain terms that

British soldiers are taken entirely from the lowest orders of society. . . . I do not see how you can have an Army at all unless you preserve it in a state of discipline, nor how you can have a state of discipline unless you have some punishment. . . . There is no punishment which makes an impression upon any body except corporal punishment. ("Report" 324)

But the Commission also heard testimony from Frederick Fitzclarence that "a judicious system of reward is much required" ("Report" 159). They heard further from Major General Sir John Wilson about the value of rewards in contrast to brutal and debilitating penalties. He clearly stated his opinion that "the men must be made directly instrumental to their own moral improvement, if that improvement is to be solid or lasting," and recommended that "mental and moral improvement" in the ranks should be promoted by the introduction of "healthy and amusing games" and the establishment of schools and libraries ("Report" 127). Thus libraries as places of sober entertainment and civilized sociability were embraced by the military establishment in the general order of 1840 as part of a new regimen of self-policing and improvement in the condition of the troops.

The barracks libraries that developed from this reconsideration of military discipline seem to have been a success. In Halifax, as appears common elsewhere, the library was paired with a reading room, which evolved into a soldiers' social club with the addition of a recreation room including games and a refreshment bar (Crook 1077). According to Lefroy's 1859 report on military libraries, there were two garrison libraries at the Halifax complex, one of which was located in the Citadel barracks that housed the common soldiers (Lefroy 54). Each library contained over 1,000 books, which circulated so regularly that many needed to be replaced. By far the most popular were novels, while religious works remained on the shelves. The meticulous Lefroy points out that of the 264 books that "worn out by fair use" and required resupply, fully 205 were works of prose fiction (Lefroy 57). That almost 78 percent of the men's favorite reading was prose fiction is given some perspective by the fact that, according to Lefroy, the General Catalogue of Garrison Libraries shows that fiction constituted about 24 percent of the overall holdings. Among the books most popular with the men were the works of Scott and James Fennimore Cooper, novels by Dickens and Captain Marryat, Ann Radcliffe's *The Italian*, Charlotte Smith's *The Old Manor House*, along with *Emma, Mansfield Park, Northanger Abbey*, and *Pride and Prejudice* by Jane Austen (Lefroy 219–221).

The actual reading practices of these soldiers have left little trace. But one ordinary soldier at least has left a reminiscence of how indispensable the military library was to him during a colonial posting. Sergeant J. M. MacMullen was a failed tradesman who enlisted in the hope of travel and adventure. He found himself posted to India with his regiment, the 13th Light Infantry, where he endured the heat and boredom as best he could. He laments the almost constant drunkenness of the other men and the intense profanity of their language; although occasionally sliding into bad habits himself, he finds profound solace in the salutary space provided by the library:

There was a host [of] old novels and romances, the larger part of the last century; but among this collection I was so fortunate as to ferret out, after much searching for something worth reading, an old edition of Scott's works, the half-defaced pages of which were conned and re-conned over by me, til I had almost got them by heart. I feel it is impossible to describe what pleasure it afforded me after returning from office, to stretch myself on my charpoy, raising my head as high as I could by doubling up my pillow, and thus to read 'Guy Mannering' until I fell into my customary sleep at three o'clock.... Libraries are indeed invaluable to the soldier in India, and should, therefore, be as well chosen as possible. (MacMullen 155)

MacMullen was perhaps not untypical of the well-intentioned and moderately educated soldier who appreciated the efforts of the authorities to improve the condition of the troops and to offer them more constructive amusements.

CONCLUSION

In offering instruction and delight for both officers and men, however, military libraries served larger goals of policy. Empires may be won by the sword, but they are governed by the pen. A new kind of soldier was needed to administer an empire, a soldier who was literate and knowledgeable about the world, and who was also sober and capable of setting a moral standard. Subscription libraries were thus embraced by the British Army as places of sober entertainment and civilized sociability. Their reading rooms provided opportunities to sharpen the skills needed for promotion in the ranks, and were a storehouse of knowledge for good government. They offered an alternative to places of bad resort, and enforced norms of civility. Their club-like atmosphere and the recreational facilities commonly attached to them were a world away from the drinking, swearing, whoring, and gambling of the tavern and the brothel. In some larger sense, then, these libraries can be seen as instruments of discipline, offering positive incentives instead of the traditional sanctions of corporal punishment and incarceration. These military libraries were more than storehouses of books. The garrison library was a space for socialization: it was a site of social interaction, a resource for intellectual improvement, and a device for moral control. Whether attached to the officers' mess or associated with games rooms and tea rooms, libraries for officers and men served the purposes of the new army that would run an empire.

REFERENCES

Baxter, Ian. "The Establishment of the First Libraries for European Soldiers in India." *South Asia Library Group Newsletter* 40 (1993): 25–30.

Burroughs, Peter. "Defence and Imperial Disunity." *The Oxford History of the British Empire: The Nineteenth Century.* Ed. Andrew Porter. Oxford: Oxford UP, 1999, 320–345.

———. "Imperial Institutions and the Government of Empire." *The Oxford History of the British Empire: The Nineteenth Century.* Ed. Andrew Porter. Oxford: Oxford UP, 1999, 170–197.

Catalogue of the Books in the Gibraltar Garrison Library. Gibraltar: Garrison Library Press, 1837.

Cromer, Earl of. "The Government of Subject Races." *Edinburgh Review* 207 (1908): 1–27.

Crook, E. M. Razzolini. "Research Memo: Soldiers' Club (Recreation Room/Coffee Bar and Garrison Library/Reading Room)." *Research Memos, Halifax Defence Complex Restoration,* vol. 4, pp. 1077–82. 20 October 1983.

Dalhousie, Earl of. *ALS to Sir John Coape Sherbrooke.* 29 December 1817. Scottish Record Office GD 45/3/4, pp. 55–57.

———. *Personal Journal. May 1816–December 1818.* Scottish Record Office GD 45/3/541, pp. 126–27.

Dyott, William. *Dyott's Diary 1781–1845.* Ed. Reginald W. Jeffery. 2 vols. London: Constable, 1907.

General Order No. 544. "Rules and Regulations for Soldiers' Libraries." Horse Guards, 5 Feb. 1840. Nova Scotia Archives and Records Management HQ 32.

Hamlyn, Hilda. "Eighteenth-Century Circulating Libraries in England." *The Library* 5th ser. (1) (1947): 197–222.

Harvey, D. C. "The Intellectual Awakening of Nova Scotia." *Dalhousie Review* 13 (1933): 1–22.

James, Lawrence. *The Iron Duke: A Military Biography of Wellington.* London: Weidenfield and Nicholson, 1992.

Laffin, John. *Tommy Atkins: The Story of the English Soldier.* London: Cassell, 1966.

Lefroy, Brevet-Colonel John Henry. *Report on the Regimental and Garrison Schools of the Army, and on Military Libraries and Reading Rooms.* London: Eyre and Spottiswoode, 1859.

Longford, Elizabeth. *Wellington: The Years of the Sword*. London: Weidenfeld and Nicholson, 1969.

MacMullen, John Mercier. *Camp and BarrackRoom; or, The British Army as it is, by a late Staff Sergeant of the 13th Light Infantry*. London: Chapman and Hall, 1846.

Moorsom, William Scarth. *Letters from Nova Scotia*. London: Henry Colbrun and Richard Bentley, 1830.

Raddall, Thomas H. *Halifax: Warden of the North*. Toronto: McClelland & Stewart, 1948.

Regulations and Catalogue of the Quebec Garrison Library. Quebec: T. Cary, 1821.

"Report from His Majesty's Commissioners for Inquiring into the System of Military Punishments in the Army." Great Britain. Parliament. *Sessional Papers*, 1836, vol. 22, no. 59. HMSO London.

Rules and Catalogue of the Halifax Garrison Library. Halifax: John Munro, 1835.

Stewart, Col. W. K. *Reminiscences of a Soldier*. 2 vols. London: Hurst and Blackett, 1874.

Strachan, Hew. *Wellington's Legacy: The Reform of the British Army, 1830–54*. Manchester: Manchester UP, 1984.

Teall, Major G. H. *A Short History of the Gibraltar Garrison Library*. Gibraltar: Garrison Library Press, 1934.

Tunstall, W. C. B. "Imperial Defence 1815–1870." *The Cambridge History of the British Empire*. Ed. J. H. Rose, A. P. Newton, and E. A. Benians. 8 vols. Cambridge: Cambridge UP, 1929–1963. II, 806–41.

3

Libraries in Public before the Age of Public Libraries: Interpreting the Furnishings and Design of Athenaeums and Other "Social Libraries," 1800–1860[1]

Adam Arenson

Ph.D. Candidate in History, Yale University, New Haven, Conn.

INTRODUCTION

When it comes to the origins of the public library in America, there is no easy answer. As Jesse Shera described in his authoritative history *Foundations of the Public Library*, depending on whether the emphasis is on municipal ownership, free access and use, location or social function, many institutions could vie for the title of "first public library." Shera argued that early public collections, held in district courts, state houses, or even in colleges, hardly seem to lead up to the opening of the Boston Public Library building in 1859. Instead of tracing mere governmental control, Shera told the history of the public library as an institution through the history of "social libraries," a term he applies to the founding, in 1731, of the Library Company of Philadelphia (31). Given the intellectual and social goals of Benjamin Franklin's "Junto," this was a social library indeed—a place to converse as well as read, debate publicly as well as study quietly. In short, the earliest American libraries in public were a space apart, from both work and home—and their special uses can inform us how the space of libraries is used to this day.

This paper examines the design, decoration, and furnishing of "social libraries" and searches for what these material forms can tell us about the social function of these libraries in the years of their prominence, 1800 to 1860. Using the methods of Barbara G. Carson's *Ambitious Appetites: Dining, Behavior, and Patterns of Consumption in Federal Washington* to embed the analysis of architecture, furnishings, decoration, and design into the historical narrative of library development, I bring forward a variety of statements and insights from the documentary record. My work also uses a variety of sociological, anthropological, art-historical and historical approaches to illuminate the lost details of these vital institutions, and to see what they suggest about the leisure activities of urban workers. By understanding the character of the architecture and furnishing of the social libraries, in conversation with private forms as well as with other newly created public spaces, I hope to provide a rich picture of what libraries in public meant in the first half of the nineteenth century.

UNCOVERING THE PLACE OF SOCIAL LIBRARIES

I focus this study on "social libraries" because I agree with Shera's insight, namely, that these institutions set the tone for the development of the modern public library, especially in this period. In fact, the founding librarian of the Smithsonian Institution, C. C. Jewett, conducted a remarkable study of libraries in 1851, where he singled out "athenæums, lyceums, young men's associations, mechanics' institutions, mercantile libraries, &c.," as "social libraries," which he defined as "generally composed of popular works for reading rather than for reference" (189). These were semiprivate, membership-only institutions, established by the leading merchants of a community, either for their own exposure to fine arts or for civic debate—the athenæums and lyceums—or for the benefit of their workers, educating clerks striving to join the elite—the young men's associations and mechanics' institutions. Mercantile libraries, a more ambiguous term, could describe either type of institution. (While Shera has included public institutions like court libraries in his use of "social libraries" and has described these groups by mode of organization as either proprietary, partnership libraries, or subscription libraries [58–62], I will use "social libraries" to describe these overlapping types, and my term "libraries in public" for the broader group.)

The social library emerged at a time when young men seeking their fortunes moved into the cities, redefining the American landscape. America in the nineteenth century was an exceedingly diverse place, as freed blacks, Irish and German immigrants, Texan ranchers, and Southern planters populated a contentious, changing landscape. Yet this will be a narrower tale. In the nineteenth century, Americans opened trade to China, conquered land from Mexico, and crossed a continent in search of gold and farmland, but social libraries remained New England in spirit and, often, in geography. The product of young, white, middle- and upper-class aspiring entrepreneurs, social libraries sprouted up in the Northeast and, to a lesser extent, through the "Yankee Diaspora" where they sought their fortunes, from the Ohio Valley to St. Louis and California. Espousing a free-thinking, confident tone and valuing education and debate, these men built institutions free and open to their peers but exclusive, as Dana Nelson has argued—shunning those who were not white, not English-speaking, and, at times, those who were not male (Nelson). Regrettably, this account will ignore those that the social library ignored, but it felt fitting to mark the absence.

The organization of social libraries reached its peak in the Northeast in the years 1825 to 1835, and aspiring merchants moving West continued to found these libraries until the end of the nineteenth century (Shera 72–79; Glynn 371; Beckerman 5; Luckingham). These social libraries appeared at the same time that rooms in private homes were being specialized into libraries and parlors, sitting rooms, and bedrooms. In the following decades, weaker institutions closed or merged: for example, the amalgamation of the elite Social Library of New Haven and the New Haven Young Men's Institute, in 1841, or the joining of the books held by the St. Louis Lyceum with the St. Louis Mercantile Library collections in 1851 (New Haven Young Men's Institute; St. Louis Mercantile Library). Leaders of the social libraries also came to concentrate their efforts on the founding of modern public libraries, notably in the involvement of the Boston Athenaeum members in the creation of the Boston Public Library and other public libraries in the region (Story 196–197; Breisch). Some of those leaders even suggested donating their own institutions' collections to start the public libraries (Shera 123–124). By the time the Boston Public Library opened its own building in 1859, the era of the modern public library had begun, and the importance of social libraries as libraries in public had waned.

Perhaps because of this later fadeout, the layout and construction of social libraries have received scant attention, often placed among other libraries in public, and examined only for how their components are reflected in later modern public libraries. Kenneth Breisch's *Henry Hobson Richardson and the Small Public Library in America: A Study in Typology* described the "small libraries" H. H. Richardson planned and built, often for benefactors who were members of the Boston Athenaeum. Breisch considered the confluence of social factors, particularly class concerns, at play in the architecture and design of these "small libraries," and in his introduction, he approvingly quoted historian Dee Garrison's *Apostles of Culture: The Public Librarian and American Society, 1876–1920* arguing that public libraries were a "rich focus for expressive meaning in Victorian America." The history of libraries is revealing, Garrison wrote, because

the belief that America was a radical democratic experiment in government; the sense of urban crisis and chaos; the fear of immigrant intruders; the emphasis upon family as guarantor of tradition; the discontent of women and labor; the hope that education would right the wrongs of poverty and crime; the hunger for education among the poor; the ambiguous paternalistic and humanitarian motives of reformers—all were as important to the content of library ritual [and decoration and design, we might add] as the need for a contented, disciplined, and busy wage force (Breisch, 14–15).

Yet when Breisch turned to predecessor libraries in public, he grouped the Redwood Library in Newport, Rhode Island (1748–1750), with Jefferson's Rotunda library at the University of Virginia (completed 1826), and the Yale College Library, the current Dwight Hall (1842–1846), in a run-up to declaring the first Boston Public Library building "the vanguard of modern library design" (56–77). Though three social libraries, the Redwood Library, the Library Company of Philadelphia's 1790 building, and the Boston Athenaeum's edifice (built 1847–1859) received mentions, Breisch's survey does not consider their design and decoration in any serious way. My work here is to recover some of that history.

THE LIBRARY IN THE HOME

In antebellum America, any reasonably successful young man could hope to own a home. While room specialization—separate rooms for different classes of activity—was just beginning to take hold, by the Civil War, the elite home would include a personal, private library (Clark 40). But at the beginning of the nineteenth century, ownership of books and a writing desk would not necessarily mean a dedicated library, even for the elite. In a painting from 1801 (Figure 3.1), James Prince, a wealthy merchant from Newburyport, Mass., gathered with his son by a desk for a portrait. Though the desk has shelves of books, the eye focuses on the quill and letter in Prince's hand, suggesting the importance of business over erudition. Historical records confirm that Prince and his son, at this early date, sit not in a library but merely in the corner of a first-floor, multipurpose room (Brewster, *James Prince and Son, William* [1801]; printed in Peterson, 1979, plate 13).

Figure 3.1   John Brewster Jr., *James Prince and Son, William*, oil, 1801. Courtesy of the Historical Society of Old Newbury.

Room specialization was a product of material prosperity. The various tasks of the eighteenth-century room, from entertainment and business during the day to sleeping at night, could now be parceled out to bedrooms and drawing rooms, parlors and libraries (Clark 40). Even with differentiation, though, a separate library was not the highest priority. In their influential pattern books for new standalone houses, neither Samuel Sloan nor the partnership of Alexander Jackson Davis (designs and illustrations) and Andrew Jackson Downing (strident text) included designated libraries in any of their more modest designs (Davis and Downing; Sloan). "Few cottages of moderate size have a room specially set apart for a library," Downing wrote, and he suggested that a hanging bookcase in any spare corner would suffice (432). For Sloan, the fourth ground-floor room after the dining room, parlor, kitchen, marked "C" "would make a delightful sitting-room or library, according to the choice of the occupants" (Figure 3.2), while only larger homes could provide both a drawing-room and a library (166, 172). Only in Downing's "villas"—houses with five rooms on the ground floor and "requiring the care of at least three or more servants"—did he clearly designate a room as a library (257).

Beyond having enough rooms, there was the question of what the library was for. Sloan described it as a "library or office, where the gentleman of leisure can enjoy his books and newspapers, or inhale the essence of a fragrant 'Havana'" (83). The library was male space, where the comforts of elite life could be relished. For the aspiring class, the library was a refuge from both home and work responsibilities. Architecture historian Bainbridge Bunting, in describing life in Boston's Back Bay, noted that the merchant's exchange would close at two in the afternoon and dinner would not be served until three, so the library could "provide a quiet retreat where [the man of the house] might spend his afternoon in study or with his accounts" (Bunting 130). Downing, in contrast, saw the

DESIGN XX.

Country House for any Climate.

Fig. 79.

Fig. 80.—Principal Floor.   Fig. 81.—Second Floor.   (170)

Figure 3.2 Design XX, "Country House for any Climate," Figs. 79, 80, and 81, engraving, in Sloan, p. 170. The room marked "C," Sloan wrote, "would make a delightful sitting-room or library, according to the choice of the occupants." Samuel Sloan, *Sloan's Homestead Architecture*, 1861, p. 172.

library more broadly: as "a separate apartment . . . devoted to intellectual culture," it was merely "a retired and secluded room," one that was "cosy and home-like," which "will probably be the sitting-room of the family" (359, 324–325). For Downing's audience, the male, business concerns of the library were shared with its role as an informal gathering place for family.

Whatever its use, everyone agreed on what made a room the library—the books. As a room for reading, good lighting and space for bookcases were necessities. Sloan prescribed "tastefully arranged and decorated book-shelves," telling us that they should be "of course incorporated as a permanent fixture of the room" (153–154). Downing noted that, with a bay window, the room "will be lighted more agreeably than if the walls on each side were pierced with two smaller windows," while on the other walls "an unbroken space is afforded on both sides for books" (306). Downing and others feared that the towering bookcases threatened to make the library "stiff," but suggested it could remain "a room pleasant to work or play in" (Edis 189–190). This could be effected through the use of subtle colors "that never tire and always please," utilized in wallpaper and stained glass (Davis and Downing 335–336). A place for the husband to

FIG. 197.

Figure 3.3   "Library Furniture," Fig. 197, engraving. Sloan, *Sloan's Homestead Architecture*, 1861, opposite p. 345.

work as well to relax, a refuge for the family and a place of education—the library could fulfill all of these duties if it could "partake of a mixed character" (Cooper 8).

Sloan suggested stately libraries; Downing was attuned to their mixed uses. But in their sections on furniture, both provided the ideal, elite-coordinated suites of furniture, beginning with the finest individual items. "Library chairs should be rather heavy and solid, compared with those of the drawing-room or dining-room," Downing explained. Bookcases were similarly weighty, shielding books with "glazed cases," and were topped "with Grecian architraves and mouldings." Library tables were "more massive than any other tables," "inlaid upon the top with morocco or cloth, to afford a smooth surface for writing." The businessman would of course need the pedestal library table, with its "drawers on both sides" and "a rising flap on the top, which may be raised to any height, to write or read upon; and when not required, it can be let down flush with the top of the table" (424). "A quaint arm-chair," chosen for comfort, would be "very suitable for the library," Downing wrote, while for novelty, he suggested the "tête-à-tête," a chair which "holds but two persons . . . to face each other in conversation" (455). The tête-à-tête suggests a social space for courting, but Downing averred, saying it was "an agreeable piece of library furniture in the winter evening," so that "the wife can sit towards the light, sewing, while her husband sits towards the fire with his book to the light, in the best position for reading" (455–456).

The pattern book illustrations held the full complement of library furnishings, done in the best ways. Downing noted that in these elite libraries, the Elizabethan style was often chosen, and antiques were much sought after. "Oak or black-walnut" were the woods of choice, with "a richly-carved bookcase, sofa, and table" providing the basic set (457, 348). Sloan upped the ante by providing a sense of "the most elaborate character" of these items (Figure 3.3), showing a bookcase with carved finials, a kneehole desk, and ornately decorated drawers, illustrating the full extent of the table and the texture on the chair (facing 345). The lavish library of this type at Lyndhurst, a Hudson Valley mansion,

Figure 3.4   Jack Boucher, "General View of North Library," 1971, Historic American Buildings Survey, HABS NY, 60-TARY, 1A-38, Library of Congress, Prints and Photograph Division. Accessible online via: http://hdl.loc.gov/loc.pnp/hhh.ny0869.

which was designed by Davis for New York merchant George Merritt (Figure 3.4), has been restored, while an 1838 portrait of General Stephen Van Rennselaer—amidst signs of opulence like a marble bust, velvet table coverings, and large collection of ornate books—provides a contrast to the portrait of James Prince discussed earlier (Boucher, "General View of North Library" [1971], Historic American Buildings Survey; see also Peterson plate 141; Chester Harding, attrib., *General Stephen Van Rennselaer* [c. 1838] in Peterson, plate 52). These libraries brought all the proper elements together—the portraits and the glazed cabinets, the hefty pedestal table, and the carpeting. An illustration from Henry Lawford's 1856 furniture catalog went even further, showing an impossibly large library, filled with an enlarged suite of coordinated furniture and holding books behind ornately carved cabinet doors (plate IV). These arrangements show that, even though often not practical for the individual to own, the elite merchant thought clearly about how to construct the ideal formal space for reading and writing.

These scenarios would be mere dreamscapes for all but the very rich, of course. For the middle class, able to afford a home with a library but unable to purchase these elaborate suites of furniture all at one time, the documentary evidence suggests that they assembled a workable set of chairs and desks, bookcases, and ornaments. The library of Philadelphia's Episcopalian bishop, William White, was such a room, painted by John Sartain as it looked after White's death in 1836 (John Sartain, *Bishop White's Study*

[1836] in Peterson, plate 50). Un-upholstered Sheraton chairs and a Windsor chair filled the room, though perhaps they were brought in from the dining room visible through the doorway; in any case, they were not a suite for the library. The late bishop's best chair seems to fit Downing's model of a "quaint arm-chair," designed to recline for the reader, but White's desk was modest in size, and he clearly had more books than he could (afford to?) put away in bookcases, stacked as they are above the cabinets. Small paintings and prints, rather than vases and busts, marked the mantle. Similarly, the library of the Smithsonian Institution Secretary Joseph Henry's residence on the Mall, photographed in the 1860s after his death, showed glass-fronted bookcases on undecorated walls and next to two mismatched chairs, one of them a cane-bottomed folding chair (*Joseph Henry's Library* [1860–1870] in Peterson plate 123). These imperfectly stylish libraries, decorated with as-available items, may nevertheless seem more "cosy and home-like" to the modern viewer than the fancy furniture of the idealized, "stiff" elite libraries.

This brief investigation of the library form in the private home provides a number of lessons for the more general question at hand. Given that a library was the fourth or fifth room specialized in mid–nineteenth-century designs, it is clear that a library was a luxury, one where furnishings could further articulate the level of refinement the family could afford (Ames). For the wealthy, a whole suite of specialized furnishings, with valued objects and classic tomes, promoted the idea of the library as a preserve, a place where the man of the house could do his reading or bookkeeping without interruption. For others, notably those of more modest means, the library could provide some of these functions while also allowing for family leisure activities from conversation to sewing. There, a mixed set of chairs and utilitarian items for holding books would do. A library, after all, was about the books; Downing wrote that "the walls of an humble cottage sitting-room," hung only with a small set of bookshelves, "have a higher meaning there than those of the most superb picture-gallery in a villa." This, he insisted, was because "we know that it [a bookcase] signifies intellectual taste in the former case, while it [the picture gallery] *may*, perhaps, be only a love of display in the other" (423). The library was a site of tradeoffs and compromise in the private home. An examination of libraries in the public realm demonstrates similar tensions that, as in the home, are reflected in the way library rooms were furnished.

PARLORS IN PUBLIC

The pattern-book authors took the country villa as their model: standalone homes set on ample parcels of land, far enough from their neighbors but close enough to the city so as to allow the man of the house access to his business. As those who could afford it moved to "streetcar suburbs" in this ideal middle distance, others drawn to work in the city found residence in newly constructed rowhouses or rented rooms in early apartment buildings. Convenient but small, these arrangements did not allow for a personal library, of any size or decor. Yet residents of these apartments—in this era, the familiar demographic of white, single young men, who had come in to the city from farms or from abroad in search of a livelihood—also needed a place to relax in the evening, to read, or to converse with friends (Luckingham; Barth). Social reformers, grappling with the challenges of the industrializing city, understood that, in the words of historian Tom Glynn, "education would provide an alternative to drinking, gambling, and other dangerous and immoral pursuits" (351). How could these need be fulfilled in the public sphere?

One way was by simply providing the private rooms on a public scale. In her study of the parlor and its furnishings, art historian Katherine Grier noted that the first half of the nineteenth century was "a world full of parlors," not just at home but on steamboats and trains, in hotels and attached to theaters (Grier 53). Grier found "astonishingly elaborate and expensive" parlors established in the cities by working-class groups, such as firefighters, to provide places where they could socialize (51–54). These spaces, decked out with oil paintings, a fancy sideboard, the company's "award silver," and populated in engravings by firefighters in top hats, represented allegiance to middle-class aspirations—even if they had to be fulfilled in fraternal, rather than individual, terms (53).

In her catalogue of such public parlors, Grier included an account of the New York Atheneum reading rooms from the November 15, 1850, *Daguerreian Journal*, where the author described "three very spacious rooms" of "great size and height." The rooms, he said, "had a costly look" and created "the imposing effect of interiors devoted to social intercourse"—that is, much like a sitting room or library in the elite home (qtd. in Grier 51). Grier described how, in the following decades, the parlor would be co-opted for commercial purposes, often in the guise of a "palace," mentioning the "palace hotel" and "dry goods palace" as examples (56). But Grier argued that from 1830 to 1850, public parlors "were essentially large-scale versions of the fashionable drawing-rooms in private houses." Different in room size, but not in type of decoration, these parlors in public held repeated individual furnishings, like upholstered chairs and pier tables—rather than immense individual items that Grier called "more grand and less home-like," like a gargantuan chandelier or an endless sofa, as became the custom in hotels and other public halls beginning in the 1850s (57). Grier included athenaeum reading rooms in her review of *parlors*, despite the greater similarity between the athenaeums and private *libraries*. By including the athenaeum with the firefighters' parlors and session rooms, re-creations of the home parlor in public, Grier's work suggests a model for understanding the social library as a private library in public.

Before returning to the question of libraries and reading rooms directly, it is interesting to consider whether the parallel between the hotel parlor and the library in public is a good one, and how public spaces provided a different sort of refuge than a home library. This task is best begun with Paul Groth's book *Living Downtown*, which investigated the history of residential hotels from the beginning of the nineteenth century through 1930, the end of their heyday. Groth found that residential hotels were often the place newcomers chose to live. Located close to the commercial and social centers of the city, they provided easy entrance into the right circles. In the early nineteenth century, slave markets and stock exchanges often were located in hotel lobbies, uniting the residential with the commercial (57, 59). In describing how the public spaces in hotels were furnished, Groth quoted an 1855 account on how these rooms were "furnished in a far more costly manner than a majority of young men can afford," a comment that echoes Grier's findings (qtd. in Groth 61).

Groth argued that the combination of modest private rooms and more ornate public parlors made it difficult to determine the class markers of boarders, lodgers, and apartment-dwellers. The use of public places for socializing, dining, and relaxing—the functions of a private drawing-room, dining room, and library, now projected into public space—allowed hotel dwellers a degree of mobility (5–8, 20–22). Groth wrote that "there was little of the social and cultural opposition that theorists require for a true division between classes" (22). Instead, the middle class "often emulated the truly wealthy," and "with their best clothes and manners . . . could infiltrate the palace hotel dining room for a memorable meal," even though, Groth reminded us, "they could not live like that every day" (21; see also Bourdeiu). The hotel, therefore, allowed the young man residing there to live out part of his dream of a home of his own. The ability for urban young men to move in such surroundings was seen as a privilege of city life—and it was one that the elite tried to curtail (Levine). When, in 1844, a New York hotel began to offer hotel guests meals in private dining rooms, a newspaper editor sternly protested that private dining was an affront. "Going to the Astor and dining with two hundred well-dressed people and sitting in a splendid drawing room with plenty of company" afterward, the editor argued, was a privilege of city life, a sign of the "tangible republic" that marked America as different (qtd. in Groth, 29–30). For this editor, the public dining room had a civic function; it was more than merely a substitute for the private dining room of those staying at or living in hotels. This was not just a private room on a public scale; to call it a sign of the "tangible republic" suggested more was at stake than individual aspirations.

THE SEARCH FOR A GREAT GOOD PLACE IN THE CITY

Thus, while Katherine Grier, focusing on the decorations, made parallels between the private and public parlors, the mid–nineteenth-century social commentators which Paul Groth cited suggest that there was a communal need being served in the public parlors and social libraries—that these places had a public identity unrelated to a private form. In *The Great Good Place*, sociologist Ray Oldenburg focused on the social function of the "third place," his term for one of "a great variety of public places that host the regular, voluntary, informal and happily anticipated gatherings of individuals beyond the realms of home and work" (Oldenburg 1989 16). Chronicling the importance of the French café, the German *bier garten*, the English pub, and modern American coffeehouses, bookstores, and diners, Oldenburg said that the third place provides "the kind of thing Tocqueville marveled at" in his descriptions of voluntary associations on the American landscape in the 1830s (Oldenburg 2001 2).

Oldenburg argued that third places tend to share certain features. A third place is on "neutral ground" (i.e., not in someone's home); it has a group of regulars; it is accessible, both nearby and open convenient hours; and it is a "playful" place, where conversation is shaped by the "exercise and display of wit" (Oldenburg 1989 37). While some of these characteristics may be hard to judge about a third place of two centuries ago, other ideas on Oldenburg's list speak quite clearly to the nature of social libraries. In third places, the urge to converse dominates, and regulars feel "at home," perhaps more so than in their own houses—ideas reflected in the privilege and pride that the newspaper editor felt about the hotel dining room and its place in the "tangible republic." The third place is a leveler, Oldenburg wrote; "the charm and flavor of one's personality, irrespective of his or her station in life" is the coin of the realm, and people can be "enjoined, accepted, embraced, and enjoyed" in the third place "despite their 'failings' in their career or the marketplace" (24, 25). While nineteenth-century third places were far more likely to maintain class divisions in their focus on individual improvement and material as well as social success, Oldenburg's basic outline is familiar.

In considering how the social libraries of the nineteenth century might be understood as "third places," it is also important to remember how new the need for a third place would have been. Young men were, for the first time, confronted with the anonymity and strangeness of the city. Though loneliness may be an accepted fact of contemporary life, it was a revolution in the nineteenth century. No one knew they needed a third place until they contemplated the reality of the city: far from friends, off from work, the prospect of an empty rented room held little comfort (Rotundo). To find their third place, these men had to find a community; they had to understand that others were facing the same challenges. That they could do so in part through an "imagined community" of print provides a hint into the power of social libraries in these years.

Anthropologist Benedict Anderson's now-classic book *Imagined Communities* focused on the development of nationalism and "that remarkable confidence of community in anonymity which is the hallmark of modern states," but his work has been particularly helpful to cultural historians interested in how modes of communication helped create *real* communities as well (Augst). Anderson described how novels and newspapers ask the reader to link simultaneously occurring events and imagine their relation; such forms serve as more than an analogy to nation when "the newspaper reader, observing exact replicas of his own paper being consumed by his subway, barbershop, or residential neighbours is continually assured that the imagined world is visibly rooted in everyday life" (Anderson 35–36). With the market revolution, literacy became more common; with innovations in papermaking, the invention of the novel and the penny presses vastly expanded what was available to be read (Davidson). While Dana Nelson, among others, has indicated how such local and national membership could be restricted on racial, gendered, and class-based grounds, the fact that social libraries purchased novels and newspapers and could lend them out to all who asked nevertheless suggests the importance of the library as both a third place for these young aspiring men and its role in knitting them together as a community (Nelson).

Oldenburg and Anderson's theories ultimately point to separate, if complementary, aspects of social libraries. Oldenburg described the necessity of a "third place" refuge, especially, if not exclusively, for those without such recourse in their own home. Anderson found that such places were fed by a need for association among strangers, and demonstrated the importance of the local, "tangible republic" in shaping the national one, limited in the ways Nelson delineated. In turning to how the library in public evolved, it will be helpful to keep in mind the question of how social libraries interact with both the pressures of urbanization and the search for community. As we shall see, these factors shaped the library not just in its conception, but also in its decoration and design.

THE MEANINGS OF BOOKCASES AND THE "FICTION QUESTION"

The well-furnished private library and the more modest one; the private room writ large; the third place and the "imagined community" made real—all of these spaces serve as valuable models for understanding the construction and design of libraries in public. Our embedded analysis will begin with a seemingly benign description of how library bookcases should be constructed, taken from the 1859 Smithsonian report of William Rhees. For information on library construction, Rhees reprinted a section of a treatise on libraries from the *Encyclopædia Britannica*. After a quick description of bookcase materials, focusing on their strength and fire-proofing ("If it be determined that the book-cases shall be wholly uninflammable, the shelves may be made of enameled slate, and the others portions of galvanized and perforated rolled iron."), the article's author briefly mentioned that "for the bulk of a great collection of books, I see little or no advantage in the use of closed cases, whether wired or glazed." A casual reader might continue to roll through the admonition that "in all cases, the rarities and choice contents of a library should be protected by glass," but, given our interest in what quotidian library decisions meant in this era, it is necessary to examine the question of bookcases more closely (qtd. in Rhees ix–x).

Both of the private libraries we have examined, that of George Merritt at Lyndhurst and Joseph Henry at the Smithsonian, featured closed-case bookcases, suggesting that the books were as reassuring in display as edifying in use. Open shelves imply more frequent use; by advocating open shelves, the *Encyclopædia* author envisioned a library which, as Jewett defined, held "popular works for reading rather than for reference"— that is, a utilitarian-minded social library. The open bookshelf, then, suggested the social libraries could be Downing's "cosy and home-like" space, where casual conversation could mix with casual reading of popular works. Yet such casual reading was only accepted by some of the social libraries; the choice of shelving and what it stood for became a controversy between "elite" and "clerk's" social libraries over the "fiction question."

Dee Garrison, in her celebrated *Apostles of Culture*, described at length the late nineteenth-century controversy over fiction. Her distinction between a "censorship model" and a "consumership model" in the history of public library librarianship maps well to the earlier era's differences between "elite" and "clerk's" social libraries (Garrison; Denning 48–50; Carrier). In 1826, the inaugural year of the New Haven Apprentices Literary Association, a mercantile social library, the members considered for debate the question "Are novels injurious to a reader?" (New Haven Men's Institute). The town's elite Social Library had passed a resolution in 1808 stating that novels, romances, and plays were to be banned from the library unless approved by a vote of two-thirds of the membership (Shera 108–109). In the divide between the elite and their clerks, the fiction question served as a central issue for how the "dominant genteel culture" would choose to deal with the working classes, as Michael Denning has argued in *Mechanic Accents*. When it came to social function, the place of the library, Denning noted, was "contested terrain" (47–48).

Elite libraries, like the Boston Athenaeum, the Boston Library Society, the Social Library of New Haven, and the Apprentices' Library Company of Trenton, chose to ban novels, passing up that which is "so apt to captivate juvenile imaginations," in the words of the Trenton board of managers, in favor of purchasing "works of sterling value and lasting usefulness . . . on religion, morality, and science" (Beckerman 5; Glynn). As if to show the extent of these preferences, members of the Boston Athenaeum supported the founding of the Boston Public Library in part because they felt that institution could buy the popular literature, leaving the athenaeums to remain "repositories of exclusive culture" (Story 196–197).

In contrast, social libraries for clerks, such as the Cincinnati Mercantile Library, the Rochester Mechanics' Association, the New Haven Young Men's Institute, and the New York Mercantile Library, welcomed novels and the ephemera of magazines and journals (Augst; Barringer and Scharlott). They understood that patrons wanted not an esteemed collection of rare books but the popular items they saw in the bookstores but, perhaps, were unable to buy for themselves. Other libraries, such as the Apprentices' Library of New York City, the St. Louis Mercantile Library Association, and the San Francisco Mercantile Library Association, tried to strike a balance between a small collection of novels and a larger educational collection (Luckingham; Glynn). In many ways reflecting the ambiguity of the name "mercantile," these libraries tried to provide for clerks while

Figure 3.5   John C. Browne, "Artifacts in the Historical Society of Pennsylvania," photograph, c. 1868. Courtesy of the Library Company of Philadelphia.

holding a cache for merchants—a strategy that still differentiated them from the most elite libraries.

FURNISHINGS AND DESIGN: ELITE SOCIAL LIBRARIES

In the heated atmosphere surrounding the fiction question, the difference between a bookcase with a closed case and open shelves loomed large, helping to differentiate elite and clerk's social libraries and serving as a key as to how social meaning can be drawn from differences of furnishing, decoration, and design. The location of the Boston Library Society, founded in 1794 and housed in the rooms over the arch in Charles Bulfinch's new and tony Tontine Crescent, indicated an immediate unity between the most fashionable and luxurious of urban dwellings and the elite library society (*The Boston Library Society Rooms in the Tontine Crescent* [c. 1857] in Wentworth 34). With the neoclassical design matching fashionable taste of the era, the library served to crown the project and drew from the prestige of those living there. As the library stood over and above the houses, the space expressed just the right sort of haughty-yet-refined message for the "elite" library audience.

Though no images of the interior of the Tontine Crescent rooms can be found, the library of the Historical Society of Pennsylvania (Figure 3.5), founded in 1824, may serve as a fair parallel (*Artifacts in the Historical Society of Pennsylvania* [c. 1868]; reprinted in Finkel 113). In a room filled with scientific and cultural artifacts (the photographs show a teepee in the left background, a mortar and pestle in the right foreground), the walls were lined with closed-case bookcases, dark wood with a simple arch design. A

Figure 3.6   "The Athenaeum Reading Room, 1855," engraving. Charles Knowles Bolton, *The Athenaeum Centenary*, 1907, opposite p. 132.

rug was laid out on the floor, and, above the bookcases, portraits were lined up, recalling the grandeur of General Van Rennselaer's library portrait. Membership in these societies may have been to support civic advancement, but clearly the furnishing of these rooms suggested their importance as communal show-spaces even for the elite, who could do as well at home.

The Boston Library Society was ultimately subsumed by the most successful elite library in the United States, the Boston Athenaeum. Founded in 1807 by a group of aspiring businessmen from good families, the Athenaeum members began at the top and simply kept pushing up the bar of gentility. The limited number of shares rose in price throughout the nineteenth century, and were generally passed down "like Family silver from generation to generation," as one commentator put it (Story 192). The Athenaeum was first housed in a fashionable mansion on Pearl Street; in the 1850s, a purpose-built building on Beacon Street, at the nexus of commercial and political power in Boston, housed the reading room as well as a picture gallery (Story, Breisch). The Athenaeum, like the Library Society, towered over its neighbors, evoking the civic authority of neoclassicism through its engaged pilasters. The size and number of paintings in the picture gallery, and the draw the gallery provided for women, indicated something of the cultural cache of membership.

Most instructive, though, was the view of the reading room (Figure 3.6), with the space seemingly stretching on forever (Bolton opposite 132). When considering the private library, the furniture in Lawford's catalog seemed far too large, but here, in a room at least three times as large, we can see the idea of such a private library extended to its grand, dream-like scale. Busts and scrolled ironwork provided decoration, and the matched chairs and large working tables allowed for all that one could ask for in a library—with the added benefits of the community of Athenaeum members. This engraving showed how the Athenaeum reading room in 1855 was a distinctly male space. The men sat at ease while the women, all accompanied, had to be in search of a specific item. In fact, the women were escorted because they were not allowed under Athenaeum rules to enter the reading room alone; the chief librarian "reacted with shock

Figure 3.7   "Interior View of Appleton's Book Store," engraving. *Illustrated American Advertiser*, 1851, p. 305.

and horror" when such a suggestion was made in 1855 (Van Slyck 225). The bookcases were roped off, suggesting even men had to request the items they desired. The control of the space suggests both the sense of the library as male refuge in the home and the restrictiveness of membership, as described by Oldenburg and Nelson. If elite social libraries were attended by those who could afford to have their own elaborate libraries, the bonds of elite fraternity and the cache of such "conspicuous education" served as attraction (see Veblen 1889). When the first Boston Public Library reading room was completed, with a long hall adorned with classical statues and two rows of ornate tables, the mark of the Athenaeum's members in its construction was clear (*Boston Public Library, Bates Hall, Main Reading Room* [c. 1895] in Breisch 75).

These elite spaces also influenced commercial construction. Just as Katherine Grier found the "dry goods palace" and the steamboat parlor borrowing from the hotel's use of the parlor in public, advertisements showing the interior of some contemporaneous bookstores reveal the influence of the Athenaeum reading room. The Phillips, Sampson & Company display house had a grand table and the same arched doorways, and boasted of "facilities for furnishing PUBLIC AND PRIVATE LIBRARIES," while at Appleton's Book Store (Figure 3.7)—the publisher of the works of Andrew Jackson Downing and Alexander Jackson Davis—the perspective and the ceiling ornaments matched the Athenaeum reading room almost exactly (*Illustrated American Advertiser* 1856 421, 305). Marketing is about aspiration, and so expanding the rich man's private library to the gargantuan proportions of the elite social library served as the perfect model for the booksellers' store design.

FURNISHINGS AND DESIGN: CLERK'S SOCIAL LIBRARIES

From the architecture to the furnishings to the social functions, the contrast between elite social libraries and the retreats of aspiring clerks is striking. In 1847, the Nantucket Atheneum built a new building, but the library only received a section of the space. The entire upper floor was dedicated to a lecture hall; the meeting room and museum took up much of the first floor, indicating that the priority in this space was education, not ornament. The library received adequate light from its windows on three sides, but it was not arranged to impress. The long views down the aisles in the Boston Athenaeum were not repeated in this building, which was far more utilitarian in character (Nantucket Atheneum).

Clerk's social libraries were also far more likely to occupy a floor in an office building than to build a structure dedicated only to their use. This is true of the New Haven Young Men's Institute building to this day; it was also true of the nineteenth-century buildings of the New York Mercantile Library and the St. Louis Mercantile Library, each of which maintained floors above commercial space, even in buildings they owned (New Haven Young Men's Institute; Fletcher 1894 facing 50; St. Louis Mercantile Library). The clerk's social libraries often found space through the generosity of members made good; for example, when William A. Reynolds, the president of the Rochester Mechanics' Association, plowed his profits from wheat into a downtown business center, the Arcade, Reynolds gave the library space to house their books (Arenson 26).

Scholars have linked clerk's social libraries to a general interest in personal and civic improvement, a mindset that linked education not so much with refinement and pretension as with success in business and prominence in social circles (Augst; Barringer and Scharlott). In 1839, the Cincinnati Chamber of Commerce and Board of Trade was founded in that city's mercantile library, demonstrating the link between these institutions and the ambitious new business organizations (Barringer and Scharlott 393). That these libraries had been incorporated through state legislatures—using the same language as any new business—furthered this link (Shera). It was through "the education of young men," crowed a member of the San Francisco Mercantile Library Association, "that civilization, with its attendant blessings, will be carried upon the wings of commerce" (qtd. in Luckingham 32).

In the St. Louis Mercantile Library's first building, completed in 1854, the Delivery and Reading Room held some marble sculptures, glass-paned cabinets, and a vaunted death-mask bust of Napoleon, but photographs reveal modest desks, placed far closer together in a room smaller than the Boston Athenaeum and certainly without its imposing vista, as posts supporting the ceiling sprouted haphazardly throughout the room. As plans and views for a design competition held by the St. Louis Mercantile Library demonstrate, plans for a wide, symmetrical reading room and two-story bookcases were envisioned, but the funding to carry out the grand plan for the reading room was evidently not within reach. (*Delivery and Reading Room, St. Louis Mercantile Library* [1854–1887] and Architectural Drawings in St. Louis Mercantile Library Archive)

The utilitarian bent to clerk's social libraries is suggested by both the written and visual evidence. The keynote speaker at the reopening of the New York Apprentices' Library suggested how "a poor, little ragged apprentice boy" would look into the library and find a "rich repast spread before him," but that repast was less ornament and more earnest content of the books, freely available (qtd. in Glynn 35). In San Francisco, the mercantile library president reported in 1856 that the rooms were "well filled with members every evening, quiet, respectful, and attentive, giving their time and attention to the cultivation of their intellectual faculties" (qtd. in Luckingham 33). An engraving of the San Francisco Mercantile Library reading room from that year (Figure 3.8) presented a strikingly different picture from that of the Boston Athenaeum ("Library and Reading Room of the Association," Hutchings' California Magazine [May 1860], 491; reprinted

Figure 3.8 "Library and Reading Room of the Association," *Hutchings' California Magazine*, May 1860, p. 491. Yale Collection of Western Americana, Beinecke Rare Book and Manuscript Library.

in Luckingham 31). Here, the reading room again was far more modest in size; all but a few cases had open shelves, and there were no ropes preventing patrons from retrieving their own books. In the busy room, there was a minimum of ornament; as men sat at small desks, much like those in private homes, the space had been subdivided, to allow men to privately conduct their business. Though some women seem to be assisted by the men who accompany them, two other pairs were merely socializing, using the library as a parlor in public, to converse as would not be possible in their rented rooms. While seemingly modest compared to the Athenaeum reading room, this clerk's social library nevertheless served its members exactly as they needed.

CONCLUSION: THE LEGACY OF LIBRARIES IN PUBLIC IN THE AGE OF PUBLIC LIBRARIES

When the era of the modern public library began with the opening of the Boston Public Library in 1859, the concerns of both elite and clerk's libraries appeared there as well. For the elites, the library had been male space; if women were to be allowed, they reasoned, some "protection" needed to be created. It was, as architecture historian Abigail Van Slyck found, the separate ladies' reading rooms that were created reflected the goals of the elite library benefactors of the public library, who found a way to "manage" the presence of women in the library without disrupting its feel as a "gentlemen's club" (228, 224, 227). The elite benefactors had complained about women talking and giggling in their elite social libraries; that such behavior would likely be encouraged by the talkative, ambitious men in the clerk's social libraries indicated the breadth of their differences.

The separate ladies' reading rooms also entailed changes in design. "The decor . . . was noticeably less institutional," with rooms Van Slyck described as "inviting, cozy, homelike"—the exact terms Downing used to describe the private library. The ladies' reading rooms often had a "domestic character," Van Slyck said, with a fireplace, plants, and low bookcases marking the space as different from the rest of the library (230). Furniture in ladies' reading rooms was far more likely to match, as a suite, and often included the only upholstered furniture in the public library, sitting on the only carpet and near the only draperies. Even if a public library could not afford a completely different treatment, one could tell which reading room was which because, quipped one librarian, "the women's reading room held a potted palm" (qtd. in Van Slyck, 234).

Van Slyck draws many insights from these comments and described the gendering of these public libraries, but I want to focus on what they can tell us about men's reading rooms in public libraries. To contrast with the descriptions of these "domestic" female reading rooms, the main, male reading rooms, then, were starkly utilitarian, with mismatched furniture and no draperies or carpets. They served a private need in a public space, concentrating resources on buying books, not on ornamentation. In short, the men's reading rooms in the public libraries sound much like reading rooms in the clerk's social libraries, functioning as a space where function overtook form. As young aspiring men were always entering cities, these third spaces for private thought were always needed; if an elite merchant needed such a space, he could simply go to his home library. Hence the athenaeums that still exist are often more like museums, displaying fine art and utilizing their books, often rare and unique, as a research library—and further than ever from the clerk's library of circulating novels, and the branch public libraries we know today.

Social libraries were a fundamental influence on the design of the modern public library. Often intended to serve the men and women of the "clerk's republic"—those who had come to the cities, aspiring to social and business success—the first public libraries found sponsors among the ornate designs of elite social libraries, while building on the decorative as well as organizational models of the clerk's social libraries, spaces more utilitarian and modest in their design. While the elite could build on the spectacle of their own private libraries by investing in fine arts and rare books for their athenaeums, the furnishings and collections of many young men's institutes became ever more utilitarian, geared toward providing a third space for those in modest urban housing, regardless how shabby it became. In something as simple as a bookcase design, the different between an elite library built on a grand scale and a clerk's library accessible to all is evident. Only by placing the modern public library alongside the rare-book room, the high-school library, the community-college atrium and even the airport bookstore—placing it into a full vocabulary of architectural and design forms, historically and today—can we see how the library functions as a place, embedded in the dreams of city life, vital to commercial success as well as intellectual pursuits.

NOTE

1. Thanks to Edward S. Cooke, Jr., for his guidance with this paper, to the Library Company of Philadelphia, the St. Louis Mercantile Library, and the Nantucket Atheneum for providing documents about their institutions, and to the late great Juice Hut at San Diego State University, where I first encountered the idea of the third place.

REFERENCES

Ames, Kenneth L. *Death in the Dining Room and Other Tales of Victorian Culture*. Philadelphia: Temple University Press, 1992.

Anderson, Benedict R. *Imagined Communities: Reflections on the Origin and Spread of Nationalism*. Rev. ed. London: Verso, 1991.

Arenson, Adam. "Receiving and Perceiving Emerson: Examining 'The Conduct of Life' Lectures through Newspaper Reviews in Rochester and St. Louis, 1851–1860." Thesis (A.B.)—Harvard College, 2001.

Augst, Thomas. "The Business of Reading in Nineteenth-Century America: The New York Mercantile Library." *American Quarterly* 50 (1998): 267–305.

Barringer, Sallie H. and Bradford W. Scharlott. "The Cincinnati Mercantile Library as a Business-Communications Center, 1835–1846." *Libraries and Culture* 26 (2) (Spring 1991) 388–401.

Barth, Gunther Paul. *Instant Cities: Urbanization and the Rise of San Francisco and Denver*. New York: Oxford University Press, 1975.

Beckerman, Edwin. *A History of New Jersey Libraries, 1750–1996*. Lanham, MD: Scarecrow Press, 1997.

Bolton, Charles Knowles. *The Athenaeum Centenary*. [Boston]: The Boston Athenaeum, 1907.

Bourdieu, Pierre. *Distinction: A Social Critique of the Judgement of Taste*. Cambridge, MA: Harvard University Press, 1984.

Breisch, Kenneth A. *Henry Hobson Richardson and the Small Public Library in America: A Study in Typology*. Cambridge: MIT Press, 1997.

Bunting, Bainbridge. *Houses of Boston's Back Bay; An Architectural History, 1840-1917*. Cambridge: Belknap Press-Harvard University Press, 1967.

Carrier, Esther Jane. *Fiction in Public Libraries, 1876–1900*. New York: Scarecrow Press, 1965.

Carson, Barbara G. *Ambitious Appetites: Dining, Behavior, and Patterns of Consumption in Federal Washington*. Washington, DC: American Institute of Architects Press, 1990.

Clark, Clifford Edward. *The American Family Home, 1800–1960*. Chapel Hill: University of North Carolina Press, 1986.

Cooper, H. J. *The Art of Furnishing on Rational and Æsthetic Principles*. London: Henry S. King and Co., 1876.

Davidson, Cathy N. *Revolution and the Word: The Rise of the Novel in America*. Oxford: Oxford University Press, 1986.

Denning, Michael. *Mechanic Accents: Dime Novels and Working-Class Culture in America*. London, New York: Verso, 1987.

Davis, Alexander Jackson and Andrew Jackson Downing. *The Architecture of Country Houses; Including Designs for Cottages, Farm-Houses, and Villas, with Remarks on Interiors, Furniture, and the Best Modes of Warming and Ventilating. With Three Hundred and Twenty Illustrations*. New York: D. Appleton & Company, 1853.

Edis, Robert William. *Decoration & Furniture of Town Houses; a Series of Canto Lectures Delivered before the Society of Arts, 1880*. 2d ed. London: C.K. Paul & Co., 1881.

Finkel, Kenneth. *Nineteenth-Century Photography in Philadelphia: 250 Historic Prints from the Library Company of Philadelphia*. New York [Philadelphia, PA]: Dover Publications, Library Company of Philadelphia, 1980.

Fletcher, William Isaac. *Public Libraries in America*. Boston: Roberts Brothers, 1894.

Garrison, Dee. *Apostles of Culture: The Public Librarian and American Society, 1876–1920*. New York, London: Collier Macmillan, Free Press, 1979.

Glynn, Tom. "Books for a Reformed Republic: The Apprentices' Library of New York City, 1820–1865." *Libraries & Culture* 34 (Fall 1999): 347–372.

Grier, Katherine C. *Culture & Comfort: People, Parlors, and Upholstery, 1850–1930*. Rochester, N.Y., Amherst, MA: Strong Museum; Distributed by the University of Massachusetts Press, 1988.

Groth, Paul Erling. *Living Downtown: The History of Residential Hotels in the United States*. Berkeley: University of California Press, 1994.

Historic American Buildings Survey, "Lyndhurst, Main House, 635 South Broadway, Tarrytown, Westchester County, NY," HABS NY, 60-TARY, 1A-38, Library of Congress, Prints and Photograph Division. Accessible online via: http://hdl.loc.gov/loc.pnp/hhh.ny0869

Hutchings' California Magazine, May 1860.

Illustrated American Advertiser. 5th ed. New York: Prall Lewis & Co., 1856.

Jewett, Charles C. *Notices of Public Libraries in the U.S. of America.* Washington, DC: Government Publishing Office, 1851.

Lawford, Henry. *The Cabinet of Practical, Useful and Decorative Furniture Designs.* London, New York: J. S. Virtue, 1858.

Levine, Lawrence W. *Highbrow/lowbrow: The Emergence of Cultural Hierarchy in America.* Cambridge: Harvard University Press, 1988.

Luckingham, Bradford. "Agents of Culture in the Urban West: Merchants and Mercantile Libraries in Mid-Nineteenth Century St. Louis and San Francisco." *Journal of the West* 17 (April 1978): 28–35.

Lyndhurst National Historic Site, "Lyndhurst-Virtual Tour," 2005. http://www.lyndhurst.org/tour.html. Accessed Summer 2005.

Nantucket Atheneum. Floor plans. "D.R.," drafter. n.p., 1989.

Nelson, Dana D. *National Manhood: Capitalist Citizenship and the Imagined Fraternity of White Men.* Durham, NC: Duke University Press, 1998.

New Haven Young Men's Institute. "A Bit of History." n.p., n.d.

Oldenburg, Ray. *The Great Good Place: Cafés, Coffee Shops, Community Centers, Beauty Parlors, General Stores, Bars, Hangouts, and How They Get You through the Day.* 1st ed. New York: Paragon House, 1989.

———. *Celebrating the Third Place: Inspiring Stories About the "Great Good Places" at the Heart of Our Communities.* New York: Marlowe & Co., 2001.

Peterson, Harold Leslie. *American Interiors: From Colonial Times to the Late Victorians: A Pictorial Source Book of American Domestic Interiors with an Appendix on Inns and Taverns.* New York: Scribner, 1979.

Rhees, William Jones. *Manual of Public Libraries, Institutions, and Societies, in the United States, and British Provinces of North America.* Philadelphia, PA: J. B. Lippincott & Co., 1859.

Rotundo, E. Anthony. *American Manhood: Transformations in Masculinity from the Revolution to the Modern Era.* New York: BasicBooks, 1993.

St. Louis Mercantile Library. *Cultural Cornerstone 1846–1998: The Earliest Catalogs of the St. Louis Mercantile Library and the Growth of the Collections for a Varied Community of Readers.* John Neal Hoover, compl. St. Louis: St. Louis Mercantile Library, 1998.

Shera, Jesse Hauk. *Foundations of the Public Library; the Origins of the Public Library Movement in New England, 1629–1855.* Chicago: Univ. of Chicago Press, 1949.

Sloan, Samuel. *Sloan's Homestead Architecture, Containing Forty Designs for Villas, Cottages, and Farm Houses, with Essays on Style, Construction, Landscape Gardening, Furniture, Etc., Etc. Illustrated with Upwards of 200 Engravings.* Philadelphia, PA: J. B. Lippincott & Co., 1861.

Story, Ronald. "Class and Culture in Boston: The Athenaeum, 1807–1860." *American Quarterly* 27 (1975): 178–199.

Van Slyck, Abigail A. "The Lady and the Library Loafer: Gender and Public Space in Victorian America." *Winterthur Portfolio* 31(4) (Winter 1996): 221–242.

Veblen, Thorstein. *The Theory of the Leisure Class; An Economic Study in the Evolution of Institutions.* New York, The Macmillan Company; London, Macmillan & Co., 1899.

Wentworth, Michael. *The Boston Library Society 1794–1994: An Exhibition of Portraits, Views and Materials Related to the Foundation of the Society and Some of Its Early Members.* Boston: Library of the Boston Athenaeum, 1995.

4

A Grand Old Sandstone Lady: Vancouver's Carnegie Library

Ann Curry

Associate Professor, School of Library, Archival and Information Studies, The University of British Columbia, Vancouver, B.C., Canada

INTRODUCTION

Vancouver's Old Sandstone Lady was one of 125 Carnegie-funded public libraries built in Canada between 1903 and 1923. Most of these buildings (111 of them) were in Ontario, but three were in British Columbia—in New Westminster, Victoria, and Vancouver (Beckman 19). Andrew Carnegie funded over 2,500 public library buildings around the world with his philanthropic gifts because he believed that libraries were places that supported his philosophy and practice of assistance to those who were endeavoring to help themselves (Bobinski 11). Because Carnegie's assistant James Bertram distributed recommended building plans to each municipality applying for a grant, Carnegie library buildings have a "stamp" that identifies them as being a Carnegie—the magnificent columns, the wide steps to the front door, the stonework. In the early part of the twentieth century when most were constructed, these libraries "stood for the possibility of change, the thirst for beauty, the threads of memory and imagination that bind the New World to the Old, . . . for public culture, and the civic commitment to culture" (Jones xi). Despite this "family" resemblance in structure and purpose, however, each building has adapted over the decades to reflect the needs, intentions and aspirations of its community, making each a unique place infused with the triumphs and traumas experienced by its staff and patrons. Vancouver's Carnegie is such a place: the Old Sandstone Lady has adapted to drastic changes in surrounding community and type of clientele, assumed various library service/museum roles, and weathered indignities and abuse perpetrated by both city politicians and patrons while providing information, comfort, companionship and shelter to the inhabitants of Vancouver for over one hundred years. Her story is one of hope, grandeur, neglect, poverty, and rebirth: it mirrors in many ways the lives of the city's inhabitants themselves as they have rejoiced or struggled through wars, financial bonanzas, economic depressions, and addictions. After 103 years of service, she is still one of the most important places in the community.

THE EARLY YEARS

In 1900, Vancouver was providing library service from a crowded, poorly lit, and insufficiently heated room within the YMCA building. Library patrons and board members appealed to city hall regularly for newer and more spacious quarters, but these requests went unanswered. In 1901, Vancouver lawyer Alfred Allayne-Jones wrote to Ottawa MP George R. Maxwell about Andrew Carnegie's $200,000 monetary gift to the city of Seattle, which was used to build an impressive public library. Allayne-Jones stated that "the great terminal City of Canada, the gate to the Orient, needs Carnegie's name attached in that way" (Allayne-Jones).

At Allayne-Jones' urging, George Maxwell wrote to Andrew Carnegie's private secretary James Bertram in New York, who in his reply outlined the conditions for a Carnegie grant: the City of Vancouver would receive fifty thousand dollars if they would commit to spending five thousand (or one percent of the grant) per year to maintain the library (Bertram). Maxwell promptly wrote to Vancouver Mayor Townley and encouraged the Mayor to accept the offer. Council approved the gift and the requisite conditions in late March 1901.

Economic and political wrangling hampered the building plans right from the start. Allayne-Jones' proposal had placed the library on a plot of land owned by the Canadian Pacific Railway (CPR) and bound by Howe, Hornby, Georgia, and Robson streets (Read 4). City Council rejected the CPR land due to problems with location and cost, and instead approved in July 1901 the purchase of several lots near Pender and Hamilton streets, only to be informed later that another group already claimed this land (Read 4). Site selection for the new Carnegie was further complicated by rivalries between the east-end residents in the "old" heart of the city near city hall, and residents in the newer west-end area, to which businesses were beginning to relocate in the early 1900s. City councillors finally selected two sites—one in each area, and conducted a plebiscite on August 1901 to settle the issue. Vancouver City Librarian Edgar S. Robinson, writing in 1937, lamented the result:

West End versus East End interests fought it out on a personal and selfish basis with little regard for the welfare of the city as a whole, or for the library either. . . . The Eastenders turned out in force and swamped their enemies by a 746 to 407 vote. This is an important matter settled by a group of voters who know nothing about the factors entering into the location of a central building, and cared less. (Robinson 3)

In September 1901, the library board accepted architect G.W. Grant's plans—a three-story building to accommodate the stacks, circulation areas, separate reading rooms for men and women, lecture hall, and picture gallery, with sandstone and granite from local quarries as the main construction materials ("Cornerstone"). A year later in September 1902, a parade down Granville Street to Hastings led by the Grand Lodge of the Masonic Order celebrated the laying of the building cornerstone. The Mayor, Aldermen, Library Board commissioners, civic officials, and citizens conducted the prayers and speeches that accompanied the stone-laying ceremony, which was followed by burying near the cornerstone a special capsule containing Vancouver's Act of Incorporation and coin and stamp samples used in 1902 (Read 9).

On November 11, 1903, the Board directed librarian Edwin Machin to open to the public the new Lending Library room, as they felt that a sufficient number of new books had been processed to fill the shelves (by the end of 1903, the total collection had 8,100 items). Machin was also instructed by the Board to ensure proper behavior and conduct among patrons in the new building, with the specific directive that boys younger than fifteen were barred from the library after 6 p.m. (VPL). The four existing staff members struggled to cope with more users in the new building, including many "dozers" in the reference room, but the Board refused to add more staff positions. Instead, they recommended that the new building assume more social responsibility in the community by developing its role as a social meeting place, particularly for those who might be lonely or unemployed. To this end, the Board approved the playing of chess and checkers in the new library, forbidden activities in the old library facilities, and they directed Chief Librarian Machin to make available the game boards and pieces for users who requested them (VPL Feb. 1904).

The Library did not occupy the entire building when it opened—the Vancouver Art, Historical and Scientific Society (the Museum) occupied the upper floor. The City Council considered both as "cultural" organizations, and therefore amiable co-tenants. Despite this cultural bond, the relationship between the two agencies was often strained, exacerbated by City Council's inept budget department. Right from opening day, city council failed to pay the costs of providing light and heat to the Museum, despite an arrangement to do so. This tension between the Museum Society and the Library Board boiled over in October 1905 when the Board debated cutting power to the upper floor, but stopped short of actually pulling the switch (VPL—Oct. 1905). After the Board reported to Council that they were short of funds, Council offered in March 1906 to pay a portion of the Museum's monthly bill (Cardin 5–6). Library budgets remained tight, however, and Librarian Machin decided to cut costs by reducing the candlepower of the lights from ten to six.

The new library also struggled with its "cultural" role. Librarian Machin had purchased a sizable collection of books in French (including many novels) for the new Carnegie Reading Room to enrich and lift the literary quality of the collection, but not everyone favored this cross-cultural opportunity. After a patron questioned the merit of a French-language novel in August 1906, all the French-language books were pulled from the shelves while the Library Board compiled a list of the French "smut books" and sent it in December to the Library of Parliament in Ottawa. A librarian there made note of the books considered objectionable and also noted others objectionable only for youths (Cardin 7). This classified list has been lost, unfortunately, as has information about the fate of the objectionable books.

The population of Vancouver continued to grow rapidly during 1905–1910. Many single men from across Canada travelled to the city seeking work, and they enjoyed reading the library newspapers or playing chess or checkers after work hours or while securing employment. The Carnegie mandate to act as a social gathering place did concern several librarians who objected to "loungers" in the Reading Room who wished to chew and then to spit tobacco, offending other patrons, particularly women. The city police chief recommended that the Library prosecute offenders for spitting in a public place, but as an alternative, the staff converted space in the basement for the tobacco-chewing loungers to use (Cardin 5–6).

By 1908, the Carnegie was already cramped for space as Vancouver's population continued to grow rapidly. Inadequate temperature control had been a problem since the building opened. In summer, the crowded reading rooms were stifling, smelly, and unpleasant, while in winter the uneven coal furnace heating caused some rooms to be overly hot (Cardin 10). The elegant but ill-secured marble staircase had begun to list dangerously and banisters tempted young boys for a quick but dangerous two-floor ride, much to the irritation of staff and patrons.

The neighborhood surrounding the library was changing as the Carnegie celebrated its first decade. The cultural, financial, and retail center of Vancouver moved ever westward, away from the Library, as did the many of the upper- and middle-income families. The Library Board and City Council worried about this loss of clientele—in only ten years, the Library envisioned as the cultural and educational heart of the city was being sidelined (Cardin 11).

Tensions between the Library and the Museum (still located on the third floor) worsened after three burglaries occurred between 1907 and 1909. Entry had been gained though windows that neither the Library nor the Museum would pay to secure with bars. Security concerns about the collection surfaced in 1909 when the Library moved to open stacks, prompting the hiring of uniformed employees to ensure that items were not taken from the premises and to guarantee proper patron decorum in the stacks (Cardin 12).

Mr. James Edwin Machin, chief librarian since 1890, retired in early 1910 due to injuries suffered when he was hit by a tram, and passed away in April. Mrs. Machin and her daughter, both of whom had worked in the library for many years, stepped in to assume managerial responsibilities for the Library, assisted by former City Alderman Goodman who served as a temporary librarian (15, p. 15). The biggest challenge of that year was the reclassification of the entire 14,000-volume collection from the former "home-grown" classification system to the Dewey Decimal System, an initiative that cost the Library $200.

THE SCHOLARLY TEMPLE

Mr. Goodman was replaced on January 31, 1911, by Mr. R. W. Douglas, a scholar who lacked library training but possessed considerable zeal for the job. His vision for the Carnegie was that of a scholarly reference library, not a popular reading room, and he set out immediately to weed the collection and replenish it with more erudite books (Cardin 19). By 1913, the Library had nine branch libraries in separate buildings or storefronts, and circulation was booming in all outlets except the Carnegie, whose cramped facilities and focus on scholarly materials did not encourage more public attendance (Cardin 20). City Council approved a Library operating budget of $50,000 for 1914, and the Library system appeared poised for growth and perhaps a renovation of the beleaguered Carnegie, now only eleven years old, but overcrowded with books and patrons. The outbreak of World War I, however, dashed any hopes for a building refit as circulation declined immediately when citizens focused their attention on the war effort rather than reading. The system was "on-hold" during the war years of 1914–1918, but in 1920 the Library Board began seriously to question Librarian Douglas' scholarly vision for the Carnegie collection. They feared that the building, the services, and the collection were failing to meet the social and cultural needs of Vancouver citizens. To assess the Library, they engaged the services of Dr. Henry from the University of Washington and Mr. Jennings from the Seattle Public Library, who submitted an extremely critical report after a two-day visit. The list of the Carnegie's shortcomings was long: inadequate space, insufficient staff, problems with sharing the building with the Museum, poor selection methods, and inadequate community services to meet the city's social and cultural needs (Cardin 31–32). Henry and Jennings' final recommendation was to get rid of the Carnegie Library as soon as possible: they felt that the building failed abysmally to provide the vibrant public space needed by one of Canada's fastest-growing cities. This criticism of space and services led to further Board criticism of Librarian Douglas, but no moves to abandon the Carnegie.

To reestablish Vancouverites' relationship with their Library, the Board tried to increase access to materials and visibility in the community. Lending department closing times were changed from 8 p.m. to 9 p.m., and the children's library shifted from opening only during morning hours to 2 to 6 in the afternoon and 10 to 7 on Saturdays. Circulation of children's books increased significantly after this change, which signaled an important shift in clientele focus: children coming to the Library after school, unaccompanied by their parents, were now welcomed as library patrons. Although the Board knew that the Library's physical facilities were woefully inadequate, they felt that marketing Library services might improve the Carnegie's profile in the community, so they urged Carnegie's librarians to contact the news media more frequently so stories about Library events would appear in the papers (Cardin 36).

THE PUSH FOR RESPECT

The new Board members who took office in 1924 felt that it was time to end Douglas' tenure. Faced with this lack of support, Douglas resigned, and was replaced with trained librarian Edgar Stewart Robinson, who brought an unfailing devotion to books, public libraries, and library users (Curry 130). He was eager to promote the joy of books, dismayed at alliterate citizens like the Vancouver City alderman who boasted of having read only three books in his life (Gatz 3), and determined to make the Library a symbol of civic pride among Vancouverites. In his first annual report to the Board he wrote,

To take its rightful place in the City of Vancouver today and on par with library systems in the more progressive cities on the continent, the public library must first of all have adequate quarters. . . . It now remains for the citizens of Vancouver to show their recognition and appreciation of the work of this institution to that end that we may be enabled by their support to make the library take its proper place in the community. (Robinson)

His challenges were many, however. The Library had few support staff; working conditions and pay were poor; most staff members lacked professional training, and the backlog of books awaiting cataloguing was daunting.

As early as 1926, Robinson wanted to replace the Carnegie with a newer building. In an interview for the *Province* newspaper, Robinson stated that the building was unattractive, lacked form and function, the staircase was useless and the brick walls were oppressive (Vancouver's Library 3). Robinson also recognized the difficulties the Carnegie faced in fulfilling a double mandate—that of Central Library and also neighborhood library. As a Central Library, the overcrowded building needed to provide social space and library services for all Vancouver's citizens; as a neighborhood library, the building needed to serve the large number of Chinese citizens now in the area plus the large transient population of newly arrived immigrants and seasonal workers, many of whom worked in the logging industry. During the late 1920s, City Councillors proposed that a new cultural complex be built that would house the city library, art gallery, and museum, but Robinson rejected this plan because the location was remote from the business district. Although desperate for new space, he feared that such a partnership would consign the library to the fate of staid cultural artifact, the antithesis of the vital social and economic force that he hoped the library would be.

A PLACE OF REFUGE AND POLITICAL PROTEST

In 1929, Robinson did acquire extra space when the Library expanded into the newly vacated City Hall adjacent to the building. He converted most of this space into a newspaper reading room with it own caretaker, a particularly good decision in light of the devastating impact of the stock market crash that year and the economic depression in subsequent years. The reading room served as a refuge for unemployed or elderly men, who had lost their jobs or who were without families. The building was near the railway station—the "end of the rails" for Canada, and many men who had travelled across the country in an unsuccessful search for work found the warm, dry, and safe reading room a welcome change from boxcar living. As many as eight hundred individuals per day would read newspapers, play chess or checkers, or just doze in the Reading Room.

Most of the city and interurban lines pass in four directions on two sides of the building, heavy trucks thunder by, street signals sound, crowds gather at the nearby market, the fire department dashes through, and organizations parade with bands. It is often a real achievement to answer a telephone question, especially when a building is being erected across the street or a general election is in progress. The Japanese section lies on one side of the library, the Chinese on the other, and picturesque groups of Indians and East Indians mingle with crews from ports far and near, for the wharves are not many blocks distant. In these days of world-wide unemployment, Vancouver also has its crowds of men out of work and the library's location makes it a casual refuge, increasing the constant surge in and out. (Stockett 861)

In the space vacated by the reading room in the original building, Robinson established a new Science and Industry Department, with special reference service and a separate collection. Despite the darkening financial climate in the city, Robinson was determined not to delay any longer his initiatives to establish the Library's relevance on Vancouver's economic scene, and though crowded and far from ideal, the space did become the place where Vancouver's businessmen came for information.

As the Depression deepened through the 1930s, the Carnegie staff struggled to provide services with fewer staff and few new materials. Robinson complained that the Library was "deteriorating into a filling station" (Robinson 1930 Report) because staff were being forced to ignore reference and collection management duties so they could cope with long lines of patrons wanting to check out books. In 1932, City Council cut the library budget in half to $63,000 and cut wages by 10 percent (Robinson Report 1933). To cope with these drastic measures, Robinson laid off half the library staff, changed many full-time positions to part-time, reduced library opening hours, and closed the Carnegie down entirely for July and August of 1933. Robinson feared that such drastic cuts would hasten social revolt, "making 'reds' among other peaceful folk" when they realized that City Council considered "the dollar . . . more sacred than human welfare" ("City Librarian" 3).

In 1935, social unrest did occur, with the Carnegie at the center of the revolt. The Old Sandstone Lady became the protest rallying point for angry relief camp workers in an incident known thereafter as "The Occupation of Carnegie." The relief camp men worked in poor conditions in government camps for very low wages, but after several years of "food and shelter pay" they were restless and discouraged: they did not want soup kitchens, they wanted real jobs. If they left the camps, however, the government considered them to be on strike, and cut all social assistance ("All Must" 11). Hundreds of these "striking" relief workers had gathered in Vancouver to protest this federal unemployment relief policy, and to draw government attention to their cause, a group 250 strong stormed the Carnegie on Saturday May 18, 1935. The striking workers promised not to break anything (which they didn't), asked all the staff to evacuate the building, and then occupied the entire building. They set up "headquarters" in the third-floor Museum so they could use the windows to communicate their message to the huge crowd that gathered around the building. Although the occupation was illegal, the strikers had considerable support from Vancouver citizens and even from Mayor MacGovern, who called the federal relief program "a failure" ("Strikers" 1). Members of the public showed their support by attaching parcels of coffee, tea, sandwiches, and cigarettes to ropes lowered from the third-floor windows. At the end of the day-long siege, the City offered the men immediate cash relief funds and promised not to prosecute if they left the building, offers that the men accepted ("Mayor" 2). The Occupation of Carnegie provided the impetus for the "On to Ottawa" trek, a 3,000-kilometre railway freight car journey to force the federal government to heed their plight. That the workers chose the Carnegie as the rallying point for this important protest is significant: although tattered with age and suffering from neglect, the Grand Old Sandstone Lady was still a public building that symbolized pride and justice, and the perfect platform from which to launch a political protest.

SUPPORTING THE WAR EFFORT

With the outbreak of war in 1939, library staff once again played a role in the war effort, which prompted staffing changes. Many male staff members enlisted and the shortage staff led to hiring of page girls and married women for the first time. Similar to the situation during First World War, circulation figures dropped as Vancouver citizens were occupied with the war effort.

As the war arena shifted to the Pacific, the threat of Japanese invasion on Canada's west coast increased and more military personnel were stationed in British Columbia. To prepare for an attack, library staff practiced black-out exercises, which proved difficult with the Carnegie's large and magnificent windows. They wrapped old, valuable, and out-of-print materials in fire-proof asbestos sheets and placed them in underground vaults.

When the Second World War ended in 1945, Robinson felt that the Carnegie should be a key place for de-mobbed soldiers and civilians to come for help in adjusting to the postwar economy. To this end, the Library bolstered its collection of business, technical, and trades books to assist those wanting to start a small business or study a trade (Robinson 1947 3). Demand on the science collection was particularly high just after the war; in fact, library staff reported that these books were so scarce and sought-after that they were frequently the target of thieves. Robinson felt strongly about the Carnegie playing her part to support Vancouver's postwar economic boom, but the paucity of the collection, the scarcity of staff, and, most of all, the inadequacy of the building hampered his efforts. His September 1947 report to the Board (published in the local newspaper) that staff and patrons frequently confronted rats "as big as cats" that had wandered over from the public market, did stir some discussion ("Rats, Arson").

PLANS TO REPLACE THE CARNEGIE

A group of library supporters determined to have the library take its rightful place as a center of civic pride formed the Friends of the Vancouver Public Library in February 1945. Their objectives were to bring the public and the library together; to promote library services; to advise and work with the Library Board and staff that deal with policy concerns for the good of the institution; and to provide a springboard from which users could offer their opinions (Friends). The underlying purpose of the Friends group was to convince Vancouver citizens to pass a by-law that would fund new library buildings and, to this end, the group organized public "forums, talks, discussions, musical evenings, and free film showings" at which the importance of improved library service was promoted (Gatz 20). Replacement of the Old Sandstone Lady seemed imminent when Vancouver citizens passed the first by-law for a new main library and three branches on December 12, 1945, with a majority of 83 percent. Political infighting at City Hall about a possible site for the new library began almost immediately, however, and persisted for the next ten years.

As the squabbling about a new site and funding continued, the Library Board focused on being progressive. They commissioned a series of three surveys (1949, 1954, and 1957) that examined the library's operation, resources, facilities, administration, services, and financial circumstances. John Adams Lowe, director of the Rochester, New York Public Library, and John S. Richards, director of the Seattle Public library performed the 1949 study. Their report was very critical of the Carnegie. Newspaper coverage quoted passages from the report that said working conditions were "shocking": "Crowded workrooms . . . wretched ventilation . . . inadequate restrooms . . . hazardous in case of fire . . . odors from the adjacent market and alley are so obnoxious that the windows are kept closed in summer" ("Library Facilities" 8).

The Adams/Richards report strongly recommended that the Main library "divorce" itself from the Museum (which still inhabited the third floor after nearly fifty years), and that a new main library be located in a more central location. The report also lambasted the Library for its poor collection and resulting lack of usage: the American Library Association (ALA) standards recommended 1.5 volumes for each registered borrower, Vancouver had 0.44; ALA recommended a minimum of $1.50 be spent for each registered borrower, Vancouver spent $0.77; ALA noted that in most cities registered users comprised at least 30 percent of the population, in Vancouver only 13 percent of citizens were users; and these users took out only 2.31 volumes per capita, well below the 6 volumes ALA prescribed (Lowe).

Newspaper columnist Jean Howarth supported the consultant's recommendations: she urged citizens to lobby municipal and provincial officials for better facilities and services so that Vancouver's public library could be a "centre for learning and a pleasant place where you can find like-minded people . . . a living room for people to enjoy magazines, . . . a place for information" (Howarth).

Although the Carnegie had been a source of civic pride in 1903, this was definitely not the case when City officials (at Robinson's urging) toured the building in 1950. They declared it to be a hazardous place where staff worked in dusty vaults and used newspapers to keep dust from seeping in through the windows. The building was "terrible . . . incredible . . . a fire-trap" ("Ancient Trap," "City Group"). The building was not a place of civic pride for many library patrons either. Allan Roy Evans wrote letters to the local newspapers complaining about "chronic coughers and explosive sneezers" (Evans—Jan 30), and how hard it was to "try and find a seat in the reference department any rainy afternoon or evening!" because many people were "asleep with accompanying snores" (Evans—Jan 27). As people and shelf space had become tighter over the years, the Carnegie had evolved into a place of tension and conflict—a reference library with tightly packed seats, leaving no room for distance between groups with different needs. The middle-class users wanted a quiet, "gentile" environment, while the low-income or homeless residents desperately needed reading room/living room space.

Setting aside the 1906 incident in which all the French-language novels were pulled from the library shelves, the Carnegie in its first fifty years of operation was known as an important place to expand one's mind. During his thirty-three years as chief librarian, Edgar S. Robinson promoted the Library as the quintessential civic space where good citizenship is nurtured:

Good readers make good citizens and the Library is the ounce of prevention which will keep our people informed, balanced in their judgment and firm in their belief in democracy as our way of life. An intelligent vote cannot be cast by an ill-informed citizen. A public library is truly an "Arsenal of Democracy." (Robinson "Half a Century" 3)

He boasted publicly in the 1940s that the Library collection contained publicly unpopular books such as Hitler's *Mein Kampf* and Anne Morrow Lindbergh's *Wave of the Future*, which appeared to be pro-Nazi. In 1954, Robinson faced a strong intellectual freedom challenge when the Vancouver Junior Chamber of Commerce (JCC) organized a book burning to foster the love of classic tomes in children who read comic books and horror stories. A book burning in Canton, Ohio, that inspired the event had encouraged children to trade ten comics or horror stories for a hardcover classic novel selected by the Canton public librarian ("City Library"). The JCC, led by a Mr. Harrison, had assumed that the Library would be the perfect place to serve as a depot for the dreaded comics and horror novels, but Robinson was adamant that the Library not be associated with book burning:

[w]hat Mr. Harrison believes to be a subversive book, others might not. I don't think we have any subversive books—that is those which advocate the overthrow of the government by revolution. But we have all kinds of books on Communism and the people want to read what we have, both for and against Communism. The Library has books, for instance, for and against capitalism and other subjects (Robinson "No Burning").

Despite the Library's opposition, the JCC decided to continue with the book burning, because they believed that the focus of the event was the removal of trash from people's homes, not censorship ("Jaycee Comic").

Vancouver's long-awaited new main library edged slightly closer to reality in 1951 when the City selected a site at the corner of Burrard and Robson, and completed the land purchase the following year. But controversy dogged the purchase even after nearly fifteen years of bickering, as some residents wanted a site closer to the new post office building ("Public should fight") while others opposing this Westside location resurrected the Eastside/Westside rivalry first heard when the Carnegie site was selected in 1901 ("Groups seek"). Robinson strongly supported the Burrard/Robson location because it was near the city's business center. He had always believed that the Library should be a key player in Vancouver's economic sphere, and this location would certainly enhance this role. Construction for the new library started late in 1954 and the new building opened on November 1, 1957, but without the library's greatest booster. Edgar S. Robinson passed away on October 24, a week before the library opened ("Robinson's Library").

Amid the excitement of the new building, the neighborhood residents who had used the old Carnegie as their second home were largely forgotten. The old men were fiercely loyal to the Old Sandstone Lady, and most of them did not make the long trek or take the bus to the new library. They worried that Carnegie Library would be closed, and their fears were justified, as the City discussed how the building might be donated to the museum. The Library staff hoped the city's social service department would step in and provide a reading room at Carnegie for the patrons they had seen on a daily basis for so long, but their hopes were dashed when the Carnegie closed its doors on November 1 ("New Library," "Old Faces"). Some of the older men waited on the steps for a few weeks, but gradually they dispersed when the doors to "their" library remained firmly locked ("Bid for Old Library").

THE CARNEGIE AS CITY MUSEUM 1958–1968

When the Library moved its central branch services from the Carnegie building to the new Robson Street location, the Old Sandstone Lady was closed for almost a year for renovations. She reopened September 4, 1958, as the Vancouver Museum, which now occupied all three floors. The Museum showcased in its enlarged space a diversified collection which one could kindly call "eclectic": it included a large collection of First Nations' items, an Egyptian mummy, a suit of fourteenth-century Japanese armour, and a 500-item collection of BC birds (the largest collection of its kind in the world) (Hood).

Throughout the decade that the Carnegie housed the Museum, the area around the building tumbled further into social despair. Boarded-up buildings were stark evidence of the flight of businesses from the area, shabby hotels and rooming houses replaced more reputable establishments, and alcohol and drug addiction thrust many area residents into a life of homelessness, poverty, and prostitution. The Carnegie was at the center of this area, now characterized as the "Downtown Eastside." The wide expansive steps leading up to the Carnegie's monumental pillared entrance caused concern as they provided "outdoor seating" to those who still considered the building a community gathering place. Reflecting the prejudices of the time, the museum curator Thomas Ainsworth complained to the City Clerk about the number of "Chinese and Hindoo" men who sat on the steps and hindered access to the front entrance of the museum. Faced with declining visitor numbers, the Museum finally closed November 6, 1968. The city put some items in storage and auctioned off others, such as a Chinese bamboo temple, to raise a total $2550.25 (Warner).

THE EMPTY YEARS

The Old Sandstone Lady remained empty and abandoned for twelve years while City Council considered and rejected numerous proposals for her use. During those years, the area continued to struggle with the issues of drugs, alcohol, prostitution, poverty, and social housing, and the Carnegie suffered injuries and indignities reflective of those suffered by the vulnerable and homeless citizens who huddled on her steps. Some politicians advocated demolishing the building because they felt it no longer had a place on the city landscape, but in 1972, the Carnegie was declared a historical building, prohibiting it from being torn down or renovated without due care to preservation (Hood).

The Carnegie remained empty year after year, and downtown Eastside residents groups became increasingly disturbed that no use was being made of this building at the center of their community. In response to this pressure, the City tried to sell or lease the building in 1974, but received no reasonable bids. The *Vancouver Sun* advertisement noted, "The purchaser or lessee will be required to undertake to repair and retain the exterior appearance of the building" (Ad for Sale or Lease), a daunting task as the building had been vacant for over five years. In 1975, the City tried again, but this time, only a lease bid was solicited. Once again, no acceptable offers were received. It appeared no one wanted the Old Sandstone Lady.

The Carnegie suffered yet another indignity when Mayor Phillips tried to "give away" the building to the highest bid, however small it might be, but City Council defeated his motion and instead asked for proposals for use from local community groups. Two of these groups—the Downtown Eastside Residents Association (DERA) and the Native Courtworkers and Counselling Association of British Columbia—were eventually asked to design a plan to share the facilities ("Carnegie Centre"). The DERA proposal, which included a library/reading room seemed to garner the most support.

Before anyone could use the Carnegie again, however, it needed extensive repairs and renovations. An assessment conducted in 1974/75 listed many severe building problems resulting from years of neglect, including a large hole in the third floor wall that had allowed in both the rain and thousands of pigeons that had roosted in luxury under the Romanesque Renaissance dome and created an unbelievable mess (City Maintenance). City Council approved the required repairs and renovations in 1976, but the $1.2 million funding was not granted until 1978.

THE GRAND REOPENING

The new Carnegie Community Centre, including the library/reading room, finally opened its doors on January 20, 1980, with a grand opening that included informal tours for the public, and opening ceremonies in the brand new theater that were attended by many politicians. After being neglected for decades, the Downtown Eastside and its residents—some of the poorest in Canada—were finally gaining political attention. Viewed cynically, the Carnegie was becoming the place where politicians could demonstrate publicly their social conscience, and the grand reopening of the building presented a perfect opportunity for such a display.

The architectural firm Downs Archambault won the 1981 Award of Honour from the Canadian Heritage Foundation for their renovation of the Carnegie. Major structural changes were necessary to make the building structurally sound, and to meet new building codes required nearly eighty years after initial construction, but the architects managed to retain the key monumental and signature aspects of the building—the dome, the spiralling marble staircase and the beautiful stained glass windows (Hood).

The Centre offered in 1980 and continues to offer many services to the community, including a lounge, theater events, exercise room, billiards, ping-pong, card table, chess, a cafeteria, and arts and crafts activities. The opening ceremonies program reveals that a variety of educational programs were offered during the renovated Carnegie's first months. English as second language (ESL) classes were available for the Vietnamese refugee "boat people" who had recently arrived in Vancouver: many of them had settled in the Carnegie area because of the strong Chinese presence. Other programs presented were basic college-level criminology courses, a course on how to cook on a hot plate (for men only), and a nutrition course for First Nations women (Opening Ceremonies).

The new library/reading room, which occupied part of the main floor, was managed as a special Vancouver Public Library Branch with borrower regulations adjusted for the area's clientele, for example, no proof of permanent residence required. A librarian and several assistants staffed the Library and managed the collection, which had 7,000 popular paperbacks, daily papers (including several in Chinese), a small hardback book collection, and magazines. With only 1,500 square feet of public floor space, the Library is small but busy. In 1980, the Library was open 324 days, circulated 68,139 materials, registered 3,741 patrons, and answered nearly 600 reference questions. In 1981, the entire Carnegie Centre was closed for three months due to a civic strike, but even with nine months open, the Library did brisk business, circulating 73,702 materials and answering over 9,000 reference questions (Cotterall).

GOVERNANCE UPHEAVALS

For most of the 1980s, the Carnegie Centre was rocked with turmoil as the various community organizations and city departments represented on the Carnegie Community Centre Association (CCCA) Board tried to manage operations and finances. The continuing ineffectiveness of the CCCA, exacerbated by public displays of animosity amongst Board members, caused the City Social Planning Department to suspend working agreements with the Association. The Carnegie was unlike the city's other community centers—it had different services, different regulations, different clientele, and its place in the Downtown Eastside Community was far more pivotal than that of other centers in their community. As a drug- and alcohol-free "oasis" within an enclave of violence and despair, the Carnegie literally saved lives. Governance of Carnegie required special skills and flexibility of all constituent members. In September 1987, working relations between the City and the Centre were reestablished, and although communication is occasionally tense, the CCCA remains an important advisory board to the Director of City Social Planning ("Council Urged" A13). The Library staff calmly and professionally continued to provide services through this period of governance turmoil: the Library's circulation continued to climb, and the number of patrons visiting the Library increased steadily. During the 1980s, the Carnegie Library established itself as a place where all were treated with respect, no matter how poor or ill-dressed, where one could find a friendly atmosphere very different from the shabby hotel room, litter-strewn alley, or cold dumpster where patrons spent many hours alone. At the Carnegie, even patrons who had veered farthest from society's norms were treated "like everyone else"—valued as having intelligence and a right to access information and read for pleasure.

NOT A GENTLE PLACE

Providing a sanctuary amid the hard and unforgiving reality on the streets outside is not always easy, and the Carnegie library staff have special mettle, deeper compassion, and true grit. It is not uncommon for drug addicts and alcoholics to be using the Library facilities at the same time as senior citizens and children. Drug use inside the Carnegie

Centre, however, is strictly prohibited and if a person is suspected to be intoxicated they are generally refused entry, as are people with a history of inappropriate behavior.

In 1991, Vancouver was setting a new record for homicides in a single year when in November the fortieth homicide victim died on the front steps of the Carnegie. He had been beaten at a local hotel and had dragged himself to the Carnegie Centre, presumably looking for help. While tragic, it is a testament to the Centre and its services that a fatally injured man would go to the Carnegie Centre for help ("City Sets" A1).

The Centre as whole has a strong educational mandate because the illiteracy rate in the area is high, and the Library is a full partner in the Centre's many literacy programs. The Library staff have many stories about patrons whose lives have changed when they became literate through these instructional programs and through reading library books. Staff at the Centre, including those in the Library, speak of the Carnegie "family." They care about the people in the community as individuals, greeting many of them by name as they enter the facility. The staff are well aware that many of their patrons are living life "on the edge"; so seeing someone during the day has special meaning—it means they are still alive. The population of the Downtown Eastside community served by the Carnegie Library in 2005 is approximately 11,500: 50 percent are between twenty-five and forty years of age, 10 percent First Nations, and 30 percent Chinese (6 percent of whom are from Mainland China). The collection has not increased much since opening day, due to space restrictions, and now numbers about 11,000 books, and many of those are paperbacks. Westerns remain the most popular fiction choice. Special collections in the Library include a First Nations collection, Chinese-language collection, small Spanish collection, and a focus on books related to social and health issues in the area such as poverty, addiction, housing, and physical and mental health. The Library is open from 10 a.m. to 10 p.m. every day, and usually every holiday (including Christmas!) if staff are available (VPL, Carnegie Reading Room). The Carnegie Kitchen within the Centre is also open long hours: it serves large nutritious meals, like chicken pasta and salad, for a small price—$1.87. To help bring members of the community together, the Carnegie Centre publishes a twice-monthly free newsletter that is a casual forum for news, poetry, community advertisements for events, and opinions, and always includes a column about Library happenings: http://carnegie.vcn.bc.ca/index.pl/newsletter.

CONCLUSION

When the Old Sandstone Lady was built in 1903, she was a symbol of civic pride that announced to the world that Vancouver had grown from a raw lumber town into a major city that was Canada's gateway to the Pacific. The building's magnificent dome, majestic columns, and the stained glass windows depicting Shakespeare, Milton, and Spenser represented Vancouver's commitment to progress through cultural and educational pursuits. Abigail Van Slyk in her book *Free to All* says that Carnegie "library buildings themselves were viewed as forces for good or evil, beyond their stated purpose and apart from the human activity they were built to house" (Van Slyk 159). Vancouver's Carnegie was considered a force for good in 1903, and she has carried that value in the eyes of the community for over a century—through two world wars, the Depression, and now as a force for good in a neighborhood ravaged by the evils of poverty, crime, alcohol, and drug addiction and dealing. Despite limitations of structure and space, the Old Sandstone Lady tried her best to meet the changing needs of Vancouverites over the years—to be a center for academic study in the early 1900s, a resource for culture and popular reading in the 1920s, a safe haven for the unemployed during the 1930s, a resource for economic recovery in the 1940s, and an information center for all citizens in the 1950s. But the Carnegie is perhaps providing the most good in her last incarnation as the Community Centre that holds the Carnegie Library, providing a refuge and a sanctuary (Whitney). When one surveys the thirty chairs in the library reading area, all occupied by people for whom living each day is a victory, all of whom are reading or visiting with others, it is obvious that this building plays a pivotal role in the community.

Vancouverites have a grudging respect for the Old Sandstone Lady: she has survived the ravages of time, the indignities of neglect, and the exploitation of her patrons. The millions of footsteps that have pounded up the wide marble staircase have worn a dip several inches deep, but the staircase endures and continues to welcome visitors. The Old Sandstone Lady's benefactor Andrew Carnegie said, "There is not such a cradle of democracy upon the earth as the Free Public Library, this republic of letters, where neither rank, office, nor wealth receives the slightest consideration." The building's century of service is fitting tribute to Andrew Carnegie's mandate.

ACKNOWLEDGMENTS

The contributions to this project of SLAIS student research assistants Jen Bradley and Andrea Lam, the Special Collections staff of Vancouver Public Library, and the wonderful staff at the Carnegie Branch Library whom I much admire, are gratefully acknowledged.

REFERENCES

Ad for sale or lease of Carnegie Centre by City of Vancouver. *Vancouver Sun* 2 July 1974.

"All Must Cooperate: Gainful Occupation Instead of Relief in the Aim of Your Government." *The Vancouver Province* 18 May 1935.

Allayne-Jones, Alfred. *Letter to George Maxwell.* Northwest Collection Pam NW 027 N55m. Vancouver Public Library.

"Ancient Trap Kills Mouse as Officials Visit Library." *News-Herald* 21 October 1950.

Beckman, Margaret, Stephen Langmead, and John Black. *The Best Gift: A Record of the Carnegie Libraries in Ontario.* Toronto: Dundurn Press, 1984.

Bertram, James. Letter to George Maxwell. Northwest Collection. Pam NW 027 55m. Vancouver Public Library.

"Bid for Old Library as Shelter Denied." *Vancouver Sun* 14 November 1957.

Bobinski, George S. *Carnegie Libraries: Their History and Impact on American Public Library Development.* Chicago: American Library Association, 1969.

Cardin, R.V. "Growing Pains: 1903–1924" in *The History of Vancouver Public Library*, an unpublished collection of essays edited by Stanley Read, 1975. Special Collections, Vancouver Public Library.

"Carnegie Centre." *Vancouver Sun* 17 January 1975.

City Maintenance Services Memo. n.d. Vancouver City Archives: 22-E-4 File 2.

"City Librarian Criticizes Council." *The Vancouver Province* 10 February 1934.

"City Library Not To Adopt Book Burning." *The Vancouver Province* 10 September 1954.

"City Group Tours Dingy Library." *The Vancouver Province* 21 October 1950.

"City sets homicide record." *Vancouver Sun* 21 November 1992.

"Cornerstone of the New Free Library Laid amid All the Pomp & Circumstance of the Ancient Craft of Freemasonry—An Interesting Ritual." *News Advertiser* March 1902.

Cotterall, Charles. Letter to Mayor Mike Harcourt and City Council, 20 May 1982. Vancouver City Archives.

"Council Urged to Renew CC Ties." *Vancouver Sun* 14 September 1987.

Curry, Ann, and Gary Carre. "Edgar S. Robinson: Canada's Longest Serving Public Library Director." *Épilogue* 13: 117–36.

Evans, Allan Roy. "Library Loungers." *Vancouver Sun* 30 January 1950.

Evans, Allan Roy "To The Editor: 'Library for squatters.'" *News Herald* 27 January 1950.

Friends of the Vancouver Public Library. *Aim: To Secure and Maintain Adequate Library Services for Vancouver Citizens* Vancouver: Friends of the Vancouver Public Library, 1945. Pamphlet, Special Collections, Vancouver Public Library.

Gatz and Maley. "The Robinson Era: 1924–1957" in *The History of Vancouver Public Library*, an unpublished collection of essays edited by Stanley Read, 1975. Special Collections, Vancouver Public Library. (Note: Special collections staff suggested that the authors are Betty Gatz and E. Madeley.)

"Groups Seek Injunction." *The Vancouver Province* 23 June 1951.

Hood, Pat. *The History of Carnegie Centre*. Vancouver: Carnegie Centre Publications, n.d. Carnegie Library Special Collections, Vancouver Public Library.

Howarth, Jean. "This Column." *The Vancouver Province* 13 February 1950.

"Jaycee Comic-Burning Proceeds Despite Snub." *The Vancouver Province* 27 November 1954.

Jones, Theodore. *Carnegie Libraries across America: A Public Legacy*. John Wiley & Sons: New York, 1997.

"Library Facilities Termed Disgraceful." *The Vancouver Province* 11 February 1950.

Lowe, John Adams, and John S. Richards. *A Survey of the Vancouver (British Columbia) Public Library*. Vancouver: Vancouver Public Library, 1949.

"Mayor Howled Down in Church, Siege of Museum Lifted Quietly." *The Vancouver Province* 20 May 1935.

"New Library Open on Nov 1." *Vancouver Sun* 19 October 1957.

"Old Faces Missing From Vancouver's New Library." *Vancouver Sun* 1 November 1957

Opening Ceremonies Program, 1980. Pamphlet. Special Collection, Vancouver Public Library.

"Public Should Fight Library Site Choice." *News Herald* [1951?]. Vancouver Public Library Clipping file—1951, Special Collections, Vancouver Public Library, Vancouver.

"'Rats, Arson' Disturb Library Board Meeting." *Vancouver Sun* 13 September, 1947.

Read, Stanley. "The Great Breakthrough: The Library and Carnegie." In *The History of Vancouver Public Library*, an unpublished collection of essays edited by Stanley Read, 1975. Special Collections, Vancouver Public Library.

Robinson, Edgar S. "Half a Century of Book Lending." *The Vancouver Province* 13 November 1937.

Robinson, Edgar S. Quoted in "No Burning of Books Wanted." *The Vancouver Province*, 28 January 1955.

Robinson, Edgar S. *Report of the Librarian, 1924*. Vancouver: Vancouver Public Library, 1924.

Robinson, Edgar S. *Report of the Librarian, 1930*. Vancouver: Vancouver Public Library, 1930.

Robinson, Edgar S. "Library Meets Need of Expanding City." *The Vancouver Province* 20 May 1947.

Robinson, Edgar S. *Report of the Librarian, 1933*. Vancouver: Vancouver Public Library, 1933.

"Robinson's Library Now Open to Public." *The Vancouver Province* 2 November, 1957.

Stockett, Julie. "The Vancouver Public Library: A Six Years' Record of Growth." *The Library Journal* 55 (November 1, 1930):861–862.

"Strikers." *Vancouver Sun* 18 May 1935.

Vancouver Public Library (VPL) Board Meeting Minutes. 11 November 1903. Special Collections, Vancouver Public Library.

Vancouver Public Library (VPL) Board Meeting Minutes. 10 February 1904. Special Collections, Vancouver Public Library.

Vancouver Public Library (VPL) Board Meeting Minutes. 13 October 1905. Special Collections, Vancouver Public Library.

Vancouver Public Library. "Carnegie Reading Room. Accessible online via: http://www.vpl. vancouver.bc.ca/branches/Carnegie/home.html. Accessed February 13, 2005.

"Vancouver's Library Needs: An Outline of Requirements to Cope with Future Demands." *The Vancouver Province* 13 February 1926.

Van Slyck, Abigail A. *Free to All: Carnegie Libraries & American Culture 1890–920*. Chicago: University of Chicago Press, 1995.

Warner, Gerry. "Vancouver's Carnegie Library." *Westworld* (March/April 1977).

Whitney, Paul. "A Refuge and a Sanctuary: Vancouver's Carnegie Library as Civic Space." Unpublished paper, 2004.

Section II

Libraries as Places of Community

5

The Fruit and Root of the Community: The Greensboro Carnegie Negro Library, 1904–1964

Julia A. Hersberger

University of North Carolina at Greensboro, Department of Library and Information Studies, Greensboro, NC

Lou Sua

Media Specialist, Clara J. Peck Elementary School, Greensboro, NC

Adam L. Murray

Head of Acquisitions, Murray State University Library, Murray, KY

INTRODUCTION

Public libraries often function as central institutions in the daily life of individuals who live in small communities. When a small public library also serves a minority constituency, it can impart a great sense of place to that community. In this paper, we will analyze one particular library, the Carnegie Negro Library of Greensboro, North Carolina, and how it was first established to serve the users of a specific "community within a community." We also will explore how it continued to grow, expanding its original user base to become an even more vibrant and integral neighborhood meeting place.

The title of the paper, "The Fruit and Root of the Community," is taken from the first history of the Greensboro Carnegie Negro Library written in 1944 on the 20th anniversary of the library's existence. Mrs. Martha J. Sebastian, head librarian, wrote in this document, "In conclusion, I hope that the Carnegie Negro Library will grow in size, grow in influence, grow in usefulness, until it will be, indeed, worthy of being counted among the great libraries of the world; these libraries that have been well-styled 'the fruit and root of all great civilizations.'... And I have one more hope, which is, that I will live to see that day" (Sebastian 5). While it is debatable as to whether the Greensboro Carnegie Negro Library rivaled the greatest libraries of the world, it certainly had a great influence on members of the African American community of that time. For many decades after its establishment, the library focused on meeting the educational, informational, and, most importantly, the social and cultural needs of the local African American community. The historical accounts of the library's place in the community indicate that it was a symbol of great community pride.

Figure 5.1   In a 1928 newspaper article, the Carnegie Negro Library is referred to as a "miniature library" and one longtime user called it a "dollhouse." Photo used with permission from the Greensboro Public Library.

AFRICAN AMERICANS AND COMMUNITIES AS PLACES

Communities lend themselves quite easily to an analysis of a sense of place. Traditionally, the term "community" carries two different place-based connotations. The first implies a territorial or geographic element, or simply a "fixed place." The second is based on interests and concomitant relationships unbounded by a sense of place (Creswell 7–12). However, sense of place is not simply an attachment to a geographical location; it combines geographical elements of a physical setting with the emotional aspects of "spirit of place" or *setting* (Steele 11–13). The term *setting* connotes an emotional connection to a place. A strong positive sense of place provides a feeling of belonging and can instill a perception of security to individuals or groups.

Public libraries can conceptually function as both a place and a setting where the physical building itself and the social factors within which it is embedded combine in ways that result in a strong psychological community impact. The building itself may become a positive symbol that represents larger communal issues and the progress of that specific population. In a bounded community setting, common experiences of the members often indicate similar emotional connections. It is in these patterns of experienced feelings where a shared emotional bond truly emerges.

The sense of place and place attachment in African American communities has a unique development pattern throughout history in the United States. Strong African American communities developed during slavery as a form of survival bonding. A resilient, ethical sense of mutuality, where individual needs were subordinated for the greater good of the larger community, provided much needed social support in the face of a brutally dehumanizing system of slavery (Nieman viii). The existence of an externally oppressive system that succeeded in the rigid separation of races created an internally diverse population strongly united against powerful outsiders (Blackwell xvii).

These communities, based on survival bonding, evolved into "communities of exclusion" of freed slaves prior to 1860. Political rights and economic prosperity continued to be denied to African American communities for decades following the Civil War. State laws established the separate-but-equal doctrine that allowed a semblance of autonomous institutions, although any real measure of political or economic power was carefully monitored and controlled. These communities of exclusion began to build their own political and economic infrastructures in many urban settings as a survival mechanism (Hudson 147).

Religious institutions played a critical role in African American communities. In addition to their traditional religious role, African American churches also met the secular needs of their community by supplying material needs, playing a political role in the community and being the impetus for the organization of mutual aid societies (Nieman xviii). However, the church was not a seamless provider of community benefits. The religious community was often fractured due to the rivalry and competition between denominations. Religious affiliation also was tied to a class structure in the African American community, which caused fissures in the community. The public library, on the other hand, was viewed as a neutral and potentially less divisive community institution; it often became a central meeting place that supplemented the important roles the church played in these communities. Accordingly, in this paper, the Greensboro Carnegie Negro Library is analyzed both in terms of its role as a physical space making visible the pride of this African American community, as well as its importance as a place in the unfolding history of African Americans and their struggle for recognition and equality.

COMMUNITY AS A CONCEPTUAL FRAMEWORK

In the process of conducting a literature review on African American libraries and librarianship, a clear analytical framework did not emerge. The majority of articles are from the professional literature and focus on collection development/resources for or about African Americans. For example, articles such as those by Olson, Byerly, and DuPree, present information about African American nonfiction, African American Web sites, and Diversity Resources. Another theme in the literature addresses the lack of African American librarians and the causes and solutions to this issue. E.J. Josey's work on recruitment of African Americans into librarianship is an indicator of this theme; so too is the work by T.M. Morris.

Two final themes in the literature are the historical accounts about specific library figures in African American librarianship, and the history of library service to African Americans. Explorations of the contributions of particular African American librarians can be found in the works of Walker and Kemp, who detail the efforts of African American librarians at the Library of Congress and elsewhere. Wilson exemplifies the studies into library service to African Americans by presenting data on library service to African Americans in Kentucky.

Two articles of particular note upon which this study drew are Sarah Anderson's "The Place to Go" and Cheryl Knott Malone's "Autonomy and Accommodation: Houston's Colored Carnegie Library, 1907–1922." Malone remarks that "Buildings constructed for the use of African Americans, including library branches, have been 'part of the ritual of memory, struggle, and hope' as Elsa Barkley Brown and Gregg D. Kimball have put it" (Malone 95–96). Malone continues on to note the dearth of studies on the establishment of separate library facilities for African Americans in the early part of the twentieth century. It is hoped that this study adds to a growing body of literature focused solely on the efforts of various communities, including African American communities, to establish their own public libraries.

How does a place grow beyond its physicality to develop deep meaning and emotional connection for a community? To explore this question, we draw upon the conceptual framework of McMillan and Chavis (1986), who propose four criteria of what defines and constitutes a "community." Many of the frameworks that may be used to study community focus, especially with regards to the African American community, on disintegration and dysfunction, rather than integration and involvement. The model presented by McMillan and Chavis was chosen because it offered a broad framework for analyzing the baseline elements of community.

According to McMillan and Chavis (9), the four building blocks of a community are (a) membership, (b) influence, (c) integration and fulfillment of needs, and (d) a shared emotional connection. Although McMillan (315) expanded his original work to reflect a more affective analytic framework using concepts such as "spirit," "faith," and "trust," these are better suited when one is working with a current population and can interview a critical mass of members. For the purposes of this historical approach, the original conceptual framework is more appropriate.

To demonstrate how these concepts are operationalized, we briefly describe each analytical unit and provide working definitions.

> **Membership:** A sense of belonging, an investment by an individual in a community that results in a feeling of a "right to belong." Boundary setting is an artifact of membership establishment. Positive elements of boundary setting are security (including emotional safety), a sense of identification, personal investment, and a common symbol system. For this study, having a library card and/or visiting the library or using the library in some manner will constitute the primary form of membership (McMillan and Chavis 9–11).

> **Influence:** A bidirectional concept where not only the individual potentially affects the community as a whole, the community also wields influence over the individual. Cohesiveness and conformity are artifacts of influence. People from the community had great influence on the establishment and running of the library. Library programming is another aspect of influence that can be examined bidirectionally: community leaders and library users influenced what programming was developed and presented, while library staff developed programs that also had a great influence on the community, especially on children and young adults (McMillan and Chavis 11–12).

> **Integration and Fulfillment of Needs:** Operate through positive reinforcement and are examined through variables that address needs, including status, values, and reciprocal social capital. Recognition that the library was able to meet the needs associated with the community's values transforms the library's services into a motivator for continued use. How the library meets the needs of the community can be examined by studying the services provided by the library, particularly in the area of programming (McMillan and Chavis 12–13).

> **Shared Emotional Connection:** Based in part on a shared history. May also be based on shared attributes. The seven features that characterize this criterion are interpersonal contact, quality of interaction, closure to events, importance of shared events, investment, effects of honor and humiliation, and spiritual bonds (McMillan and Chavis 13–14). How people remember the library, and in particular how they remember the library as a social center and meeting place for the community, will provide insights into this critical component of the library as a sense of "place" (McMillan and Chavis 13–16).

The examination of the Carnegie Negro Library in Greensboro, North Carolina, is a case study, exploring not only background information on the historical development of the library, but also the role it played in the African American community and, in turn, the impact that the African American community had on the library as an evolving place. The McMillan and Chavis conceptual framework will be used as the lens with which to examine the relationship between the African American community and this particular library, and the role of the library as a place within that community.

The research questions that guided the study include the following:

1. What role did the African American community play in the establishment of the Carnegie Negro Library in Greensboro, NC?
2. What role did membership play in situating the Carnegie Negro Library as a "place" in the African American community between 1904 and 1964?
3. What was the impact of the library on the community and the influence of the community on the library?
4. What were the needs of the community and how did the library meet those needs?
5. Most important, what was the shared emotional connection that situated the library as a high-quality "place" experience?

Analyzing these critical aspects of community within the context of the experience of the library as place within the African American community will give us a clearer snapshot of how a local, public institution becomes an anchor institution for a traditionally excluded population.

METHODOLOGY

For this research project, we have taken a historical approach, combined with a social science focus. While the chronology of events in this particular library plays an extremely important role in understanding the ties of the African American community to the library, this is not a library history study per se, but rather a study of a library within the historical context of a specific community. According to Powell, this type of research would be termed "new social history" as it is based in social science–type analysis (Powell 167).

Methodology: Data Collection

Historical documents have been acquired, mainly from the Greensboro Public Library records. These documents include official records such as copies of original library reports, board minutes, etc., newspaper accounts from copies of original news articles and photographs, letters, oral evidence (videotape of oral histories and interviews), schedules/agendas, manuscripts, and one recent historical study of the Greensboro Public Library. Both primary and secondary sources were accessed for the study. It should be noted that although the literature on "place" provides a methodology for measuring "sense of place" (Jorgensen 238–40) which involves multiple models, including three-factor, single-factor, and higher-order analysis, we were unable to enact this methodology. We were able to interview a few of the patrons, most of whom are now elderly, who once used the Carnegie Negro Library in its later years, but we could not contact a large enough number to rigorously measure place attachment.

Data Analysis

To reduce the large amount of textual data to relevant information based on the established research questions, a content analytic approach was used. In order to code the documents, we undertook the basic steps of defining categories and units, assessing reliability, and establishing coding rules (Weber 21–24).

Three limitations should be mentioned. First, it must be duly noted that the majority of the data examined was from the official files kept by the library staff. These files are mainly internal documents and thus are skewed toward a positive image of the library. Newspaper accounts offer critical views of the library, providing a diversity of opinions of the library service over time, but these accounts are also overwhelmingly positive. It is possible that there was dissent over the value of the library in the African American community; however, if it existed, it was not documented. The level of unity experienced by the community may have played a role in limiting negative comments. Nonetheless, the documents that were collected are as representative as is possible.

A second limitation to the study is that it focuses on one single library, geographically situated, whose history of community symbolism may or may not mirror the development of other libraries and communities. Finally, a third limitation is the decision of the researchers to focus solely on the library as a place within this one African American community. Although references may be made to certain large-scale historical developments that affected the Greensboro Carnegie Negro Library, it is not within the scope of this study to extend the analysis far beyond the boundaries of the local community. To that end, there are many excellent sources which examine the historical context of segregation in the American South.

HISTORICAL BACKGROUND

With respect to creation of the Carnegie Negro Library in Greensboro, two particular historical factors were of prime importance. First, the general development of public libraries in the South lagged behind other regions of the country. As late as 1921, just prior to the construction of the Carnegie Negro Library, at a meeting of the American Library Association (ALA) in Swampscott, Massachusetts, it was noted that "the public and association libraries of Salem, Massachusetts (at that time a city of 43,000 inhabitants) contained more volumes for public use than all the public libraries of Asheville, Charlotte, Winston-Salem, Greensboro, Durham, Raleigh, Goldsboro, and Wilmington, North Carolina . . . other statistics show that the situation in North Carolina was typical, if not better than that of many other southern states" (Gleason 12). Thus, the citizens of Greensboro in general and the Greensboro African American community in particular had very poor access to public library resources in their city.

Another important historical fact that affected the building of the Greensboro facility was the 1903 state legislative act entitled, "An Act to Incorporate the 'Charlotte Carnegie Public Library'" that established a library for the white population but also contained the proviso for a separate institution to serve the African American population under the governance of an independent board (Gleason 20). From this legislative act, the concept of a library building for the "colored people" of Greensboro was brought about and presented to the Board of Aldermen by Mr. E.P. Wharton in 1905.

According to Mr. Wharton, Andrew Carnegie had offered a sum of $10,000 for the building provided the City would appropriate $1,000 annually for its support. Following Mr. Wharton's report, the Mayor of Greensboro appointed an investigative committee and the Carnegie Negro Library took its first step to becoming a reality. Three months later, on March 12, 1906, the President of the Agricultural and Mechanical College (now North Carolina A&T State University) appealed to the Board of Aldermen to consider Mr. Carnegie's proposition for a library for colored people, who constituted a significant proportion of the population. The 1900 Census records show that the total population for Greensboro at this time was 10,035 with the "Negro" population totaling 4,086 (Twelfth 633). While detailed census records are not available for the 1920s (since demographics were not aggregated for cities with populations under 25,000), it is likely that the ratio of whites to African Americans was similar to that of 1900.

Greensboro accepted the offer and the money was set aside for the building, though a number of impediments prevented the library opening immediately. However, although African Americans made up about 40 percent of the population of Greensboro in the early part of the twentieth century, the building of a library to serve them was delayed for two decades due to political wrangling. The major obstacle was finding a location for the library, which caused a great deal of discussion and difference of opinion. In 1916, the Board of Trustees of the proposed library for colored people went before the Board of Aldermen and offered a lot on East Washington Street, which was a part of Bennett College (in 1926 the coeducational college became the Bennett College for Women). At the same time, a different group of citizens opposed this location and requested that a piece of property be bought on East Market Street for the library. The Bennett site would place the library more in the residential section of the colored part of town, while the East Market site would locate the library more in the business section of the Negro community. In the midst of this conflict, Andrew Carnegie died and by 1923 the Carnegie Foundation notified city leaders that if the money was not spent, the offer of building funds would be withdrawn. Following the receipt of the Carnegie Foundation letter, plans were quietly made and the Carnegie Negro Library was erected in the winter of 1923–24 at the East Washington site.

During this time, it was brought to the attention of the City Council that the yearly operating costs of the library would be more than the original 1905 offer of $1,000. Mr. W.B. Windsor stated that, "[The] cost of living was very high, including the cost of materials and labor, I think all of us are aware that had the library been erected in 1905 instead of 1924, we would have a finer, larger, more adequate building in every respect than we have" (Sebastian 2). Also, the Library Board that had originally been appointed had dwindled to only three members in the early 1920s. In the winter of 1923–24, Mrs. Martha Sebastian, the wife of a prominent physician in the Negro community, was approached to take charge of the library (see Figure 5.2). She accepted the position, and it was under her strong leadership that the library began to flourish.

THE EARLY YEARS

When the Carnegie Negro Library opened on the first of October 1924, it was "an empty building with the exception of a few bare shelves around the walls, a couple of tables and a few chairs. There was a box of books on the floor" (Sebastian 3). This box of 150 books had been selected by the Superintendent of Public Schools in Greensboro and purchased by the City of Greensboro. The main floor housed both a reading room and a reference room, with the librarian's small office in the rear. In the center of the open stacks was the circulation desk. The basement floor had one large room, which later served as the Children's Department. Also in the basement were a furnace room and two restrooms (Radio 1).

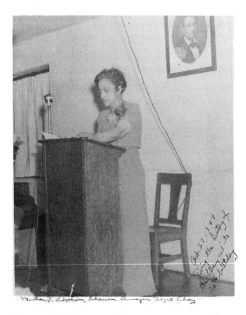

Figure 5.2   Mrs. Martha J. Sebastian served as
the head librarian of the Carnegie Negro Library
from 1924 to 1948. She referred to the library as
the "fruit and root of the community."

The librarian's salary in 1924 was $50 a month, while the only other position for which
funds were available, a janitorial position, was cut. Although the City of Greensboro
funded the yearly operating costs of the Carnegie Negro Library, providing $1,000
per year, the library itself functioned as a separate and independent institution due
to segregation in the South. While Mrs. Sebastian did provide annual reports to the
Greensboro City Council on the status of the library, the Carnegie Negro Library had
its own Board of Trustees. For the first five years of operation, the budget remained
stagnant at $1,000.

In 1929, the Library Board was reorganized. This Board was comprised of very
prominent members of the African American community, including the Supervisor of
Negro schools, a local dentist, and a teacher from the public schools. The library was
able, with the efforts of the Board, to win appropriation increases from time to time.
Through the efforts of the Board, such luxuries as Venetian blinds, an electric fan, and
an ice-water container were added to the library. In addition to such value-added service
objects, the library, under the direction of Mrs. Sebastian and the Library Board, was
redecorated every two or three years. The building, not more than 2,000 square feet of
space, was quickly filled to overflowing with books and people and, as such, space was
always at a premium. According to the reports from Mrs. Sebastian, requests for a larger
facility were repeatedly brought to the attention of the City Officials, with no effect.

LIBRARY GROWTH AND INFLUENCE

The collection of the Carnegie Negro Library was built with contributions from the
community, both white and African American. From the initial box of 150 volumes,

the library collection grew during Mrs. Sebastian's tenure of twenty-four years. Toward the end of her administration, Mrs. Sebastian fought for, and received, permission for countywide service to Negro communities outside of Greensboro, with the Carnegie library providing these services. Following Mrs. Sebastian's death in 1948, Mrs. Willie Grimes, who had served as the library assistant from 1931 to 1937, was hired as the head librarian. By 1950, the population of Greensboro had increased to 74,389, up from 10,000 in 1900. It is likely that this increase was the result of a change in the city limits. The white population totaled around 60,000, with the African American population counting for about 12,500 residents (1950 Census 33–63).

After the Supreme Court decision of 1954 in *Brown vs. Board of Education*[1] dismantled the legal foundation for racial segregation in the South, the Carnegie Negro Library continued to serve the African American community in both the city and in Guilford County. Mrs. Grimes served as head librarian until 1963. In a 1957 document, Mrs. Grimes presented a revised ten-year plan to the City of Greensboro. She noted that, despite the building having reached its optimum capacity years before, it was unlikely a new building would be built. She wrote, "As far as getting a new building in a different location, it seems very doubtful in the near future. The city is planning a new central library which will be used by all citizens" (Grimes, *Revision* 1). In her 1960 report titled "Description of the Functions of Carnegie Library" (1), Mrs. Grimes noted that the library had space for about 20 readers, had a collection of 36,000 volumes and served a city and county population of about 4,500 cardholders. Circulation totaled 83,984 books for the previous year. The library was so crowded that the tops of the stacks were used to hold books while many "useful books" were packed away due to the space shortage.

Still, the library remained a very active community center. The staff comprised six full-time workers, one janitor, and a page who worked part-time. There was a bookmobile serving the entire county, including a housing project, another section of town called Warnersville, and four schools. Mrs. Grimes notes that the library "is used extensively by the elementary and high school students after school hours and on Saturday and by many of the college students" (Grimes, *Description* 1). In addition to the school students, three nursery school groups came to the library weekly, and the library provided a weekly afternoon story hour for older children. There were two Winter Book Clubs plus the Summer Reading Program for children. According to the report, the library had an attractive teenage corner, with both adult and children's films shown frequently.

Adults too met at the busy, popular small facility. Discussion groups, book review forums, film forums, a world affairs forum, and a lecture series met regularly at the library. In addition, the report notes that the "staff works with community clubs inside and outside the library" (Grimes, Description 2). In a separate report on the lack of county funding for the bookmobile services, she notes "the real value of any library to its community lies in activities which do not readily lend themselves to quantitative reporting" (Report 4). In 1950s and the early 1960s, the Carnegie Negro Library was still a very active community institution, even with the physical space problems.

Even though Mrs. Sebastian noted in her twenty-year history of 1944 that the library had reached maximum space capacity, it was not until Mrs. Grimes' tenure that plans to build a newer and larger facility within the expanded African American community came to fruition in 1963. At this time in history, the Carnegie Negro Library was merged with Greensboro's Main library as one city system. With the desegregation of the library system, the Board of Trustees of the Carnegie Negro Library was dissolved and the governance of the city library system was turned over to an all-white Board of Trustees.

African American community members still retained their own branch[2] and were also allowed the use of the facilities at the Main library.

In its forty years of service to the African American community in Greensboro and Guilford County, the building itself stood for hope with its educational and recreational opportunities. Since its closing in 1963, the little library building has been used in various capacities by Bennett College. It was renovated in 1997, keeping much of the interior charm of the old Carnegie building and now houses the offices for Institutional Advancement for the college. The sign over the front door, once boarded up, reads "Carnegie Negro Library," for all to see.

FINDINGS AND DISCUSSION

Reading and analyzing a large amount of data concerning the establishment and evolution of the Carnegie Negro Library, including its later incarnations as the Southeast Branch and Vance H. Chavis Lifelong Learning Branch of the Greensboro Public Library, a great sense of community ownership and concomitant pride in the library emerges. The sense of "place" represented by the library in the African American community is multifaceted. In the early decades, the library served as a neutral meeting place regardless of whether or not one could read. The library also had a very close connection to education, supporting self-education and formal education in the local schools, colleges, and universities. The library cemented its status as a community space by being the place where one could find out the latest news and events occurring in the African American community.

In order to take a broad view of how the library's sense of place developed in the Greensboro African American community, we examine the library focusing on McMillan and Chavis' community building blocks of (1) membership, (2) influence, (3) integration and fulfillment of needs, and (4) shared emotional connection.

Membership

The first building block of communities established by McMillan and Chavis is that of membership and connotes a sense of belonging. A sense of belonging is critical to establishing and building a sense of place. The most obvious methods of analyzing membership, especially given that this is a historical study, are circulation data and patron registration. Historical records indicate that patron registration increased from 1,230 in 1928 to 5,931 in 1956 (Only) (Report, 9). Circulation records demonstrate this same trend: circulation in 1960 was 83,984, up from 19,934 in 1945 (Circulation 1).

According to the McMillan and Chavis framework, membership is constituted by a number of subcategories, including the establishment of boundaries and the development of a sense of belonging and identification. Emotional safety and personal investment are also aspects of membership; however, much of the data applicable to these aspects are discussed at length in subsequent sections.

Boundary Setting. McMillan and Chavis define boundary setting as providing "members with the emotional safety necessary for needs and feelings to be exposed and for intimacy to develop" (McMillan and Chavis 9). Boundaries are in place to protect a group or place from outsiders that may pose a threat, in this case the white community with different privileges due to segregation. In the early years of the Carnegie

Negro Library, boundary setting was primarily related to the geographic limitation of service within the city limits, with support funding coming from the City Council. An early pamphlet bearing Mrs. Sebastian's name as Librarian[3] includes the following "Rules and Regulations":

Membership
The library is open to all Negroes of Greensboro over six years of age.
All applicants not listed in the city directory must have application signed by tax-payer of city or county.
All applicants under 18 years of age must have applications signed by parents.

General Rules
All shelves are open to the public.
Quiet shall be observed by all patrons in the library.
Circulating petitions or soliciting subscriptions for any purpose is prohibited.
Eating and the use of tobacco are not permitted in the library.
Immediate notice of change of residence must be reported.
Persons who have repeatedly abused the rules of the library shall be deprived of its privileges.

Each of the rules helped delineate boundaries of membership. One needed to be listed in the city directory, establishing a geographical boundary, and one had to be African American, establishing a racial boundary, and finally, one had to be over the age of six as an age boundary. There is not, however, evidence in the data that these boundaries caused difficulties or excluded many members within the city limits. On the contrary, these boundaries promoted the library's position as a community institution in a community of exclusion, providing for the African Americans a location where they could achieve survival bonding; interacting and uniting for greater rights and service.

Later, in 1945, boundaries expanded as the demand for library services grew from the larger community of African Americans. County library service was begun with several outreach sites where books were available to those rural communities. Twelve adult and children book depositories were established across the area. It is important to note that the majority of Guilford County residents at the time were African American. Four years later, bookmobile services were established to reach even more rural sites. There was one bookmobile to service the white rural population and one that visited the African American communities until the early 1960s, when the library was merged with the larger Greensboro system. A newspaper article from 1952 (News) reports:

The Carnegie Negro Library Bookmobile circulated 2,079 books during October, a record month since the bookmobile began operating in 1949. The unit added 600 new borrowers to its registry and increased its stops by 21.

The bookmobile serves every member of the family from Junior to Gramps. There are hero stories of adventure, history, poetry and travel. We have adult books on home improvement, agriculture, economic problems and world affairs.

To satisfy the great urge to continue one's education when school days are over and to accomplish what is sometimes called self-education, is hardly possible today without good books. All citizens of Guilford County should take advantage of the service the bookmobile offers.

Historically, the struggle to simply build the Carnegie Negro Library united the African American community in Greensboro. This collective investment in the establishment of a community institution also built a high rate of use.

Sense of Belonging. Another marker of membership is a sense of belonging. Sense of belonging is "the feeling, belief, and expectation that one fits in the group" (McMillan and Chavis 10). With a developing sense of belonging, one can identify with a group or institution and view it as being "mine." There are some measures of this factor. The number of cards issued, the percentage of the African American population registered, and materials circulation all represent the outcome of the sense of belonging. The Carnegie Negro Library was noted as having the highest circulation of the nine public libraries in the state for Negroes in a bulletin issued by the state library (Greensboro B9). From 1929 to the 1960s, the number of volumes housed in the library jumped from 3,500 to 35,872; circulation went from 14,846 to 83,984. As mentioned above, patron registration increased from 1,230 in 1928 to 5,931 in 1956 (Only) (Report, 9).

Even the dispute over where to situate the library demonstrates this sense of belonging. Some leaders wanted the library more centrally located within the African American business section of Greensboro, while others felt that the library should be built on a parcel of land on the grounds of Bennett College, a historically African American college and presumably closer to the African American residential neighborhood. Eventually the city voted to build the library on the Bennett College site bringing what Mrs. Sebastian refers to as "a tedious controversy" to an end (Sebastian, 2).

Emotional Safety. Within the African American community, there were different factions with different points of view. The library's sense of neutrality made it a meeting place that local churches and local schools did not provide, even though these institutions also served as important community organizations. The Carnegie Negro Library served as a safe place for the African American community to meet and discuss issues. This will be discussed in more detail under the point "Influence: Conformity & Cohesiveness."

Personal Investment. According to McMillan and Chavis (10), another indicator of membership is the personal investment of individuals from the community. The details of the personal investment data collected are covered under *Influence*, but it is important to note the efforts of a significant number of individuals in establishing and maintaining the Carnegie Negro Library.

The African American community in Greensboro worked diligently from 1905 until 1924 to gain a public library facility. High use of the facility once the library was built points toward a strong sense of belonging and ownership, providing evidence of membership.

Influence

The concept of influence in analyzing the Carnegie Negro Library and sense of place is a bidirectional element. Specific individuals in the white and African American communities were influential in both the establishment of the library and in guiding its evolution over the next several decades. Concomitantly, the library itself had an impact on not only the community at large but on individual users.

Influence of Individuals. Although the major influences on the Carnegie Negro Library were members of the African American community, there were a number of citizens from the white community who contributed to the founding of the library. E.P. Wharton, a local businessman, wrote the original letter to Andrew Carnegie suggesting funding for the Negro library. Mrs. Sebastian refers to Mr. Wharton as "The father of library services in Greensboro" (Sebastian 1). Among others, Mrs. E. Sternberger,

Dr. Charlotte Brown, Watson Law, and Miss Fort are noted for their donations of books, money, and other resources. Mrs. Julius Cone helped increase the library collections from 150 to 10,500 of the "best and most up-to-date books that may be found in any library, north, east, south or west" (Sebastian 5).

The key influences on the library remained the movers and shakers of the African American community. James B. Dudley, president of the Agricultural and Mechanical College[4] was one of the main leaders of the original project, as was S.A. Peeler, president of Bennett College. W.P. Windsor, W.D. Siler, D.C. Suggs, Dr. J.F. Pellinger, and others were involved in the discussion on where to situate the library. Many of these men served on the first Board of Trustees. Mrs. Sebastian's 20th Anniversary history is literally a who's who of the local African American community in naming board members over this time period (Sebastian 3).

In addition to local citizens, the library staff made an important contribution to the sense of the library's place in the community. The efforts of Martha Sebastian cannot be underestimated. It is clear from the documents that survive that it is through her efforts that the library thrived and that she was the main gardener in growing the "fruit and root" of the community. A "History Book-o-Mark" (circa 1947 or 1948) notes, "Since 1924 Mrs. Martha Sebastian has served as Librarian continuously and under her guidance and leadership the library has become one of the strongest Negro libraries in the South and today it is serving not only Greensboro proper but the whole of Guilford County" (1).

An example of Mrs. Sebastian's efforts can be found in a report she wrote to Mr. Weatherly, County Manager of Guilford County in 1946. She writes, "Since the above mentioned date [September 25th, 1945] I have made 60 trips to these areas [twelve outreach sites in the county] covering 982 miles, using my own car for the purpose. The Negroes living in Rural Guilford will have read 6650 books to day" (Memo 1).

Mrs. Sebastian continued to be a force as the head of the Carnegie Negro Library until her death in 1948. Mrs. Sebastian was succeeded by Mrs. Willie Grimes, who continued the development of the Carnegie Negro Library as a strong influence in the African American community. She retired in 1963 after thirty-one years working in libraries, fifteen years as the head librarian at the Carnegie Library. Under the direction of Mrs. Grimes, more programming was added in addition to expanding the collection from 14,000 volumes to around 36,000 volumes in 1960.

Influence was exerted on the library not just from individuals, but from clubs, groups, and organizations as well. The local Civitan Club is recognized for their generosity in donating hundreds of books in the library's bleak financial periods (Sebastian 5). Mrs. Sebastian notes there were many other key individuals and groups that came to the aid of the library over the years. Such generosity of spirit is further evidence of the library's sense of place in not only the African American community but in all the communities of Greensboro.

Influence on Individuals. The influence of the library on individuals will be analyzed more specifically in the section on *Shared Emotional Experience*, but here the influence of programming will be noted. In addition to collected program papers, numerous pages are devoted to articles in several library scrapbooks. Programs were provided for all age groups. Reading and storytelling programs were aimed at children and young adults. Many adults also frequently used the library for group meetings and programs. An example of this is the Heritage Club, a group that met to discuss local history and community issues.

Figure 5.3   The Heritage Group met frequently at the Carnegie
Negro Library. Standing in the back at the left is the head librarian,
Mrs. Willie Grimes (circa 1955).

Conformity and Cohesiveness. The bidirectional nature of influence establishes an
environment where conformity and cohesiveness are nurtured in a community. Historical
accounts gathered by the library and preserved in their scrapbooks indicate that the
library provided a measure of conformity and cohesiveness in the community as many
exercised their influence and rights of membership in the library over the years. As
previously mentioned, local churches were not always able to act as a neutral space for
community-wide interaction and discussion. Carnegie Negro Library offered a forum
free from denominational conflict in which community leaders and members could meet.

One important meeting held at the library on February 18, 1932, brought together
members of the community to formally organize the Jesse Moreland branch of the
Young Men's Christian Association (YMCA). An article found in the library scrapbook
notes that the group had already been meeting for three years at the library when a
local industrialist, Caesar Cone II, gave the group a building worth $60,000 and that
the men had raised $5,000 for the purchase of the lot (Small). Carnegie Negro Library
also served as host to the Greensboro Art Center and the 1944 North Carolina Negro
Library Association's annual meeting (State). Meetings held in the local library aided
in the growth of other cultural and social organizations outside the library, verifying its
seminal position in creating conformity and cohesion in a minority community.

Integration and Fulfillment of Needs

Positive reinforcement is the major cornerstone of the concept of integration and
fulfillment of needs in a community sense (McMillan and Chavis 13). Negative reinforcement would result in an unenthusiastic or unconstructive sense of place; consequently a library would not impress a high quality place experience upon its users. The
data gathered is primarily from the library's point of view, but there are sufficient other

sources, such as newspaper and personal accounts, that demonstrate whether sense of place was positively or negatively reinforced in the African American community in Greensboro in the early to mid-1900s.

Reinforcement and Need Fulfillment. The perception by large numbers of the African American community that the library was able to fulfill their needs served as positive reinforcement to continue using the library. In an undated script for a radio talk, Mrs. Sebastian notes that "The objectives of a public library are different from those of the Research, College and University or School library in that it provides books, materials and other means of communication for all the people for the purposes of individual and social well-being and enlightenment. It meets the needs of the community as a whole (Radio 1–2)." Her reception to input was not limited to the Board of Trustees, but included the library users as well. For a community with restricted rights, especially regarding education, Mrs. Sebastian recognized a community need for resources pertaining to self- and continuing education. Written accounts, in the form of thank-you letters kept in the library scrapbooks, note her responsiveness to different requests. One teacher in the Poplar Grove School stated that she wished the bookmobile had provided library access years earlier, as she noted marked improvement in her classes. She felt that former students would have done better in their class work if they had had library access (Memo 1).

In the efforts to meet the library service needs of rural county areas, Mrs. Sebastian wrote of the need for the local school teachers to assist in promoting awareness of the bookmobile and its services, "The results [of the added bookmobile stops] have been amazing. More people are borrowing books than ever before. . . . We are trying to show people that education does not stop upon completion of a number of grades but is a continuous process. The public library supplies all kinds of information to people who want to keep up or who have been denied the privilege of advanced training. The teachers play a very important role in educating the community to take advantage of the bookmobile" (Carnegie 1).

Programming to various interest groups and on various topics were also very popular and based on local community needs and interests. Figure 5.4.

In the Radio Talk script, Mrs. Sebastian notes that "Aside from the Children's Story Hour on Wednesday afternoon, the Teenagers Library Club, the Children's Summer Reading Club (for the young group) the joint sponsoring with Bennett College of the Great Books group and a prospective 'Friends of the Library Club' we feel that much more should be done along this line" (Radio 3).

Rewards and Values. While Mrs. Sebastian realized the community need for the library to serve as a resource for self and continued education, the community could not have achieved the integration they did without recognizing this need as a shared value, or perceiving the rewards of utilizing the library toward this end. Education, particularly the opportunity to continue one's self-education, was a remarkably important underpinning value to the African American community.

Even though the African American community recognized the rewards associated with utilizing the library, and while the city of Greensboro and Guilford County appreciated the efforts and results derived from the work of the Carnegie Negro Library's staff, they were not always quick to reward them with additional support. In a report

Figure 5.4   Mrs. Willie Grimes conducts a reading program in the children's department of the Carnegie Negro Library (circa 1950).

dated September 29, 1949, a report noted that the building was in a poor location after twenty-five years of growth in the area and that it was "run down and too small" and "no new funds should be spent renovating the building" (Recommendations 2). The same report recommends that a new library be built in the East Market Street area—the other site choice debated decades earlier when the library was first built. As with the struggle to build the original library, the African American community had to labor for the next seventeen years to generate recognition of the need for and completion of a new library facility. Thus, while the shared values of the African American community were cohesive, and while the white community appeared to reap the benefits of having an educated minority population, progress for the library was not forthcoming without persistent actions.

Individual Needs. The library managed to meet not only these macro level needs of the African American community at large, it also fulfilled the needs of the various individuals of this community. Various informants have noted that they either extended their knowledge gained in school efforts at the Carnegie Negro Library or that they self-educated where the privilege of public education had been denied them. In turn, the African American community, particularly at the county level, felt that the public library service made accessible through the Carnegie Negro Library benefited their communities. Although data is sparse from the points of view of individual users at this time, newspaper articles that represent a community sense of value of the library are very complementary, especially concerning the rewards gained by the extension of library services countywide. Also, documents from the city of Greensboro, the County Commissioners, and County managers support a general sense of rewards being reaped not only by the individuals of the African American community but by the larger communities of the city and the county.

Shared Emotional Experience

According to Hay, "Sense of place differs from place attachment by considering the social and geographical context of place bonds and the sensing of places, such as the aesthetics and a feeling of dwelling" (Hay 5). While there certainly exists evidence that people in Greensboro's African American community appreciated the library with respect to its geographical and aesthetic setting, it is the emotional sense of an attachment to the place that is strongly held in the memories of past library users. *Investment* and *honor and humiliation* are other factors that constitute shared emotional experience. The framework links *honor and humiliation*; however, our data revealed no evidence of humiliation. Honor played a large part in motivating the personal investment of individuals of the community and as such was discussed under the section dealing with *Influence*. The same applies to *investment*. This lack of data on humiliation may be symptomatic of the limitations detailed earlier under *Methodology: Data Analysis*.

Interpersonal Contact. McMillan and Chavis hypothesize that the more people interact, the closer they become (McMillan and Chavis 13). The library was more than a place to read and check out books, it became a central meeting and gathering spot for the African American community (Sebastian 5). A 1928 article notes "How eager the people whom the library serves are to take advantage of the opportunity is shown by the manner in which they throng the building. Oftentimes, the building is filled to overflowing with all chairs occupied, those who cannot find another place to sit on the steps" (Only 1).

Quality of Interaction. The more positive the experience and the relationships, the greater the bond (McMillan and Chavis 13). The reports of high use of the facility throughout the forty years of service would support an assertion that the quality of interactions contributed to a high-quality experience of place at the Carnegie Negro Library. The African American population in Greensboro was a tight-knit community during the years that the Carnegie Negro Library was in operation. The library served as a central institution not only to the city residents but also connected those in the county to those in the city.

Closure to Events. Group cohesiveness is inhibited if interactions are ambiguous and tasks are left resolved (McMillan and Chavis 14). No data was discovered that led researchers to believe that any issues were left unresolved. This might be due to the fact that the Carnegie Negro Library evolved into the new Southeast Branch (later renamed the Vance H. Chavis Lifelong Learning Branch) of the Greensboro Public Library. The community never lost its sense of their "own" library.

Importance of Shared Events. McMillan and Chavis hypothesize that the more important a shared event in a community, the greater the bond (McMillan and Chavis 14). The African American community bonded together in a struggle to get the Carnegie Foundation's money spent on a library facility—a struggle that lasted from 1904 to 1924. This effort initially united the community and held them together as they continued to struggle for resources and, eventually, a new library building.

Spiritual Bond. The final analytical element of a shared emotional connection found in a community is that of a spiritual bond or a "community of spirit" (McMillan and Chavis 14). The African American community of users of the Carnegie Negro Library demonstrated a great deal of local spirit as is evidenced by the many articles noting the important role the library played in bringing people together. In 1998–1999, for the seventy-fifth anniversary celebration of library service in the African American community, a group called the Heritage Quilters produced a memorial quilt, which is still on display at the Chavis Branch building. On the quilt are sections with, among others, a picture of Mrs. Sebastian, the names of the library directors, a picture of Mrs. Grimes, a picture of the Carnegie Library, and the names of those who staffed it. Several of the quilters had been users of the old library and stories were shared about using the library.

Mary Rogers Scarlette grew up half a block from the library and is a retired administrator at Bennett College. She recalls, "Everything went on here. That's why this building [the Carnegie Negro Library] is so important to the community. . . . This building always made people feel good by being in it" (Copeland B2). Just being in the building after its renovation in 1997 brought back many memories for Mrs. Scarlette. She goes on to describe how the building still had the smell of books in it even after Bennett College had renovated the building for office space. "It was like the smell was embedded in the walls" (Copeland B2). Some of the books from the Carnegie Negro Library were given to Bennett College when the library moved. Mrs. Scarlette found her favorite children's book, *The Water Babies* by Charles Kingsley, on the shelves of the university's library. It still had its original checkout card in the back and her name, she noted, was written on the card "nine or ten times" (Copeland B2). The library still holds a strong sense of place and place attachment to those who were library users during its forty-year tenure.

CONCLUSIONS

The Carnegie Negro Library opened on the Bennett College campus in 1924. The library was a symbol of an opportunity for advancement for the African American community. Education was seen as the key to a better life for all African Americans, especially for the children in the community. The library was more than just a place to check out a book or to just read—it became *the* place for gatherings and meetings.

The library served as headquarters for the Greensboro Art Center, which provided art instruction for African American adults and children from 1936 to 1940. It served as a place to plan for the Hayes-Taylor YMCA and for advocating for the first African American police officer in Greensboro. It served as a gathering place for numerous other groups and organizations in the community. The library was seen as the location for the community to meet and plan strategies for the betterment of the community. The library was seen as "the place" rather than "a place"—the place where decisions were made that would affect the entire community, where community changes happened, the place that was most important to the educated and undereducated, and the place where everyone could better themselves.

People remember Carnegie Negro Library as more than just a building but as a place where all members of the community could be considered as equals. It was a neutral place, a place where everyone may be coming for different reasons but where their needs could be met.

Lola McAdoo, on the Carnegie Negro Library:

What I remember most about the Carnegie Negro Library is that it was in my community. The community was the neighborhood where Bennett College for Women and Washington Street School was situated; in a community that focused on educating the child and extending reading outside the home. In my home, we visited the library called "the center'. We selected our books according to the level we were reading. Our teachers at Washington Street School and the neighborhood used the library as extended reading. My mother and especially, my grandmother were avid readers and often sent us to the library. It was within walking distance. I remember the librarians there being very friendly. I recall the railing, it's still there. It was a very friendly atmosphere, a quiet atmosphere. Often times, many community activities were held at the Carnegie Library. We had Girl Scouts held there and the Y-Teens would meet in the lower level of the library because they had an activity room where we could come and have little teas and read and be read to. It was a center in our community, in the Black community. This was the only place that had a public library that people could come and read. And also many of the neighbors who did not take the daily newspapers could come to the library and read the paper. During that time there were a lot of people who could not afford to buy the newspaper. It was a time, a very hard time with the types of jobs but people knew they could come to the library after work and read the newspaper. There were a lot of papers then that are not in print now that talked about the local black activities, social, educational, sports here and around the areas. The *Journal Guide* was one of those papers that I recalled that we could know what was going on in Burlington, High Point, and Winston Salem. Carnegie Negro Library meant that there was a place, where a lot of things going on, not just for reading but for social activities.

In 1999, the Carnegie Negro Library was renovated and rededicated by Bennett College and the building was reopened as offices for institutional development. During the preparation for the celebration of the rededication, the President of Bennett College convened a group of retired educators, former and current community members, and staff from the V.H. Chavis Branch Library (the successor to the old Carnegie Negro Library) to discuss their remembrances of the Carnegie Negro Library. Among those in attendance were Mr. Vance H. Chavis, Mrs. Nannie Dick, Mrs. Cummings, Mrs. Mary Chavis, Mr. Alexander Watson, and Mrs. Bea McAdoo-Shaw. As former members walked through the building, they eloquently spoke of their memories, vividly painting images of how the library used to be. Each seemed to step back in time and remember events in the library—as a child, principal, or teacher in the school system, an employee in the library, a community member who was affected by the closing of the library or as a young mother using the library as a resource. As each told their story another piece was added until the story was completed and one could understand what the Library meant to the community. The Carnegie Negro Library was not just "a place," it was what defined the community—it was "our place" or "my library" which was, as Mrs. Sebastian termed it, "the fruit and root of the community."

ACKNOWLEDGMENT

The authors would like to acknowledge the indefatigable efforts of Rohit Singh, whose assistance in the data collection and early editing phase of this project was invaluable.

NOTES

1. Brown v. Board of Education, 347 U.S. 483 (1954) (USSC+). To access a copy of the U.S. Supreme Court decision see http://www.nationalcenter.org/brown.html.

2. The Carnegie Negro Library evolved into the Southeast Branch of the Greensboro Public Library System. It was later renamed the Vance H. Chavis Lifelong Learning Branch.

3. While the pamphlet is not dated, Mrs. Sebastian's tenure as the Librarian was from 1924–1948. This pamphlet is most likely from the 1930s.

4. Now called North Carolina A&T.

REFERENCES

1950 Census of Population: Characteristics of the Population. Volume 2.33, North Carolina.

Anderson, Sarah A. "The Place to Go: The 135th Street Branch Library and the Harlem Renaissance." *Library Quarterly* 73 (4) (2003): 383–421.

Blackwell, James E. *The Black Community: Diversity and Unity*, 3rd ed. New York: HarperCollins Publishers, 1991.

Byerly, Greg. "African American Websites for Black History Month and All Year Long." *School Media Activities Monthly* 21 (6) (2005): 38–39.

"Circulation Statistics 1945–1965." Carnegie Negro Library Scrapbook.

Copeland, Tom. Renovation reveals sign of the past. *Greensboro News & Record* 19 June 1997: B1–B2.

Cresswell, Tim. *Place: A Short Introduction.* Oxford: Blackwell Publishing, 2004.

DuPree, Sherry. "Dissolving Boundaries: A Roadmap to African American and Diversity Resources." *Florida Libraries* Special Edition (2005): 55–61.

Gleason, Eliza.A. *The Southern Negro and the Public Library: A Study of the Government and Administration of Public Library Service to Negros in the South.* Chicago: University of Chicago Press, 1941.

"Greensboro's Negro Library Heads List of Nine Public Libraries in State." Carnegie Negro Library Scrapbook 28 September 1931.

Grimes, Willie M. "Revision of Suggested Ten-Year Plan." Carnegie Negro Library Scrapbook, 1957.

———. "Description of the Functions of the Carnegie Library." Carnegie Negro Library Scrapbook, 1960.

Hay, Robert. "Sense of Place in Developmental Context." *Journal of Environmental Psychology* 18 (1) (1998): 5–29.

"History Book-O-Mark of Carnegie Negro Library." Carnegie Negro Library Scrapbook.

Hudson, J. Blaine. *Diversity and Community: An Interdisciplinary Reader.* Ed. Philip Alperson. Malden: Blackwell Publishing, 2002.

Jorgensen, Bradley S. and Richard C. Steadman. "Sense of Place as an Attitude: Lakeshore Owners Attitudes toward Their Properties." *Journal of Environmental Psychology* 21 (3) (2001): 233–248.

Josey, E. J. "The Need for the Recruitment of African American Librarians." *Culture Keepers III.* Black Caucus of the American Library Association, 2000.

Kemp, Roberta. "The Secrets of My Success." *Wilson Library Bulletin* 68 (1994): 35–37.

Malone, C. K. "Autonomy and accommodation: Houston's Colored Carnegie Negro Library, 1907–1922." *Libraries and Culture* 34 (2) (1999): 95–112.

McMillan, David W. and David M. Chavis "Sense of Community: A Definition and Theory." *Journal of Community Psychology* 14 (1986): 6–23.

McMillan, David W. "Sense of Community." *Journal of Community Psychology* 24 (4) (1996): 315–325.

"Memo to Mr. Weatherly." Carnegie Negro Library Scrapbook, 30 May 1946.

Morris, Teresa. *African Americans in Library and Information Science Programs: Recruitment Strategies Examined.* Thesis: University of North Carolina at Chapel Hill, 1998.

"News of Carnegie Library Bookmobile." *Future Outlook* 8 November 1952.

Nieman, Donald G. *Church and Community Among Black Southerners 1865–1900.* New York: Garland Publishing, Inc., 1994.

Olson, Ray. "Top 10 African American Nonfiction." *Booklist* 101 (1) (2005): 934.

"Only Carnegie Library for Negroes in North Carolina is Located in Greensboro." *Daily Record* 15, December 1928.

Powell, Ronald R. *Basic Research Methods for Librarians*, 3d ed. Greenwich: Ablex Publishing, 1999.

"Radio Talk—The Library System: Carnegie Negro Library." Carnegie Negro Library Scrapbook.

"Recommendations to Improve the Carnegie Negro Public Library." Carnegie Negro Library 29 September 1949.

"Report on a Study of Library Services Provided and Appointment of Cost Between the City of Greensboro and Guilford County." Carnegie Negro Library Scrapbook, 2 May 1956.

"Rules and Regulations." Carnegie Negro Library Scrapbook.

Sebastian, Martha J. "History of the Carnegie Negro Library." Carnegie Negro Library Scrapbook, 1944.

"Small Group Formed First Negro Y.M.C.A. In City." Carnegie Negro Library Scrapbook, 16 November 1940.

State Negro Librarians Open Bennett Meeting." *Greensboro News and Record* 8 October 1944.

Steele, Fritz. *The Sense of Place.* Boston: CBI Publishing, 1981.

The Twelfth Census of the United States Taken in the Year 1900: Population of States and Territories, etc. Volume 1.1. New York: Norma Ross Publishing, 1997.

Walker, Billie. "Black American Pioneer Left a Legacy at LC." *American Libraries* 35 (2) (2004): 44.

Weber, Robert P. *Basic Content Analysis*, 2d ed. Newbury Park: Sage Publications, 1990.

Wilson, J. R. "Library Service to African Americans in Kentucky, from the Reconstruction Era to the 1960s." *College & Research Libraries* 64 (6) (2003): 509–510.

6

Locating the Library as Place among Lesbian, Gay, Bisexual, and Queer Patrons

Paulette Rothbauer

Assistant Professor, Faculty of Information Studies, University of Toronto,
Toronto, Ontario, Canada

INTRODUCTION

There are two commonsense understandings of how the library might come to constitute a place: through its physical features such as the contours of its building architecture, the layout of its floor plans, and the mapping of its internal spaces; and through a consideration of its location within a larger community of other structures, other services and other agencies. However, in this paper, I argue that the physicality and locationality of the public library tell only one part of the story of how the library functions as place in the lives of its users. Library uses can also be analyzed within a framework of spatial practices informed by ideas from recent geographies of sexuality, identity, and place.

As Gill Valentine explains in her book *Social Geographies*, space is a central organizing concept in geography that has over time been used to describe the earth's surfaces in order to find "universal spatial laws in order to understand the way the world worked" and to predict human patterns of behavior within mapped locales and regions (2). Explaining a positivistic perspective on geography, Valentine writes,

Space was conceptualized as an objective physical surface with specific fixed characteristics upon which social identities and categories were mapped out. Space was, in effect, understood as the container of social relations and events. Likewise, social identities and categories were also taken for granted as "fixed" and mutually exclusive. (3)

Influenced by poststructuralist thought, social geography begins with the assumption that social identities are "multiple, contested and fluid." Furthermore as Valentine goes on to explain, "so too space is no longer understood as having particular fixed characteristics. . . . Rather, space is understood to play an active role in the constitution and reproduction of social identities; and social identities, meanings and relations are recognized as producing materials and symbolic or metaphorical spaces" (4).

Cara Carmichael Aitchison provides a chronological classificatory framework for geographical studies of gender, leisure and place in which she describes one genre of analysis as that which conceives of "place as an objective and locational reality and space as the social and cultural manifestation of such locations. In this way, place can be conceived of as fixed while space is fluid and subject to transformation as a result of social and cultural change" (71–72). Aitchison notes that this corresponds to Michel de Certeau's conceptualization of space as "practiced place" (74). It is worth citing de Certeau's articulation of space at length as it offers a promising perspective on the spatial practices of lesbian, gay, bisexual, and queer (LGBQ)[1] library patrons within the place of the library:

A *space* exists when one takes into consideration vectors of direction, velocities, and time variables. Thus space is composed of intersections of mobile elements. It is in a sense actuated by the ensemble of movements deployed within it.... In contradistinction to the place, it has thus none of the univocity or stability of a "proper." In short, *space is a practiced place*. Thus the street geometrically defined by urban planning is transformed into a space by walkers. In the same way, an act of reading is the space produced by the practice of a particular place: a written text, i.e. a place constituted by a system of signs. (117, italics in original)

The notion of spatial practices articulated by de Certeau corresponds to the recent destabilizing geographies of lesbian, gay, and queer space and place in which the conversion of place into space relies on conceptualizing place "as that endowed with significant meanings by and for individuals and groups, often for the making of identity" (Skeggs et al. 1840). The 1967 police raid on a gay male bar resulting in the Stonewall riots in New York City is commonly understood to mark the emergence of visible gay neighborhoods within the boundaries of larger heterosexual cities (Valentine 219). There have also been several studies that function as cartographies of gay and lesbian enclaves located in large cities around the world (see Valentine 219–22 for a brief review). In this body of work LGBQ sexualities are seen to be constituted, in part, through interaction with particular spaces and places that either permit or deny the public and private expression of such sexualities:

Sexual identities depend to some extent on particular spaces for their production (for example, an individual's sexual identity may be read as lesbian or gay from the space they occupy, or a person may only feel able to 'come out' and identify as gay in a lesbian or gay space). Spatial visibility has thus played a key part in the development of sexual dissidents' rights. In turn, space is also produced through the performance of identities. (Valentine 222)

The foregoing conceptualizations of space, society, and social identity as mutually constitutive support the following discussion of the public library as place among LGBQ patrons. Using a spatial frame for an analysis of library uses among LGBQ patrons as reported in a number of published studies helps to disrupt the ways in which the public library is commonly understood as a fixed place that supplies or provides information and reading material on the subjects of sexual orientation and sexual identity.

There are now several studies that consider the role of the public library in reconstituting the public sphere and thereby carrying the potential to contribute to a revitalized civil society (see e.g., Leckie and Hopkins; Buschman; Greenhalgh; Greenhalgh and Worpole; Alstad and Curry). In their article "The Public Place of Central Libraries" Leckie and Hopkins provide empirical evidence of the vital positioning of the centrally located public libraries of two large Canadian cities as important places that are used for serious study and information-seeking behavior, but that also invite a variety of social activities. The public library as a site for recreational and cultural activity is taken up by Given and Leckie in a second report of the Canadian urban public libraries study in which reading, writing, "talking to other patrons," and "using the computer" (381–82) were the most commonly observed patron behaviors. When taken together with all other observed social activities, the authors conclude "that even large, complex central libraries are vibrant social spaces" (384). However this finding is not borne out in the context of library use reported by the research participants in my dissertation study nor by those in other studies of lesbian, gay, bisexual, and queer patrons, not even in those studies that occur in large, urban cities. More common are reports of barriers to access to desired texts and needed information. LGBQ patrons also failed to perceive the public library as an inviting social space. Participants did not perceive a "place" for themselves within the place of the public library—neither in its physical layout nor in its collections.

LIS LITERATURE ON LESBIAN, GAY, AND BISEXUAL PATRONS

Several articles have appeared in the professional and scholarly library and information science literature that report on the actual and perceived uses made of libraries by gay, bisexual, and queer adults. Creelman and Harris published the first empirical study of the information needs of lesbians; indeed, as Joyce points out in his review of public library service to LGB patrons, this was the first LIS study of any lesbian, gay, bisexual, or queer population (272). Prior to the article by Creelman and Harris, the small body of LIS literature concerned with alternative sexual identities and sexual orientation were commentaries that focused on collection and professional issues rather than reports of research. For example, in one of the earliest calls for improved service to gays and lesbians, published in 1978, Ashby lists five levels of service to lesbian and gay patrons that would emerge from a renewed commitment to the professional values of librarianship: staff training and awareness; a comprehensive materials selection policy; effective selection practices; finding aids and access guides; and promotion of services to the target population (54). A year later, Wyatt urged librarians to collect materials beyond those that dealt with "medical or pseudopsychiatric aspects" of homosexuality (88). In an article published ten years later, Malinowsky provides an introduction to reference materials "for or about gays and lesbians" (1647).

Since the early nineties several more calls for improved service to LGBQ patrons, including young people, have been published. Most of these calls continue to be embedded in discussions of LGBQ collections. Raaflaub cited problems with indexing language and classification schemes as well as heterosexist and homophobic attitudes as causing significant barriers of access to lesbian literature (20). Ellen Greenblatt and Cal Gough, the pioneering editors of the handbook *Gay and Lesbian Library Services* have been advocating for years for more inclusive subject headings, cataloguing procedures and, in general, for more inclusive library services. Other studies examine the nature of specific collections and dimensions of access to them with the assumption that a well-indexed and deep collection of materials offers a meaningful point of service that can meet the information needs of LGBQ patrons (see, e.g., Sweetland and Christensen;

Rothbauer and McKechnie; Boon and Howard). However, studies like these stop short of any sustained examination of the actual information behavior of LGBQT people.

In the study cited above, Creelman and Harris identified the primary information needs of adult lesbians as (1) coming to terms with a lesbian identity; (2) sharing this identity with others, colloquially known as "coming out" to others; and (3) finding others (39). A large majority of the women interviewed perceived the library to be an important resource for information about homosexuality, yet they predominantly expressed dissatisfaction with the materials they found there. More than half of the research participants claimed that reading "printed sources" did not help them with their information needs because they could not find relevant, lesbian-oriented, practical, and current information.

Stenback and Schrader's study of the information-seeking behavior of adult lesbians found that libraries, in particular, and printed sources, in general, were ranked as being more important sources of information than were other lesbians (43). This finding corresponds to an earlier study by Whitt that surveyed a much larger sample of lesbian participants (275). Yet all three studies of the information needs of adult lesbians cited here conclude that one of the most frequently expressed initial uses of the public library is for information related to meeting other lesbians in an attempt to establish a connection with a larger community—a need for information that was consistently unmet by libraries.

Studies of other populations of lesbian, gay and bisexual patrons provide much of the same evidence. Garnar reported in his survey of 169 lesbian and gay adult library patrons in Denver, Colorado, that the public library took second place to lesbian and gay bookstores and community centers as sources of material that met information needs related to sexual identity and sexual orientation. In a survey of lesbian, gay, and bisexual library patrons of two U.K. public libraries supporting a lesbian, gay, and bisexual collection, Norman concludes that a separate LGBQ collection aids access to information. Using survey instruments, Joyce and Schrader captured the perceptions of gay male patrons of the Edmonton Public Library. In a general way, their findings support the earlier empirical studies of adult lesbians: the library is identified as the most significant source of information about sexual orientation and the primary information need corresponds to a desire to gain a sense of belonging to a larger community (33–34). In his more recent dissertation, "The Discursive Construction of Lesbian, Gay and Bisexual Identity," Steven Joyce cites the emergence of Web-based resources that are displacing the library for information about alternative sexual identities among his young adult participants. In my dissertation, "Finding and Creating Possibility," I focused on the role of voluntary reading in the lives of seventeen self-identified lesbian, queer, or bisexual young women between the ages of eighteen and twenty-three years. A major thread of this inquiry included an examination of sites and sources of information about gay, lesbian, and queer reading materials including libraries, bookstores and the Internet (Rothbauer "The Internet"). Uses of the library and of the Internet frequently resulted in unsatisfactory searches for reading materials, while bookstores were more likely to be regarded as reliable, accessible and satisfying sources of books with LGBQ content (Rothbauer "People" 69–70).

This brief review of library and information science studies clearly illustrates that the library, often the public library, *is* granted a place in the lives of lesbian, gay, bisexual, and queer library patrons both by research subjects and the researchers themselves. In the following section I examine how the dominant metaphors of library as safe place and library as storehouse work together to materialize the library as closeted space.

LIBRARY AS A SAFE PLACE IN THE COMMUNITY

There is a commonsense understanding that libraries are one of the primary locations for lesbian, gay, bisexual, transgender, and queer people to find information about what it means to declare an alternative sexual orientation or a nonmainstream sexual identity. So common is this notion, in fact, that *Cassell's Queer Companion* includes an entry for the term *library* defined as "one of the main sites of self-discovery for lesbians and gay men" (as cited in Curry "If I Ask" 56). Pioneers in the call for service to LGBQ patrons, Cal Gough and Ellen Greenblatt, also cite anecdotes from authors' accounts of the role the library played as they came to terms with their gay and lesbian identities ("Services" 59). In this same article, Gough and Greenblatt go on to write: "These writers discuss the key role libraries played in the discovery of their emerging sexual identities. So central is this step of the "coming out" process that gay and lesbian literature abounds with such anecdotes" (59).

As the previous literature review shows, the growing body of library and information research also supports the notion that the public library functions as an initial site of information about sexual identity and orientation to LGBQ patrons—a site of access, moreover, that relies on the metaphor of library as safe place. The public library is represented as a place to access information and reading materials on alternative sexualities that invites a private, anonymous encounter with the collection by people who are perceived to be at risk due to the potential stigmatization associated with their sexual identities and sexual orientation. Frequently, calls for library services to LGBQ patrons are justified by the need for refuge or safe space in which to explore and research sexuality without fear of either disclosure or scrutiny. Consequently, this perceived need for refuge gives rise to the notion that one of the primary ways to support this patron group is to establish a place within the library that permits gays and lesbians to surreptitiously search library holdings. Below are a few representative excerpts from early calls for service to LGBQ patrons that illustrate the offers of anonymity and objectivity that situate the library as a safe place:

For the gay/lesbian library patron—especially if that person happens to be unsure or anxious about his/her sexual identity—it's partly the complete or near complete anonymity surrounding the use of library materials that brings a gay person into the library in the first place. (Gough and Greenblatt "Gay" 5)

Reading in libraries is more important than we may realize. It is a relatively private and safe way to sift out the positive from the negative, to discover the gradually improving quality of material available about homosexuality. The library is a place to find solace. (Monroe 45)

When a sense of isolation and "being different" are the strongest elements of the early gay experience, the chance discovery in a library or bookshop can change a life. . . . Many gay people do not want to be identified as such by asking for particular titles and even a simple list of authors can be a tremendous help to finding the way to novels or biography with a gay theme. (Ashby 154)

However, the library cannot always ensure anonymity for its patrons as simply being observed reading or browsing through materials that contain lesbian or gay content may create a fear of being observed and therefore raise the possibility of censure or harassment. That such fears and needs are reported to be more common among LGBQ people when they are in the initial stages of coming to terms with their sexual identities is supported by data taken from my interviews with lesbian, bisexual, and queer young women. When asked about library use participants in my dissertation study indicated that the library was unable to provide satisfactory access to lesbian and gay materials due to inadequate collections and due to the frequently expressed fear of the possible disclosure of one's sexual orientation occurring within its walls. For example, Keri,[2] a twenty-year-old self-identified lesbian, recalled her fear of being noticed in the library:

[I]f you're just coming out and you want more information you don't want to take those books from the library, you know. . . . Like I remember going to the library . . . and I'd be reading [books] there in the aisle—like I wouldn't take [them] to the table.

Keri's library experience was recalled by many of the participants in my research and it is commonly found in biographical anecdotes of other lesbians and gays. The following excerpt provides another cogent example of library as safe place; written by a lesbian teenager it is taken from a book of photographic essays by Adam Mastoon featuring lesbian and gay youth:

I found the most hidden corners of the library, the carrels that fit in the corner so no one could see the reader. I even tucked my legs beneath so nobody could identify my sneakers . . . I hid, often, in the library and between the stacks. (80)

So while librarians advocate the library's chief function as providing safe access to information about alternative sexualities, hiding, risk, and fear continue to characterize firsthand accounts of visits to the library by LGBQ patrons. Furthermore, positioning the library as a safe, anonymous, and private place, a place of solace, a place that affords hiding space for LGBQ patrons, reinscribes the values of the homosexual closet. The limits to accessibility that are created are described by one theorist by defining the features of closet space in relation to other rooms:

The closet is not far away from the room, and it is certainly accessible, but one must look for it. One must open its door to see its contents, or to move into or out of it. So by definition a closet has a certain kind of spatial interaction with its room. It is separate and distinct too. It segregates, it hides and it confines. Closets are spatial strategies that help one arrange and manage an increasingly complicated life. (Busch 1999 as quoted in Brown 7)

When viewed this way, libraries can be seen as both limiting and encouraging two levels of service to LGBQ patrons: use of internal library space and use of library holdings. Library space is presently limited by the perceived need for safe space in which LGBQ patrons negotiate systems of access designed to protect their sexual identities or sexual orientations from public disclosure. Use of LGBQ collections (another kind of library space) continues to be hampered by a certain mystique of access that frustrates even the most experienced and determined of searchers (Rothbauer "The Internet"). The reliance on the metaphor of library as safe place materializes the closet by privileging concealment, secrecy, and fear. LGBQ patrons are *placed* in libraries as silent, fearful, anxious, and *closeted*. However, closets are also defined by how people move in and out of them and can be seen as spaces of movement and interaction with other locations within larger communities[3] (Brown 46, 141).

Many studies locate libraries among competing community sources of information such as bookstores and various social services agencies (see e.g., Rothbauer "Finding", Stenback and Schrader, Garnar, Norman). The representation of the library as a safe and neutral place marks its distinct location within the larger LGBQ community, and strategies designed to make library services to the LGBQ community visible may unintentionally threaten its members' perceived needs for security and anonymity. One of the ways that the public library is situated within its LGBQ communities is through assumptions held by patrons regarding access to information about such communities that might foster connections with other members. However, the potential for the library to support community building is often defeated by the perception of poor collections and of inscrutable systems of access (see Stenback and Schrader; Joyce and Schrader; Rothbauer "People"). This despite the finding of all empirical studies of the information needs of lesbian and gay patrons indicating that the public library initially functions as kind of a taken-for-granted place to get information about local lesbian and gay communities. On the surface, the research would seem to give some evidence of the public library's potential to support the more general claims that the public library functions as place by becoming "one of the focal points of its community" (Gorman 45). However, a closer reading of the context of the information behavior of lesbians and gays reveals that the focal point does not hold as the provision of library services is almost always perceived to be inadequate and unsatisfying, leading to lowered expectations among patrons as well as a search beyond the walls of the library for more rewarding and fruitful sources and sites of information.

Libraries are also positioned by their geographical place or by their location within a larger community (Leckie 233). In the context of the studies cited in this paper, this positioning is often performed through competition in the provision of LGBQ information within a wider community of gay and lesbian people, agencies and services. In empirical studies of the information needs of lesbians public libraries are ranked among other physical sites of information such as gay bars, gay and lesbian organizations, women's bookstores and gay coffee shops (Stenback and Schrader 42–43; Creelman and Harris 38). Stenback and Schrader suggest that the effects of the size and type of community influences the role of the public library as well:

> there were many resources readily available to those living in the largest urban centers that were not accessible in [small or rural] communities, for instance, lesbian and gay community centers, gaylines or phone services, gay bars, and womens' bookstores. Furthermore, because the women in small centers were well known to others in their communities, they did not view the local public library as a safe, private place that they could go for information. Instead, they felt compelled to leave their own communities in order to seek information that was vital to self-identity and development as lesbians. (47)

The emphasis that Stenback and Schrader put on the geographical location of the public library in relation to the needs of its patrons illustrates that the public library takes on meaning as place only in relation to other social agents and institutions. Participants in my study confirmed this finding in their reluctance to visit libraries that were perceived to carry little of interest or that were too far out of the way of daily travels (Rothbauer "Finding" 145). The library collection seems to be the most meaningful axis of service to LGBQ patrons. The place of the library is defined largely by what it can offer its patrons in terms of reading materials and, as such, invites comparisons to other sites that are frequently deemed to be more reliable and accessible sources of books and magazines containing representations of LGBQ experience.

LIBRARY AS STOREHOUSE

Often the library is wholly identified with its collections, as if it has no place in the lives of LGBQ patrons external to its holdings. By far, and perhaps not surprisingly, studies of LGBQ materials and collections comprise the largest degree of scholarship within library and information science. By privileging collections of materials researchers and writers rely on the storehouse metaphor to justify or explain services to LGBQ patrons. Articles that explore collections of LGBQ materials very often make an explicit link between the levels of library service and the quality of the library collection as illustrated by the following selection of excerpts:

Evaluating public library collections for the inclusion of young adult (YA) fiction with LGBT content provides a means of assessing how well libraries are serving LGBT youth. This study aims to provide an impetus to librarians to ensure that the needs of this group are met. (Boon and Howard 133)

A library that consistently fails to provide appropriate materials concerning gay and lesbian themes runs the risk of failing, to some degree, up to ten percent of its clientele. (Kilpatrick 80)

If a search for current and relevant materials with LGB content is not stymied by inadequate and problematic cataloguing, it may be altogether halted by the nonexistence in libraries of such materials. (Joyce 276)

Studies of LGBQ collections and materials tend to emphasize specific types of literature rather than an analysis of the entire holdings of a particular library or group of libraries. For example, Sweetland and Christensen investigated the holdings of adult gay, lesbian, and bisexual literature identified in the *Lambda Book Report* (34). Carmichael used the OCLC WorldCat Database to examine literature retrieved using the subject headings "homosexuality," "gay men," and "gays" (65–66). Potts followed this study by conducting her own search for adult lesbian fiction using the online catalogues of the book retailer Amazon, the Library of Congress, and the British Library (162). Curry looked at the collection management practices of free gay and lesbian newspapers in Canada and the U.K. ("Collection"). Others begin their studies with checklists of GLBQT young adult fiction (see Spence; Rothbauer and McKechnie; Boon and Howard). All of these articles contain sometimes implicitly, sometimes directly stated calls for more responsive information systems with which to access LGBQT materials—calls that merge with professional values of intellectual freedom and democratic access to information. Such a position suggests human user–oriented perspectives on the provision of library services that are built upon the development and maintenance of quality collections of LGBQT materials. Underpinning this position, however, is the static metaphor of the library as storehouse. It is a fixed and passive collection of books, serials, videos and online resources that is seen to hold the most promise for meeting the information needs of LGBQ patrons—promise that can only be met when such patrons are connected with LGBQ materials in a direct and unequivocal manner. The storehouse metaphor forecloses on other possibilities for the library as place (i.e., as a shifting, dynamic social ground) as it forces us to see the library solely as a kind of container that changes depending only on what gets put into it or taken out of it. This conceptualization of the place of the library corresponds to the notion of space as a fixed, objective surface that allows social identities to be "read off" of it.

LGBQ library patrons similarly conceive of libraries as storehouses when they see the inadequacy of the library holdings of LGBQ materials as representing the entire measure of what the library can offer to them as they negotiate their nonmainstream sexual identities and sexual orientations. For example, participants in my dissertation research would visit the library hoping to find some reading materials with lesbian or queer content and when they could not find any books or they had exhausted their carefully compiled lists, the library ceased to be useful to them. In many cases the library was no longer seen to be even a source of LGBQ reading materials. The library lost ground to gay and lesbian and feminist bookstores that were perceived to be more reliable sources of better (i.e., more relevant and more current) reading materials. The following excerpt from my interview with Barb illustrates her expectations of the public library collection: she knew that the public library would carry major bestsellers and various classics of lesbian literature, but did not expect it to provide more recent works:

The public library has stuff like Ann-Marie Macdonald, Jeannette Winterson . . . I'm sure it had some more classic texts, probably Virginia Woolf, E.M. Forster or people like that. But the ones, when I wanted to find something more contemporary. . . . I don't know if it had *Rubyfruit Jungle*, but there was a bookstore in [mid-sized Ontario city] that I went to a couple of times, and [it was] well-priced, so that's where I actually bought the books. (Rothbauer "Finding" 147–48)

Calls for improving access to materials with LGBQ content through more relevant and sensitive subject headings (Campbell), through signage and shelving practices, through deeper indexing, and better catalogue interfaces mark the library as a place that could employ strategies to create and support effective and efficient access to LGBQ materials. Such calls seek to shore up the traditional level of service to LGBQ patrons—the passive and conservative approach advocated by Helma Hawkins in 1994 of "providing some fairly private places to read in the library, without being observed by everyone who walks by" (30). The concept of the library as a safe place for LGBQ patrons is entrenched in the services provided to this patron group and it circumscribes the extent to which the library can be positioned as an active, engaged, and social place for LGBQ patrons.

LIBRARY AS PLACE: TENSION AND AMBIVALENCE

The persistent belief expressed by LGBQ patrons as reported in all empirical studies of the information behavior and library practices of this patron group is that libraries will provide access to some kind of information about what it means to be lesbian, gay, bisexual, or queer. However, access to LGBQ library materials will always be limited by its embeddedness in the contexts of the production and distribution of such materials— by official strategies of publishing, shipping, purchasing, and circulation. Or in other words, LGBQ patrons can only find access to materials that exist, that are published, purchased, catalogued, and circulated. If the sole avenue of service to LGBQ patrons is simply to make such materials available, the library will continue to be defined as a static (and inadequate) repository of books whose relevance will continue to be questioned. The implications of this dilemma are twofold: on one hand a call could be made for an increase in the share of the publishing market dedicated to LGBQ materials, thereby increasing availability of texts with gay and lesbian content and increasing potential reader satisfaction. On the other hand, a call could be made to review the traditionally passive approach to service to LGBQ patrons to move beyond an emphasis on "the collection" to begin to consider the meaning of the collection in the lives of its perceived audience of readers.[4] The tension between these two competing mandates of service to LGBQ patrons ameliorates the capacity to which the public library can function as a successful public place for these patrons.

The need for a safe, private space in the library that is useful or helpful to people dealing with nonmainstream sexual identities seems to trump the need for a vital, engaged social realm that might augment social connections among people. The distribution of booklists and pathfinders to gay and lesbian texts, improved shelf access, the adoption of better cataloguing practices, the creation of private and safe spaces within the library, and the purchase and circulation of materials with LGBQ content are necessary, even foundational aspects of library services for LGBQ patrons. Following Michel de Certeau, this array of professional practices can be said to function as "official strategies" defined as practices that work to represent the library as a recognizable, official place in the ongoing conceptualization of service to LGBQ patrons (Rothbauer "The Practice"). However, so long as library services are developed using the place of the public library as a starting point, they will always rely on what the system can "officially" provide, rather than the uses that are made of what is provided. For example, the expressed fears regarding unintentional disclosure of one's sexual orientation may be more broadly interpreted than solely as a need for a safe, *private* place in which to read and browse materials containing LGBQ content. The participants in my dissertation study suggest that safe, *public* spaces might function just as well by allowing them to "come out" in a space that gives access to much sought after representations of a range on non-mainstream sexualities *and* that offers protection by actively censuring anti-homosexual and homophobic activities within its walls.

The lesbian and queer young women who participated in my study gave many salient illustrations of the concept of safe and what they perceived to be public[5] places when they spoke about the role of gay and lesbian or feminist bookstores. My research participants made unequivocal declarations of support for independently owned and locally situated booksellers. Moreover, financial support of independent booksellers, especially women's and gay bookstores, expressed a show of solidarity for gays and lesbians. Bookstore use was also a way to publicly enact a lesbian or queer identity—supporting lesbian and gay "friendly" stores was construed as a political, consumer-oriented act that granted legitimacy, visibility, and recognition of non-mainstream sexualities. There is an emergent body of research in cultural studies of marketing that examines politically motivated consumption among lesbians and gays (see e.g., Kates and Belk; and Penaloza). The establishment of lesbian and gay space, represented by specialty bookstores, offers not only sites of access to lesbian and gay literature and information, thus mirroring typical library uses, but also functions as a solid ground from which consumers can find reflection of lesbian and queer sexual identities. This, in turn, legitimates the enactment of such identities. The difference between specialty bookstores and libraries, in this analysis, lies in the persistent belief that libraries need to be safe, private, anonymous sources of LGBQ information, so much so, perhaps, that they render invisible LGBQ patrons and their uses of library materials and library spaces.

The persistent perception by LGBQ patrons of the inadequacy of library holdings and library access to information about sexual identities and sexual orientation suggests a tension between the traditional notions of the library as a safe place and as a storehouse. A consideration of the ways in which the place of library is produced or perhaps reproduced as space offers a new interpretation of this tension: regardless of negative perceptions of library holdings and methods of access to LGBQ materials, the public library is consistently granted significance in accounts of emergent and ongoing negotiations of what it means to claim a lesbian, gay, bisexual, or queer identity. In other words, the library remains an important initial ground of information seeking and continues to be placed in narratives of information behaviour of LGBQ people. In a study on the virtual spaces of lesbian and bisexual women's electronic mailing lists, Wincapaw explains that these spaces are created by electronic social interactions that are valued for the provision of places to meet with other women, of opportunities to explore identity, and of refuge from hostile and discriminatory personal and social environments (48–49). The idea of the safe space is evoked here but it is the opportunity to "make a connection with other lesbians and/or bisexuals" that was valued most (57). Although thus far there has been little evidence that the public library supports the creation of lesbian or gay space, the possibility of a spatial frame is not altogether lost for public libraries, not when we consider the spaces produced by the act of reading (de Certeau 117). The distribution by libraries of materials that contain LGBQ content *can* be viewed as one of the most powerful, progressive, and positive levels of service to LGBQ patrons, regardless of consistently poor evaluations of the depth and breadth of LGBQ collections, or as I have argued here, regardless of the ambivalence of place. As Curry writes of free gay and lesbian newspapers in libraries in the United Kingdom and Canada, "[b]y being distributed in public places, they also proclaim to the straight majority that a gay/lesbian community exists" ("Collection" 14). The power lies in promoting the collection, in promoting the materials, and by announcing support for the larger LGBTQ community. Such support should be defined in terms of community building and community engagement rather than by reinscribing the boundaries of the "homosexual closet," which are always defined by limitation, fear, secrecy, privacy, denial and erasure (Brown 5).

It is precisely through the traditional mode of service to LGBQ patrons—namely through access to texts—that libraries can contribute to the creation of queer spaces. In an analysis of the sexual geographies of reading in postwar London, Richard Hornsey argues that "the space of reading, knowledge and commodification were placed into a certain (hetero-)sexual geography, structuring the terms through which everyday spatial practices were performed, be they regulated or resistant" (372). Following Hornsey, I would like to suggest that library services to LGBQ library patrons are regulated within a similar heterosexual geography that fixes the library as storehouse and library as safe place by privileging the values of the homosexual closet (i.e., safety, privacy) that denies the potentiality of the creative, social capacity of the place of the public library among LGBQ patrons. Spatial tactics can be used to claim membership in a public place as exercised through activities such as the daily occupation of space, visible uses of space, and welcoming invitations to "take up space" (Brown 252). This kind of membership is denied to LGBQ patrons with the persistent conceptualization of public libraries as storehouses and safe places that renders invisible any spatial tactics due to a singular emphasis on the needs for privacy and anonymity.

FROM CLOSET SPACE TOWARD QUEER SPACE: A CONCLUSION

The heterosexist concept of the homosexual closet, defined to mean the concealment and erasure of gays and lesbians (Brown 5), underpins the library's approach to services to LGBQ patrons despite a competing ethos of tolerance. The dimensions of the homosexual closet delineate the official place of the public library in the lives of LGBQ patrons through two metaphors of library as place: the dominant metaphor of library as safe place and the secondary metaphor of library as storehouse. Among members of this patron group the public library struggles to maintain even its traditional role as a static repository of books as it is persistently viewed as a failure in the provision of desired reading materials to LGBQ library patrons. Nor do LGBQ patrons always value the public library as a focal point of service within a larger lesbian and gay community. It is, paradoxically, the creation of access to LGBQ materials as the primary mode of service to LGBQ patrons that ensures the place of the library in their lives and, at the same time, it invites them to look elsewhere for representation and social connections. The conventional ideas of the public library as *place* (i.e., as repository or refuge) fail in the context of the library uses of LGBQ patrons, but an analysis of reading, conceived of as a creative practice that produces social and ideological space, offers the possibility for the public library to contribute to the creation of *space*.

According to de Certeau, reading is an exemplary spatial practice of everyday life that allows people to wander through an imposed system—that of the text, but also of the circuits of writing, publishing, distribution and reception of texts, circuits in which libraries are clearly embedded. The creative production of the reader, the spaces created through the act of reading, permit readers to exercise a degree of social power that is detached from the text's origins (de Certeau 169). And as Michael P. Brown writes, "Space does not just represent power; it materializes it" (3). If we take the origins of the texts to include the strategies mounted by public libraries to connect collections with LGBQ patrons, we can begin to see a wider view of how the place of the public library might function in the lives of these users. It allows us to see the emancipatory potential of LGBQT collections, even though they receive poor evaluations by all participants in most studies of LGBQ patrons. The readers in my study found the LGBTQ collections to which they had found access to be inadequate, and yet such texts supported the creation of social and ideological spaces that allowed them to claim spaces within their communities—communities within which libraries are situated as members by virtue of their provision of textual representations of lesbian, queer, bisexual, gay, and trans experience. This spatial frame privileges the meanings of the library in the lives of its users, rather than assigning meaning based solely on the limitations of its collections.

NOTES

1. I use the acronym LGBQ in the most inclusive sense possible in an attempt to represent the diversity of sexual identities and sexual orientation declared in all studies cited in this paper. Readers should not mistake the use of the acronym as an attempt to unify such identities to one homogeneous group of library patrons. The omission of the "T" that signifies "transgender" is

intentional as I have yet to encounter a study of the information behavior of this group. Variant use of the acronym indicates how others have used it in their work.

2. The names of all participants are pseudonyms. Other identifying characteristics have also been altered or removed in order to protect identities of participants.

3. I believe it is possible to talk about a "queer community" without accepting it as a unitary, stable, reified social structure. As others (Weston, Seidman, Gamson) argue, the concept of a distinct community of lesbians, gays, and other sexual minorities provides a site for social affinity arranged along the trajectories of sexual identity, sexual practices, and sexual orientation. And rather than see collective identity as unchanging across individual enactments and historical moments, we can follow Gamson, who posits collective identity as a process of collective action that continually reconstitutes notions of collective identity.

4. Readers may recognize the obvious influence here of Wayne Wiegand's 2003 call for inquiries of this nature.

5. "Public" in this sense would be more accurately described as "pseudo-public," as retail bookstores and other kinds of commercial spaces are not, in fact, public in the same sense as public libraries that typically rely on public funding.

REFERENCES

Aitchison, Cara Carmichael. *Gender and Leisure: Social and Cultural Perspectives.* London and New York: Routledge, 2003.

Alstad, Colleen and Ann Curry. "Public Space, Public Discourse, and Public Libraries." *Libres* 13.1 (2003). Retrieved 11 October 2005 from http://libres.curtin.edu.au/libres13n1/.

Ashby, Richard. "Library Services to Gay and Lesbian People." *Assistant Librarian* 80.10 (1987): 153–55.

Boon, Michele Hilton and Vivian Howard. "Recent Lesbian/ Gay/ Bisexual/ Transgender Fiction for Teens: Are Canadian Public Libraries Providing Adequate Collections?" *Collection Building* 23.3 (2004): 133–38.

Brown, Michael P. *Closet Space: Geographies of Metaphor from the Body to the Globe.* London and New York: Routledge, 2000.

Buschman, John E. *Dismantling the Public Sphere: Situating and Sustaining Librarianship in the Age of the New Public Philosophy.* Westport, CT: Libraries Unlimited, 2003.

Campbell, D. Grant. "Queer Theory and the Creation of Contextual Subject Access Tools for Gay and Lesbian Communities." *Knowledge Organization* 27.3 (2000): 122–31.

Carmichael, James V. "Effects of the Gay Publishing Boom on Classes of Titles Retrieved Under the Subject Headings 'Homosexuality,' 'Gay Men,' and 'Gays' in the OCLC WorldCat Database." *Journal of Homosexuality* 42.3 (2002): 65–88.

Creelman, Janet E. A., and Roma Harris. "Coming Out: The Information Needs of Lesbians." *Collection Building* 10.3–4 (1990): 37–41.

Curry, Ann. "Collection Management of Gay/Lesbian Materials in the U.K. and Canada." *Libri* 50.1 (2000): 14–25.

———. "If I Ask, Will They Answer? Evaluating Public Library Reference Service to Gay/Lesbian Youth." *Reference and User Services Quarterly* 45.1 (2005): 65–75.

de Certeau, Michel. *The Practice of Everyday Life*, translated by Steven Rendall. Berkeley, CA: University of California Press, 1984.

Gamson, Joshua. "Must Identity Movements Self-destruct? A Queer Dilemma." *Social Problems* 42.3 (1995): 390–407.

Garnar, Martin. "Changing Times: Information Destinations of the Lesbian, Gay, Bisexual, and Transgender Community in Denver, Colorado." *Information for Social Change* 12 (Winter 2001). Retrieved 11 October 2005 from http://www.libr.org/ISC/articles/12-Garnar.html.

Given, Lisa M., and Gloria J. Leckie. "'Sweeping' the Library: Mapping the Social Activity Space of the Public Library." *Library & Information Science Research* 25.4 (2003): 365–85.

Gorman, Michael. *Our Enduring Values: Librarianship in the 21st Century*. Chicago and London: American Library Association, 2000.

Gough, Cal, and Ellen Greenblatt. "Services to Gay and Lesbian Patrons: Examining the Myths." *Library Journal* 117.1 (1992): 59–63.

———, eds. *Gay and Lesbian Library Service*. Jefferson, N.C.: McFarland, 1990.

Greenhalgh, Liz. "Public Library as a Place." Comedia Working Papers #2: *Future of Public Libraries*. Bournes Green: Gloucestershire: Comedia, 1993.

Greenhalgh, Liz and Ken Worpole. *Libraries in a World of Cultural Change*. London: UCL Press, 1995.

Hawkins, Helma. "Opening the Closet door: Public Library Services for Gay, Lesbian, and Bisexual Teens." *Colorado Libraries* 20.1 (1994): 28–31.

Hornsey, Richard. "The Sexual Geographies of Reading in Post-War London." *Gender, Place and Culture* 9.4 (2002): 371–84.

Joyce, Steven. "The Discursive Construction of Lesbian, Gay and Bisexual Identity: How Symbolic Violence and Information Capital Mediate the Coming Out Process." Ph.D. diss., University of Western Ontario, 2003.

———. "Lesbian, Gay, and Bisexual Library Service: A Review of the Literature." *Public Libraries* 39.5 (2000): 270–79.

Joyce, Steven, and Alvin M. Schrader. "Hidden Perceptions: Edmonton Gay Males and the Edmonton Public Library." *Canadian Journal of Information and Library Science* 22 (April 1997): 19–37.

Kates, Steven M., and Russell W. Belk. "The Meaning of Lesbian and Gay Pride Day: Resistance Through Consumption and Resistance to Consumption." *Journal of Contemporary Ethnography* 30.4 (2001): 392–429.

Kilpatrick, Thomas L. "A Critical Look at the Availability of Gay and Lesbian Periodical Literature in Libraries and Standard Indexing Services." *Serials Review* 22.4 (1996): 71–81.

Leckie, Gloria J. "Three Perspectives on the Library as Public Space." *Feliciter* 50.6 (2004): 233–36.

Leckie, Gloria J., and Jeffrey Hopkins. "The Public Place of Central Libraries: Findings from Toronto and Vancouver." *Library Quarterly* 72.3 (2002): 326–72.

Malinowsky, Robert H. "Reference Materials For or About Gays and Lesbians." *Booklist* 84 (June 1, 1988): 1647–48.

Mastoon, Adam. *The Shared Heart: Portraits and Stories Celebrating Lesbian, Gay, and Bisexual Young People*. New York: William Morrow and Company, 1997.

Monroe, Judith. "Breaking the Silence Barrier: Libraries and Gay and Lesbian Students." *Collection Building* 9.1 (1988): 43–46.

Norman, Mark. "Out on Loan: A Survey of the Use and Information Needs of Users of the Lesbian, Gay and Bisexual Collection of Brighton and Hove Libraries." *Journal of Librarianship and Information Science* 31.4 (1999): 188–96.

Penaloza, Lisa. "We're Here, We're Queer and We're Going Shopping: A Critical Perspective on the Accommodations of Gays and Lesbians in the U.S. Marketplace." *Journal of Homosexuality* 31.1–2 (1996): 9–41.

Potts, Hilary. Searching the Databases: A Quick Look at Amazon and Two Other Online Catalogues. *Journal of Homosexuality* 45.1 (2003): 161–70.

Raaflaub, Yvonne. "Problems of Access to Lesbian Literature." *RQ* 31.1 (1991): 19–23.

Rothbauer, Paulette M. "Finding and Creating Possibility: Reading in the Lives of Lesbian, Bisexual and Queer Young Women." Ph.D. diss., University of Western Ontario, 2004.

———. "The Internet in the Reading Accounts of Lesbian and Queer Young Women: Failed Searches and Unsanctioned Reading." *Canadian Journal of Library and Information Science/La Revue canadienne des sciences de l'information et de bibli;oéconomie* 28.4 (2004): 89–112.

————. " 'People Aren't Afraid Any More, But It's Hard to Find Books': Reading Practices That Inform the Personal and Social Identities of Self-Identified Lesbian and Queer Young Women." *Canadian Journal of Library and Information Science/La Revue canadienne des sciences de l'information et de bibliothéconomie* 28.3 (2004): 53–74.

————. "The Practice of Everyday Life". In *Theories of Information Behavior: A Researcher's Guide*. Eds. Karen Fisher, Sanda Erdelez, and Lynne (E.F.) McKechnie. Medford, NJ: ASIST, Information Today, 2005: 284–88.

Rothbauer, Paulette M., and Lynne (E.F.) McKechnie. "Gay and Lesbian Fiction for Young Adults: A Survey of the Holdings in Canadian Public Libraries." *Collection Building* 18.1 (1999): 32–39.

Seidman, Steven. *Beyond the Closet: The Transformation of Gay and Lesbian Life.* New York and London: Routledge, 2002.

Skeggs, Beverley, Leslie Moran, Paul Tyrer, and Jon Binnie. "Queer as Folk: Producing the Real of Urban Space." *Urban Studies* 41.9 (2004): 1839–56.

Spence, Alex. "Gay Young Adult Fiction in the Public Library: A Comparative Survey." *Public Libraries* 38.4 (1999): 224–43.

Stenback, Tanis L., and Alvin M. Schrader. "Venturing from the Closet: A Qualitative Study of the Information Needs of Lesbians." *Public Library Quarterly* 17.3 (1999): 37–50.

Sweetland, James H., and Peter G. Christensen. "Gay, Lesbian, and Bisexual Titles: Their Treatment in the Review Media and Their Selection by Libraries." *Collection Building* 14.2 (1995): 32–41.

Valentine, Gill. *Social Geographies: Space and Society.* Harlow, England: Pearson Education/ Prentice-Hall, 2001.

Weston, Kath. *Families We Choose: Lesbians, Gays, Kinship.* New York: Columbia University Press, 1991.

Whitt, Alisa J. "The Information Needs of Lesbians." *Library & Information Science Research* 15.3 (1993): 275–88.

Wiegand, Wayne A. 2003. "Broadening Our Perspectives." *Library Quarterly* 73.1 (2003): v–x.

Wincapaw, Celeste. "The Virtual Spaces of Lesbian and Bisexual Women's Electronic Mailing Lists." In *From Nowhere to Everywhere: Lesbian Geographies*. Ed. Gill Valentine. Haworth Press: Harrington Park Press, 2000.

Wyatt, Michael. "Gays and Libraries." *New Zealand Libraries* 41.3 (1978): 88–93.

7

Behind the Program-Room Door: The Creation of Parochial and Private Women's Realms in a Canadian Public Library[1]

Pamela J. McKenzie

Associate Professor, Faculty of Information and Media Studies, University of Western Ontario—London, Ontario

Elena M. Prigoda

Instruction and Liaison Librarian, Gerstein Science Information Centre, University of Toronto, Toronto, Ontario

Kirsten Clement

Educational Outreach and Young Adult Librarian, Brantford Public Library, Brantford, Ontario

Lynne (E.F.) McKechnie

Associate Professor, Faculty of Information and Media Studies, University of Western Ontario—London, Ontario

INTRODUCTION

Much has been written recently on the role of the public library as a commons where members of the public may gather (Nelson) or as a site for the building of "social capital" (Goulding). However, the research into public library use tends to focus on the use of collections, services, and specific resources (e.g., Zweizig and Dervin, Shoham, Gross, Dresang, and Holt) without considering the ways that the library *as a place* is used: "Although there have been hundreds of studies of library users and their information-related behaviors, relatively little of this research has focused on libraries as a type of social activity space" (Given and Leckie 372).

This chapter describes the use of public space in two programs, a knitters' group and a young child/caregiver storytime, attended by women in a single branch of a large (>100,000) Ontario public library system. We analyze the ways that these women transformed the space of a public library program room into semiprivate or private realms, and discuss the implications of those transformations. We therefore build on the research of Leckie and Hopkins by extending observation and analysis from central to branch libraries and to less visible but still publicly owned areas of the public library. We consider the social spaces located within the library as a physical space (Leckie and

Hopkins, Dixon et al., McKechnie et al., Miller) and the library in the life of the user (Wiegand).

PUBLIC SPACE AND THE PUBLIC REALM

Leckie and Hopkins argue that "given the murkiness surrounding the identification of which spaces are public and which are private or semiprivate, it seems rather futile to define public space by a characteristic, such as ownership, or a physical attribute such as openness. Contemporary public spaces can perhaps be more usefully thought of in terms of the activities that take place within them and the sociocultural functions that these spaces perform" (330). Lyn Lofland ("World" 11) concurs that public spaces are inherently social and has been central in studying urbanites' use of public city spaces and analyzing the meanings of those spaces for users.

Lofland defines public space simply as "accessible or visible to all members of the community" ("Public" 8). One of the most important characteristics of public space is that it comprises a *world of strangers*, or people "with whom one has not had personal acquaintance" (Lofland, "Public" 7). Life in a world of strangers is made possible by "an ordering of the urban populace in terms of appearance and spatial location such that those within the city could know a great deal about one another by simply looking" (Lofland, "World" 22). Urbanites use such ordering to identify and classify strangers, to seek out or avoid interactions with them, and to create smaller pieces of private or semiprivate space in public space.

Lofland posits that city life consists of three distinct but interrelated *realms* ("Public" 9–12, "World" 119–20). Realms are social rather than physical spaces, and are defined by the relationships among the people occupying them rather than by physical characteristics. The public realm is characterized by the presence of people who are personally unknown or only categorically known to one another, for example a customer and shop owner who interact intermittently and infrequently. The parochial realm is characterized by a sense of commonality among acquaintances or neighbors who are involved in interpersonal networks that are located within "communities." There are "regulars" in a parochial space, and patrons have nodding or speaking acquaintances with their fellows. Many of Oldenburg's "third spaces" fall within the parochial social realm. The private realm is characterized by ties of intimacy among primary group members who are located within households and personal networks.

There is nothing inherent in a physical location to make it one type of realm or other. Thus, a legally "public" place can be sociologically "parochial," a family home can become a public realm when opened for a charity tour, or a public zoo can be the site of a private realm where family and caregiving relationships are enacted (DeVault, "Producing"). Because realms are social rather than geographic, they are quite fluid and can change over time. The higher the number of close relationships in a space and the more intimate the inhabitants' knowledge of the space, the closer the space is to functioning as a private realm for its inhabitants, and the more likely it is that those inhabitants will treat the setting like their home, using the space for their own private purposes apart from those originally intended, behaving in informal and casual ways, and adopting an attitude of proprietary rights toward the setting. The complaints of Leckie and Hopkins' participants about the noise of other patrons may be taken as evidence that not all users consider the public library to be a public realm space. As McKechnie et al. found, central and branch public libraries were the sites of a great deal of socializing, eating, and drinking in addition to reading and quiet study. The same physical spaces may be used in a variety of ways by different patrons, possibly at the same time, and may function variously as public, parochial, or private realm spaces.

This chapter seeks further to explore patrons' uses of program-room spaces in a public library branch. The two studies described here explored how library storytimes for young children and their adult caregivers and a public library–hosted knitters' group functioned as social spaces for their inhabitants.

METHODS

Both studies used naturalistic participant observation (Lincoln and Guba), which allowed us to witness the use of the St. Stephen's Green Library first-hand rather than relying on the memories and descriptive abilities of participants. In the fall of 2003, McKechnie and McKenzie, with the assistance of Moffatt, observed and audiotaped a full five-week session of a storytime program as part of a larger study (McKechnie and McKenzie). We stood in the room as unobtrusively as possible and made notes as we observed. Between 8 and 16 young children from birth to 24 months attended storytime with their caregivers each week.

In the fall of 2004 Prigoda, assisted by McKenzie, observed and audio-recorded meetings of a branch-hosted knitters' group. We participated actively, knitting and chatting as we observed, and recorded our observations after leaving the library. Weekly attendance at the knitters' group was about fifteen, although a total of twenty-five women attended over the course of the fall.

All four authors contributed to the framing of the studies and the data collection. McKenzie is responsible for the analysis and the writing of this chapter, which is based on McKenzie's, Prigoda's, and Moffatt's field notes from both studies, and a total of fifteen transcripts reflecting seven sessions (five storytime and two knitters' group) and eight interviews (one focus group and two individual interviews with storytime participants, five individual interviews with knitters'). We developed interview schedules following the field observation (Warren).[2] Both studies conform to the ethical guidelines of the University of Western Ontario and the Tri-Council policy statement on research with humans (Tri-Council Policy Statement).

SPATIAL ORDERING OF STRANGERS

Urbanites make use of two distinct principles of ordering strangers. Clues to a stranger's identity are provided simultaneously by his or her appearance (appearential ordering) and location (spatial ordering). "Appearential ordering allows you to know a great deal about the stranger you are looking at because you can 'place' him with some degree of accuracy on the basis of his body presentation: clothing, hair style, special markings, and so on. In contrast, spatial ordering allows you to know a great deal about the stranger you are looking at because you know a great deal about 'who' is to be found in the particular location in which you find him" (Lofland, "World" 27).

In preindustrial cities, Lofland argues, appearential ordering was the most useful means of identifying strangers. A variety of diverse activities (e.g., begging, busking, educating children, eliminating wastes) took place in public space, and a stranger's appearance (clothing, language) allowed him or her to be categorized. Modern cities, on the other hand, are characterized by the specialized use of public space and the spatial segregation of activities. Many activities formerly carried out in public space are licensed, limited, or relegated to private spaces. Urban residents are segregated by age (in schools and seniors' homes), class, and ethnicity (in neighborhoods). In addition, appearance is no longer such a useful indicator of category. The young person wearing jeans and a sweatshirt could be a high school student, a vagrant, or a corporate CEO. As a consequence,

> the modern urbanite, in contrast to his preindustrial counterpart, primarily uses location rather than appearance to identify the strange others who surround him. In the preindustrial city, space was chaotic, appearances were ordered. In the modern city, appearances are chaotic, space is ordered. In the preindustrial city, a man was what he wore. In the modern city, a man is where he stands. (Lofland, "World" 82)

This is not to say that appearance and behavior are unimportant, rather that they are most reliable when used in the context of spatial knowledge.

In this particular case, library users could have several forms of categorical knowledge, both spatial and appearential, available to them about one another by virtue of their presence in the library. Numerous studies have profiled the demographics of library users (for a summary, see I. Smith), but McNicol offers insights into the kinds of spatial ordering that are available to a stranger by virtue of a person's regular presence in a public library. She used data from a British mass-observation archive to gather opinions of the kinds of people who use libraries. Respondents offered several impressions: "School children, the middle aged and older people ... Other user groups mentioned were mothers and toddlers; men out shopping with their wives, and non-working married women. In general, library users were seen as people with reasonable amounts of spare time ... avid readers." (83). Regardless of the degree to which these impressions correspond with the characteristics of actual British library users, this list of criteria provides evidence that urbanites do make inferences about people related to their use or non-use of a library. For example, one of McKechnie's informants described the neighborhood public library as "an environment that you assume people are friendly because they all use books" (110).

Someone coming into the St Stephen's Green library for the first time could infer several kinds of categorical knowledge about the strangers inhabiting the space based merely on their presence there. First, they have chosen to be present in a public library and could therefore be expected to value public libraries and at least some of the services they provide. Second, they have been permitted to remain. Libraries, like bookstores, "provide places where hanging out is indeed welcomed yet where 'security' is preserved by the ... manager's right to reject undesirable visitors" (Miller 395). We observed a library staff member asking a library visitor to leave for behaving inappropriately.

Presence in this particular public library further signals that a stranger may be affiliated (or want to be affiliated: one of the knitters' called herself a "St. Stephen's Green wannabe") with the neighborhood and share some of the social characteristics of its residents. St. Stephen's Green is an older residential neighborhood, containing many small businesses and services and located on easily accessible bus routes and walking/bike paths to downtown.[3] The neighborhood is relatively affluent and is known locally for its liberal sensibilities. The unemployment rate is less than 1 percent, and 25 percent of the population have a university degree. Family income is above the provincial average and more people are employed in white-collar professions and fewer in the trades, processing, and manufacturing than in either the city or the province. The neighborhood is both ethnically and linguistically homogeneous.[4] People encountering strangers in this neighborhood could therefore expect to meet mainly white, well-educated, socially liberal people.

When taken in conjunction with spatial ordering, appearance and behavior can provide further clues about the identity of strangers. Our field notes provide evidence of the ways that we categorized strangers in this setting:

There is a woman in her thirties wearing a bike helmet and a backpack using one of the computer terminals; she is only there for a brief time before leaving the library, almost as though she were checking something on her way to work. [KM][5]

The woman's location in a bicycle-friendly neighborhood, her presence in the public library at the beginning of the work day, her behavior while in the library, the duration of her stay, her perceived age, and her appearance combine to provide clues that allow the observer to categorize her, rightly or wrongly, as a commuter on her way to work. Lofland contends that this kind of categorization is part of what urbanites do regularly when dealing with strangers.

In addition to the categorical knowledge associated with a stranger's presence in the library itself, presence in the program room at the beginning of storytime or the knitters' group additionally demonstrates an awareness of library-sponsored programs and some understanding of what libraries do and how they do it; an interest in participating and congruence with at least some values associated with the program or the activities performed therein; the organization, motivation, and transportation needed to get there at a particular time; and the flexibility to participate during the normal work day. A participant's ability to be present at the library on a weekday morning or afternoon suggests that she is unemployed, retired, on leave, working at home full-time, employed away from home part-time, or that her full-time employment is structured to permit this kind of schedule.

Within the context of this spatial ordering, a number of appearential clues could supplement categorical knowledge about a program participant. First, a woman's own apparel, the apparel of her child, and the color and style of the chosen knitting project could invite taste and possibly income categorizations. Her level of experience could be inferred by the age of her child or the complexity of the knitting project chosen and the degree to which she asked for assistance. The age of the woman or of her child could provide an indicator of her status in the workforce. A woman over sixty-five is likely to retire and one whose youngest child is over a year old is probably no longer on a paid parental leave.[6]

The combination of spatial and appearential clues therefore provide a newcomer to the scene with many tools with which to categorize a stranger:

[Ten minutes after the beginning of the program] my attention is distracted by a woman coming into the room. She has a soother on a ribbon on her shirt and is carrying a diaper bag and an infant car seat. I thought she looked tired and harried, and that observation combined with the infant car seat, her lateness, and the presence of the soother on her rather than on her baby led me to guess she had a very young baby [PM].

When a newcomer arrives at the program room door for storytime or knitting, several kinds of evidence are available to her and she can already guess a lot (rightly or wrongly) about the kinds of people she will meet inside. A relationship initiated in such a setting is therefore not a relationship among strangers, but rather a relationship among categorically known others, for whom the categories are quite sophisticated. By virtue of their very co-presence in this space participants are communicating that they likely have a lot in common, even before the first word is spoken.

WOMEN, WORK, LEISURE, AND SPACE

Despite evidence that women make extensive use of public libraries (I. Smith) and despite the oft-cited claim that the library "is often one of the few places in a busy city centre where people, particularly women, of all ages go alone and spend time without worry" (Greenhalgh, Warpole, and Landry 52),[7] we know surprisingly little about the ways that women use public libraries (see King, Rothbauer). This absence may be due in part to the focus on the library as a site for a number of "productive" and "purposeful" activities.

Leckie and Hopkins found that "[t]he evidence from the seating sweeps was revealing in confirming that the central library is considered by most patrons to be a place of purposeful study.... The central library acts primarily as a public work space and not a recreational space" (355). Cartwright likewise found that "the library is more widely seen and used as a place for study, information and defined 'retrieval', whilst the bookstore is more widely seen and used as a place for recreation, socialising and browsing" (22). Wiegand (371) argues that these impressions are characteristic of a larger trend: "over time the LIS community came to regard as most important the kinds of information that address questions related to work, or help people become informed citizens, intelligent consumers, and educated people."

Feminist scholars have long questioned the fixed boundaries between public and private spaces and have sought a more nuanced understanding of the nature and organization of the work and leisure activities that take place within them:

In the classic traditions of sociological theorizing, the labels "public" and "private" were taken as referring to two great realms organized very differently (and associated with men versus women and adults versus children, respectively). There were good reasons for thinking this way because these new forms of social organization developed with industrialization; the labels "public" and "private" pointed to large social transformations that were positioning men, women, and families quite differently than in predominantly agricultural societies. For at least three decades now, however, feminists and others have been emphasizing the permeability of the ostensible boundaries between these territories and the connections that make the appearance of bounded space possible. (DeVault, "Families")

Commensurate with a recognition of the permeability of the public/private divide, feminist scholars have argued for a more inclusive definition of "work" which values the sorts of activities that comprise the often invisible work done, frequently by women, in private spaces. These include exactly the activities commonly disregarded by LIS researchers as "non-instrumental activities–sitting, waiting, chatting, reading and watching" (Greenhalgh et al. 74–5).

Defining work inclusively has two important implications for the consideration of public and private spaces. First, defining leisure merely as "recreation from paid employment" risks overlooking the kinds of activities that take place in "everyday leisure spaces": the "'hidden' forms of leisure associated with the home, with children, or related to household work, shopping, or everyday consumption" (Aitchison 74). Conversely, associating family work only with the physical environment of the home risks falling prey to the erroneous assumptions

that family happens, especially for the youngest children, primarily within the bounded walls of the private home and that the "outside world" becomes relevant only as children mature. I would argue, on the contrary, that even as infants children begin to experience the larger physical and social environments in immediate proximity to their homes, as well as those they travel through and to with other family members. (DeVault, "Families" 1302)

This analysis therefore troubles the binary of "work" and "leisure" along with that of "public" and "private." A brief introduction to the physical space and participants in each setting, and an overview of the literature on women's participation in child care and textile handwork activities will serve to situate our two programs physically and theoretically in terms of these binaries.

STORYTIME: "A REALLY HAPPY PLACE FOR BABIES TO SPEND SOME TIME"

Storytime at St. Stephen's Green library was held on a weekday morning. Each session was attended by infants, babies moving toward sitting and crawling, and some able to stand and/or walk. The formal program lasted about 20 minutes and was followed by an opportunity for informal discussion and interaction with library materials. On the first day of storytime, the librarian provided an overview:

We'll start with an opening couple of songs and rhymes and we'll sort of work through a routine that we'll follow every single week where we'll do some tickle rhymes and we'll do some action rhymes and then we'll do a little bit of singing and it will be mixed up with some stories in between. And at the very end of all of that, I'll put some board books down in the middle and we'll have a little time to just chat amongst ourselves and you can have a look at some books that are good for babies and get to meet each other. You'll notice that the babies' names are on the top of your nametags and underneath that is the name of the person who's brought the baby today, so it makes it easier to talk to them and get to know them a little bit. Also, I have, for babies who are old enough, I have an animal cracker, a little one.

Stooke ("Healthy") reported that children's librarians identified the creation of a welcoming space as a necessary component of the work they carry out on behalf of young children's literacy. This librarian had created a particular physical space: her low stool was placed against one wall, with all the props and books stored unobtrusively nearby. A rug indicated the area where families should sit, and families arranged themselves in a horseshoe, its end open to the stool. Some families staked regular territory while others changed position from week to week. A nearby table bore nametags, pamphlets on library programs, extra copies of the books used in the program, other books on the same themes, and the abovementioned board books. The room, a utilitarian and generic space, was thereby transformed into the kind of space that could support the goals of storytime, and the work of women caring for young children.

Much of the caregivers' work was facilitated by their copresence in the program room with other caregivers. In addition to providing a way to identify and exchange social support (Tardy and Hale), Tardy found that the mundane conversations occurring when mothers and children gather together in a playgroup served "to construct the women's identities, particularly as mothers" (Tardy 436). The actual talk, independent of any outcomes, was part of the evidence of the caring work of good motherhood. Griffith and Smith contend that twentieth-century parent advice literature based on child psychology research has focused increasingly on the mother's role in the child's psychosocial development. "How mothers related to their children came to be held to make the difference between the possibilities of the child reaching his or her full potential and the social waste of his or her unrealized development" (37). It is a widely held part of this "mothering discourse" (Griffith and Smith) that the work of nurturing young children's literacy "must be shared by all of us who work with children" (Kupetz 28), including librarians and teachers, but primarily supported by parents (Stooke, "Many"). Parents' work in support of their very young children's literacy development, including participating in a library storytime program, may therefore fulfill a need be a particular sort of parent.

The program room, set up to facilitate the sharing of books and fingerplays with young children simultaneously facilitates the formation of supportive social ties, the exchange of information relevant to caregivers, and the enactment of the appropriate mothering role.

THE KNITTERS' GROUP: "A KIND OF WOMEN'S SUPPORT GROUP"

The knitters' group had been running for a number of years as a weekday afternoon program of the library. Most members had learned to knit as children or young women but for many there were long hiatuses for childrearing and/or paid employment. Most were retired and had grandchildren, although at least one had a school-age child at home and at least one worked part-time. We heard more than one story of being unemployed or on leave from paid employment. Knitters' had varying degrees of expertise and commitment to finishing projects. Field notes indicated that some knitters' "hardly knit at all" [EP] and that others seemed to have a finished project to show every week.

Textile handwork often takes place in groups such as guilds, fairly formal and organized groups with regular meetings. Members meet to work on and discuss current projects in one another's company. Some guilds provide formal educational programs and workshops, and the combination of novice, experienced, and master crafters in the guild setting allows members both to participate in a leisure activity and to interact with and learn from others sharing a common interest in a craft (see Schofield-Thompson and Littrell, Piercy and Cheek, Cerny et al.).

At its inception, the St Stephen's Green knitters' group provided formal instruction but over the years it had became much more informal in structure. A long table in the middle of the room provided the physical focus for the group's activity. Knitters' sat around the table, on which they could set their work. Most sat in regular seats, or at least regular areas of the table, from week to week. A storage cabinet in the room was allocated to the group and held some supplies. At the beginning of the meeting the organizer or another member might call the group to attention for news of former members or announcements of sales at a local craft shop, local and nearby knitting and craft shows, or upcoming library activities.

While the group was called to order, anyone with a finished project was invited to show and talk about it to the assembled group. Often these projects were passed around: "Knitter 6 showed finished project—pattern said was for advanced knitters' only. Wanted to show what she had accomplished" [EP]. Stalker found that home crafters saw knitting as an activity that enabled them to avoid idle time, a means of occupying the mind to stave off worry or loneliness, a link with past and future generations, an appropriate demonstration of their competence as women and mothers, and a source of accomplishment and pride as they decoded a difficult pattern or finished a garment. The finished project served as a physical manifestation of a knitter's effort, talent, and productive use of time.

Studies of quilting guild participation identify the importance of this kind of show-and-tell for communicating both the significance of the textile objects themselves and the meaning incorporated in their making (Schofield-Tomschin and Littrell 42). Piercy and Cheek (22) argue that the show-and-tell contributes to the negotiation of a female identity as "the guild member publicly documents her achievements and receives validation from other quilters. . . . [A]ll participants are welcomed and applauded for their efforts."

After the focused part of the session, participants knit and had informal conversations in pairs, trios, or larger groups. Those having difficulty asked others for knitting assistance. It was unusual but not unheard-of for the entire group to participate in a single discussion. Knitters' passed around patterns, books, newspaper articles, and finished projects, sometimes systematically circulating them, sometimes placing them in the middle of the table and retrieving them as needed. Knitter 3 summarized the kinds of topics that were discussed:

Well we certainly discuss patterns, and knitting, and how-to things. . . . We discuss what's going on here in the library. . . . We talk about people's health problems because sometimes people are away for various reasons. We talk about the charities that we might make things for, and getting that stuff together. Who's going to deliver stuff to the [local women's shelter], things like that. We talk about movies, or there'll be something in the news. . . . I think we talked about the [upcoming 2004] US election. And, we talk about local politics. And like, "Who's going to fix the potholes on a such-and-such a road?" things like that. And, oh yeah, recipes, we exchange recipes. Plans for our [group social events] . . . Family is a big thing. Everybody talks about who they're knitting something for, and what their grandchildren are up to.

Handwork guilds have been identified as "particular examples of 'feminine culture'" (Piercy and Cheek) and researchers have argued that guild participation involves a socialization process whereby individuals draw on a shared ideology and a collective knowledge of handcraft tradition to express themselves individually through their handwork. This juxtaposition of shared feminine identity and individual self-expression is a common theme in three studies. Schofield-Tomschin and Littrell found that participation in textile handwork guilds supports both development of the self through the production of the craft, and development of the self with others through interpersonal interactions within the guild setting. Cerny et al. argue that the socialization process associated with guild membership helps women to understand handwork traditions, identify as crafters, and affirm their female identities. The guild is therefore "more than a community in which women make quilts: it is a community where quilting is intimately linked with being female" (Piercy and Cheek 20).

When physically arranged for and occupied by the knitting group, the generic public space of the program room is transformed into a community space where knitting and female identity are intertwined.

WOMEN'S RELATIONSHIPS IN THE PROGRAM ROOM

When inhabited by women jointly engaged in traditional women's work, the public space of the program room becomes a site, not only for the sharing of stories and of knitting, but also for the enactment of women's identities and the performance of caring. The ethic of care has been found both to constrain women's use of public space (e.g., because of fear for children's safety) and to generate possibilities for women to give and receive care (Day). Use of public spaces therefore affords both work and leisure, potentially simultaneously: Women's experiences of public space frequently involve giving or receiving care or reinforcing relationships with friends and family. In interviews, women described use of public spaces as opportunities to sustain relationships, and to exchange assistance, affection, rewards, and gifts with others (Day 110).

Sociologists have traditionally distinguished between "primary" relationships infused with warmth and intimacy, and "secondary" relationships characterized by relative anonymity and lack of caring, and have valued primary relationships as fulfilling and essential and secondary relationships as shallow and irrelevant. Lofland ("Public" 61–63) challenged this distinction by identifying two types of relationship that blur the boundaries between "primary" and "secondary": while the individuals may only be categorically known to one another and the relationship may be of short duration, both types can be supportive and infused with emotional warmth and caring. We observed both in the program room.

A *quasi-primary relationship* is an "emotionally colored relationship of 'transitory sociability' which takes place in public space. . . . Quasi-primary relationships are created by relatively brief encounters (a few minutes to a few hours) between strangers or between those who are categorically known to one another" (Lofland, "Public" 56), for example dog walkers (Patterson) or customers of a laundromat (Kenen) or second-hand clothing store (Wiseman). The spatial and appearential knowledge available to our participants makes it possible for relationships to exhibit "primary" characteristics even at the initial meeting.

Lofland ("World" 170) observed that people accompanied by children "appear to be legitimately 'open' to other persons similarly encumbered," meaning that such people collectively understand that they may legitimately talk to a stranger about his or her baby, and conversely that their own children are likely to be commented on. A common opening in a conversation among strangers at storytime involved asking a neutral question about someone else's child. This exchange took place the first week of storytime:

Unidentified caregiver: Hello! What's her name?
Older baby 3's mother: [Gives name]
Unidentified caregiver: [Repeats name]. And she's how old?
Older baby 3's mother: Seven months.

Babies sometimes facilitated interactions that their caregivers might not otherwise initiate:

Older baby 5 is sitting on her mom's lap, but begins to lean to the right toward Toddler 3's mom. She reaches out her hands and puts them on Toddler 3's mom's knee; Toddler 3's mom takes one of her hands and holds it for a minute, smiling at Older baby 5's mom [KM].

While knitting at a laundromat indicated that customers were possibly amenable to interaction but not anxious to chat (Kenen), the shared activities and supplies associated with a project in the knitters' group, including the pattern, yarn, and ongoing handwork served as nonthreatening conversation starters. "Knitter 7 was making socks in a bright kelly green yarn with red, yellow, and blue flecks. Quite late in the afternoon I asked to look at them" [PM].

Women themselves, "as a group, are regarded as 'socially open' in public space. Compared with men, women smile more, listen more, talk less, self-disclose more, are more emotionally expressive, are more likely to move out of the way, take up less space, and are approached more often by strangers. . . . [W]omen's public behaviors—emotional expressiveness, self-disclosure, listening, approachability—facilitate communication and promote social interaction, sense of community, and a climate of citizenship" (Day 116). A polite interest in someone's child or her knitting project was generally received as supportive and often led to further conversations on a variety of subjects. Many of the activities undertaken in both programs were centered on home and family, and participants easily and frequently discussed their private lives, even with newcomers.

Intimate-secondary relationships are likewise emotionally infused but differ from quasi-primary relationships in that they are the relatively long-lasting relationships of "regulars" who may never interact outside their hangout (Lofland, "Public" 56). Wireman (3) developed the concept of intimate-secondary relationships, which

have the dimensions of warmth, rapport, and intimacy normally connected with primary relationships yet occur within a secondary setting and have some aspects of secondary relationships. The dimensions are: intense involvement, warmth, intimacy, sense of belonging, and rapport; mutual knowledge of character; minimal sharing of personal information; minimal socializing; involvement of the individual rather then the family; a commitment that is limited in time and scope and with a relatively low cost of withdrawal; a focus on specific rather than diffuse purposes; consideration of public rather than private matters; and a preference for public meeting places.

Lofland hypothesizes that intimate-secondary relationships may in fact involve socializing, diffuse rather than necessarily specific purpose, and the sharing of personal information. She argues that "the routinized relationships of people who 'know' one another only categorically seem especially capable of being transformed into connections of an intimate secondary sort" (Lofland, "Public" 58). The examples she provides (grocery clerks, bartenders, hairdressers, employees from adjoining shops) share many characteristics with library staff and co-users of the same library space.

Because we observed in the same location for several sequential weeks we observed changes in people's relationships over time and found evidence of intimate-secondary characteristics. Older baby 2's mother was new to the city and did not know anyone on her first day at storytime. By week 3 it was clear that the mothers knew something about one another's private lives whether or not they were interacting outside of storytime:

Older baby 1's mother: Did she miss your husband when he was away?
Older baby 2's mother: ((inaudible)). But when he came back she was all lit up for him.
Older baby 1's mother: That's nice. That's great!
Older baby 2's mother: She hadn't forgotten about him.

Milestones, such as finished knitting projects, provide more good examples of the development of intimate-secondary relationships. In order to recognize and celebrate something as a milestone one needs both to see the accomplishment and to acknowledge its difference from what happened before. A baby standing unaided is extraordinary only if the observer recognizes this as something new:

PM [to Older baby 1]: Hey Stander!
Older baby 1's mother: Yes!
PM: I saw you standing with no one holding onto you today!
Older baby 1's mother: Pretty soon she's gonna be [walking]!

Some relationships initiated in these worlds of strangers therefore developed characteristics of intimacy. Others provided evidence of intimacy extending beyond the local site. Relational forms are not static but can transform into one another. The fluidity of the relationships is particularly evident as time passes and relationships develop. Quasi-primary and intimate-secondary relationships may begin as fleeting or routinized connections, and may return to a more distant status or may develop to extend beyond the particular location in which they were formed to become friendships or romantic ties.

This characteristic of fluidity takes on special import when we recall again that the proportions and densities of the relational types present in them is what give specific pieces of space their identities *as realms*. A public setting in which the once dominant intimate-secondary relationships have all been transformed into friendships that both exist in but transcend the setting may still—legally and commonsensically speaking—be a public setting. But it is no longer part of the public realm. (Lofland, "Public" 60)

We observed several relationships in the program room that also existed beyond it. Some participants knew one another before coming to the library program, and in fact some joined in order to be with their friends. Others met at the program and extended the relationship beyond this setting. One of the most visible indications that relationships initiated in the program existed beyond it was the stroller walking group started by one of the storytime mothers:

Older baby 5's mother: I'm starting a walking group
Older baby 3's mother: What day do you do it?
Older baby 5's mother: Tuesday mornings. Here.
Older baby 3's mother: Oh OK. Thanks for thinking of me.

The walkers met in front of the library after storytime every week and we saw them as we debriefed over coffee and later left the scene. Our field notes contain several references to it, on succeeding weeks: "As we sit in the coffee shop, the stroller walking group passes by twice, once heading east, then later back west down St. Stephens Green Avenue" [KM]. Some of the knitters' had developed friendships and other kinds of extended relationships, including two who spoke a common non-English first language and a young retiree who regularly drove some of the most senior members to and from the library.

Finally, the program room was a site for the enactment of private family relationships. This use was most evident around the physical care of children. We observed diaper changes and feedings including snacks that technically violated the library's no-food policy. This flexibility is not unique to this branch and we observed the same kinds of things happening in other libraries. As Lofland notes, urbanites with more intimate knowledge of a public space may gain the acquiescence or even the overt assistance of those in control of the space to make uses that might otherwise be unauthorized (Lofland, "World" 127).

DISCUSSION

A program room, which is a flexible, and therefore fairly generic, publicly accessible space, may be transformed into very different kinds of realms, both through the specialized layout of furniture and equipment to suit the activities going on within it, and through the interactions of the inhabitants. We argue that, although there are important differences between storytime and the knitters' group, there are also important parallels. A number of things are going on within the program room "in the lives of its users" that warrant further attention from LIS researchers.

First, participants shared material resources, both those brought from home and those owned by the library itself. Knitters' regularly brought in their old pattern books, knitting magazines, and excess yarn to share. Hand-me-downs filled a similar function at storytime and we witnessed the transfer of a pair of shoes from one family to another. We saw participants doing reference and reader's advisory work for one another, and recommending and sometimes obtaining library resources:

Knitter 2 had a book out open in front of her, *Knitting Without Tears*, with a library spine label. We talked about it and she said she'd been needing some help and Knitter 3 suggested this book [PM].

Second, we observed what we call "learning the library." Lofland posits that the skill of coding locations and understanding behavior appropriate to them is developed in childhood: "By example, admonitions, and tongue-lashings, the parent is teaching the child such crucial matters as these: that a grocery store is a place to shop, not to play . . .; that playgrounds are places to play, not to eliminate waste materials; that libraries are places to read, not to engage in shouting matches, and that one must learn to distinguish such places from one another" (Lofland, "World" 101-2). At storytime we observed a number of examples of very young children learning the library as a place and the librarian as a person. This observation was made during the fifth week of storytime. Toddlers 1 and 2 had been very active participants from the beginning:

Librarian puts down the board books and it is amazing to see this week how many babies are right there as soon as the books hit the ground—and it isn't just Toddler 2 and Toddler 1 either: Toddler 3, Older baby 2 and Older baby 1 immediately move forward and Older baby 5 soon does too. [KM]

Third, we witnessed many kinds of work, in particular those traditionally done by unpaid family members for one another. Although these twenty-first-century Canadian women could pay someone else to do their knitting or introduce their babies to books, their foremothers would not have had this luxury. The overall purpose of both storytime and the knitters' group is therefore in tension. "As studies of women's leisure continue to show, time synchronization and time fragmentation dominate most women's lives, which has led them to taking 'snatched' spaces for leisure and enjoyment, rather than planned activities" (Green 262). Many women therefore perceive that they have "no right to leisure," particularly if they are without paid employment (Aitchison 52). Responsibility for childcare, housework, and other domestic responsibilities have further been identified as constraints on women's use of public space (Day 107-8). As programs facilitating purposive activities in line with household and child care obligations, storytime and the knitters' group allow for the simultaneous performance of family-based caring work and the experience of leisure with other women.

Indeed, the reasons participants gave for coming to both programs emphasized both elements. The first question we asked in the storytime focus group was, "Why do you come to storytime?" Initial responses were related to "leisure" activities ("Well it's a social thing, you know. Otherwise you're in your house all the time and not talking to other people with kids your age.") But the next response fit clearly within a particular discourse of mothering (Griffith and Smith) ("And it's good, you know, you're supposed to be reading to your babies, so if you don't get a chance to all the time at least you know they get that here"). For the knitters', "work" took the form of seeking instrumental help with a knitting project, but most of the interviewees described the knitters' group in terms of the fellowship and emotional support they experienced.

Fourth, the program room provided women with a venue for engaging in informal conversation with one another. This function of the program room has several important implications. Informal talk may itself be constitutive of women's friendship (Green) and the conversations of both groups of women showed evidence of emotional support and caring for one another. Women's mundane conversation in company with other women may further serve to construct, reorient, and challenge their identities as handcrafters (Cerny et al.), as mothers (Tardy), and as women (Green).

Finally, Lofland hypothesized that quasi-primary and intimate-secondary relationships promote the informal exchange of information. We observed participants asking for and giving information both about the topic immediately "at hand" (knitting, child care, and early literacy), and about an extremely wide variety of other topics including child development, health (from birth stories to end-of-life planning), consumer information, community information, how-to, and travel.

CONCLUSION

Although the public library is commonly regarded as a public space, and therefore part of the world of strangers, the "strangers" joining a public library program for the first time may not in fact be strangers at all, and the public space of the program room may be operating entirely apart from the public realm:

I look around the room and notice that many of the moms have actually taken their shoes off upon arrival—this seems like a sign that they are making themselves comfortable and that they are really *present* at storytime, not just stopping in for 20 minutes; also, more evidence that there is no pressure to appear a certain way at this library [KM].

When this excerpt is read alongside the terms that participants in the Leckie and Hopkins study used to describe other public library users (respectful, kept to themselves, orderly, considerate, studious, polite), it is clear that the social realm of the central library stacks and reading areas is quite different from the realms created by the participants we observed in the program room. The public library cannot then be seen as a single kind of space, but should rather be understood as a site that supports a variety of relationships and hosts a variety of realms.

Given and Leckie considered the importance of acknowledging the "library as in-teractive place" versus "library as quiet space." We would go further, and propose that attention to the relationships among library users, between users and staff, and between users and the library space, can free us to reconceptualize both library use and informa-tion practices in entirely new ways. Further studies with this kind of focus will contribute to a better understanding both of the library as a physical space and of the library as a social environment in the lives of its users.

NOTES

1. The authors would like to thank the public library system, the branch head and children's librarian of the St. Stephen's Green Branch, and the organizer of the knitters' group for providing access and for their ongoing support of our research, the American Library Association for financial support of the storytime study through the Carroll Preston Baber grant, and the library users, both children and adults, who let us into their spaces and realms.

2. The storytime interviews contained questions such as, "Why do you come to this program? What other things do you do with your child(ren)? Is this program different from/similar to other things you do? How?" The knitter interviews contained questions such as "Tell me about yourself as a knitter. Why do you come to the knitters' group? What kinds of things are (and are not) talked about? Have you received any information or referrals from other knitters'?"

3. More of its inhabitants walk or bike to work than in the city as a whole or the province. All comparisons presented in this overview have been calculated from 2001 Canadian Census data for the region in question (Statistics Canada).

4. Visible minority population is 4.0 percent for the neighborhood, 10.9 percent for the city, and 19.1 percent for the province. The percentage of the population having English as the first language is 89.2 percent for the neighborhood, 79.8 percent for the city, and 70.6 percent for the province (Statistics Canada).

5. Field notes identify their author by her initials.

6. The Canada Labour Code provides for a total of up to 52 weeks of combined maternity leave and parental leave that may be shared between parents (Human Resources and Skills Development Canada). Mothers claim the bulk of the leave time; according to Marshall, approximately 10 percent of fathers claimed parental benefits in 2001.

7. Lofland offered a similar observation in 1973 when she explained that one of her informants "knows from prior experience (as well as from what she has been taught) that she can go into a library or museum for free, that she can hang around in them for a period of time without being thought odd and she, a woman alone, is unlikely there to be either bothered or molested" (Lofland, "World" 105).

REFERENCES

Aitchison, Cara Carmichael. *Gender and Leisure: Social and Cultural Perspectives*. London: Routledge, 2003.

Cartwright, Helen. "Change in Store? An Investigation into the Impact of the Book Super-store Environment on Use, Perceptions and Expectations of the Public Library as a

Space, Place, and Experience." *Library and Information Research* 28.88, Spring (2004): 13–26.

Cerny, Catherine A., Joanne B. Eicher, and Marilyn R. DeLong. "Quiltmaking and the Modern Guild: a Cultural Idiom." *Clothing and Textiles Research Journal* 12.1 (1993): 16–25.

Day, Kristen. "The Ethic of Care and Women's Experiences of Public Space." *Journal of Environmental Psychology* 20.2 (2000): 103–24.

DeVault, Marjorie. "Producing Family Time: Practices of Leisure Activity Beyond the Home." *Qualitative Sociology* 23.4 (2000): 485–503.

DeVault, Marjorie L. "Families and Children: Together, Apart." *American Behavioral Scientist* 46.10 (2003): 1296–305.

Dixon, Christopher M., et al. "Latte Grande, No Sprinkles: An Exploratory Observational Study of Customer Behaviour at Chapters Bookstores." *Beyond the Web: Technologies, Knowledge and People/Au-Dela Du Web: Les Technologies, La Connaissance Et Les Gens. Proceedings of the 29th Annual Conference of the Canadian Association for Information Science.* Ed. D. Grant Campbell. s. l.,: Canadian Association for Information Science, 2001: 165–74.

Given, Lisa M., and Gloria J. Leckie. "Sweeping the Library: Mapping the Social Activity Space of the Public Library." *Library & Information Science Research* 25.4 (2003): 365–85.

Gross, Melissa, Eliza T. Dresang, and Leslie E. Holt. "Children's in-Library Use of Computers in an Urban Public Library." *Library & Information Science Research* 26.4 (2004): 311–57.

Goulding, Anne. "Libraries and Social Capital." *Journal of Librarianship and Information Science* 36.1 (2004): 3–6.

Green, Eileen. "'Women Doing Friendship': an Analysis of Women's Leisure as a Site of Identity Construction, Empowerment and Resistance." *Leisure Studies* 17.3 (1998): 171–85.

Greenhalgh, Liz, Ken Warpole, and Charles Landry. *Libraries in a World of Cultural Change.* London: University College London Press, 1995.

Griffith, Alison I., and Dorothy E. Smith. *Mothering for Schooling.* London: Routledge, 2005.

Human Resources and Skills Development Canada. *Pamphlet 5—Maternity-Related Reassignment and Leave, Maternity Leave and Parental Leave. Part III of the Canada Labour Code (Labour Standards).* 2004. Retrieved 31 August 2005 from http://www.hrsdc.gc.ca/asp/gateway.asp?hr=en/lp/lo/lswe/ls/publications/5.shtml&hs=lxn.

Kenen, Regina. "Soapsuds, Space, and Sociability: A Participant Observation of the Laundromat." *Urban Life* 2 July (1982): 163–83.

King, Geraldine B. "Women Library Users and Library Users of Traditional Women's Subjects." *Reference Librarian* 49/50 (1995): 179–93.

Kupetz, Barbara N. "A Shared Responsibility: Nurturing Literacy in the Very Young." *School Library Journal* 39 July (1993): 28–31.

Leckie, Gloria J., and Jeffrey Hopkins. "The Public Place of Central Libraries: Findings From Toronto and Vancouver." *Library Quarterly* 72.3 (2002): 326–72.

Lincoln, Yvonna S., and Egon G. Guba. *Naturalistic Inquiry.* Newbury Park, CA: Sage, 1985.

Lofland, Lyn H. *The Public Realm: Exploring the City's Quintessential Social Territory.* New York: Aldine de Gruyter, 1998.

———. *A World of Strangers: Order and Action in Urban Public Space.* New York: Basic Books, 1973.

Marshall, Katherine. "Benefiting from Extended Parental Leave." *Perspectives on Labour and Income* 4.3 (2003): 5–11.

McKechnie, Lynne E. F. "Opening the "Preschoolers' Door to Learning": an Ethnographic Study of the Use of Public Libraries by Preschool Girls." Unpublished PhD dissertation. University of Western Ontario, 1996.

McKechnie, Lynne E. F., et al. "Covered Beverages Now Allowed: Public Libraries and Book Superstores." *Canadian Journal of Information and Library Science* 28.3 (2004): 39–51.

McKechnie, Lynne E. F., and Pamela J. McKenzie. "The Young Child / Adult Caregiver Storytime Program As Information Ground." *Library Research Seminar III*.

McNicol, Sarah. "Investigating Non-Use of Libraries in the UK Using the Mass-Observation Archive." *Journal of Librarianship and Information Science* 36.2 (2004): 79–87.

Medical Research Council of Canada, Natural Sciences and Engineering Research Council of Canada, and Social Sciences and Humanities Research Council of Canada. *Tri-Council Policy Statement: Ethical Conduct for Research Involving Humans*. Ottawa: Public Works and Government Services, 2003.

Miller, Laura J. "Shopping for Community: the Transformation of the Bookstore into a Vital Community Institution." *Media Culture & Society* 21.3 (1999): 385–407.

Nelson, Sandra. *The New Planning for Results: A Streamlined Approach*. Chicago: Public Library Association, 2001.

Oldenburg, Ray. *The Great Good Place: Cafés, Coffee Shops, Community Centers, Beauty Parlors, General Stores, Bars, Hangouts, and How They Get You through the Day*. New York: Marlowe & Co., 1997.

Patterson, Mike. "Walking the Dog: An Urban Ethnography of Owners and Their Dogs in the Glebe; Where Can 'Lassie' Go? Territoriality and Contested Spaces." *Alternate Routes* 18 (2002): 5–70.

Piercy, Kathleen W., and Cheryl Cheek. "Tending and Befriending: The Intertwined Relationships of Quilters." *Journal of Women & Aging* 16.1/2 (2004): 17–33.

Rothbauer, Paulette M. "Finding and Creating Possibility: Reading in the Lives of Lesbian, Bisexual and Queer Young Women." The University of Western Ontario, 2004.

Schofield-Tomschin, Sherry, and Mary A. Littrell. "Textile Handcraft Guild Participation: A Conduit to Successful Aging." *Clothing and Textiles Research Journal* 19.2 (2001): 41–51.

Shoham, Snunith. "Users and Uses of the Public Library Reading Room." *Public Library Quarterly* 20.4 (2001): 33–48.

Singleton, Royce, et al. *Approaches to Social Research*. New York: Oxford University Press, 1988.

Smith, Ian M. "What Do We Know about Public Library Use?" *ASLIB Proceedings* 51.9 (1999): 302–14.

Stalker, L. Lynda Harling. "Wool and Needles in My Casket: Knitting as a Habit among Rural Newfoundland Women." Unpublished Master's thesis. Memorial University of Newfoundland.

Statistics Canada. *Census of Canada: Census of Population, Census of Agriculture*. 2001. Retrieved from http://www12.statcan.ca/english/census01/home/index.cfm.

Stooke, Rosamund K. "Healthy, Wealthy and Ready for School: Supporting Young Children's Education and Development in the Era of the National Children's Agenda." The University of Western Ontario, 2004.

Stooke, Roz. "'Many Hands Make Light Work' but 'Too Many Cooks Spoil the Broth': Representing Literacy Teaching As a 'Job for Experts' Undermines Efforts to Involve Parents." *Journal of Curriculum Studies* 37.1 (2005): 3–10.

Tardy, Rebecca W. "'But I *am* a Good Mom': The Social Construction of Motherhood through Health-Care Conversations." *Journal of Contemporary Ethnography* 29.4 (2000): 433–73.

Tardy, Rebecca W., and Claudia L. Hale. "Bonding and Cracking: the Roles of Informal, Interpersonal Networks in Health Care Decision Making." *Health Communication* 10.2 (1998): 151–73.

Warren, Carol A. B. "Qualitative Interviewing." *Handbook of Interview Research*. Ed. Jaber F. Gubrium and James A. Holstein. Thousand Oaks, CA: Sage, 2002.

Wiegand, Wayne. "To Reposition a Research Agenda: What American Studies Can Teach the LIS Community about the Library in the Life of the User." *Library Quarterly* 73.4 (2003): 369–82.

Wireman, Peggy. *Urban Neighborhoods, Networks, and Families: New Forms for Old Values.* Lexington, MA: Lexington, 1984.

Wiseman, Jacqueline. "Close Encounters of the Quasi-Primary Kind: Sociability in Urban Second-Hand Clothing Stores." *Urban Life* 8.1 (1979): 23–51.

Zweizig, Douglas, and Brenda Dervin. "Public Library Use, Users, Uses: Advances in the Knowledge of the Characteristics and Needs of the Adult Clientele of American Public Libraries." *Advances in Librarianship* 7 (1977): 231–55.

8

Seattle Public Library as Place: Reconceptualizing Space, Community, and Information at the Central Library[1]

Karen E. Fisher
Associate Professor and Chair of the MLIS Program, and Lead Investigator, IBEC (Information Behavior in Everyday Context), The Information School, University of Washington, Seattle, WA

Matthew L. Saxton
Assistant Professor, The Information School, University of Washington Seattle, WA

Phillip M. Edwards
Doctoral Candidate, The Information School, University of Washington, Seattle, WA

Jens-Erik Mai
Professor, Faculty of Information Studies, University of Toronto, Toronto, Ont.

INTRODUCTION

"Place" as a research phenomenon has occupied scholars in such fields as sociology, anthropology, and human and cultural geography for decades. Of late, it has also proven a useful concept for understanding the multifaceted dimensions of libraries, how they are perceived and used by different stakeholders but most specifically, library users. Difficulties lie, however, in how "place" is understood and operationalized by different researchers. Such confounding inhibits our knowledge of libraries' roles in society. In this paper we address two primary frameworks for understanding libraries as "place" by drawing upon findings from a field study of the newly constructed central building of the Seattle Public Library.

Early approaches to understanding "place" tended to focus on describing its characteristics. Geographer Fred Lukermann, for example, in the 1960s—as highlighted by Relph—characterized "place" as being where (1) location is fundamental, (2) nature and culture are involved, (3) spaces are unique but interconnected and part of a framework of circulation, (4) spaces are localized, and (5) spaces are emerging or becoming, and have a historical component (Relph 3). While this framework is useful for an elementary understanding of place, it adds the complex, related notion of "space" and does not address the myriad ways in which one may interpret "place," such as a physical place (a lakeshore), an activity (e.g., place of worship) and a figure of speech ("she was put in her place"). "Place" can also be explored in a cultural sense, as was the recent focus of Feld and Basso's *Senses of Place*, which contains ethnographies of what "place" means to such populations as the Apache of Arizona and the Kaluli people of New Guinea in terms of expressing and knowing. Lippard in *Lure of the Local: Senses of Place in a Multicentered Society* similarly discusses "place" by blending history, geography, cultural/social studies, and contemporary art.

In the library and information science (LIS) literature, similar treatments of place have occurred, many of which resemble thought-pieces, polemics, or focus heavily on user satisfaction in addition to focusing on library as a place of social, political, cultural, and physical dimensions. For example, Curry, Dunbar, George, and Marshall surveyed over 500 library users in four branch libraries in British Columbia, Canada. The researchers asked library users about satisfaction with individual features and components of the building and facilities; the most highly ranked features across all settings were windows and lighting, particularly natural lighting. Numerous works thus abound of how libraries design diverse services and engage physical space and objects to address users' needs beyond those of such time-tested sources as monographs and serials. Allen and Watstein, Ginsburg, Albanese, Shill and Tonner, and Engel and Antell, for example, discuss college libraries; Weise, and Ludwig and Starr focus on health libraries; Wagner, Gosling, St. Lifer, Demas and Scherer, McKinney, Ranseen, Saanwald, Alstad and Curry, Bryson, Usherwood and London, Bundy, Wood, and Worpole address public libraries; Crumpacker suggests ways that school libraries can be more inviting while an entire issue of the regional journal *Alki* (December 1999) was devoted to professional renderings on "the library as place."

In introducing an issue of *American Studies* on "The American Library as an Agency of Culture," Augst proposes that libraries function as place in three ways: as social enterprises, as part of the physical/public infrastructure, and as sites of collective memory. Thomas employs a social constructionist approach to discursively view academic, public and school library practices architecturally. A different twist emerged from Block's interviews with non-LIS staff from the nonprofit "Project for Public Spaces (pps.org)." She reported that libraries' staunch internal focus relegates them to "community living room[s], at best" as opposed to the community front porch—a place to launch activities and contacts with other people, instead. Four intrinsic qualities for great public spaces include access and linkages (easy to get to, connected to surrounding community); comfort and image (safe, clean, and attractive); uses and activities (as many things to do); and sociability (place to meet other people). Exemplar libraries were the New York Public Library, Multnomah County Library in Portland, Oregon, and the Beaches Toronto Branch Library.

In-depth studies of the ways in which individuals, families, neighborhoods, and communities benefit from libraries have tended not to use "place" as a framework. For example, Durrance and Fisher in *How Libraries and Librarians Help* discuss ranges of library outcomes as does Nancy Kranich in her edited work *Libraries and Democracy: The Cornerstones of Liberty* (2001, 49–59) and Molz and Dain in *Civic Space/Cyberspace: The American Public Library in the Information Age* (1999). Fisher, Durrance, and Hinton (2004), albeit, use Fisher's related notion of information grounds (Pettigrew 801) to interpret findings from their study of Queens Borough Public Library system and its immigrant users. Consequently, LIS does not have a robust framework for analyzing the roles of libraries in terms of "place"—a problem noted by Wiegand who laments the "cost to LIS of ignoring 'place' and 'reading,'" and by Gorman in emphasizing the wide-ranging values that the public attributes to libraries and yet is little systematically documented.

Leckie and Hopkins presented a "place"-based framework in examining the public place of the Toronto and Vancouver central libraries. They conducted over 1900 user surveys, 100 user interviews, staff interviews, and observational seating sweeps to gather individuals' perceptions and common usage patterns of library materials and facilities. In critiquing an interdisciplinary literature on the nature of "public space," especially in terms of public rights, privacy, and access, they highlighted Oldenburg's (1999) assertion that "highly successful public places" (aka "third places"), comprise eight key characteristics. While Leckie and Hopkins did not revisit Oldenburg's framework in discussing their findings, they reported that (1) central libraries are unique, necessary, and heavily utilized places, (2) new information technologies augment as opposed to diminish the role of these places, and (3) the encroachment of private interests (e.g., ongoing commercialization) is threatening to "transform the fundamental nature of libraries" as public places (Leckie and Hopkins 360). Similarly, the notion of "sense of place (SoP) in the context of regionalism" was highlighted by McCook. Like Oldenburg, she defined sense of place as "the sum total of all perceptions—aesthetic, emotional, historical, supernal—that a physical location, and the activities and emotional responses associated with that location, invoke in people" and further asserted that public libraries, having exemplary sense of place to its constituents, can help communities keep their distinct characters (McCook 294).

CONCEPTUALIZING PLACE

To understand library as place we selected two frameworks to guide our empirical investigation: Oldenburg's notion of the third place, and Creswell's extended five-part definition of place. These frameworks illuminated the research problem by making core terms (e.g., place and space) explicit and operationalizable.

In his popular book *The Great Good Place: Cafes, Coffee Shops, Bookstores, Bars, Hair Salons, and Other Hangouts at the Heart of a Community,* Oldenburg introduced the phrase "third place" and inspired the title of many community-oriented businesses such as Seattle's "Third Place Books." According to Oldenburg, public places such as cafes and hair salons function as "third places," that is, where people can be found when they are not at home or work. A veritable and necessary social good, Oldenburg describes several third places and conceptualizes on their nature, which as neighborhood locales must exhibit eight characteristics to be successful and attract people:

- Occur on neutral ground where "individuals may come and go as they please, in which none are required to play host, and in which all feel at home and comfortable" (Oldenburg *Great Good*, 22);
- Be levelers, inclusive places that are "accessible to the general public and does not set formal criteria of membership and exclusion" and thus promote the expansion of social networks where people interact with others who do not comprise their nearest and dearest (24);
- Have conversation as the main activity—as Oldenburg explains, "nothing more clearly indicates a third place than that the talk is good; that it is lively, scintillating, colorful, and engaging" (26); moreover, "it is more spirited than elsewhere, less inhibited and more eagerly pursued" (29);

- Are accessible and accommodating: the best third places are those to which one may go alone at most anytime and be assured of finding an acquaintance (32);
- Have "regulars" or "fellow customers," as it is these, not the "seating capacity, variety of beverages served, availability of parking, prices, or other features," that draw people in—"who feel at home in a place and set the tone of conviviality" while nurturing trust with newcomers (33–5);
- Keep a low profile as a physical structure, "typically plain," unimpressive looking from the outside, which "serves to discourage pretension among those [who] gather there" and meld into its customers' daily routine (37);
- Have a persistent playful, playground sort of mood: "those who would keep a conversation serious for more than a minute are almost certainly doomed to failure. Every topic and speaker is a potential trapeze for the exercise and display of wit" (37);
- Are a home away from home, the places where people can be likely found when not at home or at work, "though a radically different kind of setting from home, the third place is remarkably similar to a good home in the psychological comfort and support that it extends" (42).

Oldenburg further espouses third places in terms of their personal benefits, which include novelty, perspective, spiritual tonic, and friendship; societal good in terms of their political role, habit of association, role as an agency for control and force for good, recreational spirit, and importance "in securing the public domain for the use and enjoyment of decent people" (83)—in addition to the negative or down-side of third places such as segregation, isolation, and hostility. In many ways, Oldenburg's work suggests that third places build social capital, popularized by Putnam and Feldstein as "making connections among people, establishing bonds of trust and understanding, and building community" (1). Oldenburg, however, omits libraries as a potential third place, including from his 2002 edited work of nineteen examples of third places from across the country that include coffee shops, a bookstore, a gym, and urban streetscape. Putnam, on the other hand, acknowledges the pivotal role of public libraries in building and maintaining social capital in his case study of the Chicago Public Library's Near North Branch Library (Putnam and Feldstein).[2]

Oldenburg's strict focus on the public or social dimensions of place alerts one to the need for addressing other nuances. In this respect we turn to Cresswell, a professor of social and cultural geography at the University of Wales who crafted *Place: A Short Introduction*. He asserts that place can be defined in five ways, the first three of which he borrows from political geographer John Agnew:

1. Location: the fixed objective position or coordinates (Cresswell 6);
2. Locale: "the material setting for social relations—the actual shape of place within which people conduct their lives as individuals" (7);
3. Sense of Place: "the subjective and emotional attachment people have to place" (7);

To these Cresswell adds:

4. Space: a more abstract concept than "place," space separates places and is "a realm without meaning" (10);
5. Landscape: "the material topography," whether natural or human-made; people do not live in landscapes, they look at them (11).

In terms of libraries, Oldenburg's and Cresswell's frameworks offer insightful orientations for understanding the roles of libraries within society. Whereas Cresswell discusses five distinct facets of place, Oldenburg focuses more specifically on the social side. Noticeably absent from both frameworks if applied to a library setting, however, is the concept of information. Although information may be loosely equated with Oldenburg's third concept of conversation and books may be regarded as part of Cresswell's locale (i.e., the material setting), neither framework explicitly incorporates information seeking and consumption as a core aspect of place. Thus the current study may contribute to the foregoing frameworks by adding "information" to the repertoire of place.

THE CURRENT STUDY

On Sunday, May 23, 2004, the 152-million-dollar Central Library building of the Seattle Public Library (SPL) was unveiled to the public, garnering international media attention as an innovative experiment in library architecture and services. The new building is an intriguing research object in several respects: the design choices regarding allocation of functional and social space, the revision of the staffing model to accommodate a new mix of service points, and the reorganization of the nonfiction collection as a "book spiral," i.e., an unbroken, concentric run of materials arranged by Dewey Decimal Classification (DDC) that ascends four floors. The building has two street-level public entrances and an elevator connecting to the underground parking garage.[3] From the 4th Avenue entrance, users access the checkout desk, the book return, a colorful Children's Center, English-as-a-Second-Language (ESL) materials and a 425-seat auditorium. From the 5th Avenue entrance users enter a high-ceilinged atrium filled with natural light that leads to the fiction collection, young adult resources, the SPL Foundation gift shop, and an espresso stand. Stairways lead to the fourth-floor meeting rooms; escalators to the fifth level arrive at the "Mixing Chamber," which has over 100 public access computers and the reference collection, where librarians freely move about using GPS-enabled Vocera wireless communication devices. Levels 6 through 9 contain the book spiral; the tenth level features a 12,000-square-foot reading room; the eleventh level houses the administrative offices (see Figure 8.1).

In the art journal *Metropolis*, the rationale behind the building design was explained in the following words:

The firm [OMA] divided [SPL's] program into two categories—stable areas, which hold a range of predictable activities, and unstable areas, whose future uses are unpredictable. By combing through the board's program, OMA discovered five stable functions: the headquarters (administrative offices); a spiral-shaped book-storage system, along which the library's collection could expand or contract (rather than dividing the collection room by room); the meeting areas (anything larger than a conference room); the staff areas (where books are ordered, repaired, and sorted); and the parking garage. The design treats each of these five programmatic areas—called "boxes"—as independent buildings with their own mechanical and structural systems. (Ward 141)

To better understand the perceptions of Seattle's denizens toward the new building, considered the world's most avant garde public library, we drew upon the earlier frameworks of "place" to derive the following primary research question:

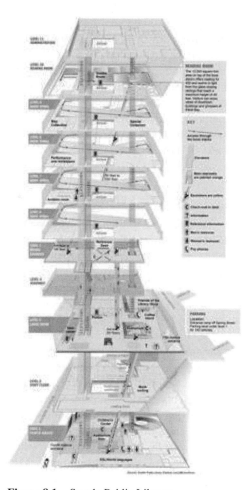

Figure 8.1   Seattle Public Library.

What does the SPL Central Library mean as "place"—socially, politically, culturally, and economically—to library users and passers-by?

In addition, we wanted to examine the impact of the book spiral. Some of its presumed advantages were ease of access, especially for disabled users, and ease of maintenance for library staff.[4] Thus, a secondary research question comprised:

How does the book spiral affect users' understanding of how the collection is organized?

METHODOLOGY

We interviewed three groups of informants: (1) people in the book spiral, (2) people in other parts of the library, and (3) people walking by outside (passers-by), who could be users or non-users. This pool purposefully included different segments of the service population, including residents, commuters, and visitors. Users were asked thirty open and closed questions (Appendix A); passers-by were asked seventeen of the same (Appendix B). Questions reflected three categories of people's perceptions of the SPL as a

- *physical place* (i.e., what they liked or disliked about the structure and its surroundings);
- *social place* (i.e., how they interacted with other people, sense of community); and
- *informational place* (i.e., perceptions of library materials and specifically the design and structure of the book spiral).

Following questions about visit frequency, participants were asked about the building and the role of the SPL in their daily lives, finishing with free association to discover the concepts that they associated with eight basic terms: architecture, books, community, free speech, learning, librarians, reading, and technology. Participants were encouraged to respond to the free association terms with a phrase. The sequencing of the terms, however, varied across interviews to control response bias.

Rooted in early experiments by Galton in the 1880s, free association is a popular social science research method but has been rarely used in LIS. In one of the earliest descriptions of the free association method, Wheat said that difficulty lay with selecting words that could be understood in the same way by all people, especially as ethnicity, regionalism and English-as-a-second language can affect word interpretation. He also noted that word types can make a difference in responses as nouns result in more common responses while verbs, prepositions, and conjunctions cause more abstract and less common answers. More recently, Nelson, McEvoy, and Dennis assert that people who have similar experiences and come from similar social units are likely to have shared associations between stimulus and response words that should not be expected from others.[5] After the free association terms, the interviews concluded with demographic questions to determine how well the sample resembled a cross section of the Seattle population in terms of age, gender, ethnicity, income, education, and occupation.

Data collection was randomly scheduled during the mornings, afternoons, and evenings to reflect the SPL's opening hours over three weeks (October 8, 2004–November 7, 2004). This time period was considered typical as schools and colleges were in session and no federal holidays occurred. Rather than drawing a proportionately representative sample, we sought a diverse sample to maximize the different perspectives available and thus utilized a non–random-sampling technique. Interviewers varied who they approached by alternating between sexes, ages, styles of dress, and apparent ethnicity. As an incentive to participate, respondents received a Starbucks espresso coupon. Two uncontrollable factors, however, may have affected people's perceptions of civic institutions, needs for information, and sense of community, namely the co-occurrence of (1) the U.S. presidential election, which may have resulted in greater awareness and interest in political issues (e.g., the term "free speech" during the free association component), and (2) controversial U.S. military operations in Iraq—the perceptions and attitudes of the Seattle population toward government may have been more personally affected given the numerous military installations in the surrounding counties.

Interviewers recorded responses as phrases and key words using the informant's own words, which were entered along with field notes (operational, methodological, theoretical) into QSR NUD*IST 5 (qualitative data management software). Through content analysis, we identified themes that reflected our theoretical frameworks as well as emergent themes, counterexamples, and anomalies. Following an overview of our respondents' sociodemographic characteristics, we address their perceptions of the SPL as a physical, social, and informational place in downtown Seattle to determine what, if any, symbolic or practical meaning they attribute to the library.[6] We conclude by revisiting our two theoretical frameworks and sharing suggestions for future research.

THE SPL CENTRAL LIBRARY: ITS USERS AND PASSERS-BY

We conducted 226 interviews over three weeks; 259 people declined to participate, resulting in a response rate of 46.6 percent (about twice the response rate for a typical survey). Two-thirds of the interviews occurred with users inside the building (151 interviews), and one third occurred with passers-by (75 interviews).

Almost 80 percent had an SPL library card, indicating that the sample largely comprised library users. Participants were evenly split between men (51.7 percent) and women (48.3 percent). The majority was White (67.3 percent) and spoke English as the primary language at home (86.7 percent). Asian (12.4 percent), Black (7.5 percent), and multiracial (6.1 percent) persons also participated. Ages ranged from 18 to 82, representing individuals from diverse stages of life. Education levels reflected the larger Seattle population (*American Community Survey*): 96.0 percent graduated from high school and 56.2 percent had a four-year degree. Participants' occupations varied, though many were students (14.1 percent), unemployed (11.5 percent), or retired individuals (9.7 percent). Almost half earned less than $30,000, and close to a third earned between $30,001 and $75,000.

SPL as Physical Place: Structure and Architecture

I'm a warm and cozy person, so when I first saw it, it seemed cold. But now that we're here, we've made it our own place.

The preceding quote best typifies the reaction expressed by many regarding the theme of the SPL as physical place. The architecture of the central library is modern, challenging in terms of being unlike any other place in Seattle, and presents an environment that cannot be assimilated all at once. Even after a dozen visits to the site, we found new features, rooms, and spaces of which we were previously unaware. The great majority of all users and passers-by expressed strong feelings about the new building, regardless of whether they "loved it" or "hated it." In their responses, participants frequently used superlatives (e.g., greatest, ugliest, most exciting, coldest, loveliest) to describe their feelings and reactions to the physical structure. However, regardless of whether they initially admired or despised the structure, most expressed a sense of ownership of the space and recognized that this was "their" library.

One of the most common emergent themes was that of civic pride and the role of the central library building as a symbol of modernity and forward thinking. Such comments were more common from passers-by, those who live and work in the vicinity of the structure, but were also echoed by those within the building. While perhaps such comments may initially sound cliché—such as one might hear from a city "booster"— they were nonetheless the exact terms and sentiments expressed by most informants. Far from being labeled as an archaic institution in the age of the Internet or being associated with a predigital past, the library was identified as "new," "modern," "vibrant," "exciting," "innovative," and "visionary," as explained by the following respondent:

Sometimes we get stuck in notions of how things ought to be—what's appropriate and what's not. This gives us an opportunity to go out of the mode of what we think of as urban structures. Not a lot of embellished finishes. Things are open and exposed. Don't have to have all that to make it a great space.

The informants also recognized the structure as a "spotlight," "showcase," "attraction," "landmark," and "icon." Following the Space Needle as a city icon, the SPL has captured the public's imagination as a unique element of the city's landscape and a point of interest for locals and visitors alike. As a respondent observed, "This is one of the greatest additions to Seattle that I've seen in a long time. Sometimes, I purposely walk by just to pass it." Another echoed these thoughts with, "It's a change from how people think of libraries. I keep coming back. Sometimes, I walk through just to walk through the library."

Focusing on the interior of the structure, another popular theme to emerge is the sense of light and spaciousness throughout the structure. Glass walls provide a sense of openness on all floors. Even within the stacks of the book spiral, a glance to right or left will provide a vista of the streetscape and neighboring towers. Many observed that this had an inspirational effect, using terms such as "inspiring," "bright," "airy," "never crowded," and "open" to describe the atmosphere. One stated, "I like the transparency between the inside and the outside. Still feels like it's part of the city even though it's a huge building." Far from the idea of a library as a place of separation or seclusion, the structure gives the reader a feeling of greater connection with the surrounding city.

The visitor is presented with balconies and open views to the main floor at a number of places, resulting in mixed responses of delight and uneasiness, as expressed in the following observations. One expressed, "You can go up nine to ten levels and look down over rail. The rail comes up to my hip. You know how you get that stomach feeling, when it lurches? I love that!" while another had a negative reaction, stating, "I was immediately taken by the suicide platform at the top." While agoraphobics may seek out spaces toward the interior of the building that are less exposed, most informants expressed pleasure with the spacious views and grand open spaces within the structure.

The minority of informants who disliked the structure almost exclusively referred to a sense of coldness or bleak quality in the modern style. They used terms such as "cold," "uncomfortable," "unfinished," "austere," "intimidating," and "grey" to describe their perceptions. The predominance of "concrete" and lack of carpeting contributed to this feeling. The building was likened to a "warehouse" and a "minimal security prison." Several of these respondents sought to soften their criticism by suggesting that they didn't "care for modern architecture" regardless of purpose or setting, and went on to make many complimentary statements about how important the library was to them. This distinction between the library as a structure and the library as a service organization indicates a depth of thought and reflection on the purpose of library in the community. One observed, "The building isn't worth it, but the library is."

During the word association exercise, both positive and negative responses to the term "architecture" were consistent across both users and passers-by alike (Table 8.1).

Table 8.1. Sample of Reponses from Word Association—"Architecture"

	Users	Passers-by
	Adventuresome	Amazing
	Amazing	Beautiful
	Artistic	Creative
	Beautiful	Cutting edge
	Brilliant	Daring
	Crazy (good)	Discovering
	Delightful	Exciting
	Funky! It's free-spirited	Eye catching
	Futuristic	Fantastic
Positive	Inviting	Fascinating
	It fits in	Form of art
	Liberating	Functional
	Modern	Hope
	Outstanding	Inspiring
	Spectacular	Stimulating
	Tripping	Striking
	Unique	Superb
	Very sharp	Unique
	Wonderful	World class
Negative	Brutalism	A freak
	Funny looking	Atrocious
	Futuristic	Dangerous
	Ingenuous	Egotistic
	Overblown	Expensive
	Striking	Imposing
	Ugly	
	Unfinished	

The last theme to emerge is the identification of the new library as an improvement over the old. Subjects described the old facility as "tired," "crowded," "worn," "deplorable," and "falling apart." Such criticisms of the old building are probably vocalized more frequently now as users make mental comparisons to the new structure. Beyond the aesthetic considerations of the architecture itself, informants recognized the new facility as providing more technology, more space, and more resources than the previous facility. The building draws new users, as one indicated, "I know more people who have come to this library than the old one. They're excited about this library." Whether the impressions regarding the size of collections are justified or not, users expressed a sense the new building has more books, more magazines, and more CDs to offer than the old facility. Despite the ease with which materials can be shipped to any branch, several informants noted their primary motivation to visit the downtown library is to review sources that are not available at their local branch, indicating that they value "seeing" items all in one physical space. Informants also reaffirmed the downtown location as a "convenient" site for the library in that it provides access to both public transport and local freeways. The library has been located on this specific block in Seattle for over a century, and the residents continue to value its central location in the prime commercial heart of the city.

At the end of the interview, users were asked if they had anything else they wanted to say to the City Librarian or Board of Trustees. One subject noted, "I congratulate them for having the courage to make this happen," and another said, "It means a lot for Seattle to support something that was so controversial and to move on through it. . . It is a testament to accomplishing things and realizing the public sector deserves the best that we can give them." Several echoed this sentiment of courage as reflected with the decision to go with a modern architectural style and to build such a grand structure for a public institution in the face of a weakening economy. The building becomes a statement about the values and priorities of the city's residents, and the determination and strength it requires to make those priorities real in a physical sense.

The SPL as Social Place

I will bring a friend next week for the very special purpose of seeing the building and each other. It's a destination, a very special building.

To come here is a kind of a social event for me. People are checking it out, which is good but it's not like I come here to find dates. Not yet, at least.

While public library mission statements have long focused upon educating the masses, librarians have been well aware of the social functions that libraries play, from the toddler who learns to share books at baby storytimes to the teenager who meets rambunctiously with peers in the computer room, and from the homeless who seek nooks for rest to the seniors whose only public outing may be the weekly book club meetings. Aside from a few key works (e.g., Durrance and Fisher, McKechnie and McKenzie), however, little basic research has systematically addressed the social role that the public library plays in the lives of its users. The new SPL building was designed with the express purpose of bringing people together via its meeting rooms, collaborative work spaces, coffee stand, atria, use of color, lighting, and furniture. Indeed, the third floor of the SPL is called the "Living Room." But how effective are these efforts?

Our survey comprised several questions regarding the social effects of the new SPL. First, we were interested in whether people came to the SPL with other people, meaning was there a social aspect in the simple act of visiting the SPL? Of the users, 76.2 percent said that they had come alone that day while 23.8 percent had been accompanied by someone else. However, when asked if they *ever* come with others, over half (53.6 percent) replied "yes." Analysis determined that these companions were invariably close family, friends, or associates. Others included roommates, elderly neighbors, coworkers (en route to or from work), paid caregivers, and out-of-town visitors. The heartening finding thus here is that the SPL serves as a connector, providing social opportunities for people to interact across the generations. As shown in Table 8.2, responses regarding *why* people come to the SPL together ran the gamut: from using services and obtaining materials to sharing an experience to the pragmatic of saving parking fees. These themes were typified by users who said, "I came with visitors from out of town; they read about the library in the newspapers and wanted to see it," "I visit with friends at the library," "I come with my children and husband for schoolwork. We take turns watching the kids and using the library," and "I come with my wife and the other members of the genealogy club."

Table 8.2. Reasons that People Come to the SPL with Other People

- Part of looking after children who are not in school
- To use the computers/Internet
- To look for books, magazines, movies (kids have a bigger selection than at branches)
- To read to children
- To go to an activity such as baby storytime
- So kids can work on school projects
- Friends come together to work on projects, do research (e.g., genealogy)
- For "transportation practice"
- To date or to study
- To visit/socialize
- To have lunch together, run errands
- Part of sightseeing
- Parking is easier
- To translate for someone who speaks/reads English poorly

Respondents were further asked "Do you ever come to do things for other people?" Of the 32.5 percent who said "yes," the recipients of their generosity included family members, friends, roommates, and neighbors as well as students and members of groups such as the Sci-Fi Museum, book clubs, and community-based organizations. Activities that users perform on behalf of others ranged from borrowing and returning materials (books, movies, CDs), doing research using the collection, using the computers to search the Web, check email, write and print documents, and working on school projects. Most representatively and memorably we were told:

- "I look at Arab books for my woman."
- "Sometimes I compare financial news for friends."
- "My sister's in jail because of her manic depression condition. I want to help her get treatment and want to learn about what it's like for her."
- "I used the computers to produce a newsletter for a volunteer position I hold."
- "I have an invalid friend and I sometimes get CDs for her."
- "I come to do things for my son because he has a very busy schedule and my parents because they are home bound."

Like many libraries, the SPL features regular presentations for the public on an array of topics. Of our respondents, however, only 9.4 percent had ever come to a public presentation—which was not surprising given how recently the building had been opened. The types of presentations they attended included children's storytime, the Opening Day Welcoming Ceremony, Chinese dancing, music concerts, the Warsaw Uprising 60th Anniversary, and the September Project.

One third of users indicated that they used the SPL for work. While the most frequent reason was to find a job, other responses included for research, to print documents, use the computer, get materials, and write documents and presentations. Our examples show that people who work in varied positions rely on the SPL to get the job done. Occupations for which the library was a key resource included teachers, who use it to get materials for their lessons ("I'm a teacher, I look for children's book on various subjects"), chefs

("I'm looking for recipes of Thai food to cook in the restaurant where I work" and "for work, I'm checking on specialized cooking for Italian or French cooking"), and business owners ("My business is container gardening so I look for books on this subject"). Other respondents described their work-related uses as "I looked up stuff about the Americans with Disabilities Act and ASL—American Sign Language," "I [used the computer] to get an application for a professional exam," "I'm here to get educational material, technical information related to my job," and "I research patents, children's book ideas on bees, and textile resources." Two separate authors said that they use the SPL as a place "to write" and to meet with editors.

Thus far we have addressed the more obvious social aspects of the SPL such as with whom people visit and why. Deeper understanding of the SPL's social dimensions, however, lurks in the undercurrents of people's views of the SPL and community, its architecture, its books and librarians, and the relationship between the SPL and freedom of speech. Results from the word association method using the term *community* were rich and mainly positive. Users and passers-by alike replied that together "SPL and community" largely signified an important melding of varied people in a warm environment. Illustrative remarks ranged from the basic: "Everybody gets together here," "It's good for the community to have a library," "This is a good service to the community," "It brings everybody together, you feel like you're part of something," "It's a building that brings different populations together," "It feels like a place where people come together," and "Lends itself to community; good informal public spaces," to the more analytic, such as,

Buildings always represent community. This is a community that is really out there and willing to test the waters. Many communities would never have let this happen. [SPL] is forward looking.

And,

I think of the library when I think of the city . . . it's a major component. I'm trying to learn to use it better.

The few negative observations were along the line of the following: "This library is trying to be conducive to building community, but there's a lack of information about the events here. They have the right idea, but they don't market it very well. I see advertisements about what's going on at Kane Hall [auditorium at the University of Washington] but not here. I don't know what's coming," and "[It's] forced. They're trying to create a sense of community, but forgetting some groups of people. I think this building represents a narrow-minded sense of community."

While architecture and the trappings of physical comfort à la furniture, open space, greenery, lighting and refreshments can do wonders for the heightening of a building and its inhabitants' sociability—as discussed earlier under "architecture"—to people who truly know books and librarians, the latter are also intrinsic elements in the social life of a library. While responses to the word association method regarding "books" are shared in our discussion of physical place, they also bear mentioning here because of the pervasive ways in which both users and passers-by spoke frequently of books as their "friends"—friends that you could meet at the library or friends that could accompany you home or elsewhere, courtesy of the library. Moreover, respondents spoke about books using such terms as "love," "exciting," "needed" and "take you away." As a thirty-seven-year-old female library user gushed, "anything you want is in a book except human contact, and even then if you're engrossed in the story that is a form of contact."

Users' and passers-by's views of librarians were somewhat similar if in a less openly emotive way. As a social type librarians were invariably cast as nice, kind, friendly, helpful, educated, knowledgeable, and, yet, quiet women who wear glasses and provide people with advice and aid in searching. While the users provided more comments on "librarians" than their passer-by counterparts, their tenor was similar. A more colorful remark "They know everything! If I say, "I read this book once and it had this girl in it," they're like "I know that book, it's right over there." General confusion over who exactly a librarian is from amongst all a library's staff, however, still exists in the minds of at least some users, which results in negative comments. For instance, one passer-by said "They don't know how to use the equipment, a lot of them haven't been trained," while a user sniped "Too overzealous. Every time I go to have a smoke I have to hide books or they stash them in a back room for a couple of days." Another theme was that respondents felt that they did not see or interact enough with librarians. Responses along these lines included: "Librarians are very talented. . . . I wish there was more opportunity for us to have one-on-one contact with librarians," "Haven't met one in this library but I admire librarians," "[Librarians are] concentrated on the fifth floor. I wonder how visible they are," "They've been nice to me but I don't have much contact with them," and "Unlike many of the public places that I go where I know people's names and addresses, I haven't yet gotten to know any of these librarians or their names." On the one hand, this suggests that the public is savvy; they know that the person behind the circulation desk or providing security is not a librarian; on the other hand, it further suggests that perhaps librarians have become invisible, that the few who haven't been replaced by technicians or paraprofessionals are mainly behind the scenes, and that a lack of name badges or other prominent signage is keeping them from being easily identified. Whatever the reasons, the public—at least those of the SPL—admire their librarians, know their worth, and want to see and interact with more of them.

The final element in our analysis of the social dimensions of "SPL as Place" relate to the notion of free speech. Long considered a fundamental principle of library service by librarians and those who have benefited from librarians' support of free speech, such as film director and author Michael Moore, whose work *Stupid White Men* was only published due to the efforts of librarians, freedom of expression is a nebulous concept that we were unsure that the public might connect with libraries. Results from the word analysis method indicated that this was somewhat the case in that many comments pertained to the notion of free speech itself and not in connection to free speech in terms of the SPL. Moreover, due to the overlap in timing of our study with the national election, several responses reflected anti-Bush and anti-Republican fervor in the predominantly Democrat stronghold of Seattle. However, many respondents did have lengthy remarks that clearly illustrated an understanding of the relationship between freedom of expression and libraries. On the negative side, one user said that "You're not allowed to talk in the library," while another asserted that free speech was "ignored" and added "a display on the first floor is very offensive to the President, the Republicans and our participation in the war. I have complained about it. I also asked for a typewriter to be available but never heard from anyone." On the positive side of the relationship between the SPL and freedom of speech, many comments were made, from the basic "That's what libraries are for," "Ask questions, they'll freely help you here. Very helpful in there," "No problems with free speech at the library," "Relates to library policy of non-discrimination," and "[They have] literature of different opinions," "Definitely, [SPL] is a public space, at least on the first floor. You can talk freely there," and "It's pretty good, I liked the September project, the painting." Other responses centered around the SPL's practice of not divulging borrowers' records, for example: "I think it's terrific they don't give out patrons' records. Who's that guy? Ashcroft? I think he's a Nazi," and "It's good, [the library is] protected, records are destroyed." Perhaps the most illustrative if not oddest came from the user who said:

I yelled at a librarian the other day. Actually he was a technician. I couldn't get logged in and he said that the computer was reserved. I said I only wanted it for 5 minutes and he said "okay," but by that time someone else had taken it and there were no others for me. So I yelled at him. I didn't get kicked out, so I guess that's free speech.

From the responses of participants, it is very clear that the public using the SPL have not only a wide-ranging understanding of multifaceted aspects of free speech, but also see the library as a place where free speech is practiced and upheld in a variety of different ways.

SPL as Informational Place

Informants readily identified the Central Library as a place for obtaining information, reading for pleasure, and learning. While this observation is not surprising, the comments of those interviewed indicate a deep recognition of the importance of information and education in their lives and also illustrate a high social value placed on learning both for themselves and for the community as a whole. Coupled with this recognition, the concept of free access was also highly valued and frequently mentioned by those surveyed. While they did not use a term such as "digital divide," users and passers-by alike identified the communal social benefit to providing access to the Internet and access to computers to all segments of the population regardless of ability to pay.

One of the most common terms used by all subjects was "find," regardless of what it was being sought. Informants were highly aware of the library as a place to "find," "seek," "locate," "get," "explore," "discover," or gain "access" to information, or as one informant worded it, "things you need." They used terms such as "gateway" and "catalyst" to describe the library's function. As one user commented, "It's like a treasure for me. I can get anything I want if I have time." Another stated "There are more computer terminals than I've seen anywhere else. It's a real tool." These quotes reflect two important characteristics. First, the library is perceived as an endless source of information, a thought echoed by another informant who used the term "no boundaries." to describe what the library meant to them. Second, the informant recognized the library as a place where they must commit something of themselves, in this instance "time," or use a "tool" in order to gain benefit.

One evident difference between the perceptions of users and passers-by appeared in how both groups characterized what people wanted to find. Passers-by tended to define the search in terms of objects. They described the library as a place to find "books," "newspapers," or "CDs." In contrast, users more frequently spoke of "information," "research," or "knowledge." One explanation may be that users who frequent the physical library may come to know the resources and collections better that the casual observer.

This difference may indicate deeper reflection on the part of the users, or perhaps a problem-solving perspective that is not necessarily shared by nonusers. While passers-by placed a value on the library as a warehouse of materials, users tended to focus on what they gain from these materials. One commented, "At this point in my life, it's a place for seeking and understanding." This thought illustrates that the library is associated with the process of thinking and not only obtaining information.

Many of those interviewed also described the role of librarians and staff in helping them find information. Almost all statements were favorable (informants who felt free to criticize the building may have been less willing to criticize individuals) and many expressed gratitude for the assistance they have received. While it's possible that responses about libraries and librarians may be influenced by a halo effect, numerous participants gave concrete explanations of why they were pleased with assistance. One typical comment was, "Librarians deserve whatever break they can get. The go out of their way to be helpful." The librarian is perceived as doing more than expected in terms of finding information. Another shared perception was that librarians are patient and tolerant of those who don't know "simple" things, as explained by the following respondent:

I'm sure they are asked many simple questions like how to find this [he holds up a piece of paper with a call number on it] and they never seem to mind answering. I've never had problems getting help.

Such observations are in direct contrast to the stereotype of the librarian that permeates popular culture as an impersonal, condescending, and rule-bound individual.

In addition to finding and seeking, participants frequently discussed themes related to life-long learning, learning resources, and learning environment. Users were far more likely than passers-by to discuss the library as a place for learning. While both groups commented on the nature of learning as a "lifelong" process, users were more likely to describe learning as something that is "constant" or occurring "each day." One user commented it was the "main reason I come to the library." An analysis of responses to the term "learning" during the word association exercise indicates that the library as a place supports learning by providing resources and creating a conducive place for learning. Both users and passers-by noted the importance of collections as sources for study, but users were more likely to comment on the environment within the building. As one stated, "The most important aspect of the library for me is that it is a playful place. It redefines libraries and it links libraries to exploration." The connection between place and learning is clearly recognized by the library's users.

A second emergent theme pertaining to learning involves the concept of education as a public social good and the importance of providing the opportunities for learning to the community. Respondents used terms such as "necessary," "fundamental," "progressive," "growing," and "empowering" to describe the library's contribution to learning. One noted, "I think it provides the opportunity for everyone in the city to attain individual growth." Special emphasis was placed on the importance of the library as a learning place for children, as typified by one who stated, "For me and my children, it represents a learning tool to give my children an opportunity for higher education. We couldn't live without it. They love school now." In this quote, the notion of library as "tool" is again illustrated. The concept of place for learning is closely tied to the concept of a place for free access. One commented that the library provides "the opportunity to improve yourself at no charge. A free public education."

Informants were highly vocal in how they emphasized the need for "free" access.When asked whether the library building was worth the cost, the overwhelming majority responded affirmatively and used terms such as "bargain," "opportunity," and "free" to explain their reasoning. As one participant concisely stated, "It is less than the cost of buying books each year." Reasons for justifying cost fell into three categories: assisting people with low income, personal savings, and cost-effectiveness for the community. First, many observed the importance of free access promoting equity in the community, especially for the economically disadvantaged. Statements such as "Poor people can use the Internet" and "Everyone can have a membership" exemplify this concern. Another responded to questions about cost by saying, "A society without public libraries is going nowhere." Social good, above and beyond personal benefit, is perceived as a core value in favor of spending on libraries. Others voiced a second, more pragmatic rationale explaining that the library saved them much more than it cost in terms of purchasing books and movies. As one person observed, "Books and movies are expensive," and users and passers-by alike identified the trade-off of borrowing versus purchasing items for oneself. This was recognized most clearly by those who also expressed a large appetite, as one who stated, "I like to read fiction, but if I bought all the new romances, it would burn a hole in my pocket . . . I'm very grateful that membership at the library is free." A third argument was voiced by those who suggested the cost was "cheap" in comparison other public expenditures, such as the amount spent on a sports stadium or the proposed monorail project aimed to improve public transportation. Others noted that they "spend more on lattes" each week than the estimated per person annual cost of building the new library.

The most common criticism related to cost pertained to hours of operation. Rather than decrease the quality of service or reduce levels of staffing, the Seattle Public Library has addressed past cuts in the operating budget by closing all facilities for two weeks each year (once in winter and once in spring). A small number of informants suggested that the library should have increased hours rather than build a new facility. These observations may be naïve given that the cost of construction came from bond funds rather than operating funds, but such comments do indicate that the closures have the desirable effect of making budget cuts visible to a public that keenly desires more services and access, and feels the temporary loss.

DISCUSSION

At the outset of this paper we introduced two frameworks for understanding libraries—the SPL specifically—as "place": Oldenburg's notion of the third place and Creswell's five component lens. Conceptually we found that that both frameworks served their primary purpose of orienting us toward our research phenomenon, meaning they helped us understand nuances among different cognate terms such as "place," "space," and "landscape." Along this vein, they also provided initial insights into how data analysis might be approached. We now return to these frameworks to discuss how well they served in these capacities and how we potentially enriched them in the course of this research.

Oldenburg's third place framework, which, as noted, has been cited severally by LIS researchers but not applied in-depth, was of primary interest for its focus on the social aspects of libraries as place. While we heartedly agree that libraries are a veritable and necessary social good, our data did not support all of Oldenburg's eight propositions in establishing libraries, at least the SPL, as a third place. Thus, in answer to the broad question "Is the SPL Central Building a third place?" results from our study suggest that while it may be a third place in spirit, it fully meets few of Oldenburg's criteria. For example, our data supports the following assertions:

- Occurs on neutral ground, where "individuals may come and go as they please, in which none are required to play host, and in which all feel at home and comfortable;"
- Be levelers, inclusive places that are "accessible to the general public and do not set formal criteria of membership and exclusion" and thus promote the expansion of social networks where people interact with others who do no comprise their nearest and dearest;.
- Are a home away from home, the places where people can be likely found when not at home or at work, "though a radically different kind of setting from home, the third place is remarkably similar to a good home in the psychological comfort and support that it extends."

However, the following criteria or propositions were not borne out (or partially at best) by our analysis:

- Have conversation as the main activity—while conversation occurs freely, it is not the central activity featured at the SPL notwithstanding the library's efforts at facilitating conversation via its third-floor living room and other communal areas;
- One may go alone and be assured of finding an acquaintance—while groups may meet at the library, visitors cannot always expect to find a friend or acquaintance, especially given the sheer size and complexity of the building;
- Have "regulars" or "fellow customers" who nurture conviviality and trust with newcomers—persons may frequent the library and get to know others who regularly visit at the same time, but little or no special outreach is made to the new visitor;
- Keep a low, unimpressive profile as a physical structure—Koolhaus, the architect, intended to make a bold statement with the design of the structure, and the visitor is meant to experience the physical nature of the building and as well as use the library's resources;
- Have a persistent playful, playground sort of mood—users clearly indicated the serious nature of the work and learning they performed in the library, and while some commented that the place was fun or playful, the mood was one of productivity, study, and reflection.

While our analysis of the SPL Central Building does not support the third place propositions noted above, it is consistent with other third place characteristics that Oldenburg notes, as offering such personal benefits as novelty, perspective, spiritual tonic, and friendship via its collection, staff, services, and clientele. In addition, the SPL was highly regarded by our respondents as a societal good in terms of its political role, habit of association, recreational spirit, and importance "in securing the public domain for the use and enjoyment of decent people" (Oldenburg *Great Good*, 83). We found little evidence, other than the odd respondent who felt that the homeless should be barred from the library, that the SPL harbors such negative third place characteristics as segregation, isolation, or hostility. In this sense, our analysis also supports Putnam and Feldstein's observation that libraries foster social capital by facilitating human relationships via trust and understanding and hence nurture community. More significant, we found that the SPL supports two distinct forms of social capital, bonding and bridging, because in addition to linking together people of similar ilk they also promote diversity by assembling people of different types—themes that echo Putnam and Feldstein's observations of the Chicago Public Library's Near North Branch. Given the misfit between Oldenburg's framework and the SPL central building (strong agreement on only three of the eight criteria), we ask to what degree might the framework better account for the nature of a library branch? In other words, might the smaller scale and tighter cohesiveness of a branch library make it more fully reflect the attributes of a third place? According to Oldenburg, bookstores fit the bill as a third place (Oldenburg 2002), so why not a branch library?

Our second framework, Cresswell's five-part definition of "place," was useful for helping clarify the differences among overlapping terms. Using this framework, responses can be classified as follows:

> *Location*: This concept was of particular interest given the history of the site being used for the downtown Central Library for over a century. Respondents confirmed the importance of the location in terms of ease of accessibility and prominence in the heart of the city. The site is well situated for low-income residents, who were recognized as primary beneficiaries of the services, collections, and technology.
>
> *Locale*: The variety of the settings within the structure accommodate a range of user's needs and purposes, including interacting with others or individual efforts. Users frequently commented on material features (plants, lights, furniture, coffee stand, colors, etc.) as they related to the activities they were conducting.
>
> *Sense of Place*: Respondents expressed a range of feelings and emotions associated with the building, specific structural features, collections, and the importance of the library in their own lives.
>
> *Space*: Cresswell's discussion of space helped differentiate our understanding of place, but does not apply to the analysis of individual responses concerning the Central Library as a single place.
>
> *Landscape*: Respondents shared their thoughts and feelings regarding how the Central Library fits into the greater topography of the city and the downtown area.

Cresswell's framework, like Oldenburg's, is a useful lens for understanding the importance of libraries as places within contemporary society. Neither, however, adequately addresses the concept of information as it figures in the broader notion of place. While information may be loosely equated with "conversation" in Oldenburg's framework and "books" may be regarded as part of "locale" or material setting in Cresswell's terms, neither framework explicitly incorporates information seeking and consumption as a core aspect of place. Thus the current study may contribute to the foregoing frameworks by adding an "informational" component to the place-based characteristics noted in these frameworks. We suggest that an "informational place" can be operationalized as comprising all themes regarding information finding and seeking, reading, life-long learning, learning resources, and learning environment.

Beyond extending past research on the roles that libraries play in people's lives and the values ascribed to them by employing a strong place-based framework, our study examined the perceptions of both users and passers-by in addition to employing the free association—a population and method rarely included in past studies. Moreover, the study was timed to occur a few months after the opening of the new SPL Central Building, an unprecedented effort in library design and hence a unique opportunity for field research. We are currently expanding our study by interviewing SPL staff about their thoughts and feelings toward the new SPL building as place. We are also applying our study design to understanding the views of various stakeholders toward new SPL branch libraries. This would be of particular interest for determining whether branches exhibit more third place characteristics as hypothesized from the results of the current study.

APPENDIX A: INTERVIEW SCHEDULE FOR LIBRARY USERS

Interviewer: _____   Date: _____

Tally the number of individuals who declined to participate at this location: _____

Location (mark one):   Day (circle one):
                                        Su   Mo   Tu   We   Th   Fr   Sa

◻ Fiction (3rd floor)
◻ Children's Room (1st floor)   Start Time:_____
◻ World Languages (1st floor)
◻ Mixing Chamber (5th floor)   End Time:_____
◻ Book Spiral

                                        Sex (circle one):   Male   Female

Hello! My name is {xxxxx}. I'm from the University of Washington. I'm asking people what they think about the new library building. I have a few questions that will take about 10–15 minutes as explained in this information sheet, which includes the names of contacts in case you have any future questions about this project. All questions are optional. As thanks, you will get a coupon for a free Latte at Starbucks. Would you like to participate?

1. How long have you been visiting the Central Library, either the new or the old building? {years or months}
2. How often do you visit this library? {Record verbatim response; code AFTER interview}

    ◻ Daily   ◻ 2–3 times per month   ◻ First time
    ◻ 2–6 times per   ◻ Once per month
       week
    ◻ Once per week   ◻ Less than once per
                              month

3. Is this building your local branch? {Yes / No}
    [if NO] Was your main reason for coming downtown to visit the Central Library?
4. What do you think of the new building? {Open-ended response}
5. How do you feel this building fits with downtown Seattle? {Open-ended response}
6. What do you like the most about this building? {Open-ended response}
7. What do you like least about this building? {Open-ended response}

8. Do you usually come by yourself? {Yes / No}
    [if NO, skip to second prompt associated with question 12]
9. Do you ever come with other people? {Yes / No}
    [if YES] Who do you come with? For any particular reason? {Open-ended response}
10. Do you ever come to do things for other people? {Yes / No}
    [if YES] Who have you done this for? What have you done for them? Why? {Open-ended response}
11. Have you ever come to a public presentation at this building? {Yes / No}
    [if YES] Which ones? {Open-ended response}
12. Have you ever used this library to do something for work? {Yes / No}
    [if YES] What sorts of things have you done for work? {Open-ended response}
13. How would you find a book without asking a librarian or using the computer? {Open-ended response}
14. In general, libraries arrange their books in several ways. Can you describe how the books are physically arranged and organized in this library? {Open-ended response}
15. In this new building, some books are organized in a spiral. Do you think this helps you locate what you need? How? {Open-ended response}
16. I'm going to read you a list of words related to this library. Please say the first thoughts that enter your mind. {Open-ended responses}
    a) Reading
    b) Free Speech
    c) Learning
    d) Community
    e) Technology
    f) Librarians
    g) Books
    h) Architecture

17. In summary, what does this library mean to you? {Open-ended response}
18. For this building, 152 million dollars of the cost was financed by a twenty-five-year municipal bond. This makes the cost of the building about $10 per person a year for the people of Seattle. Do you feel this building was worth the cost? Why or why not?
19. Is there anything you would like the City Librarian or Board of Trustees to know about the services or design of the new Central Library? {Open-ended response}
Now I'd like to ask you a few quick questions about yourself.
20. What is your age? {Open-ended response}
21. What is your occupation? {Open-ended response}
22. Did you go to college? {Yes / No}
    [if NO] Are you a high school graduate? {Yes / No}
    [if YES] What is your highest degree attained? {Open-ended response}
23. What is your ethnicity? {Open-ended response}
24. What is the primary language spoken in the home? {Open-ended response}
25. Is your household income above or below $50,000? {Above / Below}
    [if NO] Is it above or below $30,000? {Above / Below}
    [if YES] Is it above or below $75,000? {Above / Below}
26. Do you live in Seattle? {Yes / No}
    [if NO] Do you live in King County? {Yes / No}
27. Do you have a seattle Public Library Card? {Yes / No}
Thank you for answering my questions. Here is a coupon for your free Latte. Thanks again!

APPENDIX B: INTERVIEW SCHEDULE FOR PASSERS-BY

Interviewer: _____   Date: _____

Tally the number of individuals who declined to participate at this location: _____

Location (mark one):   Day (circle one):

                                           Su   Mo   Tu   We   Th   Fr   Sa

      □ NE corner

      □ SE corner   Start Time:_____

      □ SW corner

      □ NW corner   End Time:_____

                                  Sex (circle one):   Male   Female

Hello! My name is {xxxxx}. I'm from the University of Washington. I'm asking people what they think about the new library building. I have a few questions that will take about 10–15 minutes as explained in this information sheet, which includes the names of contacts in case you have any future questions about this project. All questions are optional. As thanks, you will get a coupon for a free Latte at Starbucks. Would you like to participate?

1. How often do you walk by this building?
   - □ Daily
   - □ 2–6 times per week
   - □ Once per week
   - □ 2–3 times per month
   - □ Once per month
   - □ Less than once per month
   - □ First time

2. What do you think of this new building? {Open-ended response}
3. How do you feel this building fits with downtown Seattle? {Open-ended response}
4. What do you like most about this building? {Open-ended response}
5. What do you like least about this building? {Open-ended response}
6. I'm going to read you a list of words related to this library. Please say the first thoughts that enter your mind. {Open-ended responses}

   a) Reading
   b) Free Speech
   c) Learning
   d) Community
   e) Technology
   f) Librarians
   g) Books
   h) Architecture

7. In summary, what does this library mean to you? {Open-ended response}
8. For this building, 152 million dollars of the cost was financed by a twenty-five-year municipal bond. This makes the cost of the building about $10 per person a year for the people of Seattle. Do you feel this building was worth the cost? Why or why not?
9. Do you have any other comments about the library? {Open-ended response}
10. Have you ever used this library? {Yes / No}
        [if YES] What have you used it for? {Open-ended response}

To finish, I have a few quick questions.

11. What is your age? {Open-ended response}
12. What is your occupation? {Open-ended response}
13. Did you go to college? {Yes / No}
        [if NO] Are you a high school graduate? {Yes / No}

[if YES] What is your highest degree attained? {Open-ended response}

14. What is your ethnicity? {Open-ended response}
15. What is the primary language spoken in the home? {Open-ended response}
16. Is your household income above or below $50,000? {Above / Below}
    [if NO] Is it above or below $30,000? {Above / Below}
    [if YES] Is it above or below $75,000? {Above / Below}
17. Do you have a Seattle Public Library card? {Yes / No}

Thank you for answering my questions. Here is a coupon for your free Latte. Thanks again!

NOTES

1. We wish to thank the Seattle Public Library (SPL) Foundation for supporting this study through providing participant compensation. We also wish to thank SPL staff Deborah Jacobs, Michele D'Allesandro, Andra Addison, and Lois Fenker for their invaluable assistance, and especially our MLIS student assistants: Peter Cole, Tom Dobrowolsky, Grace Fitzgerald, Betha Gutsche, Robyn Hagle, Sumi Hayashi, Carol Landry, Sarah Merner, Anne Miller, Hannah Parker, Jennifer Peterson, Christopher Rieber, and Kristen Shuyler.

2. As Jean Preer (2001) astutely lamented, Putnam omitted libraries from his popular monograph *Bowling Alone: Collapse and Revival of American Community*—an oversight he corrected after discussion with library professionals at the 2001 annual ALA meeting by including the Chicago Public Library as a case study in his book with Feldstein in which he discusses the importance of branch libraries in bringing people together and enabling access to electronic information across the digital divide.

3. Extensive illustrations and photographs of the new SPL Central Library are provided in the October 2004 issue of *Metropolis*.

4. "The majority of the nonfiction collection—75 percent of the entire collection—is located on the Book Spiral. This allows the nonfiction collection to be housed in one continuous run, and avoids the problem of having to move books into other rooms or floors when various subject areas expand. The spiral is an architectural organization that allows all patrons—including people with disabilities—the freedom to move throughout the entire collection without depending on stairs, escalators and elevators. Book shelves are not filled to capacity, so there is room for the collection to grow." ("Central Library" par. 17).

5. Numerous other works such as Crosland (1929); Siipola, Walker and Kolb (1955); Bilodeau and Howell (1965); Cramer (1968); Gerow (1977); Szalay and Deese (1978); Mefferd (1979); Silverstein and Harrow (1983); and Craighead and Memeroff (2001) also provide guidance in the selection and analysis of free association terms.

6. In a forthcoming paper we share our findings from an in-depth analysis of our knowledge organization data, particularly regarding the book spiral. Notwithstanding the usefulness of several past analyses of library buildings, we did not uncover published studies that address the effectiveness of the *physical arrangement* of materials in libraries. Given the unique characteristics of the internal space at the SPL Central Library, exploring the effectiveness of shelving nonfiction materials using a continuous run of call numbers as a means of organizing knowledge may shed new light upon patterns of library use.

REFERENCES

Agnew, John. *Place and Politics: The Geographical Mediation of State and Society*. Boston: Allen and Unwin, 1987.

Albanese, Andrew Richard. "Deserted no More." *Library Journal* 15 Apr. 2003: 34–6.

Allen, Frank R., and Sarah Barbara Watstein. "Point/Counterpoint: The Value of Place." *College and Research Libraries News* 57.6 (1996): 372–73, 383.

Alstad, Colleen, and Ann Curry. "Public Space, Public Discourse, and Public Libraries." *LIBRES: Library and Information Science Research Electronic Journal* 13 (2003). Retrieved 15 Sept. 2005 from http://libres.curtin.edu.au/libres13n1/pub_space.htm.

American Community Survey. 2003.

Augst, Thomas. "American Libraries and Agencies of Culture." *American Studies* 42.3 (2001): 5–22.

Bilodeau, Edward, and David Howell. *Free Association Norms by Discrete and Continued Methods.* Washington, DC: U.S. Government Printing Office, 1965.

Block, Marylaine. "How to Become a Great Public Space." *American Libraries* Apr. 2003: 72–76.

Bryson, Jared, Bob Usherwood, and Richard Proctor London. "Libraries Must Also Be Buildings? New Library Impact Study." *Museums, Libraries, and Archives Council Information.* Centre for Public Libraries and Information in Society. Mar. 2003. Retrieved 15 Sept. 2005 from http://www.mla.gov.uk/documents/sp024rep.doc.

Bundy, Alan. "Places of Connection: New Public and Academic Library Buildings in Australia and New Zealand." *Australasian Public Libraries and Information Services* 16.1 (2004): 32–47.

Craighead, W. Edward, and Charles B. Nemeroff. *The Corsini Encyclopedia of Psychology and Behavioral Science.* New York: Wiley, 2001.

Cramer, Phebe. *Word Association.* New York: Academic Press, 1968.

Creswell, Tim. *Place: A Short Introduction.* Malden, MA: Blackwell, 2004.

Crosland, Harold. *The Psychological Methods of Word-Association and Reaction-time as Tests of Deception.* Eugene, OR: University of Oregon Press, 1929.

Crumpacker, Sara. "The School Library as Place." *Wilson Library Bulletin* 69.1 (1994): 23–25.

Curry, Ann, Denisa Dunbar, Ellen George, and Diana Marshall. "Public Library Branch Design: The Public Speaks!" Canadian Library Association/British Columbia Library Association Joint Annual Conference. Victoria, BC, Canada, 16 June 2004.

Demas, Sam, and Jeffrey Scherer. "Esprit de Place: Maintaining and Designing Library Buildings to Provide Transcendent Spaces." *American Libraries* Apr. 2002: 65–68.

Durrance, Joan C., and Karen E. Fisher. *How Libraries and Librarians Help: A Guide to Identifying User-Centered Outcomes.* Chicago: American Library Association, 2005.

Engel, Debra, and Karen Antell. "The Life of the Mind: A Study of Faculty Spaces in Academic Libraries." *College & Research Libraries* 65.1 (2004): 8–26.

Feld, Steven, and Keith H. Basso, eds. *Senses of Place.* Santa Fe, NM: School of American Research Press; Seattle, Wash.: dist. by University of Washington Press, 1996.

Fisher, Karen E., Joan C. Durrance, Marian Bouch Hinton. "Information Grounds and the Use of Need-based Services by Immigrants in Queens, New York: A Context-based, Outcome Evaluation Approach." *Journal of the American Society for Information Science & Technology* 55.8 (2004): 754–66.

Gerow, Joshua. "Instructional Set and Word Association Test (WAT) Responses of Children and Adults." *Journal of Genetic Psychology* 130.2 (1977): 247–54.

Ginsburg, Judith Renee. "Placemaking: Case Study of How Participants Understand the Design, Development, and Function of an Academic Library." Diss. University of Oregon, 1997.

Gorman, Michael. *Our Enduring Values: Librarianship in the 21st Century.* Chicago: American Library Association, 2000.

Gosling, William. "To Go or Not to Go? Library as Place." *American Libraries* Nov. 2000: 44–5.

Kranich, Nancy, ed. *Libraries and Democracy: The Cornerstones of Liberty.* Chicago: American Library Association, 2001.

Leckie, Gloria J., and Jeffrey Hopkins. "The Public Place of Central Libraries: Findings from Toronto and Vancouver." *Library Quarterly* 72.3 (2002): 326–72.

Lippard, Lucy R. *Lure of the Local: Sense of Place in a Multicentered Society.* New York: New Press, 1997.

Ludwig, Logan, and Susan Starr. "Library as Place: Results of a Delphi Study." *Journal of the Medical Library Association* 93 (2005): 315–26.

McCook, Kathleen de la Pena. *Introduction to Public Librarianship*. New York: Neal-Schuman, 2004.

McKechnie, Lynn, and Pam McKenzie. "The Young Child / Adult Caregiver Storytime Program as Information Ground." Library Research Seminar III. Kansas City, Kansas. 15 Oct. 2004.

McKinney, William Allen. "Policy and Power: The Role of the Neighborhood Library in the Community and the Forces that Add to or Detract from its Efficacy." Diss. Temple University, 2002.

Mefferd, Roy, Jr. "Word Association: Response Behavior and Stimulus Words." *Psychological Reports* 45.3 (1979): 763–67.

Molz, Redmond Kathleen, and Phyllis Dain. *Civic Space/Cyberspace: The American Public Library in the Information Age*. Cambridge, MA: MIT Press, 1999.

Moore, Michael. *Stupid White Men—and Other Sorry Excuses for the State of the Nation!* New York: Regan Books, 2001.

Nelson, Douglas, Cathy McEvoy, and Simon Dennis. "What Is Free Association and What does It Measure?" *Memory & Cognition* 28.6 (2000): 887–99.

Oldenburg, Ray. *The Great Good Place: Cafes, Coffee Shops, Bookstores, Bars, Hair Salons, and other Hangouts at the Heart of a Community*. New York: Marlowe, 1999.

———. *Celebrating the Third Place: Inspiring Stories about the "Great Good Places" at the Heart of Our Communities*. New York: Marlowe, 2002.

Pettigrew [Fisher], Karen E. "Waiting for Chiropody: Contextual Results from an Ethnographic Study of the Information Behavior among Attendees at Community Clinics." *Information Processing and Management* 35.6 (1999): 801–17.

Preer, Jean. "Where are Libraries in *Bowling Alone*?" *American Libraries* Aug. 2001: 60–63.

Putnam, Robert D. *Bowling Alone: Collapse and Revival of American Community*. New York: Simon & Schuster, 2000.

Putnam, Robert D., and Lewis M. Feldstein. *Better Together: Restoring the American Community*. New York: Simon & Schuster, 2003.

Ranseen, Emily. "The Library as Place: Changing Perspectives." *Library Administration & Management* 16.4 (2002): 203–7.

Relph, Edward. *Place and Placelessness*. London: Pion, 1976

Sannwald, William. "To Build or Not to Build." *Library Administration & Management* 15.3 (2001): 155–60.

"Central Library: Floor-by-Floor Highlights." *Seattle Public Library*. Retrieved 15 September 2005 from http://www.spl.org/default.asp?pageID=branch_central_floors_detail&branchID=1.

Shill, Harold B., and Shawn Tonner. "Creating a Better Place: Physical Improvements in Academic Libraries, 1995–2002." *College & Research Libraries* 64.11 (2003): 431–66.

Siipola, Elsa, Nanette Walker, and Dorothy Kolb. "Task Attitudes in Word Association, Projective and Nonprojective." *Journal of Personality* 23.4 (1955): 441–59.

Silverstein, Marshall, and Martin Harrow. "Word Association: Multiple Measures and Multiple Meanings." *Journal of Clinical Psychology* 39.4 (1983): 467–70.

St. Lifer, Evan. "What Public Libraries Must Do to Survive." *Library Journal* 1 Apr. 2001: 60–2.

Szalay, Lor, and James Deese. *Subjective Meaning and Culture: An Assessment through Word Associations*. Hillsdale, NJ: Lawrence Erlbaum Associates, 1978.

Thomas, Nancy Pickering. "Reading Libraries: An Interpretive Study of Discursive Practices in Library Architecture and the Interactional Construction of Personal Identity." Diss. Rutgers, The State University of New Jersey, 1996.

Wagner, Gulten S. "Public Library Buildings: A Semiotic Analysis." *Journal of Librarianship and Information Science* 24.2 (1992): 101–8.

Ward, Jacob. "The Making of a Library: The Research." *Metropolis* 24.2 (2004): 98–141.

Weise, Frieda. "Being There: The Library as Place." *Journal of the Medical Library Association* 92.1 (2004): 6–13.

Wheat, Leonard. *Free Associations to Common Words: A Study of Word Associations to Twenty-Five Words Picked at Random from the Five Hundred Most Commonly Used Words in the English Language*. New York: Teachers College, Columbia University, 1931.

Wiegand, Wayne A. "To Reposition a Research Agenda: What American Studies Can Teach the LIS Community about the Library in the Life of the User." *Library Quarterly* 73.4 (2003): 369–82.

Wood, Mark, et al. "Better Public Libraries." *Museums, Libraries, and Archives Council Information*. Commission for Architecture and the Built Environment. 2003. Retrieved 15 Sept. 2005 from http://www.mla.gov.uk/documents/id874rep.pdf.

Worpole, Ken. "21st Century Libraries: Changing Forms, Changing Futures." Commission for Architecture and the Built Environment, 2003.

Section III

Research Libraries as Places of Learning and Scholarship

9

Stimulating Space, Serendipitous Space: Library as Place in the Life of the Scholar

Karen Antell

Assistant Professor and Head of Reference and Outreach Services, University of Oklahoma Libraries, Norman, Oklahoma

Debra Engel

Associate Professor and Director of Public Services, University of Oklahoma Libraries, Norman, Oklahoma

INTRODUCTION: HOW WE GOT HERE

Several different observations led us to become interested in studying faculty use of library space. As the new Director of Public Services at the University of Oklahoma Libraries in 2001, one of the authors instantly became the "landlord" for ninety faculty studies, and was surprised to learn just how important these small spaces were to the "tenants," some of whom had "inhabited" their studies for thirty years or more. As with other landlord–tenant relationships, this one was sometimes fraught with tension over matters that seemed rather trivial, such as window cleaning and thermostat settings. As she got to know her tenants better over time, the realization that these small spaces—mostly under 50 square feet—mattered a great deal to the intellectual lives of the faculty who used them. When one faculty-study occupant only half-jokingly declared "my blood will be on your hands if you ever take away my faculty study" (Engel and Antell 8), it was clear that these small plots of library "real estate" had a deeper value than appearances would suggest. It was time to start asking questions.

During the summer of 2002 a collaborator who was as intrigued as she was by the faculty study phenomenon and its implications about the meaning of library space in the life of the mind was hired at the University of Oklahoma. Together, the authors began to ask the questions that would lead to a study of faculty use of academic library space and ultimately to the surprising results we found on academic library as place—namely, that it has a value for scholars that goes far beyond mere access to materials. Scholars love the convenience of access to electronic resources, but they also value the physical library, often for intangible but nonetheless crucial reasons, such as its "conduciveness to scholarship." One faculty study occupant reflected the sentiments of many when she told us that "The best five paragraphs of my book were written in my faculty study" (Engel and Antell 12).

Around the beginning of this collaboration, we noted the emergence of a nationwide debate among academic librarians about the future of the library building in the digital era. In November 2001, Scott Carlson had published his provocative article in the *Chronicle of Higher Education*, "The Deserted Library." Citing increasing electronic usage and decreasing circulation, Carlson predicted that academic libraries would soon be replaced by Starbucks:

One Thursday afternoon at Augusta State's Reese Library, the computer labs are packed, but the reading areas are sparsely populated—and Reese isn't the only college library that's empty. Gate counts and circulation of traditional materials are falling at many college libraries across the country, as students find new study spaces in dorm rooms or apartments, coffee shops, or nearby bookstores. Here in Augusta this afternoon, for instance, there are more Medical College of Georgia students packed into the tiny cafes of the local Borders and Barnes & Noble than there are in the college's sprawling library. (A35)

This article provided one answer to the nagging question that had been on librarians' minds for several years: Do electronic resources signify the end of libraries as we know them? However, the overwhelming and passionate response to "The Deserted Library" indicated that, despite Carlson's claims, the question was far from settled. An online forum held soon after the article's publication attracted participants from academic libraries all over the country, most of whom countered that their libraries were bustling with students and activity, even if circulation was down.

> *David Lewis, Indiana University-Purdue University Indianapolis:* It is clear to me that the nature of the work done in libraries is changing. Libraries are no longer just quiet spaces for reflective study. They are increasingly loud places for groups, and coffee shops are OK. To me the key is to have a vibrant central space for the scholarly work of the campus—whatever this looks like—to be focused on. I think if libraries continue to play this role, people will continue to use them and they will continue to be important places on campus.
>
> *Deanna B. Marcum, Council on Library and Information Resources:* Libraries are becoming very interesting places where a lot of things happen because of the nature of class assignments that students now have, the kinds of research projects they're doing. These are no longer quiet, solitary efforts, and the experience I have with both liberal arts colleges and university libraries is that gate counts are not dropping. Students are going to the library.
>
> *Mary Reichel, Appalachian State University:* Despite the evidence that Scott Carlson found for his *Chronicle* article about the use of libraries, there is still great disagreement about whether academic libraries are being used less (Carlson, "Are College Libraries Too Empty?").

Clearly, the jury was still out on the "death of the library." But the jury seemed to be concerned only with *student* use of academic libraries. Our experience with faculty study occupants, however, led us to conjecture about *faculty members'* use of academic libraries. Perhaps students really were deserting libraries, but were the faculty—the "real scholars"—also staying away?

In the midst of this raging national debate, we started small. Over the course of the summer of 2002, we invited ten of our "occupants" to have coffee with us and tell us how they used their faculty studies. Most of the ten interviewees wanted reassurance that these conversations were not a prelude to taking away their faculty study privileges or reallocating the faculty study space to other uses. After we promised not to take away their faculty studies, however, the occupants were uniformly delighted to share with us their thoughts about their faculty studies and the role of this "real estate" in their intellectual lives. Their responses overwhelmed us with their enthusiasm and passion.

WHY THEY LOVE THESE TINY SPACES

Three themes emerged in our interview with faculty study holders (Engel and Antell).

The faculty study is an "oasis of solitude" necessary for doing scholarly work. All ten interviewees mentioned in one way or another that their faculty study represented an "oasis of solitude," the only place where they could count on having uninterrupted blocks of time alone in which to do the complicated work of scholarship.

I can count on getting work done there. I know I will be able to put in three or four good hours and finish whatever it is I need to get done. (12)

[My faculty study provides] a freedom of focus without distraction. (12)

I've always done my best work in quiet libraries. (12)

One question we asked each interviewee was "Would you like a telephone in your faculty study?" Respondents unanimously (and often vehemently) said "No." In these days of ubiquitous cell phones and *de rigueur* instant accessibility, this desire to escape from telephone contact seems particularly revealing, reinforcing the faculty spaces' importance as oases of solitude for their inhabitants. As Walt Crawford notes in *Being Analog*, "The life of the mind sometimes requires peace and quiet" (62).

"Serendipitous browsing" of the stacks is an essential element of research. One faculty study occupant told us that "there is *no substitute* for walking the stacks. It's not 'browsing'— that sounds too aimless. It is more directed—'surveillance,' really" (Engel and Antell 13). This exemplifies the second theme that emerged from the interviews: faculty studies are valuable because they offer excellent proximity to the library stacks, and *serendipitous browsing* of the stacks is necessary for conducting a thorough scholarly search. "Students today are going into the literature with a laser-like bandwidth, but they are not bending their minds around the larger, broader issues brought to them by books and by serendipitous browsing" (18).

Scholars' "academic upbringing" instilled in them the ritual of going to the library to do serious intellectual work. One interviewee told us that his "academic upbringing," starting in his undergraduate days and continuing throughout graduate school and his early years on the tenure track, had inculcated in him the principle that "you go to the library to study," to do intellectual work (18). This, he says, is why he requested a faculty study. Other faculty members echoed this theme: several had held graduate student carrels during their graduate school days and maintained that "going to the library" was one of the work habits that had helped them achieve success as an academic.

THE "STATE OF THE STUDY": 1968 AND 2002

Curious to learn more about faculty studies' role in scholars' intellectual life, we delved into the literature to find only one article. Spyers-Duran's 1968 study reported on a survey of 32 "urban libraries," 65 percent of which reported housing faculty studies (56). One aspect of the Spyers-Duran study that we found particularly interesting was its almost "grudging" attitude toward faculty study occupants. The article described faculty studies not as a public service but as a "problem" for library administrators to manage. The main problem, according to the article, seemed to be faculty members' failure to observe regulations regarding food, drink, typewriter noise, smoking, and other housekeeping issues (57–58). One of Spyers-Duran's main reasons for conducting the survey of other libraries was to find out how other libraries' administrators solved these kinds of housekeeping problems and, accordingly, to make recommendations for writing faculty study usage policies so as to minimize infractions.

Since Spyers-Duran's findings were thirty-five years old and pre-dated the widespread use of electronic information, we decided to conduct a similar survey of ARL libraries to find out the "state of the study" in 2003 (Engel and Antell). We were pleased to obtain a response rate of 56 percent and surprised to learn that 75 percent of responding libraries housed faculty studies or faculty carrels, an increase over the 1968 figure of 65 percent. However, this increase in the number of studies was offset by a larger increase in the number of faculty members during this time. This was reflected in the faculty-to-study ratio: in 1968, libraries reported having one study for every forty-two faculty members. In 2003, this ratio had decreased to one study for every fifty-eight faculty members. Despite this declining ratio, however, demand for studies was relatively low: 57 percent of responding libraries reported that they had an "adequate" number of faculty studies, and slightly less than half reported having a waiting list for faculty studies. By contrast, only 18 percent of Spyers-Duran's respondents reported having an adequate number of studies.

One lasting result of Spyers-Duran's article might be the prevalence of written policies governing the use of faculty studies. In 1968, Spyers-Duran found that only half of responding libraries had such a written policy and conjectured that this might contribute to the faculty study "problem." He recommended that libraries implement a faculty study policy and even provided a sample policy to help libraries encourage faculty members to comply with faculty study regulations. Although Spyers-Duran's emphasis on "rules" seems a bit heavy-handed to us today, perhaps his article helped bring about the shift in public services "culture" that makes his article feel somewhat foreign and dated today. In our 2002 ARL study, we found that 91 percent of libraries with faculty studies had implemented a written policy governing their use. Perhaps the prevalence of good written policies has in fact brought about better relations between faculty study holders and library administrators, enabling library administrators to focus more on the public services aspect of faculty studies rather than the "watchdog" aspect.

"ACADEMIC UPBRINGING": DOES AGE MATTER?

By January 2004, our "state of the study" findings had been published and our article had added a new voice and new knowledge to the animated cacophony that was the library as place "conversation" (Engel and Antell). We were pleased to have discovered the depth of passion and enthusiasm that our interviewees felt about their faculty studies. But our article also raised a niggling question that left us feeling there was something important still to be learned. The question stemmed from the "academic upbringing" theme. One faculty study holder had told us, "Possibly it's generational— for my generation, you go to the library to study. . . . Electronic access to journals is great, but I wish students [today] could be introduced to the library in the charming way that I was" (18). The conclusion of this first paper thus included a call for further research to answer this question about generational differences:

In the future, then, researchers will need to study how the emerging generation of academics uses and values library space. If the academic upbringing of younger faculty members does not include the practice of using the resources and space in a library, will faculty spaces soon sit vacant? (18)

This question led us to expand our inquiries beyond the realm of faculty studies. We decided we needed to find out how scholars of all ages used the physical space of the library and whether differences existed among the different age cohorts. So we designed a survey that was sent in June 2004 to all faculty members and doctoral students at the University of Oklahoma Norman Campus. Still wanting to focus on faculty members rather than students, we excluded undergraduates and master's students, on the assumption that doctoral students represented the best available proxy for "scholars in training." However, we realized that knowing a respondent's age would not tell us when he or she received his or her "academic upbringing." Some scholars receive their doctorates at the age of twenty-five, whereas others are fifty or older when they enter the academic life. Therefore, one faculty in his fifties or sixties might be the "scholarly-age peer" of a person in her twenties or thirties, meaning that they both received their graduate school enculturation at the same time. Because of this, our survey asked respondents for both their birth year and the year they received their most recent academic degree. This enabled us to compare responses both by age and by "scholarly age."

AGE, "SCHOLARLY AGE," AND LIBRARY USE PATTERNS

The survey asked for demographic information about the respondent's age, university status, gender, academic degrees, and so forth, as well as soliciting information about the respondent's use of library spaces at the University of Oklahoma: whether respondents used the physical space of the library, whether they used electronic resources remotely, what activities they engaged in while using the physical space of the library, how frequently they used the library, how long their typical library visits were, which areas of the library they used, and which activities they engaged in while at the library. Most questions were multiple-choice, but two requested a written response. The survey was sent to 1,800 people, and 241 responded, for a response rate of 13.4 percent (Antell and Engel).

Our 241 respondents fell into five different age groups and four different scholarly age groups, as shown in Table 9.1   .

We hypothesized that older scholars—both those who had been born earlier and those who had received their degrees earlier—would report more use of the physical library space than younger scholars. Not every survey question's results showed different usage patterns among scholars of different ages or different scholarly ages. For instance, all groups reported fairly similar levels of library use for conducting research, checking out books, placing interlibrary loan requests, consulting a librarian, using periodicals, and browsing new books. However, significant and surprising differences emerged in other areas, and these differences often seemed inconsistent. As we expected, younger scholars (by both age and scholarly age) were dramatically less likely than older scholars to report that they had done graduate research or written part or all of their dissertation in the

Table 9.1. Number of respondents in each age group and each scholarly age group

	Age: born in the . . .						Scholarly age: last degree earned in the . . .					
	1940s	1950s	1960s	1970s	1980s	No response	Before 1970*	1970s	1980s	1990s	2000s	No response
Number of respondents	6	73	58	86	13	5	3	26	30	71	105	6

* Because of the small number of respondents in the "Before 1970" scholarly age group, it is impossible to draw statistically significant inferences about this group, and therefore we did not include it in our analyses of the data.

library when they were in graduate school, indicating that younger scholars' "academic upbringing" included less use of the library. But, contrary to expectations, younger scholars were far *more* likely than older scholars to report that they (currently) wrote papers in the library and "spent time in contemplation" in the library. This suggested to us that "academic upbringing" might not be as important as we had originally supposed in forming a scholar's work habits. Clearly, many younger scholars who had used the library very little during their graduate school years had nonetheless formed some strong habits of library use—stronger, in many cases, than the habits of older scholars who *had* been heavy users of library space during graduate school.

THE QUALITATIVE RESULTS: 176 SCHOLARS TELL US HOW THEY REALLY FEEL ABOUT LIBRARY SPACE

Two of the survey questions asked respondents to provide a written response:

- In your opinion, are there differences between using the library remotely (using electronic resources via the Web site) and using the library's physical space? If so, what are the differences?
- If you have any other observations about your use of library space that you would like to share, please use the space below.

Of our 241 respondents, 176 (73 percent) provided answers to one or both of these questions (Antell and Engel). Many responses included more than one "statement"— for instance, "Remote access is quicker, easier … [but] if I am not sure of the exact information I need or what alternative sources exist, the face-to-face contact in the library is superior" [Anonymous survey participant]. The 176 people who responded to the narrative-response questions made a total of 390 statements. We analyzed these 390 statements to discover the major themes that arose in the narrative responses.

These two questions elicited a wealth of information that revealed respondents' feelings about library space in a way that multiple-choice questions simply could not gauge. We identified eleven themes that emerged from the 390 statements. The four most prevalent themes, which we termed "major themes," accounted for 73.5 percent of all responses and demonstrated a remarkable level of agreement among our respondents about the meaning and value of library space in their scholarly pursuits.

Convenience—electronic resources (97 responses; 24.8 percent of total). We weren't terribly surprised to discover that one in four statements reflected the idea that using the library electronically is convenient (Antell and Engel).

- Remotely is more convenient. (8)
- I would prefer an entirely electronic library. (8)

Browsability—physical library (73 responses; 18.7 percent of total). The second most frequent theme revealed that many respondents value the physical library's browsability. We also included in this category responses that praised the physical library's organization or that indicated the respondent's preference for engaging with information tactilely.

- The subject organization of the library facilitates finding useful material that I may not have come across when searching online (9).
- I pay more attention when I hold the actual book in my hands rather than paging through a virtual representation of it (9).

These comments about the physical library's browsability bring to mind the value of "serendipitous browsing" mentioned by so many of the faculty study occupants whom we spoke with during our first project.

Comprehensiveness—physical library (57 responses; 14.6 percent of total). This theme expressed the idea that the physical library's collection is more comprehensive, more current, or more permanent than the electronic collections.

- When I am in the library, I have more access to information—not every journal or book can be obtained electronically. (9)
- The most important role of the library is to deposit materials, especially professional journals, without gaps in subscription—and this cannot be guaranteed by Web access. (9)

Conduciveness to scholarship—physical library (60 responses; 15.4 percent of total). Statements in this theme expressed the sentiment that the physical library is conducive to doing scholarly work. These responses touched on many ideas that recalled the interviews with the ten faculty study holders in our first project, such as the library's "role" as a place for concentration and focused work, the library's silence and sense of "sanctuary," and the notion of truly engaging in one's work by "dialoging" with the books' authors—communicating across the ages, as it were.

- I appreciate the level of concentration I am able to achieve in that setting. (9)
- I dialogue with the authors by photocopying and making margin notes (no, I do not write in the books!). (9)

To analyze the qualitative responses, we divided respondents into two age groups and two scholarly age groups. In the discussion that follows, "older scholars" refers to those who were born before 1970 or received their last degree before 1990, and "younger scholars" refers to those who were born in 1970 or later or received their last degree in 1990 or later. Although it might seem odd to think of a 42-year-old (born in 1963) who received a Ph.D. in 1989 as an "older" person, this distinction roughly identifies as "older" those who "came of scholarly age" before the advent of electronic resources; those who came of scholarly age during the electronic age are thus "younger." Of course, some respondents belong to the older "age" group but the younger "scholarly age" group: many people born before 1970 received their terminal degrees in 1990 or later.

CONVENIENCE—ELECTRONIC RESOURCES

I actually prefer when OU Library doesn't own something because then I can request it electronically [via Interlibrary Loan] and store it on my laptop and have it with me everywhere I go. [Anonymous survey respondent]

It was no surprise that the convenience of electronic resources was the most prevalent theme emerging from our respondents' qualitative statements and that younger scholars were more likely to make statements that fell into this theme. When analyzed by age, our results showed that younger scholars were 31 percent more likely than older scholars to make statements in this theme. When analyzed by scholarly age, the difference was even more dramatic: younger scholars were 49 percent more likely than older scholars to comment on the convenience of electronic resources. These findings were unsurprising, given that the most recent degree-earners did their graduate work after the advent of electronic resources.

These results also reflected several of the quantitative findings. For instance, fewer younger respondents reported that they currently conduct research in the physical library space, indicating that younger people may rely more heavily than older people on electronic resources. Several other measures of physical library usage showed similar results: Younger respondents reported less browsing of new books, less use of periodicals, and less use of graduate study carrels. Moreover, the use of the physical library space for doing graduate work plunged sharply by age: Of the respondents born in the 1940s, 88 percent reported that, when they were in graduate school, they did some of their graduate research in the library, and 44 percent reported having written part or all of their dissertations in the library. These figures fell with successively younger groups, and, for the youngest group, these figures were 20 and 10 percent, respectively. This trend was similar, but not as dramatic, when respondents were grouped by graduation year. It seems safe to conclude that younger scholars value the convenience of electronic resources a great deal more than older scholars do.

However, this is not the end of the story by any means. The other three major themes, which made up half of all responses (and two-thirds of responses in the "major themes"), all centered on the value of the physical library, not the electronic resources. And, most interestingly, for one theme, it was the younger scholars who were the most passionate supporters of "library as place."

On a related note, Palmer and Sandler found that the convenience of electronic access was important to scholars, but they also found a preference for printed materials in some cases. One sociologist who participated in their study said, "If it's a journal article . . . I don't care. If it's a book, I prefer it in print form. . . . I like the texture of books. I like the being of books. I like the 'bookness' of books" (27). This finding, too, is echoed in the other major themes that emerge from our study of scholars' use of library space, as discussed below.

BROWSABILITY—PHYSICAL LIBRARY

Once I acquire a sense of where materials pertinent to my topic may be located, I go the library and *look* at them. I may sit down on the floor and browse through the table of contents of several years worth of a particular journal looking for articles that may touch on a topic yet that didn't show up in a keyword search because I didn't think of just the right keyword. [Anonymous survey respondent]

Nearly one-fifth of the qualitative responses mentioned the physical library's browsability (Antell and Engel). This belies the common perception among librarians that library users prefer to access everything electronically and do not appreciate the ingenious work librarians have done to organize physical collections. But the value of browsability to a scholar does appear to be related to his or her age and scholarly age.

When grouped by age, older respondents were 49 percent more likely than younger respondents to mention the physical library's browsability. When grouped by scholarly age, this figure was 42 percent.

Only a few survey questions specifically addressed browsing behavior, but the answers to these questions supported this age trend. For instance, the percentage of respondents who reported browsing new books declined from 43 percent of those born in the 1940s to 23 percent of those born in the 1980s. When viewed by scholarly age, this trend was similar but less marked. Periodicals use, which sometimes is an example of "browsing" behavior, showed a similar decline with age and scholarly age, by 68 percent and 36 percent respectively.

Andrew Abbott, a faculty member at the University of Chicago, echoes these findings about the value of browsing to scholars. "There's a lot of serendipity, and randomness, in research—the chance encounter. Stumbling across a book or idea inadvertently is held as sacred by dedicated library researchers" (Schonwald).

COMPREHENSIVENESS—PHYSICAL LIBRARY

Simple electronic access, while it has definitely enhanced the research process, does *not* suffice for complete and thorough research. [Anonymous survey respondent]

Statements in the "comprehensiveness—physical library" theme indicated that the physical library's resources were more comprehensive than the electronic collections. We were heartened to learn that a significant number of our patrons recognized this, because the spate of recent "news" articles such as Carlson's "The Deserted Library" made it seem as though our patrons no longer had any use for materials that they cannot access electronically. Clearly, the many responses in this theme indicated otherwise:

Using electronic resources is helpful but limited. [Anonymous survey respondent]

Not everything is available electronically. . . . Also, printed versions contain more information, and sometimes it is absolutely necessary to see a printed graph or a photo or a map. [Anonymous survey respondent]

Remote access often limits you to newer publications. [Anonymous survey respondent]

However, striking age differences emerged in respondents' comments about the physical library's comprehensiveness. In fact, older people (by both age and scholarly age) were twice as likely as younger people to make comments that fell into this theme, suggesting that our younger patrons might be far less aware than older patrons of the fact that not everything is available online.

Responses to the survey questions addressing materials usage supported this age trend to some extent. When respondents were grouped by age, fewer younger people than older people reported checking books out of the library, using microforms, using library materials, placing materials on reserve, browsing new books, and using periodicals. However, the results for these survey questions showed no apparent age trend when respondents were grouped by scholarly age.

CONDUCIVENESS TO SCHOLARSHIP—PHYSICAL LIBRARY

Although electronic databases and searches have *greatly* improved over the last few years, and strongly increase my research efficiency, there is still no substitute for spending time in the building. [Anonymous survey respondent]

I like the solitude and quiet of the library, one of the few places in this busy, fast-paced world where such a place can be found.... There should always be libraries. Where else can you get that musty book smell? [Anonymous survey respondent]

This theme is where our results really got interesting. "Conduciveness to scholarship" was different from the other themes because it revealed how scholars used library space *independently of library resources.* Unlike comments in the other three major themes, "conduciveness to scholarship" comments were not about materials. In fact, some of these comments patently asserted that there is more to libraries than materials:

Even if I could get all my research materials electronically and of good quality, I would still want to go to the library to work and read. [Anonymous survey respondent]

Instead, comments in this theme mentioned intangibles such as the state of mind, level of concentration, or degree of productivity stimulated by the library's physical environment:

The library is an important place not only for the obvious functions, but also as a sanctuary of solitude. [Anonymous survey respondent]

The library engenders "academic" and investigation attitudes that I cannot sustain remotely. [Anonymous survey respondent]

The solitude of the library does enable more sustained concentration. [Anonymous survey respondent]

These comments sounded almost as though our survey respondents had read and quoted our first paper on faculty study occupants. The emphasis on solitude, "academic attitude," and sustained concentration hearkened back to the "oasis of solitude" and "academic upbringing" themes that arose in our interviews with faculty study holders. As we noted in our first paper,

The faculty space is an oasis of solitude, a place for sustained, uninterrupted thinking or reading, and a quiet place for reflection.... Faculty members' "academic upbringing" has habituated them to using the library as the primary place for doing research. Going to the library is a ritual that puts them in the right frame of mind to do serious work. (Engel and Antell 12)

Contrary to all expectations, we found that *younger* scholars, by both age and scholarly age, were far more likely than older scholars to comment on the physical library's conduciveness to scholarship (Antell and Engel). When grouped by age, younger respondents were 87 percent more likely than older respondents to mention the physical library's conduciveness to scholarship. When grouped by scholarly age, younger respondents were 57 percent more likely to make comments in this theme. Because the "conduciveness to scholarship" theme reflects the value of "place" rather than the value of library materials, these results reveal a surprising trend: The value of "library as place" appears to be significantly greater among younger library users.

This finding is corroborated by the results of the survey questions that reflected on the "conduciveness to scholarship" theme. The survey did not ask explicitly, "Do you value the physical library's conduciveness to scholarship"—naturally, we could not formulate this question because we did not know before conducting the survey that this theme would emerge. But the survey did ask several questions about library activities that are suggestive of the library's role as a place that is conducive to scholarship. According to the survey results, younger scholars (by both age and scholarly age) are more likely than older scholars to do the following:

- work at a library table
- spend time in contemplation at the library
- take a briefcase or backpack to the library
- take personal books or library books to the library
- take food or drink to the library
- make frequent library visits (three times per month or more)
- make long library visits (one hour or more)
- use a study carrel
- use group study rooms
- make "space-only visits" to the library (i.e., visit the library for reasons other than using library materials or technology)

The prevalence of "settling in" behaviors among younger people was notable. Taking books to the library, taking food and drink, and using group study rooms all indicated some level of settling in to work for extended periods of time. Moreover, they all were behaviors that were consistent with what we termed the "space-only visit," in which a library user visits the library for reasons other than using library materials or technology—often for intangible reasons, as one respondent noted: "I appreciate the level of concentration I am able to achieve" [at the library].

Intangibles such as "academic attitude" and "increased concentration" cannot be measured in the same way that we can measure the number of volumes in a library collection or the percentage of journal subscriptions that are available online. But they can have very real results, such as the "best five paragraphs of my book" claimed by one faculty study occupant in our first project (Engel and Antell 12).

CONCLUSIONS: *BUFFY THE VAMPIRE SLAYER* VS. "MY MOST PRODUCTIVE INTELLECTUAL SELF"

What did we learn from our inquiries into faculty use of library space? Our data contained an almost overwhelming amount of information, but the most noteworthy conclusions are as follows.

- Faculty study holders—the scholars who deliberately seek out library spaces of their own— are passionate believers in the power of place. They appreciate the faculty study's proximity to library materials, but more than that, they value the library as a place to do sustained, uninterrupted intellectual work.

- The convenience of electronic resources is the single most common response given by scholars when they are asked about the differences between using the physical library and the library's electronic resources. This response is significantly more common among younger scholars than older scholars, indicating younger scholars' preference for electronic materials.
- The physical library's browsability and comprehensiveness, two qualities that reflect the value of library *materials*, are important to scholars, and they appear to be more important to older scholars than to younger scholars.
- The physical library's "conduciveness to scholarship," a quality that is linked to the value of library space *independent of library materials*, is important to scholars. Most surprisingly, "conduciveness to scholarship" is vastly more important to younger scholars than older scholars.

Taken together, these conclusions draw a picture of faculty library use that contradicts the popular notion of the "deserted library." Faculty members appreciate the convenience of electronic resources, but they do not think "everything is available online." They understand that "serendipitous browsing" of the physical collection is a valuable search strategy that cannot easily be replicated online. They are aware that the physical library has been organized by professional librarians for maximum access to information. They recognize that different tools are appropriate for different tasks—targeted electronic searching for a specific piece of information is not necessarily the best way to approach a comprehensive search. They like to have professional help available to them when needed. However, where library materials are concerned, scholars are somewhat segregated by age: younger scholars are more likely to value the electronic resources, and older scholars are more likely to value the physical library's materials. This provides some evidence for our hypothesis that "library as place" is less important to younger scholars, those who "came of scholarly age" in the Internet age.

But when we left the realm of materials, we found evidence that tells a contrasting story. Scholars also have strong feelings about the value of the physical library as place quite apart from its materials and technology. In the physical library's space, scholars find the solitude and sanctuary necessary for the life of the mind to flourish. And, most unexpectedly, *younger* scholars are by far *more* likely than older scholars to value this intangible aspect of the physical library as place. One faculty member, who received his doctorate in 1998 and thus is part of the "younger" scholarly age group, eloquently describes the library's "conduciveness to scholarship":

The library is a place to work, think, and be an intellectual. . . . Being in the library puts me in "library mode"—it's a completely different experience physically and psychologically. When I am in the library, I am my most productive intellectual self. [Anonymous survey respondent]

Or, put a slightly different way by a doctoral student born in the 1970s,

A library has an atmosphere conducive to studying, whereas accessing it through the Internet has an atmosphere conducive to browsing the Internet, which can lead to looking up the news, playing some games, or maybe participating in an online interactive *Buffy the Vampire Slayer* fan fiction story. [Anonymous survey respondent]

So what does this mean for the future of academic library as place? It may be too early to tell, but we wonder whether younger scholars are in fact "deserting" the physical library's *materials* but at the same time reclaiming library *space* as a sanctuary for the "encapsulating solitude" that one survey respondent claimed enabled her to do sustained intellectual work:

Comfortable chairs and couches, elegantly bound volumes, and encapsulating solitude are a necessary escape. . . . Nothing can compare to the sensation of walking into a building and being surrounded by the physical sensation of knowledge: seeing books, feeling each page as it turns, smelling the aging paper and ink, and so forth. For me, the physical space of a library creates an environment that has been specifically designed to give a physical and spiritual sensation of knowledge, past experiences, and hope for the future. Electronic resources, no matter how useful, cannot duplicate this experience. [Anonymous survey respondent]

Contrary to what one might expect, this respondent was born in the 1970s and had received her most recent academic degree in 2003—on every count, one of our younger participants. In our results, her description is just one of many testimonials about the physical library's contribution to the intellectual productivity of younger scholars. Perhaps it is precisely because younger scholars came of age in the Internet era that they so appreciate the physical surroundings of the library: because they have not had to use the library *materials* as intensely as previous generations of scholars, perhaps they have learned to seek out the library space to find the very qualities that the electronic experience lacks: a sense of sanctuary, an intellectual state of mind, a "spiritual sensation of knowledge," an "encapsulating solitude."

REFERENCES

Antell, Karen, and Debra Engel. "Conduciveness to Scholarship: The Essence of Academic Library as Place." Manuscript submitted September 2005.

Carlson, Scott. "The Deserted Library." *Chronicle of Higher Education* 48 (Nov. 16, 2001): A35.

Carlson, Scott (moderator), with Mary Reichel, and Deanna B. Marcum. "Are College Libraries Too Empty?" [transcript of online discussion]. November 15, 2001, 2:00 pm (EST). Retrieved 12 Oct. 2005 from http://chronicle.com/colloquylive/2001/11/empty/.

Crawford, Walt. *Being Analog: Creating Tomorrow's Libraries*. Chicago: American Library Association, 1999.

Engel, Debra, and Karen Antell. "The Life of the Mind: A Study of Faculty Spaces in Academic Libraries." *College and Research Libraries* 65 (January 2004): 8–20.

Palmer, Janet P., and Mark Sandler. "What Do Faculty Want?" *Library Journal* 1976 part Net Connect (Winter 2003): 26–28.

Schonwald, Josh. "University to Expand Library Collections to Prepare Next Generation of Scholars." *University of Chicago Chronicle* 24, no. 18 (June 9, 2005). Retrieved 12 October 2005 from http://chronicle.uchicago.edu/050609/library.shtml.

Spyers-Duran, Peter. "Faculty Studies: A Survey of Their Use in Selected Libraries." *College and Research Libraries*. 29 (January 1968): 55–61.

10

Setting the Stage for Undergraduates' Information Behaviors: Faculty and Librarians' Perspectives on Academic Space[1]

Lisa M. Given

Associate Professor, School of Library and Information Studies, University of Alberta, Edmonton, Alberta, Canada

INTRODUCTION—ACADEMIC SPACE AND UNDERGRADUATES' INFORMATION BEHAVIORS

Information behavior research explores the totality of human experience relating to the ways that individuals actively (or unintentionally) seek, use, ignore, or make sense of information, in a range of contexts and for many purposes.[2] University students engage in numerous academic information behaviors, from asking questions of professors to borrowing books, and they encounter a range of campus spaces (from professors' offices to the campus library) in completing their work. As Case (2002) notes, students are "one of the most widely studied [social] roles of all . . . a category that virtually everyone inhabits at some point during their lives" (269), and yet, little attention has been paid to the impact of physical space on students' academic achievements and failures. In education, countless studies explore undergraduate students' academic progress and take, as their focus, students' personal reflections[3]; in library and information studies (LIS) many researchers have explored students' experiences, from preschool through graduate life.[4] In these studies (and in library practice), a student's desire to succeed in his/her academic work guides that student's informational activities. Although Vakkari and Serola (2002), Jacobson and Fusani (1992), and others have explored the notion of relevance as it relates to successful online searching, and while such authors as McInnis and Symes (1991) examine the creation of appropriate bibliographies as one element of student success, no mention is made of the physical spaces (e.g., libraries, classrooms) in which these activities occur, let alone the social context that informs pedagogical decisions about the ways that physical spaces shape students' academic experiences.

Indeed, the university campus is filled with spaces where students read, study, listen to lectures, and relax outside of class time. The campus pub, the students union building, the academic library, all are spaces where students engage in a range of informing activities, from reading course texts to chatting with professors. Although some research explores the nature and function of the academic library,[5] and while popular culture is filled with images of the librarian as the "shushing" keeper of quiet library space, little is actually known about whether these environments are best suited to students' academic activities—or even if they are ideal given individual students' learning preferences. A number of recent studies do provide insight into university students' information behaviors. Ethelene Whitmire (2002, 2003, 2004), for example, has explored cultural, epistemological, and disciplinary differences in the ways that students' seek information for their academic work. Lisa M. Given (2002b) has examined the overlap between students' academic and everyday information needs and behaviors. Jannica Heinström (2005) has examined the ways that personality traits and study strategies can affect students' information behaviors. Other authors, such as Wendy Holliday and Qin Li (2004), have also explored the "millennial generation" of students, those who come to university with information strategies shaped by their comfort with new technologies. However, none of these projects examine the role of physical space in shaping students' informational activities. As new technologies, such as wireless computer access, alter the physical layout—and users' expectations—of libraries and library services,[6] research that examines the impact of physical space fills an important gap in our understanding of the complex and holistic nature of individuals' information behaviors.

THE CAMPUS AS AN INFORMING SPACE—A HOLISTIC APPROACH TO RESEARCH

The call for researchers to apply holistic approaches in examining individuals' experiences within their physical environments is echoed by a number of scholars in LIS and other disciplines. Christopher Lueg (2001) noted the lack of research in LIS addressing individuals' physical interactions with their environments and the implications for information behaviors, and highlights the work of researchers in artificial intelligence who have recently examined individuals' actions as situated in their environments.[7] Over the past few years there has been a marked increase in the number of studies that have examined individuals' activities in the space of the public library,[8] including the democratizing nature of this particular public space,[9] and the implications for broader urban planning.[10] Indeed, research in psychology, anthropology, and urban studies that explores person–environment interaction provides useful perspectives for LIS researchers; investigations of such topics as personal privacy, way finding, and life satisfaction offer insight into the ways that individuals use—or avoid—particular social spaces.[11]

There is also a great deal of research and commentary that explores the design of pedagogical spaces and implications for student learning, with results that are instructive for those examining (and designing) library space. Phillip D. Long and Stephen C. Ehrmann (2005), for example, explore the inadequacies of traditional classroom spaces in today's technologically driven world, while Chris Johnson and Cyprien Lomas (2005) discuss the connections between learning theory and the effective design of campus spaces. This work comes on the heels of decades of debate in education about the role of the physical classroom in the learning experiences of students. Marita Moll (1997), for example, has explored the corporatization of classrooms as they connect to the Internet (and at the expense of the students themselves). Paul Light and Agnes Blaye (1991) have examined the implications of computer-based instruction on student communication and peer interaction, as compared to traditional classroom experiences. In the higher education context, David Noble (2002) has critiqued the commodification of education as demonstrated in the rise of online "diploma mills," that pose real threats to professors' intellectual property rights and the quality of education students receive in traditional learning environments.

The field of library and information studies, however, has yet to develop a similar baseline for examining undergraduates' information behaviors within the broader context of the university campus. Although the traditional university campus may not suit today's technologies, or advances in pedagogical theory, redesign of existing space is moving forward to accommodate computer labs, wired classrooms, and other advances in the absence of research on students' academic information behaviors within these physical spaces. Research that examines the campus itself (including the academic library) in the context of individuals' information behaviors is vital for expanding our understanding of the holistic nature of students' academic experiences, and for designing campus spaces that fit students' pedagogical and information needs.

PURPOSE OF THE STUDY, METHODS, AND DATA COLLECTION

This article reports results from the first phase of a study that examines undergraduates' information behaviors, with a focus on the university as an information space. The purpose of the full study is to examine students' informational activities in the context of institutional vs. personal notions of academic success, with a particular focus on the ways that physical spaces (such as a bench on the campus grounds or a desk on the third floor of the library) facilitate or hinder students' academic achievements. The study examines a single Canadian university with an undergraduate population of approximately 28,000 students. The university is a doctoral-research intensive institution, with undergraduate and graduate programs offered across the spectrum of the arts and humanities, social sciences, sciences, health science and professional disciplines (e.g., law). The library system houses one of the major research collections in Canada, as well as a diverse range of reference and other information services; there are ten libraries in buildings across campus, representing particular disciplinary specialties.

Undergraduates' perceptions of academic success are informed by institutional markers of success (as reified by professors, librarians, and other university stakeholders), as well as their own personal views of what it means to succeed. In addition, both formal and informal sources of information (e.g., library materials, peer-to-peer information sharing, lectures) shape students' personal experiences and their achievements in university. It is important, then, to examine all of these contextual elements to understand students' academic information behaviors and the ways that they use various spaces to support their work. The influence of physical and social spaces (such as coffee shops, library reading rooms, and computer labs) on undergraduates' information behaviors is a central point of investigation in this research. The results of the study offer direction to librarians and university administrators in the design of information services (and spaces) that best meet students' diverse needs, and extend current approaches to research design by considering individuals' experiences in the evaluation of information contexts.

The results reported here examine institutional markers of academic success, with a particular focus on the design of space that facilitates or hinders undergraduates' academic achievements. This article reports findings from in-depth qualitative interviews conducted in Autumn 2003 (each lasting approximately 1 hour), with twenty-one university faculty members and librarians. Participants were recruited through campus listservs and Web sites, and ads in university newspapers. Interviewees were selected using maximum-variation sampling to achieve a broad representation of age, gender, academic discipline, position, and years of service as a university employee. The interview schedule was semistructured and examined the interviewees' perceptions of academic success, undergraduate life, information resources and facilities, and the design and availability of campus spaces. The data were analyzed using a grounded theory approach, where themes and patterns are noted and categorized as they emerge from the data. These emergent themes were then coded in *NVivo*, a software program used for managing qualitative data and analysis. In addition to providing a glimpse of the institutional context surrounding undergraduates' lives, these interviews also provide insight into the state of the modern university campus, and its role in fostering those information behaviors that enable students to succeed.

FINDINGS AND DISCUSSION

Academic Information Behaviors—the Need for Welcoming Spaces

University faculty and academic librarians play integral roles in students' academic lives. Faculty make curricular decisions, set and grade assignments, involve students in research projects, and act as inspirational beacons for those studying in their chosen disciplines. Students' information behaviors are necessarily grounded in the activities that evolve in the classroom; they read, discuss, reflect, write, and wonder in response to the academic stimuli around them. Librarians, in turn, provide advice, instruction, access to resources, and other supports so that students can complete their work to the best of their abilities. What role, then, does the physical space on campus—the design of classrooms, the layout of computer labs, the lighting in the library stacks—play in guiding students in their academic pursuits?

The faculty members and librarians interviewed in this study agreed, unequivocally, on the importance of having welcoming spaces on campus to facilitate students' information behaviors. For students to actively seek information—in the library, in computer labs, or from their professors—they must want to be on campus and spend time in spaces designed to support academic work. "Comfortable" spaces filled with "bright, natural light" were the most common descriptions of welcoming spaces. Soft chairs, spacious tables, ergonomic workstations, clean surfaces, and aesthetic details (e.g., paintings) were outlined by faculty and librarians as being conducive to on-campus study. Some spaces on campus were identified as ideal, to the point that members of the broader community (e.g., high school students) were known to frequent these spaces. As one librarian, Lana, notes:

Students sleep in the Business Library because there are some more comfortable chairs there. And I know that the Health Science Library gets people studying there that aren't in Health Sciences. They just like the space. It's open and light.

More commonly, however, campus spaces were described for those welcoming elements that were lacking, especially as a result of years of funding cuts. Ripped chair

Figure 10.1 A comfortable and welcoming space? The breezeway leading from the campus library to the "mall" student residence that houses shops and restaurants; during the academic year, many students eat, read, talk, and sleep on the concrete benches and risers along this walkway.

cushions, unlit hallways, unclean floors, and computers in need of repair, were commonly cited as evidence that the institution was failing in its attempts to provide welcoming spaces for students. For Lana, the inability to manipulate older spaces and furnishings to suit current information needs (especially those related to computers), was closely linked to issues of funding—and something that she viewed as dividing the campus along funding, as well as disciplinary, lines. As a librarian in the humanities and social sciences library, she commented on the relative wealth of the health sciences or science and technology libraries, and compared these to the "making do" approach employed in her own library:

Things have changed so much since these buildings were built and we accommodate [students' needs] as best we can. But . . . having a nice big table to spread out on, but also having a hole in it to have a computer, to sit there . . . we just don't have things like that. Or ergonomic chairs to sit at computers . . . we just don't have them.

Madeleine, another librarian in the humanities and social sciences library involved in information literacy programming for undergraduates, noted the inadequacy of the library labs in providing welcoming environments for undergraduates (see Figure 10.1):

Physical comfort, air control, light control . . . if those are not adequate, not good, then it can really detract from learning. You know, if you have a lab where people are sitting there shivering . . . those kinds of things can be really problematic. A lot of our labs don't have good sight-lines from certain areas in the room. And the students need more space. They're crowded in there if they're trying to work with any kinds of materials that are not online. Our availability to print in the labs is problematic. And [we need proctors], so that somebody is there when the print breaks down, when the machines are not functioning. There's just such heavy, heavy demand that there are often lineups and there's often machines that are out of order. That's an ongoing process, to try to keep things up to date and properly functioning.

Conversation and Collaboration—the Need for Flexible, Social Spaces

When students decide to use a campus space, be it the library, a computer lab, or a common area in the students' union building, faculty and librarians also noted that the flexibility of that space was a vital component to students' informational activities and learning processes. Classrooms were frequently mentioned as lacking the flexibility that students (and instructors) needed; as Jason notes "The classroom spaces are inflexible. . . . The rigidity of tiny little desks all in rank and file is not entirely conducive to creative work." For Alan, the prevalence of group work as a pedagogical strategy in the drama department was a classroom challenge for many students, who had to seek out other locales to engage in their academic work:

A lot of what the students do . . . is group work. They can't all work in the classroom. So immediately they go outside the classroom, down the hall, around the corner and to the nook and cranny somewhere. So our building is always filled with pockets of students playing these scenes at full bore in the hallway.

Students' willingness to manipulate space—to move the desks in a classroom, pull many chairs up to one computer station, or read with their feet up on library tables—was one of the reactions to inflexible space most commonly noted by the interviewees. As Alan says,

Student spaces need to offer the opportunity to move chairs around, move seats around. Rearrange the space, so that students can be together in bigger groups or smaller groups or pull a chair over or reconfigure something. If you have large pieces of furniture that are like three-seater couches and they're nailed to the floor and they're all nailed down and you can't move any . . . those are terrible spaces.

Despite the desire for flexible spaces, and the inadequacy of existing spaces to suit students' needs (as evidenced by their willingness to manipulate spaces to suit those needs), faculty and librarians contextualized this discussion by mentioning the difficulties involved in long-term space planning. As administrators and campus decision makers, both groups noted the challenge they faced—to make purchasing and design decisions today that would serve student populations for years to come. Many interviewees discussed the problems inherent in adapting buildings, classrooms, and libraries built decades earlier to suit the needs of a wired world. As Jason, a professor in history, notes,

Students, like everybody else, need a whole array of different spaces for different functions. . . . There is a whole hierarchy of functional spaces and one of the critical requirements . . . for pedagogical success, is that you have a variety of [spaces] easily available to you in nonintimidating fashion that can be relied upon to be there when you need them—so, quiet spaces, not-so-quiet, quite noisy and bustling spaces, places to eat and drink, and hustle and bustle, and places that are private places that are semi-public, and public.

Many faculty members believe that the academic libraries on campus serve dual purposes—fulfilling traditional roles of providing undergraduates with access to knowledge and quiet, reflective places to study, but also offering students a social space for collaboration, information sharing, or down-time with peers:

I think that we have a very heavy debt as an institution to the libraries as places that have provided a great deal of student space. I don't think it's well understood in the university community as a whole how library space has been sacrificed to providing students study and activity space. Many libraries do not do that institutional function. (Jason)

The librarians interviewed in this study also remarked on the importance of social space on campus. Madeleine, for example, notes,

I have to admit, to my surprise, you know, the library space on campus is still really important. So much can be done at home, but . . . part of being a student is being social and meeting other people and being around your friends. So I think the library as a space for undergraduate students is still really important.

For others, the social function of such gathering places went beyond allowing students to feel socially connected, but that such spaces were at the heart of the learning process. Ivan explains it this way:

The more social space [students] have, the better our university would be . . . because it does seem to me that they rely on conversations with their friends as a big part of the learning process. "Let's go meet at the students union. Let's go meet somewhere." And it's pretty tough to do that because there's not a lot of spaces to do that . . . but I walked up to the library today and I looked in all these big [reading] rooms, and they're pretty empty. And I think it's because they're too quiet. Students don't study when it's quiet. Students study with the TV on and their headsets on . . . and so it's too quiet [in the library], and they don't want to be there. But you see them in the students union and they're studying and there's an uproar around them and they're totally comfortable with that. And some people want it totally quiet when they study.

Noisy versus Quiet Spaces—Library Space and Dynamic Information Behaviors

The need for both noisy and quiet spaces was one of the most prevalent themes that emerged from the interviews. Both faculty and librarians identified the need for spaces that could accommodate noisy as well as quiet activities depending on students' academic activities and information needs. The belief that the library had not yet moved beyond its traditional role as a quiet space, and the challenges this raised for librarians in their attempts to serve students' varied needs, was discussed at length in the interviews. Alan (a drama professor) described being pleasantly surprised to find, on the day of the interview, that new signs had appeared in the humanities and social sciences library:

I noticed in the library today, a sign that says something like "this is a conversational kind of space . . . you should expect conversation here." And I think that's a good sign. You know, this is not like just "shhh," you know?

Many students also perceived the library as a space reserved for "high achievers," rather than a welcoming place designed to meet all students' academic needs. Ivan, a physical education instructor, notes,

There's also a certain lack of nerdy-ness by studying in a social place as opposed to studying in the library, right? When you go to the library to study it would mean you were one of those students who's between 90 and 100%, a keener. If you're a keener you go to the library. The other people are studying . . . but they don't study in the library.

This shift in the perceived culture of the library—from a quiet, shushing enclave reserved for "keeners" to one that is flexible enough to accommodate all students' needs was another theme raised by the librarians in this study. In part, their perspectives were informed by a recent survey of undergraduates where many students raised the issue of noise.

There is a group [of students] who want absolutely quiet space with no sound at all, and there is a group who want more group study space [to] do group projects and that kind of thing, or just where they can talk without someone telling them to "shush." And then . . . there are people who fall into both groups depending on what their mood is or depending on what their assignment is. . . . And it would be nice to be able to provide more of each. I think the first one, "Absolutely quiet, no talking," is a bit of an unrealistic demand. A library is a public space and traditionally they are places for research, so places for quiet. But when you have a whole bunch of computers around that go "bleep" every time they turn on, and librarians that have to show people how to use things . . . there's going to be noise. (Lana)

Madeleine reiterated this finding from the survey:

We certainly heard in the surveys that we've done of undergraduate students that they have a variety of different space needs. And some of them really want and need absolute silent space. They want quiet places where they will not be bothered by other people talking and rattling things and even using keyboards. There's also a huge demand that we're not able to meet, for group study space. People do have to work on projects as groups and need places where they can go and feel like they're not interrupting people or being glared at.

For many of the interviewees, these issues were not only concerned with spatial logistics, but also closely related to issues of hierarchy and power in the university. Undergraduates, typically, do not have spaces to call their own on campus. Although graduate students may have shared or single offices, and while librarians and faculty typically have their own personal spaces to conduct their work, undergraduates must typically roam campus between classes to find spaces that suit their needs when they want to study or locate information. Even so, many undergraduates do try to claim the spaces they inhabit, if only for a short time:

Some people try to stake out a spot for themselves [in the library]. I see people in the reference area, where there's a bunch of tables along the window wall, behind the stacks. And a lot of people seem to like to work over there. It's quieter and you can see outside, and there are nice tables . . . but they certainly aren't private—they're big tables with multiple chairs at them. And we don't encourage people to leave their things because there are thefts. So it is hard to come in and set up your things, go to class, come back and study . . . the students can't do that. I mean, they might do that, but they do it at risk of losing their things. (Lana)

Other librarians in this study reinforced this concern—a lack of private space on campus where undergraduates could study. And, faculty members also raised this as a concern related to academic achievement and students' abilities to engage in educational and informational activities. For Jason, the separation of students from the heart of campus—what he saw as an active segregation of undergraduate activities to the students' union building—sent the wrong message about how the institution values its students.

In his opinion, the academic library can serve an integral role in valuing students, and allowing them to have some ownership over other campus spaces:

I don't think . . . that it's at all adequate that student social and study space be provided principally in a students union. This sends out a lot of bad messages about the institution and the nature of the community . . . that it's us against them; that the student services are segregated activities inside an institution that is not as welcoming or as inclusive as one would hope for because it doesn't integrate student life spaces into the spaces of the other functions of the institution. I think that does occur here, [with this library] . . . I think it's useful that [student study space] is integrated. It makes the library much more familiar and comfortable, as an institution, for students.

THE ACADEMIC LIBRARY—A SPACE FOR THE TWENTY-FIRST CENTURY

How, then, can the modern academic library—and other campus spaces—evolve to suit undergraduates' academic information behaviors? How can the library enhance its role as a center for integrated activity on the university campus? If librarians and scholars were to take William H. Wisner's (2000) words into account, the answers to these questions might reasonably be that it cannot—that the academic library is doomed. In his exploration of the postmodern library, Wisner describes the interminable silence of the computer lab, where students engage with computers but not with one another (105). He paints a dire picture of the virtual library, where the loss of the physical library building will diminish cities, and democracy (108). If the university is a city unto itself, Wisner's vision is anything but positive. And yet, students continue to flock to these institutions in their pursuit for higher learning. What role can the physical library play in these students' academic careers?

There is no question that digital resources, and the rise of multimedia, will continue to shape the nature of information resources and the libraries that bring these resources to the fore. At the same time, traditional classroom structures (marked by lectures and physical textbooks) will continue to give way to collaborative educational models. Academic libraries must shift to reflect these changes, or risk becoming as obsolete as Wisner fears. In a recent issue of *The Chronicle of Higher Education*, Scott Carlson explores just this question, and notes that as the academic library begins to evolve to integrate new technologies and new approaches to learning, it also becomes something of an academic community center on campus. This new, contemporary version of the academic library can serve as a collaborative learning environment in a far more dynamic way than its traditional form allowed. In this new space, the old (reference desks, stacks of books, study carrels) meets the new (cafés, group study rooms, multimedia), allowing the social and the academic to blend, and thereby enhancing student learning.

This new vision of the academic library, however, appears to be slow in coming to fruition. While public libraries have embraced food, drink, and conversation, as well as new technologies, and started redesigning to position themselves as centers of their communities in the last decade,[12] academic libraries have been slower to embrace change. In Canada at least, this can be partly attributed to the lack of capital funding projects on university campuses; although banks of computers and online portals have been added, redesigning existing library spaces is a more difficult enterprise given today's fiscal realities. And yet, where students' academic work requires change, redesign must certainly follow. Students can and will shift the look and feel of existing spaces to reflect their needs (by talking in quiet spaces, or moving chairs to meet with groups), or they will simply go elsewhere on (or off) campus. The librarians in this study, for example, were very mindful of students' desire for change, and mentioned the wireless network (still in its test phase on campus) as one way to empower students, and give them more freedom to mold existing spaces to suit their needs:

Now, with the wireless network [available in the library], I think that the students are going to start redefining things themselves. I can picture groups of them all sitting in a circle on each floor with a laptop or sharing laptops because they can do their work right there. . . . I was talking with [some librarians] the other day and we were thinking we should be getting some beanbag chairs because the wireless network is going to change the way it all works. So I'll just have to keep an eye on what the students do and what they ask for. (Lana)

By listening to students' academic and information needs, and designing spaces to meet those needs, librarians and campus administrators can ensure that the academic library remains at the heart of university. Traditional library spaces now include a range of new technologies and provide remote access to online resources, but these are only the first steps. Academic libraries must also accommodate change in educational theory and practice, and reflect the ways that students interact with information resources, with instructors, and with their peers.

CONCLUSION

A desire for flexible information spaces that support a range of social activities, and allow noise and movement at appropriate times, is interesting—particularly given the fact that computer lab spaces are ubiquitous, yet are frequently designed with restrictions: a prohibition on food and drink to protect the equipment and materials; a single-user design with few spaces that support group interaction, and actively discourage conversation; a single-activity design, where if students leave their computer station to browse the stacks they risk losing their chair to another student. Could wireless computer access, then, allow universities to provide flexible spaces without sacrificing access to computerized support materials? Could librarians look to students (many of whom are already moving chairs or abandoning the physical library entirely) for guidance on how best to redesign library space? As information resources continue to be made available in digital form—in some cases, only in digital form—the ability to free computer access from the confines of computer labs or tethered workstations can revolutionize students' information behaviors. And, as educational practice continues to embrace group work and other models of collaborative learning, classrooms, libraries, and other campus spaces will need to accommodate these changes. The desire for flexible, sometimes noisy, certainly comfortable spaces is central to academic achievement. Students will actively seek out new spaces, or manipulate existing plans, to support their needs; by using their information and academic behaviors as a guide, campus administrators and librarians can offer an activity space that matches students' information-related needs.

NOTES

1. This project is part of a three-year grant from the Social Sciences and Humanities Research Council of Canada. The author would like to thank Janice Banser for her work as a research assistant on this phase of the project.

2. See Case 2002; Wilson 2000.

3. See, for example, Blimling 1999; Schlosser & Sedlacek 2001.

4. See, for example, Mellon 1986; Leckie & Fullerton 1999; Given 2002a, 2002b; Kuhlthau 2004; Saumure & Given 2004.

5. See Atkins 1991; Morgan 1995; and Budd 1998.

6. See Seadle 2002.

7. See, for example, Clancey 1997; Clark 1997; and Pfeifer & Scheier 1999.

8. See Given & Leckie 2003; Leckie & Hopkins 2002; Shoham 2001.

9. See Alstad & Curry 2003; Johnson 1999.

10. See Given & Leckie 2003; Herskovitz, Metzer & Shoham 1991; and Shoham 1991.

11. See, for example, Schensul et al. 1999; Nasar & Preiser 1999; and Wapner et al 2000.

12. See Flynn 2004 for descriptions of recent projects.

REFERENCES

Alstad, Colleen, and Ann Curry. "Public Space, Public Discourse, and Public Libraries." *LIBRES* 13 (2003). Retrieved 14 Feb. 2004 from http://libres.curtin.edu.au/libres13n1/pub_space.htm.

Atkins, Stephen E. *The Academic Library in the American University*. Chicago: American Library Association, 1991.

Blimling, Gregory S. "A Meta-Analysis of the Influence of College Residence Halls on Academic Performance." *Journal of College Student Development* 40 (1999): 551–561.

Budd, John M. *The Academic Library: Its Context, Its Purpose, and Its Operation*. Englewood, CO: Libraries Unlimited, 1998.

Carlson, Scott. "Thoughtful Design Keeps New Libraries Relevant: Not Everything Students Want and Need Is Online." *The Chronicle of Higher Education* 52 (2005). Retrieved 30 Sept. 2005 from http://chronicle.com/weekly/v52/i06/06b00101.htm.

Case, Donald O. *Looking for Information: A Survey of Research on Information Seeking, Needs, and Behavior*. San Diego, CA: Academic Press, 2002.

Clancey, William J. *Situated Cognition: On Human Knowledge and Computer Representations*. New York: Cambridge University Press, 1997.

Clark, Andy. *Being There: Putting Brain, Body and World Together Again*. Cambridge, MA: MIT Press, 1997.

Flynn, Larry. "Libraries That Wow and Welcome." *Building Design and Construction* 45 (2004): 52–62.

Given, Lisa M. "Discursive Constructions in the University Context: Social Positioning Theory & Mature Undergraduates' Information Behaviours." *The New Review of Information Behaviour Research* 3 (2002a): 127–141.

———. "The Academic and the Everyday: Investigating the Overlap in Mature Undergraduates' Information-Seeking Behaviour." *Library & Information Science Research* 24 (2002b): 17–29.

Given, Lisa M., and Gloria J. Leckie. "'Sweeping' the Library: Mapping the Social Activity Space of the Public Library." *Library & Information Science Research* 25 (2003): 365–85.

Heinström, Jannica. "Fast Surfing, Broad Scanning and Deep Diving: The Influence of Personality and Study Approach on Students' Information-Seeking Behavior." *Journal of Documentation* 61 (2005): 228–47.

Herskovitz, Sara, Dalya Metzer, and Snunith Shoham. "Development of Spatial Structure of Libraries: The Case of Tel Aviv." *Libri* 41 (1991): 121–31.

Holliday, Wendy, and Qin Li. "Understanding the Millenials: Updating our Knowledge about Students." *Reference Services Review* 32 (2004): 356–66.

Jacobson, Thomas, and David Fusani. "Computer, System, and Subject Knowledge in Novice Searching of a Full-Text, Multifile Database." *Library & Information Science Research* 14 (1992): 97–106.

Johnson, Chris, and Cyprien Lomas. "Design of the Learning Space: Learning and Design Principles." *Educause Review* 40 (2005): 16–28.

Johnson, Debra W. "The Library as Place: Cultural Programming for Adults." *American Libraries* 30 (1999): 92.

Kuhlthau, Carol Collier. *Seeking Meaning: A Process Approach to Library and Information Services.* 2nd ed. Westport, CT: Libraries Unlimited, 2004.

Leckie, Gloria J., and Anne Fullerton. "Information Literacy in Science and Engineering Undergraduate Education: Faculty Attitudes and Pedagogical Practices." *College and Research Libraries* 60 (1999): 9–29.

Leckie, Gloria J., and Jeffrey Hopkins. "The Public Place of Central Libraries: Findings from Toronto and Vancouver." *Library Quarterly* 72 (2002): 326–72.

Light, Paul, and Agnes Blaye. "Computer-based Learning: The Social Dimensions." *Learning to Think.* Ed. Paul Light, Sue Sheldon, and Martin Woodhead. London: Routledge, 1991. 205–18.

Long, Phillip D., and Stephen C. Ehrmann. "Future of the Learning Space: Breaking Out of the Box." *Educause Review* 40 (2005): 42–56.

Lueg, Christopher. "On Problem Solving and Information Seeking." *The New Review of Information Behaviour Research* 3 (2002): 99–112.

McInnis, Raymond G., and Dal S. Symes. "Running Backwards from the Finish Line: A New Concept for Bibliographic Instruction." *Library Trends* 39 (1991): 223–37.

Mellon, Constance. "Library Anxiety: A Grounded Theory and Its Development." *College and Research Libraries* 47 (1986): 160–65.

Moll, Marita. "Canadian Classrooms on the Information Highway: Making the Connections." *Tech High: Globalization and the Future of Canadian Education.* Ed. Marita Moll. Ottawa: Fernwood Publishing & the Canadian Centre for Policy Alternatives, 1997: 33–64.

Morgan, Steve. *Performance Assessment in Academic Libraries.* London: Mansell, 1995.

Nasar, Jack L., and Wolfgang F. E. Preiser. *Directions in Person–Environment Research and Practice.* Aldershot, UK: Ashgate, 1999.

Noble, David. *Digital Diploma Mills: The Automation of Higher Education.* Toronto: Between the Lines, 2002.

Pfeifer, Rolf, and Christian Scheier. *Understanding Intelligence.* Cambridge, MA: MIT Press, 1999.

Saumure, Kristie, and Lisa M. Given. "Digitally Enhanced? An Examination of the Information Behaviours of Visually Impaired Postsecondary Students." *Canadian Journal of Information and Library Science* 28 (2004): 25–42.

Schensul, Jean J., Margaret D. LeCompte, Robert T. Trotter II, Ellen K. Cromley, and Merrill Singer. *Mapping Social Networks, Spatial Data, & Hidden Populations.* Walnut Creek, CA: Altamira Press, 1999.

Schlosser, Lewis Z., and William E. Sedlacek. "The Relationship between Undergraduate Students' Perceived Past Academic Success and Perceived Academic Self-Concept." *Journal of the Freshman Year Experience* 13 (2001): 95–105.

Seadle, Michael. "The Physical Dimension of Information Space." *Library Hi Tech* 20 (2002): 6–7.

Shoham, Snunith. "Users and Uses of the Public Library Reading Rooms." *Public Library Quarterly* 20 (2001): 33–48.

————. "The Ecology of Public Library Reference Rooms." *Public Library Quarterly* 11 (1991): 43–51.

Vakkari, Pertti., and Serola, Sami. "Utility of References Retrieved for Preparing a Research Proposal: A Longitudinal Case Study." *The New Review of Information Behaviour Research* 3 (2002): 37–52.

Wapner, Seymour., Demick, Jack, Yamamoto, Takiji and Minami, Hiroufmi. *Theoretical Perspectives in Environment-Behavior Research: Underlying Assumptions, Research Problems, and Methodologies.* New York: Kluwer Academic/Plenum Publishers, 2000.

Whitmire, Ethelene. "The Relationship Between Undergraduates' Epistemological Beliefs, Reflective Judgment, and Their Information-Seeking Behavior." *Information Processing and Management* 40 (2004): 97–111.

————. "Cultural Diversity and Undergraduates' Academic Library Use." *Journal of Academic Librarianship* 29 (2003): 148–61.

————. "Disciplinary Differences and Undergraduates' Information-Seeking Behavior." *Journal of the American Society for Information Science and Technology* 53 (2002): 631–38.

Wilson, T.D. "Human Information Behavior." *Informing Science: The International Journal of an Emerging Discipline* 3 (2000): 49–55.

Wisner, William H. *Whither the Postmodern Library? Libraries, Technology, and Education in the Information Age.* Jefferson, NC: McFarland & Company, 2000.

11

The Research Library as Place: On the Essential Importance of Collections of Books Shelved in Subject-Classified Arrangements

Thomas Mann

General Reference Librarian, Main Reading Room, Library of Congress, Washington, DC

INTRODUCTION

The concept of research libraries as physical bricks-and-mortar places is under siege within the library profession, due to too-facile assumptions about the "digital library paradigm." One of the premises is that a "transition" from print to electronic sources is taking place, coupled with the belief that collections of printed books no longer require the care and attention previously given them—this, in spite of the fact that more and more printed books are being published every year (Bowker 2004 512 and "U.S. Book"). The "evolution" to digital forms, it is asserted, is simply "inevitable"; and traditional libraries that fail to make "the transition" will be "left behind" as outdated "book museums." This chapter will challenge those assumptions and metaphors and address a variety of threats to the idea that research libraries need to maintain high-quality, onsite book collections controlled by traditional cataloging and classification.

The discussion will be confined to research libraries rather than special libraries or even most public libraries. Research facilities are distinguished by three criteria: the first has to do with the "80/20" rule, which points out that roughly 80 percent of library questions can usually be answered with 20 percent of library resources (Crawford 2001 72). Research libraries are those that have the particular responsibility to answer the 20 percent of questions that cannot be answered with a core 20 percent of basic resources—the questions that require both the 80 percent of less common materials that smaller libraries cannot afford to collect and their arrangement in a manner that allows efficient "recognition" access to their contents. Second, research libraries are distinguished by their responsibility to promote scholarship rather than simply information finding, that is, to convey knowledge and understanding, not just information. Doing the former requires the systematic collection of the formats—namely books—that facilitate rather than impede the extended reading of lengthy, connected narrative and expository texts. It also requires the intelligent creation of connections, groupings, linkages, and webs of subject relationships among books that simultaneously exclude wildernesses of irrelevant keyword similarities. Third, research libraries, unlike others, have particular responsibilities for the long-term preservation of knowledge and information records.

SHARED BOOK WAREHOUSE

One of the current threats to traditional research libraries-as-places having onsite book collections lies in the misuse of the idea of remote storage facilities. A prime example appeared in *The Chronicle of Higher Education* when Richard C. Atkinson (2003), the retired president of the University of California system, outlined a radical approach to research collections. Simply put, Atkinson regards the maintenance, in his words, of "many parallel, redundant research collections" as a practice that is "outmoded and no longer affordable." He specifically labels as "self-defeating" the Association of Research Libraries' index ranking of member libraries based on the number of volumes they hold. In his view, this traditional measure of library quality "provides no incentive for consortium members to forgo acquiring holdings that are otherwise available to the system as a whole" and it "rewards inefficiency and waste.... [I]n a networked digital age, excessive attention to the local management and ownership of physical materials impedes the responsible stewardship of the scholarly and cultural record." In other words, it makes no important difference to the quality of scholarship enabled by a research library if it lacks any particular book in its classified collections onsite, as long as it can ensure timely delivery of the book either from a shared remote storage facility, or through conventional interlibrary loan. The purpose of offsite storage, in this scheme, is not simply to house little-used material; it is to eliminate duplicate book purchases throughout an entire consortial system.

There are strong, objective reasons to oppose this position. Bluntly, this is a managerial view from 50,000 feet (a theme I will return to often) that fails to recognize the way scholars and students actually use research libraries at ground level. It is conspicuously innocent of any actual experience of the range of questions researchers ask that are not capable of being answered through the kind of system Atkinson proposes. (The digital library paradigm—to which Atkinson refers as the driving reason not to have collections—will be dealt with in more detail in the second half of this paper.) The problem can be best explained through concrete examples, of which I will offer two from my own experience, presented in some detail by necessity. As I hope it will become clear, these examples get to the heart of a very important issue in maintaining traditional libraries as places—not just with books onsite, but with their proper cataloging and classification as well. These two concerns cannot be separated in any consideration of libraries-as-places. One point that should be evident is, the harder reference questions are often precisely the ones that cannot be answered by either commonly available "core" resources or by computer searches; and yet these are the kinds of questions that research libraries still have the responsibility to deal with because smaller libraries cannot.

EXAMPLE ONE: LIGHTHOUSE LIBRARIES

I once had to answer a letter from a historian seeking information on traveling libraries that circulated among lighthouse keepers at the turn of the twentieth century.

These were wooden bookcases, each with a different selection of books that were rotated among the tenders in order to relieve the boredom and monotony of their isolated lives. I initially tried searching the computer catalog of the books at the Library of Congress, with no luck. Even after searching other databases on the mainframe system and several commercial indexes to journals and dissertations, I still found nothing—only occasionally the right words in the wrong contexts. I therefore decided to skim through the full texts of the books on lighthouses in the library's bookstacks. The major grouping for this topic is at VK1000–1025 ("Lighthouse service"); this area had, by a quick count, 438 volumes on twelve shelves. I scanned all of this material, quickly paging through all of the volumes.

I found fifteen books that had directly relevant sections—a paragraph here, a half page there, a column elsewhere—containing descriptions of the book collections, reminiscences about them, official reports, anecdotes, and so on. I also found another seven sources of tangential interest—on reading or studying done in lighthouses, but without mentioning the traveling libraries. I photocopied these too for the letter writer. The primary fifteen books contained a total of about 2,100 words on the traveling libraries, including a partial list of titles. Particularly noteworthy is the fact that, of the fifteen prime sources, not one mentioned the traveling libraries in its table of contents. Nine of them (60 percent) did not mention the libraries in their index either—or did not have an index to begin with. In other words, this information could not have been found even if the books' tables of contents and indexes had been entered into a database. Equally noteworthy is the fact that thirteen of the sources were twentieth-century publications— nine of them published after 1970—and thus still probably under copyright protection (a barrier to Google Print–type republication). No surrogate catalog records, no matter how detailed, get a researcher down to that level of individual pages and paragraphs—which is often required by the questions that scholars actually ask.

With the classification scheme's arrangement of multiple books on the same topic together, within one library's stacks, the needed information could indeed be found both systematically and comparatively easily. The word "comparatively" is used in relation to the Atkinson alternative: if, in contrast, the same books had been widely distributed throughout many different libraries or stored at an offsite book warehouse to avoid "costly duplication," they could not have yielded up the depth of information I found in them, because I could not have determined in advance, via their online catalog records, which 15 of the 438 volumes had the relevant information. Nor would I have been able to search digitized versions of the copyrighted texts via Google Print, even when it progresses beyond its current small scale. Current full-text retrieval services already overload results with irrelevant hits, for instance on "Lighthouse for the Blind," an organization that provides book materials to sight-impaired readers. Retrieving four hundred books from multiple locations would be so time consuming and difficult that it would be effectively impossible in the real world that actual researchers inhabit. The Principle of Least Effort in information-seeking behavior affects senior scholars just as much as novices. It tells us that, beyond a fairly low threshold of effort, people will simply give up and settle for whatever information they can find that is easily available— even when it's not what they really want. Or, they will change the scope of their inquiry away from the direction in which they really wish to go. This principle has been verified repeatedly in user studies; indeed, it has been confirmed so often that it ranks as one of the most substantive conclusions that the social sciences are capable of delivering (Mann 1993 17–18, 91–102, 221–242).

The "depth" information books contain at the page or paragraph level is not captured by catalog records: the vast majority do not have digitized tables of contents or back-of-the book indexes (and those scheduled for digitized text searching will primarily be older works in the public domain). Also absent from the catalog records are running heads, illustrations, maps, charts, portraits, diagrams, statistical tables, highlighted sidebars, bulleted or numbered lists, typographical variations for emphasis, marginalia, footnotes, bibliographies, and binding information. All such material, however, is readily searchable by focused browsing in subject-classified book collections. *Without local aggregations of quality books shelved next to each other in subject groupings in a physical place, such depth access is essentially precluded, especially to the copyrighted books of the last century that are in the highest demand.*

Example Two: Valery and Dreyfus

A scholar from France working on a study of the writer Paul Valery and his times needed to pin down an important bit of information regarding Valery's connection to the famous Dreyfus case, in which a French military officer of Jewish descent was wrongly convicted of treason, and, only years later, acquitted. The woman had hearsay information from Valery's children and daughter in-law that the writer had once signed his name to a "petition" or "liste" connected with the affair, but had no specifics of date or place. The large online *ARTFL* database of full-text French sources did not solve the problem, nor did *Historical Abstracts*, the *FRANCIS* database, or two massive published bibliographies devoted to works by and about Valery, each of them over 600 pages long. For the actual solution, I again had to go back into the bookstacks where, at the Library of Congress, we have 186 volumes on six shelves in the classes DC354–354.9 ("Dreyfus case"). As a shortcut, I was particularly looking for one volume that a browse display in the computer catalog had alerted me to, with the subject heading *Dreyfus, Alfred, 1859–1935–Trials, litigation, etc.—Sources.* (The *Sources* subdivision indicates a published compilation of primary sources concerning the actual event.) This volume, however, did not reprint or identify the particular source having Valery's signature. On the shelf above it, however, another book caught my attention; this one, it turned out, did indeed have the necessary information. As an extra serendipitous bonus, the same volume turned out to contain additional information about one of Valery's close friends—information that solved another problem for the researcher, which she hadn't specifically asked about. Once again, a search of the computer catalog—even by call number—could not identify which one of the 186 volumes had the exact information that was needed. (Indeed, the one that I thought looked most promising—and which I would have requested via interlibrary loan in an Atkinson-type system—turned out to be irrelevant.)

In this same case, it cannot be maintained that a digitized full-text database would have solved the problem. In the first place, the relevant volume, *L'Affaire Dreyfus et la presse* (Armand Colin 1960), is recent enough to be still under copyright protection, and so probably could not be digitized to begin with. More important, however, even if it had been digitized, the scholar would not have known in advance the right keywords that would retrieve it. The "petition" in question was actually a subscription list of donors contributing funds to a widow of one of the participants in the Dreyfus affair. The list was published in the periodical *La Libre Parole* in December of 1898; but none of this information could be specified in advance for a Google Print–type keyword search. Most significantly, the keywords "petition" or "liste" do not appear in the French text, which uses the terms "souscription" and "souscripteurs" instead—words that, the scholar told me, she never would have thought of on her own. Nevertheless, when I brought her several of the volumes from the "Dreyfus case" class area to skim through, she could still recognize the relevant terms within one of the books when she saw them.

THE MEANING OF THE EXAMPLES

The difference between theorizing at 50,000 feet on the wonders of digitized libraries versus actually doing the work of scholarship on the ground couldn't be clearer in these two examples. What is required for actual scholarship is a balance and a mixture of access systems that allow searches both by prior specification of keywords (in some cases) and by recognition of unspecifiable yet highly relevant material (in others), discoverable because the information shows up within likely (and manageably limited) subject categories that exclude irrelevant contexts. For the latter cases, cataloging and classification of books—as opposed to merely weighting and ranking keyword retrievals—remains essential. (It is noteworthy that a search in Google on "Paul Valery" and "Dreyfus" produces over 3,900 irrelevant hits.) Although it is counterintuitive to those within the digital library paradigm, the larger a collection is—whether print or digital—the more necessary categorization by cataloging and classification become. Keyword-ranking algorithms are simply not efficient enough for all of the needs of advanced or "depth" scholarship; recognition mechanisms are also essential (a point confirmed emphatically by respondents to a survey noted later in the chapter).

If the books on lighthouses hadn't been *right there, right next to each other*, I could not have found the relevant information within them. That information does indeed exist— and it is discoverable through a nondigital search mechanism. Its discovery was not merely a matter of "luck"—quite the contrary. It was the system of classified shelving that was working according to its design. The word "serendipity," often used in this context, is misleading. The term by itself does not indicate the existence of the highly structured arrangement and categorization of resources that lays behind its signification in a library context.

Books are not like auto parts, whose specifications or precise capabilities can be fully described in computerized inventories. There are two reasons for this difference: first, copyright restrictions do not impede the completeness of auto parts inventories, but they do stand very much in the way of how much information about books can be searched digitally. Second, inventories are compiled on the assumption that a user already knows in advance which part(s) he wishes to see; and this is not the case with scholars "at ground level" in research libraries, who are trying to achieve an overview of all relevant sources, the range of whose unpredictable keywords they usually cannot specify in advance.

It won't do to say, "If a reader wants hundreds of books delivered from remote storage, then we will indeed deliver hundreds of books." Why not? Because, at that point, the damage to the Principle of Least Effort has already been done. Put simply: paved roads create traffic, obstructed roads diminish traffic. Even if the library system is willing to deliver hundreds of books, where will you find researchers who will put up with the hassle of having to order all of them, and then wait weeks for their delivery? Remember that in remote-storage facilities, books on the same subject are not grouped together to begin with, and so cannot be delivered en masse; each one must be requested and retrieved separately. If research facilities introduce such an access bottleneck as their initial, baseline procedure, they will inevitably diminish the flow of books to the people who need to skim their contents quickly, at a "depth" level, for recognition access. This is what working scholars "at ground level" need to do in more situations than library administrators at the 50,000-foot level care to hear about. A remote storage system effectively encourage scholars to give up on their searching, even when the information they need does indeed exist at the books' page and paragraph levels. Interlibrary borrowing and retrieval from remote warehouses are wonderful supplements to a good onsite collection, but they are terrible substitutes.

LISTENING TO USERS' NEEDS FOR CLASSIFIED BOOK COLLECTIONS

It is often asserted these days that students "expect" everything to be online, but the results of several recent and very large user studies belie that claim. The first, sponsored by the Council on Library and Information Resources (Friedlander 2003, see table 650; see also Marcum and George 2003), found, based on over 3,200 interviews, that 55.4 percent of all respondents (and 59.7 percent of undergraduates) still regard browsing library bookstacks as "an important way" to get information. The second is the College Student Experiences Questionnaire (in Kuh and Gonyea 2003 276–77) with data from more than 300,000 student responses between 1984 and 2002 which found that 65.5 percent of male students, and 63.2 percent of female students, reported that they "found something interesting [through] browsing" either "occasionally," "often," or "very often." For students in doctoral-level programs the overall percent is 67.7 percent, with almost 25 percent reporting that browsing was useful either "often" or "very often." Another study—this one commissioned by OCLC (2002), the world's largest bibliographic utility—addressed the information habits of college students, but did not ask specifically about browsing bookstacks. Nevertheless, the findings were revealing: although more than 31 percent of all respondents use Internet search engines to find answers to their questions, the same people express frustration because they estimate half of their searches are unsuccessful. Further, not one participant said they would use the same resource time and again when seeking answers; and nearly 9 or of 10 students (89 percent) report that they also use the campus library's print resources, including books, journals, articles, and encyclopedias.

Browsing library stacks for recognition purposes is a search method so important that knowledge of the technique is defined as one of the standards for measuring information literacy (ACRL 2000). Among the ACRL's performance indicators is, "The information literate student retrieves information online or in person using a *variety* of methods" [emphasis added]. Outcomes include: "Uses various classification schemes and other systems (e.g., call number systems or indexes) to locate information resources within the library or to identify specific sites for physical exploration." Browsing library stacks is a search method whose importance "cannot be overemphasized" according to yet another study—a 2004 survey of faculty attitudes toward libraries done at the University of Oklahoma (Engel and Antell 2004). This survey of faculty at Oklahoma and other research libraries noted that "part of the faculty space's value to researchers lies in its proximity to the collections of monographs and print journals. . . . 'It's that one minute out of fifty-nine, when you find that one gem on the shelf' that makes the act of browsing not only effective but absolutely vital to many researchers. As one participant emphatically noted, 'There is no substitute for walking the stacks. It's not "browsing"—that sounds too aimless. It's more directed—"surveillance," really.' ..." During the interviews, "the theme of serendipitous browsing emerged repeatedly with regard to research." It is especially noteworthy that among the "variety of methods" required for ACRL information literacy, this search technique continues to be widely ignored by academic library administrators and library science professors. Once again, there is a major disconnection between soaring information theorists and actual researchers.

Regarding another highly placed library administrator's bland assertion that "faculty and students have enormous respect and trust for libraries, but they don't use them" (Minutes 2004), yet another study is relevant here. A survey of 394 undergraduates conducted at the University of Toronto in 2001 (Dilevko and Gottlieb 2002) casts a remarkably different light on the matter. Among the conclusions of this study are that

undergraduates are significant users of online resources, going so far as to rely exclusively (or almost exclusively) on such resources for at least some of their assignments and essays. Still, they recognize that print book sources cannot be overlooked in the research process. For example, 71% of social science students used print books for their assignments at least 50% of the time... and 64.9% of fourth-year students used print book sources at least 50% of the time.... Moreover, 54.1% of all students began their research process with print books at least 50% of the time.... Some undergraduates already understand the connection between, on the one hand, increased use of print sources that are only physically available at the academic library and, on the other hand, increased academic success and real gains in knowledge. In this regard, undergraduates may have a better grasp of the true function of the academic library than the academic library itself.

(This last sentence being, as I take it, a reference to the views held by library administrators.)

Finally, yet another recent, large study is relevant, although its conclusions exhibit a spinning of results that do not adequately reflect its own data. This is the Electronic Publishing Initiative at Columbia (EPIC 2004) survey of responses from 1,233 students and scholars. A *New York Times* (Hafner 2004 A1) story on the survey immediately conveys the intended spin: the reporter quotes the director of the study as saying, "We can't pretend people will go back to walking into a library and talking to a reference librarian." Indeed, the study's own "Conclusions" section begins by saying that "electronic resources have become the main tool for students' information gathering." However, there are major problems with this flat assertion. The first is evident when the EPIC study's own data is examined in greater detail, specifically passages from the "Survey of College Students" section:

– Students are almost as dependent on the physical library (75.8%) as they are on the library's website to retrieve books and articles (81.5%).
– Books and journals are still cited by most students when writing a term paper, however the number of students citing websites does not lag far behind. Books and journals were each cited by more than three-quarters of respondents as types of resources cited in the bibliography of their last research/term paper (84.8% and 77.8% respectively), while websites were cited by 68.8% of the students.

- [F]or general assignments, students are more likely to turn to the Internet, but for in-depth research assignments, they are somewhat more likely to turn to library sponsored [i.e., restricted access] electronic resources.
- Undergraduate students are more likely than graduate students to use non-library sponsored electronic resources, while graduate students are more likely to use library sponsored electronic and library sponsored print resources.
- The majority of respondents use the physical library more than once a month (67.7%).
- Print is preferred for situations where the material is long or dense, and the reader has to fully comprehend the material. Electronic resources are preferred for situations where the reader is obtaining supplementary or background materials, for current events materials, or for looking up information for short papers/homework assignments.
- The physical library is still an important destination for students.

The actual EPIC data—in line with other surveys—indicate that the majority of students use both the Internet and traditional library resources.

The EPIC study's assertion that the Internet is "the main tool for students' information gathering" is also undercut by the study's own data. In the context of the passages quoted above, it is clear that the adjective "main" is being used to indicate that electronic resources are the first sources students turn to for information-level purposes—no surprise there, given the Principle of Least Effort. The study's overall findings, however, do not show that electronic sources are the only or even the most important resources students use in pursuing the deeper levels of learning, that is, knowledge and understanding. If the word "main" is taken in its customary sense to indicate importance rather than simple ordinal priority in a sequence, then electronic resources are not student's "main" resource "where the material is long or dense, and the reader has to fully comprehend the material"—to the contrary, in these situations "Print is preferred."

The skewing or spinning of the study's "Conclusions" not only misrepresents its own data; it also introduces a particularly insidious concealed proposition—that all levels of learning reduce to "information." Distinctions between data and information on the one hand, and knowledge and understanding on the other, however, are crucial to the higher levels of education that colleges and universities strive to promote (see Berger 2002–2003; Mann 2005). *Scholarship* is not the same thing as *information-seeking*; the former requires intellectual contexts and conceptual interrelationships that are not needed in situations where only isolated facts are required. The search techniques that are often appropriate for finding isolated facts—for example, simple keyword searching—are not adequate to promote the development of integrated conceptual frameworks necessary for understanding. For librarians to believe that "information equals understanding," or even "information equals knowledge," would undermine the very mission of research libraries to promote the highest levels of learning. The creation of conceptual frameworks and interrelationships by librarians, through categorization and classification systems, is the very mechanism that rescues information in books from isolation and "orphanage."

The EPIC study's actual, "buried" findings (unreported by the *New York Times* article) correlate well with the many other studies showing that most students and researchers do indeed want to use substantive book-length copyrighted sources, not just freely available current information for short papers. For instance, a 2001 study of 40,742 interlibrary loan requests initiated in OhioLINK (Prabha and O'Neill 2001) found that 42 percent came from undergraduates—the very people who "don't use libraries" according to the reigning paradigm. Furthermore, half of the requested books were published in the preceding seven years, and 90% since 1960.

BLIND SPOTS IN THE DIGITAL LIBRARY WORLDVIEW

The question remains: Why is it that so many digital library advocates cannot perceive the continuing need for onsite book collections arranged in classified order (see, e.g., "E-Stupidity" 2004, and Membrino 2004)—in libraries as *places*—when so many academics at all levels in disciplines other than our own can see this so clearly? I suspect there are two reasons for this, and neither is to the credit of the library profession. The first reason is that too many library administrators do not themselves use their own libraries; they thus lack the personal experience in doing research that would enable them to judge the practical adequacy of the "digital age paradigm." The second is that the "digital age" library conferences from which these administrators do gain their professional feedback are themselves distorted mirrors that do not fully reflect the reality of scholars' needs "at ground level."

As evidenced by the above surveys—which although independently conducted nonetheless dovetail in their overall thrust—the majority of faculty and students recognize *from their own direct experience* two fundamental realities that remain true in spite of the proliferation of Internet resources: (a) that focused *depth searching* of the contents of most of the copyrighted books on a particular topic cannot be realistically done in any way other than the systematic browsing of subject-classified bookstacks; and (b) that serendipitous discovery by *recognition-browsing* within carefully defined segments of library book collections is crucial to many research projects because it enables researchers to find relevant sources whose keywords they cannot specify in advance, regardless of how capacious the full-text databases available to them may be. Overlooked entirely in the massive digitization projects is that they require prior specification from blank search boxes of all keywords the searcher wishes to see. A minimum of actual experience in a library demonstrates immediately that working from a blank search box is very different from working with classified arrays of full texts on bookshelves—or from OPACs that show browse displays of unanticipated aspects of a topic and cross references to hierarchically related and vocabulary-controlled category terms. It is the creation of these latter search mechanisms by librarians that gives scholars the crucial capability to simply recognize whole arrays of unforeseen options—and to do so within bounded conceptual groupings that minimize the appearance of the right words appearing in irrelevant contexts. Once again, however, neither the existence nor the importance of these search mechanisms appear at all within the purview of the 50,000-foot theorists who, lacking practical experience, believe that "Library of Congress cataloging would not be needed in these circumstances [of full text digitization]" (Minutes 2004). It is, however, precisely the absence of LC cataloging and classification controls that would make scholarship much more difficult to pursue.

The second reason that so many library administrators and library school faculty cannot see the abundant evidence is, again, that it lies in a blind spot not covered by the digital library paradigm in which they operate. Not only is there a lack of direct experience sufficient to give them a visceral awareness of what is actually required for scholarship; the feedback that they *are* getting is itself too far out of touch with reality. When one's primary "discourse community" is formed by the agendas of library conferences rather than by actual work in libraries, then a skewing of basic assumptions is inevitable. For two decades now, these meetings have been devoted almost exclusively to online resources rather than to onsite book collections (see Mann 2002). Furthermore, the digital paradigm assumed within this discourse circle unquestioningly accepts at its base an evolutionary metaphor—that is, it takes as received dogma the notion that libraries are "evolving" into online forms just as the pepper moth is known to have evolved in the natural world in response to industrial pollution. The acceptance of this particular metaphor for change, however, also entails the silent acceptance of other unarticulated presuppositions that are dangerous to scholarship.

FLAWS IN THE EVOLUTIONARY ASSUMPTION

The assumption behind that evolutionary metaphor is that the process of change within libraries, towards digitization, is entirely natural, like the unpacking of a DNA code over time. One cannot speak of a natural process as "good" or "bad"—it simply is. The second concealed proposition is that the evolution is "inevitable"—that is, it is not something that can be rationally *planned*. It "just happens"—and must happen—whether anyone consciously agrees with its direction or not. These points are perhaps best made by contrast to an alternative metaphor, that of a judge in court (as opposed to an impersonal biological tendency), who makes conscious decisions on the appropriateness of an act based on considerations of evidence, experience, testimony, precedent, and law. The image of Justice holding a balance would be an alternative metaphor much preferable to that of a moth evolving. In assuming and reifying the evolution metaphor, the library profession is also tacitly accepting the entailed but unarticulated propositions of "unchallengeability" and "inevitability" in the digital library paradigm.

The result of this unargued acceptance is that a fundamental reality of ground-level working scholars is filtered out at what I've called the "50,000-foot level." It does not matter how many times faculty in other disciplines insist on the importance of browsing onsite library book collections; it does not matter how often they insist scholarship requires recognition mechanisms as well as prior specification search boxes; it does not matter how senior or how experienced the objectors are; it does not matter how often or how vehemently they complain when large portions of onsite collections are moved to remote storage. From the perspective of the digital library paradigm, such objectors cannot be right—they must be regarded as "naive," "quaintly inefficient," "childish," "old-fashioned," "nostalgic," "sentimental," or "resistant to change" regarding their understanding of how best to do scholarly research. Such dismissive terms are the only verbal and analytical tools available to those administrators and information scientists immersed in our profession's current worldview; objections to the digital paradigm from ground-level scholars are routinely perceived as merely emotional rather than substantively rational. To admit, along with faculty researchers, that large, onsite, classified book collections in libraries-as-places are still crucial to advanced scholarship would be to recognize the existence of a major flaw in the digital paradigm—a crack in the overall model. It would demand acknowledgment of precisely the kind of stubborn, inconvenient, and gaping anomaly—"the elephant in the living room"—that, in any other field of study, would necessitate an outright rejection of the flawed paradigm itself. It would demand the recognition that a balance of equally important print and electronic resources must be achieved, and that a mixture of both recognition and prior specification search mechanisms are necessary. What we get instead from the leaders of our profession is the uncritical assumption that a "transition" from books to digital formats, as well as from intelligent control mechanisms to uncontrolled keyword guesswork, is both inevitable and desirable, all feedback to the contrary notwithstanding.

The problem in getting library administrators and library school professors even to recognize the issue—that large, onsite collections of books arranged in classified order are still crucial to substantive scholarship—is very much like that of Galileo trying to persuade the Churchmen of his time to look through his telescope at the actual evidence for the moons of Jupiter. They believe, on an a priori basis, that the purported data must be either incorrect or insignificant to begin with, and worse, that its proponents can be patronizingly dismissed as mere "sentimentalists"—simply because such evidence does not fit the "cutting edge" paradigm's dogma that library research must now focus exclusively on "the transition" to digital formats and uncontrolled keyword search mechanisms.

INTERNET LIBRARY SOFTWARE PROBLEMS AND THE CRUCIAL NEED FOR LC CATALOGING

Although projects like Google Print may appear as an unqualified good to those at the stratospheric level, there are other considerations that are much more important to scholarship than the simple "freeing" of the books from "access boundaries" occasioned by their physical locations within library walls. Foremost among these is the loss of catalog structure, standardization, linkages, browse displays, and authority work in Internet files. Let us assume that fifteen million books will indeed be digitized in the next decade or so, and offered free via Google. If we assume 300 pages per book (Lyman and Varian 2000), 15 million volumes would contain 4.5 billion pages. The first difficulty here is that any keyword searching of such a pool for "depth access" would produce retrieval results just as garbled, jumbled, and irrelevant as those that Google already produces with existing Web sites. (Note again the strong dissatisfaction with search engine results pointed out by the EPIC and OCLC studies, above.) For example, the digitization of all copyright-free books would include tens of thousands of dictionaries (including bilingual forms), and so any words searched would "hit" in these sources as well as in the narrative or expository texts. Nor could sets be "progressively refined" by the addition of extra keyword search terms, because any such keywords would themselves "hit" in the same dictionaries. This is already a problem in a much smaller full-text database, the *Evans Early American Imprints*; but one needs experience in searching to notice the existence of such difficulties. (Online journal files such as *JSTOR* or *LexisNexis* are not comparable because they do not include dictionaries.)

Such difficulties would not be mitigated by the simple inclusion of LC subject headings and classification numbers as either metadata elements or searchable keywords, because Google does not have OPAC software that enables subject headings (and their subdivisions) to be displayed in browse menus that would segregate dictionaries into separate categories. Nor can Google searching show related classification numbers in contiguous groups, as an alternative mechanism for limiting keyword hits to appropriate conceptual contexts.

Let's reconsider my first example in the light of Google. If I wish to research the question on "lighthouse libraries" in Google Web I can type in a combination of the keywords "library" and "lighthouse" or "lighthouses" in the advanced search page. The problem is that, while it does retrieve some isolated hits, this search produces

173,000 returns; the results lack even rudimentary contextual boundaries. A Google Print database, confined exclusively to book texts, in searching 4.5 billion pages would undoubtedly produces similar chaos. Mere relevance-ranking algorithms cannot solve this endemic problem of keyword retrievals in full-text databases (Mann 2002). Any massive digitization project without the filtering, structuring, segregating, and channeling elements provided by traditional library categorizations would do much more actual harm than good—assuming, as the digital paradigm does, that digitized book collections would replace rather than supplement onsite print collections—because the efficient *categorizing of books by subject* is not a problem that technology can solve through any ranking algorithms of keywords.

Library of Congress Subject Headings (LCSH) have cross-references and menus that will lead searchers from a general topic like "divorce" to "children of divorced parents"—and it is often just such a narrower topic that researchers really desire within the very general questions they actually ask—or type into a search box. (Retrieval under the latter subject heading, by the way, includes titles with unpredictable keywords such as *Unraveled: One Woman's Story of Moving Out, Moving On, and Becoming a Better Mother*; *Stepwives: 10 Steps to Help Ex-Wives and Stepmothers End the Struggle and Put the Kids First*; and *Custody Chaos, Personal Peace: Sharing Custody with an Ex Who Drives You Crazy*.) The transition from the broad to the narrower and more focused levels cannot be accomplished in any systematic manner by Google or Amazon software. Similarly, Library of Congress Subject Headings, via OPAC browse displays, can lead searchers interested in the history of Afghanistan not just to "Afghanistan-History" but also to scores of related topical aspects:

Afghanistan-Antiquities
[numerous NT cross-references here, e.g., to Kapisa (Extinct city)]
Afghanistan-Armed forces
Afghanistan-Bibliography
Afghanistan-Biography
Afghanistan-Civilization
Afghanistan-Climate
Afghanistan-Description and travel
Afghanistan-Economic conditions
Afghanistan-Ethnic relations
Afghanistan-Foreign relations
Afghanistan-Kings and rulers
Afghanistan-Languages
[numerous NT cross-references to specific languages, e.g., Bashgali language]
Afghanistan-Politics and government

All of these other aspects could well be of interest to a historian, but their existence cannot be brought to a researcher's attention by Google or Amazon—or OCLC—softwares. A simple keyword combination of "Afghanistan" and "history" in a blank search box would miss them entirely (see Mann 2005; 2003; 2001).

The crucial point here is that the purpose of assigning controlled subject headings is not simply to enable researchers to find "something quickly," which can indeed be done already on the Internet. Online library catalogs, in sharp contrast, situate individual works within larger webs of intellectual relationships to other relevant books that use variant keywords (even in other languages); indicate the different (and unexpected) levels of the topic that are searchable; spell out the extent of related (albeit unsuspected) aspects "within" the subject; and map the range of different but related topics "outside" the subject that impinge upon it.

If we regard classified bookshelves in a research library as a large intellectual "mosaic," then Google's algorithms are such that they can efficiently extract all of the stones of any specified color, but only aggregated in piles separated from all of the other colors—thereby destroying any possibility of displaying the interrelationships of all of the stones and the overall design of the mosaic itself. Google and Amazon fail miserably at both subject categorization and structured overview-provision in comparison with online library catalogs (see Kenney 2004). It is the synergy between numerical classification systems and verbal taxonomies, and the rich collections of books organized accordingly, shelved onsite in a research library place, that makes libraries such efficient tools of scholarship rather than mere information seeking.

COMMUNITY CENTERS WITHOUT BOOK COLLECTIONS?

One further concern ties together the two dangers reviewed thus far. This common thread is the way that libraries-as-physical-places are now so often being defended by their ostensible supporters: all too many such "friends" don't even mention the need for onsite book collections. If "place" is regarded as important at all in the current library literature, it is "defended" by appeals to everything except the need to maintain localized book collections. For example, one speaker at a recent symposium justified libraries as physical places in terms of

providing spaces in which learners can use . . . resources, individually and collaboratively, in multiple ways, including ways of their own invention. Computer banks, electronic classrooms, distance learning labs, special program facilities, collaborative study lounges, copy centers, even cafes and canteens and corners for contemplation—these are increasingly valued features of libraries. *Physical* libraries (Marcum 2003)

The problem is that a "library" defined by only these characteristics might just as well be a combination of (a) an Atkinson operation for providing access to current, copyrighted books stored offsite and (b) a bank of terminals connected to Google Print in which (c) "everything" will be available (actually, public domain books in unreadable formats) only through the prior specification of uncontrolled keywords in a blank search box, with (d) social centers rather than book collections providing the reason for visitors to show up onsite. (The sheer magnitude of the omission of any reference to onsite book collections brings to mind the old joke "Other than that, Mrs. Lincoln, how did you like the play?") That such a "defense" can be offered apparently without fear of contradiction at library conferences indicates how far the library profession itself has slid towards the systematic elimination of the greatest capability scholars now have for gaining both recognition awareness and in-depth subject access to the contents of most of the books in research libraries' collections. And we appear to be acquiescing in such "defenses" because the traditional focused browsing search capability that is required for so much advanced scholarship is a nondigital search technique–and therefore literally "off the screen" of perception. We seem further to be swallowing whole the assumptions that information, which requires only shorter attention spans, is now our exclusive concern; that Internet keyword-ranking algorithms can replace the intellectual work of authority control, standardized categorization, and conceptual linkage of book records; and that books themselves, which are necessary for the transmission of the higher levels of learning that require longer attention spans, are now mere "tree flakes encased in dead cow" (Mitchell 1995 56).

CONCLUSION: THE DANGERS OF GETTING WHAT WE SEEK

Our profession has apparently forgotten that research libraries will continue to be necessary for several other crucial purposes that are not accomplished by remote storage or massive digitization of books, and not served by transformation of library buildings into mere social centers. Specifically, those purposes are

> to collect, in print form, the vast bulk of current imprints that are not freely accessible to everyone online because of copyright restrictions;
> to make such sources freely and easily available offline—that is, within the public spaces defined by local library walls, widely distributed among thousands of communities;
> to catalog—rather than merely inventory—the books in ways that create categorizations, linkages, and webs of conceptual relationships among the records—which connections can be recognized from browse menus and cross references without having to be specified in advance—while also eliminating irrelevant associations;
> to facilitate both depth-searching of subject content and systematic recognition discovery within nondigitized works by means of classified shelving that enables scholars to do focused browsing of contiguous subject-related full texts;
> to make readily and easily available to readers the one proven format of knowledge record that promotes rather than discourages the actual reading of lengthy narrative and expository texts necessary for conveying knowledge and understanding rather than mere information; and
> to preserve knowledge records for centuries, not mere decades.

Not a single one of these crucial public purposes is accomplished by replacing (or "de-placing") research libraries through the massive digitization of books. We are undermining the maintenance of the very mechanisms—local acquisition, quality cataloging, shelving in classified arrays, and preservation of books—that continue to provide the greatest access to the greatest collections of knowledge records ever assembled; and we are doing it because our leadership, floating at the 50,000-foot level, apparently does not grasp the crucial requirements of scholarship at the ground level. We are behaving as though our nation's research libraries occupy no significant niches of their own in the overall information economy, and have no significant responsibilities to provide both content and search methodologies different from what is available on the Internet. We are willfully blinding ourselves both to the strengths of real libraries and to the weaknesses of the Internet, and in our disregard of the real differences we are transforming research libraries into their very opposites: institutions barely recognizable as places, and that are capable of providing only quick information fixes rather than the sources and the mechanisms of deep and comprehensive scholarship. Nothing less than the future intellectual life of our culture is dependent on the decisions that we librarians are now making. More than anything else, we need to find a much better governing paradigm for our profession than the "digital age" delusion with which we have now straightjacketed ourselves.

(The judgments expressed in this paper are those of the author, and are not to be taken as the official view of the Library of Congress.)

REFERENCES

ACRL (Association of College & Research Libraries). Information Literacy Competency Standards for Higher Education. 2000. Retrieved Aug. 2004 from http://www.ala.org/ala/acrl/acrlstandards/informationliteracycompetency.htm.

Atkinson, Richard C. "A New World of Scholarly Communication." *Chronicle of Higher Education* 7 Nov. 2003: B16.

Berger, Sidney E. "The Future of Books and Libraries." *Against the Grain* 14 (Dec. 2002–Jan. 2003): 30–37.

Bowker Annual Library and Book Trade Almanac, 2003 Edition. New York: R. R. Bowker, 2003.

Crawford, Walt. "Exceptional Institutions: Libraries and the Pareto Principle." *American Libraries* 32 (June/July, 2001): 72–74.

Dilevko, Juris and Lisa Gottlieb. "Print Sources in an Electronic Age: A Vital Part of the Research Process for Undergraduate Students." *Journal of Academic Librarianship* 28 (Nov. 2002): 381–92.

"E-Stupidity," TeleRead: Bring the E-Books Home. 11 June 2004. Retrieved Aug. 2004 from http://www.teleread.org/blog/2004_06_06_archive.html.

Engel, Debra and Karen Antell. "The Life of the Mind: A Study of Faculty Spaces in Academic Libraries." *College & Research Libraries* 65 (Jan. 2004): 8–26.

EPIC (Electronic Publishing Initiative at Columbia) Online Use and Costs Evaluation Program: Final Report. September 2004. Columbia University. Retrieved Oct. 2004 from http://www.epic.columbia.edu/eval/eval04frame.html.

Friedlander, Amy. Dimensions and Use of the Scholarly Information Environment. 2003. Digital Library Federation and Council on Library and Information Resources. Retrieved Aug. 2004 from http://www.clir.org/pubs/reports/pub110/contents.html.

Hafner, Katie. "Old Search Engine, the Library, Tries to Fit Into a Google World." *New York Times* 21 June 2004: A1.

Kenney, Shirley Duglin. "Computers in Libraries 2004." *Information Today* 21 (May 2004): 1, 33.

Kuh, George D., and Robert M. Gonyea. "The Role of the Academic Library in Promoting Student Engagement in Learning." *College & Research Libraries* 64 (July 2003): 256–82.

Lyman, Peter, and Hal Varian. *How Much Information?* 2000. University of California – Berkeley. Retrieved Dec. 2004 from http://www.sims.berkeley.edu/research/projects/how-much-info/.

Mann, Thomas. *The Oxford Guide to Library Research.* New York: Oxford University Press, 2005.

———. "Why LC Subject Headings Are More Important Than Ever." American Libraries 34 (Oct. 2003): 52–54.

———. "Why the Cybergurus Are Wrong about Libraries: Thinking Outside the Box of the Internet." *Logos: The Journal of the World Book Community* 14 (2002): 190–98.

———. "Is Precoordination Unnecessary in LCSH? Are Web Sites More Important to Catalog than Books? A Reference Librarian's Thoughts on the Future of Bibliographic Control." *Proceedings of the Bicentennial Conference on Bibliographic Control for the New Millenium.* Washington, DC: Library of Congress, Cataloging Distribution Service, 2001: 87–134. Retrieved from http://www.loc.gov/catdir/bibcontrol/mann_paper.html.

———. *Library Research Models.* New York: Oxford University Press, 1993.

Marcum, Deanna. "Libraries: Physical Places or Virtual Spaces in the Digital World?" *The Library as Place: Symposium on Building and Renovating Health Sciences Libraries in the Digital Age.* The National Library of Medicine, Bethesda, MD, 5–6 Nov. 2003.

Marcum, Deanna, and Gerald George "Who Uses What? Report of a National Survey of Information Users in Colleges and Universities." *D-Lib Magazine* 9 (Oct. 2003). Retrieved from http://www.dlib.org/dlib/october03/george/10george.html.

Membrino, Carter. "Hospital, Library Focus at U. Assembly." *The Triangle.* 28 May 2004 Drexel University. Retrieved from www.thetriangle.org.

Minutes of the Cataloging Management Team Meeting. 24 Mar. 2004, Library of Congress.

Mitchell, William J. *City of Bits: Space, Place, and the Infobahn.* Cambridge, MA: The MIT Press, 1995.

OCLC (Online Computer Library Center). OCLC White Paper on the Information Habits of College Students. June 2002. OCLC. Retrieved Dec. 2004 from www5.oclc.org/downloads/community/informationhabits.pdf.

Prabha, C. G. and P. O'Neill. "Interlibrary Borrowing Initiated by Patrons: Some Characteristics of Books Requested via OhioLINK." *Journal of Library Administration* 34 (2001): 329–38.

"U.S. Book Production Soars to 175,000 New Titles in 2003; Trade Up, University Presses Down" press release). 27 May 2004. Bowker. Retrieved Aug. 2004 from www.bowker.com/press/2004_0527_bowker.htm.

Section IV

Libraries, Place, and Culture

12

On the Myths of Libraries

Bonnie Mak

*Postdoctoral Fellow of the InterPARES Project, School of Library, Archival and Information
Studies, The University of British Columbia, Vancouver, British Columbia, Canada*

As a cultural symbol, the library is more than a space for books or a place in which to
read them. The library is considered to be the embodiment of a collective intellectual
heritage. But its definition and social role have fallen under intense scrutiny ever since
claims were made that the World Wide Web, or at least Google, could be the new library
of the twenty-first century. While still participating in a shared scholarly heritage, the
digital library belongs to no one and exists nowhere in particular. To establish a footing
for the analysis of the new spaces of books and reading, this article will explore the ways
in which the ideal of the library has been embodied from the fifteenth century into the
modern period.

Although libraries were highly regarded in Antiquity, it was not until the fifteenth
century that such rooms were more commonly incorporated into the domestic sphere.
The *Controversia de nobilitate* was written during this period of transformation, and
outlines the significance of the library in the home. In the treatise, there is a strong
indication that the library had already become a site in which complex strategies of self-
representation could be deployed. Moreover, the material history of the *Controversia*
bears witness to the struggles that have haunted the organizational structures of libraries.
By following the trail of the manuscripts and printed books of the *Controversia*, this
article considers broader questions about traditional categories of knowledge and the
spaces that they have generated.

BUILDING THE MYTH

In 1428, Buonaccorso da Montemagno described the significance of having a library
in the home in the *Controversia de nobilitate*. Applying oneself to study is considered a
virtue, he writes, and owning a library is an indicator of one's commitment to scholarship.
Buonaccorso develops this idea in the central feature of the *Controversia*, a debate on the
origins of nobility. In the contest, two young men vie for the hand of the beautiful and
virtuous Lucretia. Each man must argue why he is nobler than the other, and therefore
more worthy of Lucretia. One suitor claims to be noble by birth; the other, of a humble
family, claims that he is noble of character. The man who is deemed the winner of the
contest will win Lucretia as his bride.

Through the course of the debate, nobility is embodied in two significantly different
ways. The first suitor, Cornelius, argues that nobility is inherited through the blood-
line. Because his ancestors are noble, he is noble. The monuments that were erected to

commemorate the deeds of his ancestors are evidence of his prestigious family connections. Consequently, Cornelius says, the stone monuments guarantee his own virtuous character. The memorial is the physical attestation of his nobility; it is importantly monumental in scale, and on public display.

Against this overt manifestation of nobility, the second man, Flamminius, presents a different case. He argues that owning of a library is a sign of nobility. Flamminius contends that he has earned and maintained a noble character through hours of study. His library is therefore evidence of his nobility. The library is imbued with the creative energies to generate a noble character, providing a stark contrast to Cornelius' static memorials. Located in the domestic sphere, it is a personal space to be shared with family and select friends. The library, and Flamminius's nobility, is not intended for ostentatious public display.

By casting the domestic library as credible evidence in the debate on nobility, Buonaccorso suggests that the ownership of such a space was highly desirable in some social circles. His observation is confirmed by other contemporary sources. For instance, Benedetto Cotrugli wrote *Della mercatura e del mercante perfetto* in 1458, in which he insists that every home should have a library for personal use. Cotrugli states, "He who delights in letters should not keep his books in the common *scrittoio* [office], but should have a *studiolo* [study], set apart in the most remote part of the house" (Cotrugli 231; Thornton 32). The study is a place in which books are stored and read, and the perfect merchant must have such a room as a complement to his office. According to Cotrugli, the library occupies a crucial place in the ideal map of the home.

While the archetypal domestic library was being explicated in these textual sources, similar spaces for books and reading were being incorporated into the guidelines and architectural plans of homes of the fifteenth century. In the *De re aedificatoria* (1450), Leon Battista Alberti discusses the practicalities of building a library. He recommends that wood panelling be installed in a room that has been designated for reading. The panelling acts as a barrier of insulation from heat and cold, and will therefore help to moderate the temperature of the room (X.xiv).[1] Following the model of ancient writers, Alberti also notes the importance of nature, tranquility, and solitude for scholarly activity (IX.iv).

These narrative sources reveal that libraries held a firm place in the imagination of late medieval and early modern writers. In concrete terms, contemporary building programs show that libraries were being incorporated into the domestic map with growing regularity. Indeed, extant floor plans and architectural remains indicate that the number of libraries and studies in the home increased through the fifteenth century.[2] These spaces satisfied a practical need for storage, but more significantly fulfilled a desire to participate in the rich tradition of scholarly activity that had its origins in Antiquity.

INSIDE THE MYTH, PART ONE

One of the most important accessories of any scholar is a collection of books. Through the fifteenth century, the possession of books began to be understood as shorthand for scholarly activity. Books increased in social value and quickly assumed a role as collectible objects. Indeed, in the *Controversia de nobilitate*, Flamminius emphasizes his collection of books as a collection of objects. His books are likened to the furniture and other domestic goods that are stored in the library; all of these belongings are prized for their value and beauty. He says to Lucretia, "There . . . you will see my library filled with books, in which I have always placed all my hope. These are indeed illustrious household goods" (Buonaccorso, *Prose* 92, Rabil 51–52). The books are understood as material commodities and are cataloged with other household possessions.[3]

Having a collection of books in the home could generate a scholarly pedigree for its owner. The books need not have been read; possessing a collection is enough to signify an intellectual heritage. There is an intimation of this phenomenon when Johannes Trithemius wrote in 1492, "If I enter your house, there is no need to ask about your studies; your books will tell me" (93). Each book is representative of a greater intellectual tradition. The books themselves become mini-memorials to scholarly activity. That is, the books are the physical embodiment of scholarship, and fabricate an intellectual identity for their owner.

Behind the urgent acquisition and exhibition of books was the desire to lay claim to a scholarly pedigree. This desire continued to escalate through the fifteenth century. As the illusion of scholarly heritage grew more elaborate, the library itself came to be valued as a part of the fiction. The library, like the collection of books that it housed, garnered a certain intellectual value by symbolising scholarly activity. Ostensibly a space of collection, it became more significantly a space to be collected.[4] The library became a fossilization of an ideal, enjoying none of the creative powers that Flaminius describes in the *Controversia*. Instead of superseding the public memorials that were so important to Cornelius, the library merely reoccupies the space and function of the monument. The library stands as a fixed symbol, representing an adopted identity, not of genealogy, but of learning. Museified are its contents and any activities that are imagined to be performed within its space. Indeed, Caroline Elam notes that the identification of the *studiolo*—the study—with collecting became so intimate that its association with the activity of reading is, in many cases, lost by the sixteenth century. In its place is a room that serves more generally as a space of collection and exhibition: a gallery, cabinet of curiosity, or *wunderkammer* (Elam 51–53).

A room that marks the moment of this transition between study space and gallery space is the *studiolo* of Federico of Montefeltro in Urbino. The *studiolo*, completed around 1476, is a small room, located on the upper floor of Federico's *palazzo*.[5] The room is accessible through two doors: one from the Duke's dressing room, and the other from the Audience Room. The walls of the *studiolo* are veneered with illusionistic inlaid panels, depicting furniture and other ornaments suitable for a study. A bank of benches seems to stand out from the walls. Cupboards appear above them with their doors ajar, revealing collectible objects on the shelves inside. Books, musical and astronomical instruments, hourglasses, inkwells, and pieces of armour are featured. The casual disarray implies that Federico has just momentarily left the room.

In addition to the inlaid panels, there is a series of portraits that also contributes to the scholarly atmosphere. Paintings of twenty-eight famous men line the walls above the marquetry, and include such personages as Plato, Boethius, Euclid, Jerome, Thomas Aquinas, Dante, and Petrarch.[6] These portraits, arranged in two rows with lay personalities in the upper register and their ecclesiastical counterparts in the lower, correspond roughly to the important fields of study at the time: the *quadrivium* of Astronomy, Music, Arithmetic, and Geometry, part of the *trivium*, including Logic and Rhetoric, as well as Moral Philosophy, Poetry, Law, and Medicine (Cheles 45). The pretence of an intellectual heritage is overt here; Federico imagines himself in the company of these writers and scholars, and, perhaps, as one of them.[7]

But this *studiolo* is not a functioning library. Federico's *studiolo* was not designed as a room for preserving books or for reading them. First, there is scant space for storage in the room; the few cupboards in the *studiolo* may even have been added later, in order to replace damaged panels. Second, although some scholars have suggested that the fold-out stool and lectern indicate the use of the *studiolo* as a place for reading, Dora Thornton observes that the furniture is too flimsy to support any substantial weight, and is moreover situated in a dark corner (120).[8] Jon Pearson Perry agrees, writing that, "even the presence of a reader seated in the room was meant above all to be appreciated visually by someone else" (158). The *studiolo* is designed as a stage for the performance of study; the owner need only sit on the stool to complete the scene.

Lastly, the location of the *studiolo* near the dressing room and the bedchamber suggests that the room functioned as a showpiece of personal space. The careful association of the *studiolo* with personal space contributes to the illusion that the room more accurately reflects the character of its owner. There is important play between "showing" and "not-showing" in this room. The *studiolo* is imagined as an intimate retreat, yet the room is on full display and encourages the viewer in turn to envision Federico at work here. Outfitted with the appropriate accoutrements for study in *trompe l'œil*, the *studiolo* was never meant to function as a library, but only to look like one. It is a theatrical space for self-exhibition, a monument and a memorial to study (Findlen 293–346; Thornton 99–127). The *studiolo* itself is an object of collection that has been packaged neatly for cultural consumption. The room permits Federico to broadcast his erudition. With the *studiolo*, he has acquired an intellectual heritage.

Now that books had been forced out of their space in the study, they needed to be accommodated elsewhere. Federico's collection was kept in a large room on the ground floor of the *palazzo*, a fair distance from the *studiolo* (dal Poggetto, "Nuova lettera" 105–118; dal Poggetto, "Il restauro" 699–705).[9] Adjacent to the entrance hall, the location of the library indicates that, like the *studiolo*, it was also not conceived as a quiet place of study. The room is situated in a high-traffic area; indeed, the library's northern window looks to the *piazza* at the main entrance. The southern side of the library faces the courtyard, and this wall is articulated by two windows and the doorway. Visitors to the *palazzo* must pass by the library on their way to the grand staircase at the eastern end of the building. Again, this purported space of reading functioned as a space of display, for the visitors would certainly catch a glimpse of the grand barrel-vaulted ceiling, the decorative frescoes, and, of course, the shelves, which were full of books.

INSIDE THE MYTH, PART TWO

According to written sources, "well-ordered" shelves once lined the long walls of the Federico's library (Baldi 56).[10] The manuscripts themselves were bound with colored materials, including silk, linen, and leather, some of which were highly ornamented. At the time of his death in 1482, Federico had amassed a collection of around a thousand books. He owned six hundred books in Latin, over one hundred in Greek, and about eighty in Hebrew. Federico also possessed works in Italian by writers such as Dante and Petrarch.

It is here in the library that Federico kept his manuscript of Buonaccorso's *Controversia de nobilitate*. The *Controversia* appears in one of the earliest catalogs of the library, the *Indice vecchio*, which was compiled around 1487.[11] Like many libraries of the Quattrocento, Urbino organized its holdings by following the classification scheme that had been established in the early Middle Ages. In this system, books were arranged according to the Seven Liberal Arts—the *quadrivium* and *trivium*. The *Indice vecchio* lists the sacred writings of Federico's collection first, beginning with bibles and psalters, followed by the Church Fathers and philosophical works. Next are the books in medicine, law, mathematics, and cosmography. The final section of the *Indice vecchio* registers the books that have been classified as history, poetry, and grammar.

Federico's copy of the *Controversia* appears in this last category, among histories and panegyrics (Stornajolo, *Codices Urbinates Graeci* cxxxv).[12] The *Controversia* was considered primarily an exercise in rhetoric. In the *Indice vecchio*, it is classified by form, grouped with other disputations, as well as with invectives and laudatory pieces. Read more for its structure of argument than content, the *Controversia*, in this environment, was understood as a rhetorical tool.[13]

But this is not the only way that the *Controversia* has been classified. From the fifteenth century to today, the text continues to be categorized in multiple ways. The history of the *Controversia* reveals the complexity of the rhetorical strategies that can be deployed in a single text. For instance, the translation of the *Controversia* in French was packaged and received as a courtly didactic text.[14] The adoption of illustrations and scripts that were traditional in romance manuscripts reconfigured the *Controversia* in its French instantiation. As a result, the translation became a part of the corpus of courtly vernacular literature, and is still understood to be a participant in that tradition today.

In recent years, the *Controversia* has become a standard point of reference for historians with regard to the development of Florentine identity. Although Buonaccorso wrote many of his works in imitation of classical models,[15] some scholars cite the *Controversia* as a crucial piece of evidence in the reconstruction of civic humanism in the fifteenth century. Because the dialogue underscores the public contributions of the suitors, the *Controversia* has traditionally been upheld as a demonstration of typical Quattrocento civic pride, as well as evidence of the rise of the middle class.[16]

The various ways in which the *Controversia de nobilitate* has been and can be classified underscores the competing strategies of representation that operate within the text and its instantiations. The treatise can be understood as a rhetorical piece, as it seems to have been in Federico's library in Urbino and more widely in Quattrocento Italy. Its French translation has been written into the tradition of courtly romance. Some scholars in the early twentieth century, however, have chosen to view Buonaccorso's work as a clear statement of civic humanist principles that were particular to Florence in the fifteenth century. In this way, the *Controversia* participates in multiple and apparently rival categories. The consequences of this flexibility will be explored next, when the rules of classification that divide the *Controversia* are concretized in architectural terms.

THE MYTH MANIFEST

The Bibliothèque nationale de France (BnF) in Paris currently holds twenty-two copies of the *Controversia de nobilitate*.[17] There are ten manuscripts and four printed editions in Latin. In addition to these books, there are three manuscripts of the French translation, three printed books in French, as well as printed editions in German and English. Depending on their form, subject, and date of production, the books have been stored at different sites of the BnF.

The separation of materials according to form is the most marked. This division is made explicit architecturally, and indeed geographically. The manuscript versions of the *Controversia* are preserved in the centrally located Richelieu building, while their printed counterparts are stored in Site Tolbiac/François-Mitterrand in the 13ème arrondissement of Paris. This institutional division springs from the perception that a fundamental change took place when books began to be produced with a printing press. According to this view, manuscripts are unruly and chaotic; they do not conform to established categories of knowledge. Print, on the other hand, is thought to be consistent and stable. But the *Controversia* contests this notion and the organizational structure of the BnF by its manifestations in the two forms. The text of the *Controversia de nobilitate* remains remarkably consistent, showing little to no variation in and across the manuscript and printed versions.[18] By bridging the conceptual gap between the two technologies of writing in this way, the *Controversia* challenges the idea that manuscripts and printed materials are necessarily and substantively different because of their method of production.

Site Tolbiac, the newest building of the BnF, was opened in 1989 to house printed materials. Subject matter is taken as the major organizational principle at Tolbiac, within and without. While the contents of the library are arranged according to subject, the architecture of the library has also been configured according to these rules. The building is composed of four large towers, each of which houses a specific subject area: Law, Science, History, and Literature. Books are stored in their appropriate tower, and may be read in an adjoining reading room that has been assigned the same subject category. In this way, the internal structure of the library is made visible by architectural space. Tolbiac embodies the classificatory scheme that governs its contents.

The books of the *Controversia* cannot escape this system of organization. The online catalog splits the *Controversia* into such subjects as Catholic theology, Church Fathers, natural law, ethics, and literature. Although the books preserve the same text, they have been sent to different towers for storage. The appearance of the *Controversia* in multiple places in the catalog and in multiple places in Tolbiac brings to light the defects of the conceptual and architectural divisions of the library, and more particularly, the system that generated these categories.

In addition to subject divisions, another layer of classification has been imposed upon the *Controversia de nobilitate*. Some of its books have been designated as rare. These particular copies of the *Controversia* are kept in the vault and are only available in the Rare Books Reserve Room. The organizational system that governs the rest of the library does not apply to books that are held in the Reserve; books that have been classified as rare are not arranged by subject. Indeed, the Web site of the BnF boasts that the contents of the Rare Books Room "are classified independently of the overall thematic divisions of the new library."[19] Its holdings are not based on subject matter, but on date of printing. In this space, then, the *Controversia* is not categorized by its form or subject, but by its publication date.

While other reading rooms are situated on the lower *rez-de-jardin*, the Department of Rare Books is located on an upper floor in Room Y. The physical distinction of the Rare Books Reserve makes manifest the conceptual break that separates the rare books of the *Controversia* from its counterparts. Moreover, the digital principles of the Tolbiac building are ignored in the Reserve. Unlike the other reading rooms in the library, seats in Room Y cannot be reserved online, nor can materials be requested through the digital retrieval system. Instead, when granted entry to the Reserve, the reader must register by hand at the desk. Requests for books must also be made by hand and submitted at the desk. In every way, Room Y seeks to distinguish itself from the rest of the Tolbiac library. At the same time, it recalls the traditional rites that continue to be exercised in the Manuscripts Room of the old Richelieu building.

The Rare Books Room of Tolbiac undermines the theoretical division that separates manuscript from print, as well as the idea that printed material is by nature orderly. The Tolbiac building is founded upon the notion that the book was crucially changed with the advent of print technology. The new library, purportedly designed for printed books, is unable or unwilling to integrate incunabula and other early printed material into its space. Moreover, it treats early printed books as if they were manuscripts by maintaining the rituals of rareness that had been established in the old Richelieu location. By doing so, Tolbiac destabilizes its own claim that manuscripts and printed books are sufficiently different to require separation.

The architectural design of Tolbiac is founded upon an underlying programme of monumental display, not unlike the principles of exhibition that governed the fifteenth-century *studiolo* in Urbino. Indeed, the Tolbiac library was conceived and built on a grand scale. The four L-shaped towers, each 79 m in height, are designed to evoke the image of open books. These towers are explicit displays of both the ownership and control of knowledge. Moreover, in the early plans of the library, the towers were intended to be made of entirely transparent materials so that the accumulation and sedimentation of knowledge could be put on public exhibition (Mandosio 46).

The four towers are connected by long passageways, creating a rectangular shape around an interior garden. The construction self-consciously makes reference to the design of medieval cloisters, and summons the same notion of scholarly life that had been of great importance to writers like Alberti. Although the central courtyard creates an ideal space for study, the reader is prohibited from entering it. The garden is purely for display; it is populated by large cables and pulleys rigged to prevent the trees from damaging the glass building. The courtyard serves a purpose only in the ideological conception of the architect, Dominique Perrault, who believed that something magical could occur in the green space (Jacques 48). But the garden is merely rhetorical, invoking the idea of contemplation without allowing such activity to take place.

The spaces of Tolbiac are clearly circumscribed: there are spaces for storing books, and there are spaces for contemplating them. There is, however, no strong central sense of a space for reading. The process of reading and researching has been forgotten (Vidler 122). The architectural emphasis of Tolbiac is on the storage of books and, by extension, the storage of knowledge. The towers display the collection and possession of information; they attempt to make visible the ownership of knowledge. A colossal space of performance, the library has become a symbol, a grand memorial to knowledge.

By following the *Controversia de nobilitate*, we have explored how the scholarly ideal has been embodied in libraries from the fifteenth century until today. This historical understanding of the library as a complex site of self-representation will serve us well as we turn our attention to the spaces of books and reading that are now emerging in the digital environment. The digital library recalls the same myths of scholarly identity that have become embedded in the cultural imagination over the centuries. It will, like its predecessors, continue to be a place in which complicated strategies of exhibition are deployed. As the library takes shape in the digital environment, we can track how its spaces are configured by the scholarly ideal, and how it, in turn, reconfigures the scholarly ideal. Furthermore, we will be present for the birth of new myths, and be on hand as these myths of the digital begin to manifest themselves in our world.

NOTES

1. See also, Serlio.

2. See Elam; Liebenwein; O'Gorman; Thornton; Petrucci.

3. The Italian, French, and German translations render the same phrase more accurately as 'fine furnishings'. Some of the extant texts of the *Controversia* provide further detail, itemising a marriage bed and other home fixtures. For the translation in French, see Vanderjagt, "Qui sa" 220; for the German, see von Wyle 312.

4. Seneca had alluded to this in *De Tranquilitate Animi*, IX.7: ". . . [F]or by now among cold baths and hot baths a library also is equipped as a necessary ornament of a great house" (249).

5. The decorations were completed at least by 1476; the artist may have been Domenico Roselli, under the architectural guidance of Luciano Laurana, who worked on Federico's *palazzo* from 1465 to 1472. See Cheles; Clough,"Federigo."

6. Probably conceived by Joos van Ghent. See Cheles 37–52; Davies 52–59; Gnudi 25–38; Tenzer 95–104. In general, see also, Clough, "Federigo."

7. Some scholars argue that the portrait of Federico and his son, Guidobaldo, now held in the Galleria Nazionale delle Marche in Urbino, was also arranged in this series of paintings. However, attempts at reconstructing the order of the frieze are still problematic. See Cheles 49; Clough, "Federigo" 281. In general, see also, Davies; Gnudi.

8. Cf. Cheles 87.

9. In general, see Rotondi.

10. Lucas Holstenio (1596–1661) relates that eight cupboards of seven shelves each lined the walls, and that the books were piled on top of each other, three or four codices high. See Vespasiano 83–114. See also, Raffaelli; Moranti and Moranti.

11. Probably by Agapito. Lorenzo Astemio appears as the librarian around 1490, and Federico Veterano appears only after 1502. See Moranti, "Organizzazione" 42–43, esp. n. 87. The *Indice vecchio* is transcribed in Stornajolo, *Codices Urbinates Graeci* xx–ccii. See also, Clough, "The Library" 101–104; Herstein 113–128; Tocci, "La formazione" 9–18. In general, see Tocci, "Agapito." Vespasiano's 'catalogue' also dates from after Federico's death, around 1482 (83–114).

12. See this manuscript again in the sixteenth-century catalogue of Veterano (Guasti 148); Stornajolo suspects that this copy might be the manuscript currently known as Bib. Apost. Vat., Urbin. lat. 1250 (*Codices Urbinates Latini* 235).

13. Robert Black believes that Florence, Bib. Ricc. 693, which includes Cicero as well as Buonaccorso in Latin, is a school manuscript (269). Other similar manuscripts containing the *Controversia* that were discarded from his study were Florence, Bib. Ricc. 660, Ricc. 671, and Bib. Laur. Ash. 1657.

14. See Vanderjagt, "Il pubblico"; Vanderjagt, "Between Court"; Vanderjagt, "Three Solutions"; Vanderjagt, "Qui sa."

15. Buonaccorso also composed an oration for Cataline against Cicero, in which he draws on Sallust's description in section 31 of *The Conspiracy of Catiline* (*Orazioni* 1–14). Francesco Tateo notes Buonaccorso's reliance on the *De inventione* for his form of argument in the *Controversia* (362 n. 8), while Hans Baron observes that the character of Flaminius has striking similarities to Marius from Sallust's *The Jurgurthine War* (420–423; Jorde 64–77).

16. Charles Trinkaus believes that the *Controversia* exposes Buonaccorso's insecurity regarding his own position in society (50). Hans Baron, Quentin Skinner, and Alexander Murray all point to the text as an indication of the changing intellectual climate in the Italian city-states (Baron 420–423; Skinner 81; Murray 180–181).

17. Latin manuscripts: lat. 14177, lat. 15087, lat. 18534, lat. 4329, lat. 6098, lat. 6254, lat. 6711, lat. 7808, lat. 7862, lat. 7167.A; Latin printed editons: C.674, Rés. Z–478 [Cologne, 1473]; Rés. E*–314, Z–1475 [Louvain, 1501]; French manuscripts: fr. 1968, fr. 5413, n. acq. fr. 10722; French print editions: Rés. D–862 [Bruges, 1476]; Vélins 412, Rés. E*–46 (Paris, 1497); German printed edition: Rés. Z–543 [Esslingen, 1478]; English printed edition: Rés. R–79 ([Westminster], 1481).

18. See Mak.
19. For general critiques, see Dawson; Durlik; Mandosio

REFERENCES

Alberti, Leon Battista. *L'Architettura [De re aedificatoria]*. Ed. and Trans. Giovanni Orlandi. Vol. 2. Milan: Polifilo, 1966.2 vols.

Baldi, Bernardino. *Memorie concernenti la città di Urbino*. 1578. Reprinted in [Bologna?]: Arnaldo Forni, 1978.

Baron, Hans. *The Crisis of the Early Italian Renaissance*. Princeton, NJ: Princeton University Press, 1966.

Black, Robert. *Humanism and Education in Medieval and Renaissance Italy: Tradition and Innovation in Latin Schools from the Twelfth to the Fifteenth Century*. New York: Cambridge University Press, 2001.

Buonaccorso da Montemagno. *Orazioni di Buonaccorso da Montemagno il Giovine*. Ed. Michele dello Russo. Naples: F. Ferrante, 1862.

———. *Prose e Rime de' due Buonaccorso da Montemagno*. Ed. Giovanni Casotti. Florence: G. Manni, 1718.

Cheles, Luciano. *The Studiolo of Urbino: An Iconographic Investigation*. Wiesbaden: L. Reichert, 1986.

Clough, Cecil. "Federigo da Montefeltro's Private Study in His Ducal Palace of Gubbio." *Apollo* 86 (1967): 278–87.

———. "The Library of the Dukes of Urbino." *Librarium* 9 (1966): 101–5.

Cotrugli, Benedetto. *Il libro dell'arte di mercatura*. Ed. Ugo Tucci. Venice: Arsenale, 1990.

dal Poggetto, Paolo. "Nuova lettura di ambienti federiciani: il Bagno cosidetto 'della Duchessa' e la Biblioteca del duca Federico." *Federico da Montefeltro: lo stato, le arti, la cultura*. Ed. Giorgio Baiardi, Giorgio Chittolini, and Piero Floriani. Vol. 2. Rome: Bulzoni, 1986. 105–17. 3 vols.

———. "Il restauro della Biblioteca del Duca e delle sale attigue." *Il Palazzo di Federico da Montefeltro*. Ed. Maria Luisa Polichetti. Vol. 1. Urbino: Quattroventi, 1985. 699–708. 2 vols.

Davies, Martin. *Early Netherlandish School*. 2nd ed. London: National Gallery, 1955.

Dawson, Robert L. "The National Library of France: A Patron Reflects." *Libraries & Culture* 39.1 (Winter 2004): 76–88.

Durlik, Andrzej. "The Bibliothèque nationale de France: My French Experience." *Libraries & Culture* 37.3 (Summer 2002): 256–68.

Elam, Caroline. "'Studioli' and Renaissance Court Patronage." MA report, Courtauld Institute of Art, 1970.

Findlen, Paula. *Possessing Nature: Museums, Collecting, and Scientific Culture in Early Modern Italy*. Berkeley: University of California Press, 1994.

Gnudi, Cesare. "Lo Studiolo di Federico da Montefeltro nel Palazzo Ducale di Urbino." *Mostra di Melozzo e del quattrocento romagnolo*. Ed. Cesare Gnudi and Luisa Becherucci. Bologna: Stabilimenti Poligrafici, 1938. 25–38.

Guasti, Cesare. "Inventario della libreria urbinata compilato nel secolo XV da Federigo Veterano." *Giornale storico degli archivi toscani* 7 (1863): 45–55, 130–54.

Herstein, Sheila. "The Library of Federigo da Montefeltro, Duke of Urbino: Renaissance Book Collecting at its Height." *The Private Library* 4 (1971): 113–28.

Jacques, Michel, ed. *Bibliothèque nationale de France 1989–1995*. Paris: Artemis, 1995.

Jorde, Tilmann. *Cristoforo Landinos 'De vera nobilitate': ein Beitrag zur Nobilitas–Debatte in Quattrocento*. Stuttgart: Teubner, 1995.

Liebenwein, Wolfgang. *Studiolo: Die Entstehung eines Raumtyps und seine Entwicklung bis um 1600*. Berlin: Gebr. Mann, 1977.

Mak, Bonnie. "(re)Defining the Page for a Digital World." PhD diss., University of Notre Dame, 2004.

Mandosio, Jean-Marc. *L'effondrement de la très grande bibliothèque de France: ses causes, ses conséquences*. Paris: L'Encyclopédie des nuisances, 1999.

Moranti, Maria. "Organizzazione della Biblioteca di Federico da Montefeltro." *Federico da Montefeltro: lo stato, le arti, la cultura*. Ed. Giorgio Baiardi, Giorgio Chittolini, and Piero Floriani. Vol. 3. Rome: Bulzoni, 1986. 19–49. 3 vols.

Moranti, Maria, and Luigi Moranti. *Il trasferimento dei "Codices Urbinates" alla Biblioteca Vaticana: cronistoria, documenti e inventario*. Urbino: Arti Grafiche, 1981.

Murray, Alexander. *Reason and Society in the Middle Ages*. New York: Oxford University Press, 1978.

O'Gorman, James. *The Architecture of the Monastic Library in Italy, 1300–1600*. New York: New York University Press, 1972.

Perry, Jon Pearson. "Practical and Ceremonial Uses of Plants Materials as 'Literary Refinements' in the Libraries of Leonello d'Este and his Courtly Literary Circle." *La Bibliofilia* 91.2 (1989): 121–73.

Petrucci, Armando. "Le biblioteche antiche." *Letteratura italiana*. Ed. Alberto Asor Rosa. Vol. 2. Turin: Einaudi, 1983. 8 vols.

Rabil, Jr., Albert, ed. and trans. *Knowledge, Goodness, and Power: The Debate over Nobility among Quattrocento Italian Humanists*. Binghamton, NY: Medieval & Renaissance Texts & Studies, 1991.

Raffaelli, Filippo. *La imparziale e veritiera istoria della unione della Biblioteca ducale di Urbino alla Vaticana di Roma*. Fermo: Bucher, 1877.

Rotondi, Pasquale. *The Ducal Palace of Urbino: Its Architecture and Decoration*. New York: Transatlantic Arts, 1969.

Seneca. *Moral Essays*. Trans. John W. Basore. Vol. 2. Cambridge, MA: Harvard University Press, 1935. 3 vols.

Serlio, Sebastiano. *On Domestic Architecture: The Sixteenth-Century Manuscript of Book VI in the Avery Library of Columbia University*. New York: Architectural History Foundation, 1978.

Skinner, Quentin. *The Foundations of Modern Political Thought*. Vol. 1. New York: Cambridge University Press, 1978. 2 vols.

Stornajolo, Cosimo. *Codices Urbinates Graeci Bibliothecae Vaticanae*. Rome: Typis Vaticanis, 1895.

———. *Codices Urbinates Latini*. Vol. 3. Rome: Typis Vaticanis, 1921. 3 vols.

Tateo, Francesco. *Tradizione e realità nel Umanesimo italiano*. Bari: Dedalo libri, 1974.

Tenzer, Virginia. "The Iconography of the Studiolo of Federico da Montefeltro in Urbino." Ph.D. diss., Brown University, 1985.

Thornton, Dora. *The Scholar in his Study: Ownership and Experience in Renaissance Italy*. New Haven, Conn.: Yale UP, 1997.

Tocci, Luigi Michelini. "Agapito, Bibliotecario 'Docto, Acorto et Diligente' della Biblioteca Urbinate alla fine del Quattrocento." *Collectanea Vaticana in honorem Anselmi M. Card. Albareda, Studi e Testi* 220 (1962): 243–80.

———. "La formazione della Biblioteca di Federico da Montefeltro: codici contemporanei e libri a stampa." *Federico da Montefeltro: lo stato, le arti, la cultura*. Ed. Giorgio Baiardi, Giorgio Chittolini, and Piero Floriani. Vol. 3. Rome: Bulzoni, 1986: 9–18. 3 vols.

Trinkaus, Charles. *Adversity's Noblemen: The Italian Humanists on Happiness*. New York: Columbia University Press, 1940.

Trithemius, Johannes. *In Praise of Scribes (De Laude Scriptorum)*. Ed. Klaus Arnold. Trans. Roland Behrendt. Lawrence, Kansas: Coronado, 1974.

Vanderjagt, A.J. "Between Court Literature and Civic Rhetoric. Buonaccorso da Montemagno's *Controversia de nobilitate*." *Courtly Literature: Culture and Context*. Ed. Keith Busby and Erik Cooper. Philadelphia: J. Benjamins, 1990: 561–72.

———. "Il pubblico dei testi umanistici nell'Italia settentrionale ed in Borgogna: Buonaccorso da Montemagno e Giovanni Aurispa." *Aevum* 70 (1996): 477–86.

———. "Three Solutions to Buonaccorso's *Disputatio de nobilitate*." In *Non Nova, Sed Nove: Mélanges de civilisation médiévale*, ed. Martin Gosman and Jaap van Os. Groningen: Bouma's Boekhuis, 1984: 247–59.

———. *Qui sa la vertu anoblist: The concepts of noblesse and chose publicque in Burgundian political thought*. Groningen: J. Miélot, 1981.

Vespasiano da Bisticci. *The Vespasiano Memoirs: Lives of Illustrious Men of the XVth Century*. Trans. William George and Emily Waters. Toronto: University of Toronto Press, 1997.

Vidler, Anthony. "Books in Space: Tradition and Transparency in the Bibliothèque de France." *Representations. Special Issue: Future Libraries* 42 (Spring 1993): 115–34.

von Wyle, Niclas. *Translationen*. Ed. Adelbert von Keller. Stuttgart: Litterarischer Verein, 1861.

13

Managing Pleasure: Library Architecture and the Erotics of Reading

Abigail Van Slyck

Dayton Associate Professor of Art History and Director of the Architectural Studies Program, Connecticut College, New London, CT

INTRODUCTION

Architecture plays a central role in shaping the user's experience of the library as place. A building's exterior forms set the tone for an individual's encounter with the institution: gates, steps, doors suggest the library's approachability (or lack thereof), its scale inspires awe (or not), and its formal vocabulary signals a kinship with other institutions of a similar style. A building's plan determines which interactions—with books, with library staff, with other users—are possible and which are impossible. The three-dimensional qualities of a building's interior spaces, as well as the furnishings and fittings in those spaces, constitute a sort of stage set that encourages users to play certain sanctioned roles, while making others seem unthinkable.

Librarians have long understood the importance of library architecture and have—from the founding of the American Library Association in 1876—campaigned for a central role in the library design process. At one level, their concern was symbolic; since their claims to professional status depended upon demonstrating mastery over a body of theory, library leaders were eager to be seen as more expert than architects in the principles of library design. At another level, however, librarians were also interested in architecture's impact on day-to-day library experience, especially their own. William F. Poole, the most outspoken critic of architect-designed libraries of the 1870s and 1880s, focused on planning inefficiencies that wasted staff time and effort (250). Yet, by the early twentieth century, librarians—particularly children's librarians—began to think systematically about using the qualities of place to affect the reader's experience as well. Clara W. Hunt of the Brooklyn Public Library argued that "a natural, friendly environment" would enhance "the child's love for the room" and (presumably) for reading (167).

Thus, it is somewhat surprising that scholars of library history have been slow to recognize the importance of library architecture to their work. Adopting historical methods that rely exclusively on written sources, they have tended to ignore material culture and the historical evidence that is built into the very walls of the library itself. As a result, these scholars have often overlooked opportunities to explore attitudes that were so ingrained in the culture that they could either not be verbalized or were not considered worthy of verbal expression.

This essay aims to demonstrate the insights that can emerge from treating library architecture as valid historical evidence in its own right. Specifically, it considers the material aspects that shape the library as place, and especially the various ways in which the library itself—its architecture, furnishings, and fittings—have shaped readers' encounters with books. Ultimately, it offers a new interpretation of the public library's institutional response to pleasure.

THE PROBLEM OF PLEASURE

In the late nineteenth century, most Americans considered the pursuit of pleasure antithetical to the serious purpose of the public library. Library advocates positioned the institution as a stabilizing force in a society buffeted by industrialization, urbanization, and mass immigration. The library's claims on public funding depended in large part upon its ability to serve the public good, accommodating only readers bent on self-improvement. Although library historians (notably Michael Harris and Phyllis Dain) have disputed the extent to which the library leaders acted in their own class interests, they concur that Victorian librarians saw the library as an extension of the public education system, and thus responsible for producing informed citizens. Public librarians and the trustees who employed them disdained the notion that the library would meet the needs of readers in search of mere enjoyment. The public library, they argued, was in the business of enlightenment, not entertainment.

Early debates about fiction reading have often been interpreted as the clearest manifestation of this ambivalence toward pleasure. Throughout the nineteenth century, public librarians paid close attention to what users read. As Dee Garrison has pointed out, they took pains to distinguish between fiction and nonfiction when reporting their circulation figures and measured their success by the number of nonfiction works borrowed (68). While some nineteenth-century librarians saw no place for fiction on the shelves of a public library, others acknowledged that some compromise was necessary. William I. Fletcher, for instance, compared the public librarian to a cook following an old recipe for preparing hare. The initial step was all-important: "first catch your hare" (quoted in Harris 2511). For many of Fletcher's contemporaries, fiction was the bait that would lure readers—the "hare"—to the library, where they would inevitably, if somewhat inexplicably, be attracted to so-called better works. Discomfited by such a laissez-faire approach, other early library leaders limited the number of works of fiction that an individual reader could check out at any one time, while imposing no such limits on works of nonfiction.

Such policies were largely dropped in the early twentieth century at the same time that many libraries adopted open shelves, service for children, and other practices that librarian Arthur E. Bostwick dubbed "the modern library idea." District of Columbia librarian George F. Bowerman rationalized the shift in 1906:

Fiction is the dominant form of literary expression to-day; it has the most universal appeal; it supplies education in kindliness, gentleness, good manners; it teaches history and geography, ethics and aesthetics, sociology and religion.

Despite his apologetic tone, he averred that "few public libraries apologize for the fact that considerably more than 50% of their circulation is fiction" (108).

This change in policy has been implicitly accepted as an indication that American library leaders had come to terms with the institution's role in the provision of pleasure reading. Yet, the debate about fiction was just one small part of a larger issue. A close examination of the physical environment of American libraries reveals that the institution's response to pleasure has been both longer-lived and more complex than the study of circulation policies alone might suggest. In fact, even in the late nineteenth century, those in charge of public libraries rarely attempted to stifle reading pleasure entirely. Instead, they used the library as place both to exploit and to manage an erotically charged interaction with books.

In order to understand this longer history and some of its implications, this essay will consider four moments in the history of American library architecture: the middle of the nineteenth century when social libraries first began to construct purpose-built facilities; the post–Civil War decades when architect Henry Hobson Richardson invented the small public library as a building type; the early twentieth century, when the small public library was reinvented under the auspices of the library-building program financed by Andrew Carnegie; and the post–World War II period, when new ideas about library efficiency led to the rise of modular libraries. At each point, the library as place supported and reinforced the cultural work of the library as institution.

VISUAL DELIGHT AND BODILY COMFORT IN SOCIAL LIBRARIES

Some of the earliest libraries built in North America were not public libraries at all, but private institutions supported by membership fees. In the early nineteenth century, these social libraries were organized and patronized primarily by elite men who used them as private clubs, albeit clubs of a distinctly edifying nature. According to Catharina Slautterback, the organizers of the Boston Athenaeum (incorporated in 1807) "desired nothing less than 'to check that dissipation which enervates and depraves' by substituting 'mental occupation for sensual indulgence'" (8). At the same time, the Athenaeum's early subscribers saw no conflict between this lofty moral purpose and pleasure. Indeed, one of their first goals was "to provide 'an agreeable place of resort' and 'opportunities of literary intercourse, and the pleasure of perusing the principal European and American periodicals'" (8). For over four decades, Athenaeum members pursued these pleasures in a series of rented rooms.

Opened in 1849, the Boston Athenaeum's first purpose-built building confirms the extent to which subscribers associated their cultural pursuits with class privilege (Figure 13.1). Located at 10-1/2 Beacon Street, the building was designed by Edward Clarke Cabot, an inexperienced, but well-connected, young man whose uncle was chairman of the Building Committee (Slautterback 34). The building's exterior evoked the forms of the substantial palazzi that architect Andrea Palladio had provided for the grandi of the Italian Veneto in the sixteenth century. In subsequent centuries, Palladian forms had enjoyed successive waves of popularity among British elites. By the middle of the nineteenth century, it was the style of choice for private clubs on both sides of the

Figure 13.1   Boston Athenaeum, Boston, Massachusetts, 1849, designed by Edward Clarke Cabot. Exterior.

Atlantic, including the Travellers' Club (1830–32) and the Reform Club (1838–40), prominent London clubs designed by Sir Charles Barry. In Boston, it was a logical choice for an institution that provided the city's cultural aristocracy with exclusive use of a library, reading rooms, natural history displays, and art galleries.

Given the elite character of the building's exterior, it is little wonder that the Athenaeum's library had an equally distinguished pedigree. Located on the second floor of the new building toward the interior of the block, the book-storage room was a long, double-height alcoved room modeled on princely and university libraries. Like those libraries, the emphasis was on a dazzling display of books, a vista that made symbolic reference to the viewer's ownership and control of the collection, while emphasizing the extent of its holdings (Figure 13.2).

At the Athenaeum, the Long Room (as this book-storage room was called) played a key role in the members' experience of the library as place. The stairway deposited members on the second-floor landing in front of a centrally placed doorway that led into the Long Room through its westernmost alcove. From that point, they could either turn left and walk the length of the Long Room (and thence into a museum room of natural history displays) or they could turn right and move into a spacious reading room, which in turn communicated with the librarian's office. All of the rooms on this floor were

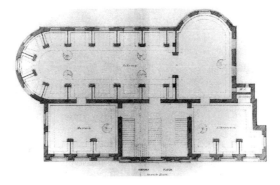

Figure 13.2   Boston Athenaeum, second-floor plan.

Figure 13.3   Boston Athenaeum, "Long Room,"
photograph from 1902.

fitted out with galleries reached from spiral stairs (although those in the Long Room
were soon relocated into alcoves).

From its inception, the Long Room facilitated an interaction between the reader and
the book that had a distinctly erotic component. The long galleried room arrayed the
Athenaeum's book collection for the visual delectation of elite male bibliophiles, while
open access policies encouraged readers to handle individual books at will, allowing
each volume's tactile appeal to figure into the book selection process (Figure 13.3).
Reading alcoves allowed readers—seated in relaxed postures—to enjoy the company of
their selected companion in a modicum of privacy.

The eroticism of this interaction may have figured into the shock and horror with
which Athenaeum librarian Charles Folsom reacted to the suggestion that women be
admitted to the library. (Although an 1855 engraving depicts a few women using the
library under male guidance, women were in fact only allowed to use the Athenaeum's art
galleries.) Folsom's argument against mixed-sex library use is fascinating in that it was
couched not in terms of any unsuitability of the female mind to serious study—an opinion
that was often expressed in other contexts—but rather in terms of sexual modesty; Folsom
pointed out, for instance, that the very idea of traversing the narrow galleries and steep
staircases should "cause a decent female to shrink"; he also worried that the unavoidable
spectacle of an active female form "would occasion frequent embarrassment to modest
men" (quoted in *Athenaeum Centenary* 41). Like the urban demi-monde that catered
more overtly to the erotic desires of respectable men, the private athenaeum library was
off-limits to "decent females."

How might we account for the gap between the stated mission of the Boston
Athenaeum (which positioned sensual indulgence in opposition to mental occupation)
and the material character of the Athenaeum library (which revealed that the two objectives were not mutually exclusive)? At one level, it seems to be the product of class
privilege, and particularly the privilege to pursue mental occupations in a place that
made books themselves the focus of sensual indulgence. At another level, however, that
gap actually played a role in defining and naturalizing class differences. By fanning the
flames of desire for books without seeming to do so, the Athenaeum—that is, the place

Figure 13.4   Winn Memorial Library, Woburn, Massachusetts, opened 1879, designed by Henry Hobson Richardson. Exterior.

itself—helped reinforce the sense that a natural, in-born taste for literary intercourse set Athenaeum members apart—and above—their less bookish neighbors. In other words, Athenaeum membership was not simply a passive reflection of privilege, but also— thanks in part to the material character of place—an active producer of class status.

TANTALIZING VISTAS IN RICHARDSON'S VICTORIAN LIBRARIES

The libraries that opened their doors to the public in the nineteenth century have a complex relationship to social libraries. Often organized by men who were already athenaeum members, public libraries (or so library historians like Michael Harris maintain) allowed athenaea to continue to function as private clubs for the community's elite. Certainly, these public libraries defined their mission quite differently from earlier athenaea, aiming exclusively at the edification of readers rather than at their delight. Yet, the buildings in which these institutions were housed orchestrated an interaction between readers and books that retained some of the erotically charged qualities of the athenaeum experience.

The Winn Memorial Library in Woburn, Massachusetts, is a case in point (Figure 13.4). Built between 1876 and 1879, it was the first of four small-town libraries built to the designs of Henry Hobson Richardson, the most prominent American architect of the post–Civil War period. As architectural historian Kenneth Breisch has demonstrated, these libraries were paid for by private funds, typically bequests from the men of families who "prided themselves on being descended from 'pure Old New England stock'" and who remained very much in control of library boards of trustees (32). Nonetheless, these libraries were open to the public and helped establish a new direction in the architecture of small public libraries for decades to come.

On the exterior, the open-lot setting, irregular massing, and Romanesque Revival vocabulary distinguished the Winn Memorial Library from the more regular, classical athenaeum buildings that typically filled their urban sites. Built in an era that historian Lawrence Levine has associated with the "sacralization of culture," the building's formal similarity to medieval revival churches was presumably also intended to suggest that the library supplemented the work of religious institutions by reinforcing moral order in a

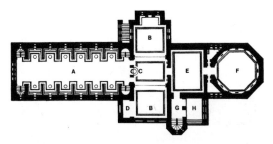

Figure 13.5   Winn Memorial Library, first-floor plan.

time of social upheaval (167–68). Local lore, however, maintains that this church-like exterior was initially mistaken for a new church, and so discouraged would-be readers from venturing in.

If the exterior of this Richardson-designed library is distinct from earlier athenaea, its interior reveals a number of similarities between the two types. Chief among these is the reliance on a long, double-height, alcoved book hall, fitted out with galleries and spiral stairs (labeled A in Figure 13.5). Another is the provision of a comfortable reading room, equipped with two alcoves, one fitted out with a massive fireplace. Finally, like the Boston Athenaeum, the Winn Memorial Library also included an art gallery and a museum room for the display of natural history specimens.

Yet, the user's experience was substantially different at the Winn Memorial Library, in large part because the library's closed-shelf policy prompted Richardson to reverse the Athenaeum's entry sequence, positioning the reading room between the entrance and the long galleried book hall (Figure 13.6). Like athenaeum members, library users could enjoy the tantalizing display of books, but unlike an athenaeum's subscribers, they were prohibited from entering the warm and visually inviting room. Not only did library policies prohibit this kind of access, but the design itself also interrupted the erotic connection between readers and books, inserting—almost prophylactically—the catalog and the librarian (seated at a prominent delivery desk) into the book selection process.

Figure 13.6   Winn Memorial Library, reading room.

Figure 13.7   Carnegie Library, Greenville, Ohio,
1901–3, designed by W.S. Kaugman. Exterior.

Another check on the erotic encounter with books was the presence of female
readers, who were accommodated in special ladies' reading rooms in many nineteenth-
century public libraries (although not in any of those designed by Richardson). As I have
argued, such rooms were ostensibly intended to safeguard the respectability of female
readers by protecting them from male leers. In many libraries, however, architectural
devices framed the view into the ladies' reading room, putting the seated, reading female
form on display in a tableau vivant of respectable behavior ("Lady" 239).

Despite the fact that the American Library Association launched a vociferous attack
on this book-storage system upon its founding in 1876, such galleried book halls remained a favorite among library boards and their architects until about 1890. Richardson
himself designed four more (in the public libraries in North Easton, Quincy, and Malden,
Massachusetts, and in the Billings Library at the University of Vermont), while his suc-
cessors Shepley, Rutan, and Coolidge included one in the Howard Memorial Library in
New Orleans. Elsewhere I have suggested that the appeal of this room type lay in its ability to give material expression to the family metaphors that sustained nineteenth-century
philanthropy (*Free* 7–8). But we can also look upon them as attempts by library boards
to exploit and then manage the user's desire to handle books, harnessing the erotically
charged encounter with books in the service of edification.

OPEN SHELVES AND BODILY RESTRAINT IN CARNEGIE LIBRARIES

In the early twentieth century, Andrew Carnegie launched a library-building program
that essentially reinvented the small public library. One of his most revolutionary steps
was to allow leaders in the library profession to articulate the planning principles that
guided the design of hundreds of Carnegie-financed library buildings (Van Slyck, *Free*
33–40). While these symmetrical, classically detailed buildings share something in
common with midcentury athenaea, they orchestrated the encounter between readers
and books in wholly new ways (Figure 13.7).

The typical Carnegie library was a single large space subdivided by low partitions
into a reading room for adults, one for children, and a workspace for the librarian, whose
central position facilitated her visual supervision of the entire building (Figure 13.8).

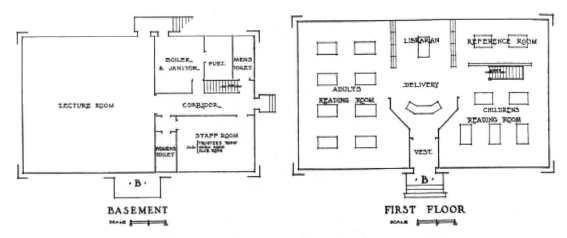

Figure 13.8 Schematic plan of Carnegie library, from "Notes on the Erection of Library Bildings [sic]" (New York: Carnegie Corporation of New York, 1911), n.p.

Books were stored in seven-foot-tall bookshelves that lined the perimeter walls of the reading rooms.

At first glance, this arrangement seems to give early twentieth-century public library users privileges that mid–nineteenth-century athenaeum members had once enjoyed. Not only were books stored in close proximity to reading areas, but for the first time in American history, public library users were also allowed to fetch their own books directly from the shelves.

Yet, if these buildings gave public library users unlimited visual and tactile access to book collections, they also tended to strip the experience of its erotic component. The seven-foot-tall bookcases may have allowed users to fetch books without recourse to a ladder or step stool, but they dampened the visual delight of books displayed in multitiered galleries. Equally important, Carnegie libraries were devoid of the private alcoves into which a reader could retire to enjoy an hour's dalliance with an attractive book. Indeed, the rationale behind the plan of such a library was to make sure that readers felt themselves under the constant visual scrutiny of the staff—more likely to be the moralizing female gaze, thanks to the feminization of small-town and branch librarianship in these decades (Garrison 180). Privacy had no place in this very public library space.

Finally, these early twentieth-century libraries ruptured the erotic connection between the reader and the book by demanding an unprecedented degree of bodily restraint on the part of the reader. Furniture layouts—which were an integral component of the schematic plans published by the Carnegie Corporation—featured orderly arrangements of rectangular tables, while official photographs highlighted approved postures (Figure 13.9). Readers—initially even young readers in the children's room—were expected to sit close together, to face the table squarely, to keep both feet on the floor, and to keep their hands to themselves. This mode of bodily restraint remained the ideal at least through the interwar period. As late as 1941, librarian Joseph L. Wheeler and architect Alfred Morton Githens recommended chairs without front rungs "to discourage 'heel-hanging' and tipping backward" (450).

Figure 13.9   Hazelwood Branch, Carnegie Library
of Pittsburgh, Pittsburgh, Pennsylvania, opened 1900,
designed by Alden and Harlow. Children's room.

These constraints were eventually only relaxed in children's rooms, when children's librarians began to apply the insights of the emerging field of child psychology to their work. Having accepted that children were not constitutionally able to behave like adults, children's librarians—like Mary Emogene Hazeltine of the James Prendergast Free Library in Jamestown, New York—envisioned children's rooms where the child "can 'tumble about' almost at will" (369). Child-size chairs, round tables, low benches, and sometimes even window seats allowed youngsters to adopt a wider range of bodily postures. Children were even allowed to sit on the floor, especially during story-hour when they gathered around a female librarian seated—often—in front of a fireplace built into a specially designed story-hour alcove. In these instances, informal postures encouraged young readers—including those from working-class and immigrant families—to perform a version of familial relations dear to middle-class hearts.

The extent to which this bodily comportment was a function of social class becomes apparent in newspaper-reading rooms established in large urban libraries in the same period. Conventional library wisdom identified the newspaper-reading room with working-class men who came to the library primarily to consult the racing form. In the Chicago Public Library at the turn of the century, readers stood in front of the newspaper racks—preferably with their hands behind their backs, minimizing physical contact with their reading material (Figure 13.10).

In short, at just the moment when the change in policy suggests that libraries had dropped their ambivalence toward reading for pleasure, the library buildings themselves tell a different story. Not only did a certain level of ambivalence about the pleasures of reading remain, but that ambivalence was also complicated by the age, the class, and—given the practice of racial segregation in many American libraries—by the race of the reader as well.

PROMISCUOUS ACCESS TO BOOKS IN POSTWAR MODULAR LIBRARIES

In the postwar period, the form of American libraries changed dramatically with the introduction of modular planning, first used on university and college campuses in the

Figure 13.10 Chicago Public Library, Chicago, Illinois, opened 1897, designed by Shepley, Rutan & Coolidge. Newspaper reading room.

late 1940s and eventually adopted in the design of public libraries as well. A reaction to the self-supporting stacks that university libraries had been using to maximize book storage capacity, the modular library was intended to reintegrate readers and bookshelves in larger libraries, while also fulfilling librarians' dreams of complete flexibility. According to David Kaser, the use of a standard construction module (established at 22-$\frac{1}{2}$ feet as early as 1943) allowed heavy bookshelves to be located anywhere in the library, while 8-foot ceiling heights offered what was considered an acceptable compromise between shelving efficiency and reader comfort (115).

Although librarians have tended to focus on its impact on library service, the modular plan revolutionized the library as place, offering an unstructured—even promiscuous—interaction between readers and books. Not only could readers fetch books for themselves, but they could also then retire with them to any one of a number of secluded areas where they could read in almost complete privacy (Figure 13.11). What is more, these reading spaces were fitted out with comfy furniture. Soft, upholstered armchairs

Figure 13.11 Charles E. Shain Library, Connecticut College, New London, Connecticut, opened 1976, designed by Kilham, Beder and Chu. Interior.

encouraged readers to assume relaxed, even languorous, postures, wrapping the book in a warm embrace. Couches—introduced to libraries for the first time in the postwar era—allowed friends to sit close to one another on the same surface. The long-standing library practice of using single chairs to individuate the body of each reader was cast aside.

Yet, when everything is permitted, the thrill is gone. Other aspects of the design worked to diminish the romance of the interaction. Uniform ceiling heights did nothing to identify the encounter with books as special, while the reliance on fluorescent ceiling light fixtures meant that lighting was ample, but not calculated to enhance the act of reading. In other words, modular libraries no longer attempted to harness the erotics of reading to serve a larger mission.

What is more, some librarians were so excited by the prospect of having achieved the long-desired goal of a completely flexible library space that they seemed to lose sight of the library as place. Kaser, for instance, criticized the design of Washington University library (opened in 1962) for introducing natural light; "since the building was amply and ambiently lit artificially," natural light was simply "not needed" (137). That readers might find it pleasant was not considered pertinent.

In recent years, there has been some recognition of the limitations inherent in conceptualizing library design solely in terms of efficiency. Hoping to entice and inspire readers, a host of brand-name architects have reintroduced both grand reading rooms and intimate spaces into public library design. Yet, the critical response continues to emphasize efficiency and especially the speed with which readers can access books (or other library materials). *Metropolis* magazine, for instance, tested the efficacy of the new Seattle Public Library (designed by a team led by Rem Koolhaas's Office of Metropolitan Architecture) by having staff members time how long it took to find back issues of the publication; from the moment they entered the building at 5th Avenue, it took a scant ten minutes, including a consultation with a librarian, an on-line key word search, and securing a printed map of the book-storage Spiral customized to their search ("Making" 100). Envisioning the institution's role as meeting a desire for library materials that was full-formed in readers' minds before they arrived at the library, even the architecturally savvy *Metropolis* staff ignored the extent to which the library as place could play a role in creating and managing that desire.

RETHINKING PLEASURE

This close consideration of the library as a physical place highlights the limitations of historical studies that rely exclusively on written records. Nineteenth-century librarians may have been reluctant simply to satisfy the public's desire for pleasure reading, but that does not mean that the pleasures of reading were ignored entirely in Victorian libraries. Instead, H. H. Richardson adopted many of the architectural features that had been used to create an erotically charged encounter between the reader and the book in social libraries, while simultaneously arranging these features in a new configuration that introduced the librarian (and his concern for edification) into the book selection process. This new library type used pleasure strategically—flaming the reader's desire for books and also seeking to control it. In contrast, the supposed freedom of open-shelf libraries of the early twentieth century was tempered by architectural and furniture arrangements that called upon readers to exercise an unparalleled degree of bodily restraint. In short, library architecture reveals aspects of the user's experience that the written record obscures.

At the same time, this consideration of library as place confirms the subtle ways in which the institution has reinforced class differences. The library spaces designed for the greatest intimacy between readers and books are those used by well-defined communities of elites (like the members of the Boston Athenaeum) or those in the process of becoming elites (like matriculating students of a college or university). Public libraries may have been called "palaces of the people," but for most of the twentieth century they required readers to prove their trustworthiness by assuming bodily postures dictated by the institution.

If this attention to library architecture highlights the public library's historic role in reinforcing class differences, it also offers a useful way to thinking about how libraries continue to engage with users across lines of difference. Do public libraries treat all members of the community in the same way? Which library users are accorded the privileges associated with the pleasure of reading? Which library users are expected to comport themselves with greater restraint? To what extent does the library attempt to heighten the user's desire for library materials? To what extent does the library manage pleasure in order to serve its mission? Perhaps one of the more important lessons from the history of library architecture is the extent to which the library as place can contribute to the library as institution.

REFERENCES

Athenaeum Centenary: The Influence and History of the Boston Athenaeum from 1807–1907. Boston: Boston Athenaeum, 1907.

Bostwick, Arthur. *The American Public Library.* New York: D. Appleton and Co., 1910.

Bowerman, George F. "The Public Library of the District of Coumbia as an Organ of Social Advance." *Charities and the Commons* 16 (April 14, 1906): 105–10.

Breisch, Kenneth A. *Henry Hobson Richardson and the Small Public Library in America: A Study in Typology.* Cambridge, MA: MIT Press, 1997.

Dain, Phyllis. "Ambivalence and Paradox: The Social Bonds of the Public Library." *Library Journal* 100 (1975): 261–66.

Garrison, Dee. *Apostles of Culture: The Public Librarian and American Society, 1876–1920.* New York: Free Press, 1979.

Harris, Michael H. "The Purpose of the American Public Library: A Revisionist Interpretation." *Library Journal* 98 (1973): 2509–14.

Hazeltine, Mary Emogene. "The Children's Room in the Public Library." *Chautauquan* 39 (June 1904): 369–74.

Hunt, Clara W. "Maintaining Order in the Children's Room." *Library Journal* 28 (April 1903): 164–67.

Kaser, David. *The Evolution of the American Academic Library Building.* Lanham, Maryland: Scarecrow Press, 1997.

Levine, Lawrence. *Highbrow/Lowbrow: The Emergence of Cultural Hierarchy in America.* Cambridge MA: Harvard University Press, 1988.

"The Making of a Library." *Metropolis* (October 2004): 97–115.

Poole, William F. "Small Library Buildings." *Library Journal* 10 (Sept.–Oct. 1885): 250–256.

Slautterback, Catharina. *Designing the Boston Athenaeum: 10-1/2 at 150.* Boston: Boston Athenaeum, 1999.

Van Slyck, Abigail A. *Free to All: Carnegie Libraries and American Culture, 1890-1920.* Chicago: University of Chicago Press, 1995.

———. "The Lady and the Library Loafer: Gender and Public Space in Victorian America." *Winterthur Portfolio* 31 (Winter 1996): 221–42.

Wheeler, Joseph L., and Alfred Morton Githens. *The American Public Library Building: Its Planning and Design with Special Reference to Administration and Service.* New York: Charles Schribner's Sons, 1941.

14

Going to Hell:
Placing the Library in *Buffy the Vampire Slayer*

Adriana Estill

Assistant Professor of English and American Studies, Carleton College, Northfield, Minnesota

> We also need the library as a place because we are human beings. 'The library' is always one of the focal points of its community. (Gorman 46)

> I don't know about the rest of you, but I'd like to get out of this place. I don't like the library much anymore. (Rupert Giles, librarian, at the end of the first season of *Buffy the Vampire Slayer*.) ("Prophecy Girl")

In early July 2004, the National Endowment for the Arts released a survey of reading in America that suggests forcefully that reading is in decline and that "it has been happening more rapidly and more pervasively than anyone thought possible" (Weber). *Buffy the Vampire Slayer* (hereafter *BtVS*) presciently charted this terrain of cultural anxiety about books and their societal role during its second season in 1997 when, after a vampire steals a book from the school library, Jenny Calendar, a computer teacher, exclaims, "Well, at least someone in this school is reading" ("Lie to Me"). In fact, the first three seasons of *BtVS* consistently addressed the cultural and social negotiations around reading, literacy, research, and, pivotally, the library's meaning as place.

Naming contemporary concerns about what roles libraries will play in a world increasingly lived online and in front of the television, Michael Gorman's recent book, *Our Enduring Values: Librarianship in the 21st Century*, declares that the "whole idea of the virtual library is an implicit challenge to the idea of the library as place" (43). Frieda Weise agrees, bluntly stating that the technological shifts we have seen in the last twenty years have led to the questioning of "the very idea of the library as a place" (6). Weise advocates for a "role for the library beyond the 'storage facility,' and even the 'access facility'" in order to "focus attention on the many other place-centered activities and services that the library can support" (12). Even a cursory survey of recent articles on libraries suggests a growing consensus that the library's quality as place matters. This quality is fundamental to everything, from its embodiment of "learning, culture, and other important secular values" (Gorman 45), to its function in building a sense of community [Demas 65; Harris 26; "A Sense of Place" 45ff], to its location as a hub for common experience (Westmoreland 138).

Yet at the same time that the physical place of the library finds numerous defenders, a recent article in *Library Quarterly* by Jeffrey Garrett suggests that the "true" library, in essence, is "an abstract system of organized data that is distinguished from all other artifacts and other physical things—as well as virtual representations—that we associate with it" (59–60). Though he separates the data from the building that contains it, Garrett does not suggest that we do away completely with the material library in his discussion of Web gateways. But he does argue that "physical space and physical geography become very secondary or even irrelevant properties of the modern library" (60). The focus on making information available discounts how the aesthetic and architectural organization of libraries not only reflect ways to access data but, more importantly, make available the means of producing knowledge and also make possible other, less informational or knowledge-based goals.

The first three seasons of the television program *Buffy the Vampire Slayer* consistently addressed how the high school library's status as place influenced its multiple uses and meanings. The series offers a portrait of how the place of the library is lived and socially produced by the characters who make use of it while in turn acting constitutively to influence their practices. In other words, the library does not act as a simple depository or retrieval space for information. Rather, the library's place enables negotiations around the acquisition of knowledge, the relationship between research and power, the drive to create community, and the desire for sanctuary. *Buffy the Vampire Slayer* thus offers a fruitful, albeit fictional, site in which to examine the continuing relevance of library as place.

The high school and its library are located within the televisual world of *BtVS*, a serial program that premiered in 1997 and had a seven-season run ending in 2003. Fictional Sunnydale appears to be a typical southern California town with almost-constant sunny weather, but it departs from the normal because it sits squarely on the "Hellmouth," a portal between this world and the demon universe. The Hellmouth's presence means that Sunnydale finds itself infested by vampires, demons, and other supernatural creatures. Luckily, Sunnydale has Buffy Summers, a high school student called to be the Slayer of the vampires and demons that haunt the town, something that almost every episode reminds the viewer of through the prefatory voice-over: "In every generation there is a Chosen One. She alone will stand against the vampires, the demons and the forces of darkness. She is the Slayer." The ritual repetition of the phrase provides historical continuity and an aural cue that we are now, as viewers, inserted into a fictional world, referred to as the "Buffyverse" in the copious writings on *BtVS*.

Over the years, viewers of *BtVS* came to know several Sunnydale spaces intimately: the cemetery, the high school, Buffy's house, and the Bronze, a student hangout. Of all these spaces, the most textured and dense is the high school with its multiple levels, intricate combination of public, private, and mixed-use spaces, classrooms that vary by function and representation, and, last but not least, the centrally located library, easily the most sustained, complex, and intriguing place in Sunnydale High. For the first three seasons, the library plays as big a role in the narrative as the principal characters: Buffy, Willow and Xander, Buffy's two principal friends and demon-fighting partners, and

Rupert Giles. Giles's job as the librarian acts as a cover and complement to his mission as the Vampire Slayer's Watcher. He trains her for combat and does the research that gives her the knowledge she needs for slaying.

Because of the library's pivotal place in the high school and in the world of demon slaying, its depiction offers us insight into the varied roles that libraries fulfill in addition to the oft-cited one of gathering and disseminating knowledge. Sunnydale's library also makes it apparent that these additional roles depend heavily on the physicality of the library, on the way that space and place are not static, fixed, or unchanging but, on the contrary, are lived and socially produced and understood. Michel Foucault has described "the space in which we live" as a "heterogeneous space":

In other words, we do not live in a kind of void, inside of which we could place individuals and things. . . . We live inside a set of relations that delineates sites which are irreducible to each other and absolutely not superimposable on one another. (Foucault "Of Other Spaces" 23)

Foucault's shift from the perception of space as static and void to heterogeneous and relational allows for a more nuanced understanding of how the library as place depends on human social practice as well as upon the aesthetic and architectural decisions of its builders. *BtVS* makes this complexity clear in its refusal to see the library as either a simple congregation of data or as an idealized embodiment of culture and secular learning. Instead, Sunnydale's library offers a portrait of paradoxes: hosting community and yet dissuading community; providing sanctuary while fostering danger; raising cultural literacy despite also endorsing moments and sites of ignorance. In each case, the show defamiliarizes the library's place for us, insisting that we understand its complex and alterable significance by moving away from the "sweeping narratives" that we associate with libraries and examine closely "one complex site traversed by many ideas and forces" (Howard 4).

INTRODUCING THE LIBRARY

The very first episode, "Welcome to the Hellmouth," opens to a nocturnal scene on the high school grounds, as the camera pans from outside the school, through walls, and directly to the library's doors. However, before entering the library, the camera swerves away toward a science classroom; the visual bait-and-switch foreshadows an impending character inversion. The camera focuses on a couple who illegally crashes into the classroom—a recent male graduate who acts like a rebel and his hesitant and frightened blonde date—and gazes on as the two reverse roles, frustrating viewer expectations for who's in trouble when she changes into a vampire and feeds on him.

And so the series's opening sequence warns viewers not to judge a book by its cover because, in the best of gothic clichés, appearances deceive. It also suggests that the camera—our mediating eye into this world—has the potential to misdirect us intentionally. In other words, both the camera work and the narrative warn us as viewers to maintain an active role because "at issue are the structure and dissemination of information itself" (McNeilly et al. par. 1). Thus the reliability of the information produced and received, whether in the show's storylines or between the televisual medium and the viewer, becomes a consistent theme that influences the library's role.

A few scenes later the camera pans the inside of the library as Buffy enters to find a history textbook she needs. At first glance the library provides an inviting space, sunny and bright because of its many windows and, we later learn, a skylight. The lower tier is occupied by a set of tables pushed together within an octagonal niche lined by low bookcases. A second tier rises above the niche and holds the stacks. The checkout desk is empty and the library appears to be deserted. The emptiness of the library, in spite of its comfortable and welcoming atmosphere and in comparison to the rest of the high school spaces, which, from courtyard to classroom, teem with first-day-at-school busyness, suggests its isolated status. But, more important, its initial barrenness implies that the library can have no meaning until people inhabit it and take part in its function.

Mr. Rupert Giles's sudden appearance from behind Buffy surprises her. Giles introduces himself as the librarian as, in almost the same moment, he recognizes Buffy as the chosen one, the vampire slayer, and greets her with the spooky "I was told you were coming." Instead of the textbook she has asked for, he offers up an old, leather tome with the title, VAMPYR, written in gold leaf. Buffy rejects this offering and flees the library.

At this point the show has foiled our expectations several times, stressing the opening scene's caveat to be wary of appearances (and our own assumptions). Neither the romantic couple, nor the library or the librarian are what they initially seem to be (or what in a typical high school drama they would be). Buffy, on the other hand, is almost instantly "unmasked." For the viewer this happens immediately after the credits as she wakes from a nightmare about vampires; shortly thereafter, Buffy drops a wooden stake in the hallways of the school, unwittingly exposing herself to the other characters. Buffy's position in these scenes of narrative duplicity highlights her desire to be the normal high school girl instead of a slayer so that her inner self would reflect her appearance. Buffy's initial encounter with the library's and Giles's doubleness ensures that the library becomes associated with the contained contradiction of expected duplicity.

Michael Curry has suggested that "we ought to look to the activities and practices that create places, and thereby to the ways in which places are supportive of the construction and maintenance of human identity" (Curry 2). In this formative first episode, when Willow recommends a book to Xander, Xander's reaction suggests that the library has no place on his mapping of the school; his practices have not occupied the library. As a result, the library supports the "construction and maintenance" of two dichotomous student identities: nerdy like Willow or academically clueless like Xander.

For the students like Xander, the library's duplicity materializes in their practice of generally refusing to see or use it in spite of their explicit role as learners in this community. Giles's singular role of willing library inhabitant means that he "takes a lot of kidding because of his perceived stuffiness ... and his apparent lack of current awareness" (DeCandido 47). Willow's gushing description emphasizes Giles' British nationality and his scholarly credentials:

the new librarian is really cool.... He just started. He was a curator at some British museum, or, or The British Museum, I'm not sure. But he knows everything, and he brought all these historical volumes and biographies, and am I the single dullest person alive? ("Welcome to the Hellmouth")

This and other cues link Giles and his nationality metonymically and functionally with the library, reinforcing the idea of the library as a culturally "high" site, one opposed, in many ways, to pop Americana, perceived as full of vulgarity and "low" culture. Not surprisingly, this vision of the library contributes to the students' expectation that the library is the exact opposite of "life" that it, in fact, represents a dead past, historical residue, instead of contemporary concerns. (Ironically, the mission to save the world from demons inextricably links Buffy and her friends to death and history, but through the lens of an arguably "low culture" genre: the vampire tale.)

Buffy finally integrates herself into the library after the discovery of a student's dead, bitten body. Giles gives Buffy a pile of books that outline the nature of Sunnydale's demon inhabitants and suggests that Sunnydale is an unusual place, a "center of mystical energy" ("Welcome"). Buffy reluctantly accepts her role through her symbolic acceptance of the books. Thus Giles and Buffy's initial interaction, initiated by refusal and abandon, segues into a more negotiated relationship that redefines the librarian's (and Watcher's) role and the library's status. In this fashion the library, in Henri Lefebvre's words, reflects the interaction of "everyday life" and "lived space": "Space is social morphology: it is to lived experience what form itself is to the living organism" (Lefebvre 95). In other words, Buffy's and Giles's joint and negotiated experiences affect the received form of the library; this episode redefines the library from a nonspace for the general student body into a space for demon fighting.

The series's introduction of the library thus serves to frame many of the principal issues that shape it as a place. While Buffy initially expects the library to provide a structure for sanctioned knowledge, the books offered to her are neither conventional nor curricular. She believes that she'll find freedom from the demon world in Sunnydale and in the library but instead discovers that it reintroduces her to danger and risk. And her first vision of the library as an abandoned space gives way to the library's incarnation as physical, intellectual, and moral center of the Slayer's strategy and organization.

THE MIND–BODY NEXUS

Particularly in the first season, the show often pokes fun at the library's undesirability. One character says to Buffy, as a prelude to asking her out, "I didn't think I'd find you [in the library] . . . you don't seem bookwormy. The type of person to lock themselves in a dark room with a lotta musty old books" ("Never Kill"). The stereotype of the library as the dark, uninhabitable, musty storehouse circulates and survives in spite of Sunnydale high school library's generally bright, pleasant, and inviting appearance.[1] The invocation of the stereotype acts as a reminder that the library's function as a source of scholarly information generally lacks an awareness of the body or of sensuality. The Bronze, the teens' hangout, serves as a foil to the library since it houses consumption, sexuality, and sensuality, all associated with corporeality. But while *BtVS* introduces these traditional narratives about the library and its "disembodied" place, it also worries at them, slowly but surely demonstrating their inadequate understanding of the library.

The initial representation of the Watcher's and Slayer's roles as complementary echo the conventional narratives: Giles represents the mind and Buffy the body. She's the fighter, he's the researcher; she's the female, he's the male. The show also relies on familiar stereotypes of librarians to feed into the understanding of the library as of the mind and not the body; Buffy and her friends routinely tease Giles because his nose is buried deeply in the books while Jenny Calendar, the computer teacher and his eventual love interest, suggests that he never left the middle ages because of his dread of technology. Giles' introduction in the first episode sets the stage for his perceived ethereal braininess, which Buffy indicates in her response to his attempts to persuade Buffy to take up her Slayer duties: "You're like a textbook with arms" ("Welcome").

But while the show's initial portrayal of the library positions it as the heart of mental and scholarly energy at the high school, in general *BtVS* draws a school map in which neither book- nor class-learning takes a central role. When students venture in, it is perceived as unexpected and intrusive [or, as Cullen puts it in his critique of Giles as a positive representation of librarians, Giles "is always surprised when students enter the library to do real research" (42)]. On the flip side, students avoid the library because, as one character puts it, she has "a life" ("Out of Mind"). The students, in other words, believe that the life of the mind is no life at all. This high school geography suggests the unwelcome truth that, for most high school students, the library exists on the *periphery* of their experience of secondary school while, in contrast, it occupies a central position for the Slayer and her helpers, generally acting as the first place they go when strategies must be planned or mysteries solved.

While the library's image as the cerebral center of high school life erodes, it gains significance as a place for Giles and Buffy and her friends (eventually nicknamed the Scooby Gang) that challenges the perception of the library as a site that only promotes the mind. While the first season of *BtVS* contains innumerable scenes of the gang sitting around the tables, with multiple books around them or engaged in intense discussion, soon the library serves as a training space for Buffy's fighting techniques. One episode's first scene places Buffy and Giles in the library, Buffy doing a step routine to a pounding technobeat while Giles upholds his staid, librarian role by complaining: "You work on your muscle tone while my brain dribbles out my ears" ("The Dark Age"). While Buffy's use of the library as a gym certainly defies its stereotypical image, by this time the library's unexpected employment is, to a degree, expected. After all, halfway through the first season we discovered that the library's cage, which seemed to contain only boxes of books and papers, also holds a weapons cabinet. The library thus provides fundamental support to Buffy's slayage in two forms: books (which provide information) and weapons (which assist combat). While the two seem diametrically opposed (like the pen and the sword), within this particular place they engage a dialectic that redefines the library for the Scooby Gang.

This redefinition becomes particularly pointed in the episode "I Robot, You Jane." Over the course of the first season the books and the library get called "musty" and "old" numerous times, as when Buffy asks Giles to get something at the video library ["it's dark and musty, you'll feel right at home" ("Teacher's Pet")] or when, after a tiff, Jenny Calendar, the computer teacher, snipes at Giles: "you'll be happy here with your musty old books" ("I Robot"). The hyperbolic accumulation of the adjective "musty" leads up to "I Robot, You Jane," which, through the characters of Jenny Calendar and Rupert Giles (and a requisite demon who enters the Internet), confronts questions about technology and knowledge, the accessibility of information, the degrees to which technology enslaves or liberates, processes of modernization (and modernity), and the relationship between the virtual and the physical. By the end of the episode, the demon has been battled and conquered, but the dialogue between Jenny and Giles continues as he tries to explain why "musty old books" mean so much to him:

Books smell. Musty and, and, and rich. The knowledge gained from a computer, is, uh, it . . . it has no, no texture, no, no context. It's, it's there and then it's gone. If it 's to last, then, then the getting of knowledge should be, uh, tangible, it should be, um . . . smelly. ("I, Robot")

These smelly, musty, rich books stand in metonymic relationship to the library, suggesting that books and the library can only serve their purpose of producing knowledge when both the body (the sense of touch and smell) and the mind (the information; the data) are joined. Accordingly, the library space in *BtVS* refuses to be idealized as a place for the mind only. This insistence on mind/body confluence occurs through a rejection of technological modernity that maintains skepticism about knowledge that comes unlinked from its material or corporeal production.

KNOWLEDGE AND POWER

"I Robot, You Jane" argues for the indispensably sensual nature of achieving knowledge while depicting a world increasingly lived online: one of the students who is helping Giles scan books into the computer growls that "information isn't bound up anymore. It's an entity. The only reality is virtual" ("I, Robot"). Echoing Jeffrey Garrett's claim that the essence of the library is the data that it contains, this student goes further by suggesting that only virtual reality matters (Garrett). The episode's narrative depicts a demon, Moloch, freed from books into the Internet when the former are scanned. Moloch finds such Ethernet dislocation ultimately unsatisfying and has his minions build him a robotic body to contain his spirit. The demon's continued need for a body, in spite of the almost unassailable power and instant knowledge the Web offers him, intimates an unspoken, vital need for physical placement. When offered a choice between a limitless knowledge flow and a robotic body, the demon chooses the body, with all its inherent limitations.

The urge not only to sensually apprehend knowledge but also to "embody" it suggests the importance of "placing" knowledge. Many *BtVS* scholars have commented on the show's focus on the acquisition of knowledge but have generally ignored the space and place of the information flow. Thus McNeilly et al suggest that "at issue are the structure and dissemination of information itself" (McNeilly et al. par. 1) while Fifarek argues that "the currency of that [slaying] system is information" (Fifarek par. 2). However, both these formulations see information as disembodied and fluid.

To ignore the spatial nature of the acquisition does a disservice to our understanding of *BtVS* and to the place of the library in general. The high school library "formally centralized and localized the Scooby Gang's researches for the majority of the first three seasons" (Wandless par. 2). To assume that the library is, to echo Foucault, "static" or "void" avoids addressing questions of the way the library architecture presents "the vast mass of library information in a way that makes it mentally and emotionally manageable" (Garrett 45). Fifarek gestures toward this idea when she argues that the secrecy of the library allows Buffy and the Scooby Gang to pursue information without "rousing suspicions" (par. 11). But the library serves as more than a guardian of secrets; its nature and architecture support a particular vision of research, information literacy, and knowledge acquisition.[2]

In the contemporary period the spatial organization of libraries finds its logic in abstract systems based in Enlightenment beliefs (Garrett 52–55). Despite the abstract, conceptual systems that organize modern libraries, in *BtVS* we get glimpses of Giles's near synonymity with the physical library as he directs the students—with nary a glance at a card or online catalog—to historical biographies or to books about entomology. Because of Giles's comfort with the library's organization, the Scooby Gang calls Giles a "superlibrarian" during the first season. However, his superpowers are consistently revealed to have their origins in the fundamentals of basic research, as we learn during the following exchange between Willow and Giles:

WILLOW: "You always know what's going on. I never know what's going on."
GILES: "Well, you weren't here from midnight until six researching it." ("Angel")

Giles's matter-of-fact response demystifies the appearance of age-related wisdom and easily acquired knowledge. While Giles's short comment reveals a deep respect for research protocols and the labor that they involve, his use of the deictic also indicates the importance of the place of the research: "here." Research might be done somewhere else but it could not be accomplished so thoroughly. In a third season episode, the importance of that "here" becomes explicitly tied to a community of learners as Willow, grounded and alone in her bedroom, accesses the Internet and, finding useful articles, then uploads them to the library's computer where everyone else awaits, circling the computer in a pose that parallels the way the Scooby Gang sits around the library table ("Gingerbread"). The crucial reception of most if not all of the demon-slaying information in the first three seasons occurs in the library, where a group can receive and use it, collectively.

The Sunnydale library encourages collective research with a collaborative workspace made possible by the central table, good lighting, and comfortable seating. The flexibility of the space also makes it useful for group work. Notably, however, as opposed to contemporary thinking about the library building that recognizes the need for design to "recognize such newer technologies as laptop computers," the Sunnydale library presents a remarkably computer-free zone (Demas 67). Indeed, it is only in this one aspect (lack of computer outlets or computers) that this high school library strays from the "effective research space" that Walt Crawford outlines (66).

The absence of technology responds to and seems constitutive of Giles's metonymic relation to the library. Giles, faithful to his stereotype, suffers anxiety around computers; they fill him with a self-admitted "childlike terror" ("I, Robot"). Since he resists computer-aided research techniques, Willow carries out the computer investigations that range from basic Web searches to unethical system-hacking. But the division of labor does not enact a trite generational gap. Indeed, Giles's fear of computers has implications for the research center that the library embodies. As DeCandido remarks, for Giles, "books are central" and are prioritized as the most useful source of information (46). While books' sensuality has a great deal to do with this, the show also represents books as a more trustworthy and principled source, especially when compared to Willow's use of the computer to access classified information.

The place of the Sunnydale library thus sets information gathering firmly within a collaborative arena, where books are privileged as sources but where each participant has the chance to contribute opinions or information and negotiate meanings and strategies. In addition, considering that the school library is "the oldest building on campus" with a "colonialist design," it becomes representative of cultural authority and capital (Sayer 106). In other words, the texts housed in this space come with the air of an official endorsement. The characters return often to the library in part for this reason: the library's place centralizes the resources and the research but, more significantly, it provides provisional endorsement of the tentative knowledge they reach.

Of course, books, the foundational bricks of any library, cannot avoid close scrutiny given that Giles's and Buffy's relationship begins with the offer of a book—*VAMPYR*—and the vocation it tenders to Buffy. The presence of this book as well as other, stranger titles differentiates this library from others and thus shapes its quality as a place. We see this foremost in the learning framework that they offer to Buffy and her comrades; as they sit around the table, which holds a pile of books, they often search for the picture of a demon that one of them saw or for an indefinable spell that may or may not work. In other words, knowledge production in *BtVS* is mentally laborious, but also fundamentally physical, rooted in matching the experienced world to the word and picture on the page. As Wandless suggests, however, the information the books contain is not always complete nor accurate (pars. 9–12). Book knowledge must be supplemented by experience and intuition. Thus the books at this library act in foundational but not limiting ways in the construction of knowledge, in spite of its presence as purveyor of cultural capital.

The kinds of books this library harbors thus become increasingly significant. As John Cullen maintains, "although the librarians are absent, the fruits of their labors remain" (42). In the case of the Sunnydale high school library, Giles's stewardship cannot be ignored since he "stocks his collection with occult works that are irrelevant to the wider student population he is supposed to serve" (Cullen 42). Housed in a high school, the library has a collection that eventually comes under fire for its irrelevance and/or danger to the general student population, eliciting Principal Snyder's snide comment, "Just how is, um, 'Blood Rites and Sacrifices' appropriate material for a public school library? Chess club branching out?" ("Gingerbread"). While, in the ideal, it is easy to argue against censorship, it is difficult not to appreciate the humor of Snyder's jibe. Giles's labor bears fruit in the form of a library, housed in a public school, whose collection reflects a private, albeit vital, purpose.

The final episode of season 1 demonstrates the limited knowledge contained in books but, in turn, highlights the importance of the library as a more complex place than as a simple repository of those books or of information. Reading the *Pergamum Codex*, Giles realizes that the Master, an ancient, powerful vampire, will rise and that the Slayer is destined to die. Giles quashes any hope that Buffy could avoid her destiny, explaining, "This is the Codex. There is nothing in it that has not come to pass" ("Prophecy Girl"), depicting the *Pergamum Codex* as textually infallible. When Buffy learns about her imminent death she confronts Giles in an attempt to find an alternate reading of the signs: "You're so useful sitting here with all your books!" ("Prophecy Girl") Buffy's words recall the binary between the life of the mind and that of the body; in this case the books and the library appear to offer her no place for agency or for body, instead spelling her doom.

After fighting the Master in his lair and being left for dead, Buffy is revived and returns to battle the Master on the roof of the library. His astonishment is compounded by the literal escape she has performed from written history: "you were destined to die, it was written" ("Prophecy Girl"). Thus *BtVS* reveals the library's books as informative but incomplete, a reminder of Borges's unlimited, infinite library and the idea that our knowledge and experiences could never be contained in any limited place, whether a book or a library. (Borges) More provocatively, Buffy's clash with the Master on the roof of the library near the skylight allows us a view of the eruption, from the floor of the library, of a three-headed worm beast. The embattled library has various defenders who attempt to stave off the demon worm while Buffy wars with the Master. This representative battle demonstrates that struggles between good and evil can only occur in the library, which has a dark and hidden underbelly below and a transparent, heaven-gazing skylight above. The library and, more particularly, the books negotiate—informationally, spatially, physically—between the two realms.

BUILDING COMMUNITY AND CAPITAL IN THE LIBRARY

Many current discussions about the library as place urge us to consider more systematically how the library brings people together. Wayne Wiegand's recent piece recognizes that "millions of patrons have demonstrated their support for the library as a place by visiting it again and again, yet we don't know very much about why they do it" (60). Kevin Harris suggests that "the effective public library will need to demonstrate a role in community cohesion and the generation of social capital" (26). Both Wiegand and Harris argue that the place of the library can act to bring people together and foster unexpected relationships. Echoing Wiegand, Robert D. Putnam and Lewis M. Feldstein, reviewing reports of the "death" of the library, report, "the library should be dead or dying, but that is not what is happening.... No longer a passive repository of books and information or an outpost of culture, quiet, and decorum in a noisy world, the new library is an active and responsive part of the community and an agent of change" (Putnam 35). *BtVS* provides a perceptive representation of the high school library and the kinds of community that it facilitates as well as those it cannot. In effect, while the Sunnydale library enables the creation of the Scooby Gang, that community formation comes at a cost: the exclusion of those perceived not to belong.

BtVS presents a limited number of what I think of as "porous" places, or, to use Ray Oldenburg's terms, the "third place" that can act as a neutral ground where people with different interests and backgrounds can build informal social ties (Oldenburg). The library and the Bronze are arguably the only two places where all the characters can converge, for a number of reasons. Buffy and her friends still live with their parents and their bedrooms still lie within a parental space and authority so that their privacy is limited and dependent upon "good behavior." Other open and social spaces in the school (the hallway, the cafeteria, the lounge) do not readily permit mixing between adults and youth. The library and the Bronze are uniquely porous, allowing both adults and teenagers in.

But, while the library is functionally, structurally and, one assumes, academically, open to the general high school public, as the first section of this paper indicates, the library is a quiet and well-ignored site at the high school. The high school students discursively understand the library as distanced and undesirable. When Willow suggests that she and Buffy meet in the library, Buffy responds quickly, "Or we could meet someplace quieter. Louder. Uh, that place just kinda gives me the wiggins." To which Willow replies, "Oh, it has that effect on most kids" ("Welcome to the Hellmouth"). Thus the Sunnydale library's initial representation precludes a sense of community, or, at the least, the community for which it was built. Yet the show does reveal a vital interest in how libraries as places can generate social capital.

In the very first episode, Xander is hidden in the stacks and overhears Giles and Buffy discussing her Slayer role, which is supposed to be a closely guarded secret. This moment introduces one of the central functions of the Sunnydale library: to protect secrets. Xander's—and later Willow's—discovery not only ensures that he's "in the know" but more important, integrates him into the group. In this way, the supposedly solitary Slayer becomes a team player; *BtVS* suggests that the shift from individual to group dynamic is only possible within the place of the library and through the discursive revelation of secrets. So in the first season the library is the only sanctioned place for discussions of slayage. When one breaches this secrecy in a public area, another remembers and shushes him or her. Thus the library becomes the only place where the Slayer and the demons of Sunnydale can be topics of conversation.

The restriction of these conversations to one place, the library, produces collective work on clandestine projects, which in turn generates considerable social capital: "social networks, norms of reciprocity, mutual assistance, and trustworthiness" (Putnam 2). Other critics of the show have also pointed out how *BtVS* challenges the myth of the superhero who "hides his true self from even his closest loved ones" by demonstrating how Buffy's success depends on the contributions of her friends and allies (Miller 38). These critics have not noticed, however, how it is the place of the library that positions the Slayer within a social network that brings with it diverse styles of learning, research, and fighting.

However, the community that the Sunnydale library engenders is less porous than what many would like to see in real life. No "perpetually open space," the high school library in *BtVS* has no pretense to being a truly neutral and/or casually inviting place (Wiegand 60). Slowly but surely the library becomes "owned" by the Scooby Gang and they no longer perceive it as a public place. Entrance into this fairly closed community means entering its secrets and sharing its worldview. When someone new does enter the library, then, their appearance often foreshadows their entrance into the mysteries and, often, their integration into the Scooby Gang.

While the absence of "real" students (or their unwelcome status when they do appear) serves as an ongoing joke about the peripheral place of the library in the student's geography, it also suggests a paradox about the kinds of places that allow community to build. As the library aids in the construction of a particular community, it also creates the conditions for perceived ownership and, eventually, exclusion rather than inclusion. At one point, Giles puts out a sign to warn students that the library is closed for filing and encourages Buffy to train there. His appropriation of this supposedly public space sets a certain tone or set of expectations for the library and its role as place.

The Sunnydale library works as a "third place" in its domination by regulars and its confirmed narrative that "every regular was once a newcomer, and the acceptance of newcomers is essential to the sustained vitality of the third place. Acceptance into the circle is not difficult, but it is not automatic either" (Oldenburg 34). Oldenburg further argues, "third place groups often seem more homogenous and closed to outsiders than they are" (35). Thus Jenny Calendar, in an attempt to understand the gang's attachment to place, exclaims, "you kids really dig the library, don't you?" ("I, Robot"). Through this dynamic the show argues that the perception of ownership over certain places (and outsiders' similar perceptions) buttresses group identity. When Willow chastises Xander and Cordelia into doing some research on a demon in season 2, she proclaims, "If you two aren't with me one-hundred-and-ten percent, then get the hell out of my library!" ("The Dark Age"). Thus the collectively owned place becomes significant at the individual level as well.

The library thus acts critically as the place that disallows the slayer's solitary efforts and instead compels the formation of a community effort. In fact, the "successful resolution of all three major crises" of the first three seasons depends on the collective thought and action of the characters (par. 12). The library makes the collaboration a possibility by providing a space that encourages it. That this collectivity can only be achieved by a certain amount of ownership, privatization, and exclusion suggests that we may need to better understand how places we think of as public actually work. Or, as Kevin Harris points out, we may need to consider whether public space and community space are necessarily synonymous and how the public library might "accommodate those expectations of civicness and at the same time... informality and the casual" (28). In other words, how can libraries remain open to all yet permit claims of specific communities? *BtVS* suggests that it is not entirely possible. In fact, the other high school students only get involved in the high school library, the Scooby Gang, and the battles against the undead at the end of season 3 when, to fight against the mayor-turned-demon, the Scooby Gang needs all the help they can get. The pivotal moment in the battle is the explosion of the library; the imperative need to destroy the library in order to save the town suggests that the demands on the library to be closed (to others, to the Hellmouth) and open (to the Scooby Gang, to potential allies, to new knowledge and strategies) are too dichotomous and impossible to maintain.

SURVEILLANCE AND SANCTUARY

Michael Gorman, in a defense of the library as place, states that "many, many people live and work in circumstances that do not offer them a quiet place to study and think. For many such students, the library is the only place that is free from the distractions of everyday life" (46). Gorman's vision of the library matches the opinion expressed by some patrons in Susan DiMattia's recent article on the sometimes noisy contemporary library, who still long for a "refuge from worldly chaos" (51). However, the contemporary library no longer holds as its ideal its qualities as refuge and sanctuary; DiMattia observes that in general the ideal of the library as silent sanctuary has been discarded. Instead, "a library is a community center, but it's also a place for study; a sanctuary, but a space that encourages active exchange of ideas" (50). While *BtVS* visually endorses the idea of the library as a sanctuary, narratively it illustrates that the library's strength lies in its creation of collaborative (sometimes loud and combative) exchanges. While it harbors secrets about slaying and vampires, it doesn't always protect those secrets. For instance, when Xander emerges from the stacks, having unwittingly been party to Buffy and Giles's discussion, the narrative does not simply shift from individual to collective action. Rather, the moment of Xander's emergence pinpoints the library's contradictory role as a place that promotes sanctuary but allows and even fosters surveillance.

Post–USA Patriot Act, it is no longer surprising to find both protection and surveillance wrapped up in one package. But to find it in 1997, in a show nominally about vampires, proves the prescience of the show's vision of the library complicated and policed by outside forces. Xander soon uses his insider knowledge to become an insider. Other outsiders, like the vampires and demons, monitor and sometimes enter the Sunnydale library without ever being able to become true insiders. Thus the library serves as the hub that arbitrates between the Scooby Gang and "the forces of darkness."[3] Another group allowed physical entry but not cultural or social entry are the parents and school officials who represent institutional authority and forces of repression and censorship.

Accordingly, the Sunnydale library significantly fails to conform to our commonly held preconceptions about how the library might or might not be violated. The library's system of surveillance depends upon what Michel Foucault has called the "docile" or "disciplined" body (Foucault *Discipline and Punish* 135 ff). Foucault's work on the disciplining of the modern individual suggests that the work of regulating action and thought occurs internally and externally through a system

> organized as a multiple, automatic and anonymous power; for although surveillance rests on individuals, its functioning is that of a network of relations from top to bottom, but also to a certain extent from bottom to top and laterally. . . . The power in the hierarchized surveillance of the disciplines is not possessed as a thing . . . ; it functions like a piece of machinery. . . . This enables the disciplinary power to be both absolutely indiscreet, since it is everywhere and always alert . . . and absolutely "discreet," for it functions permanently and largely in silence. (Foucault *Discipline and Punish* 176–77)

The Sunnydale high school library makes visible the discreet system of discipline by highlighting its character as a place that offers security but that also permits and even encourages the confrontation with danger. During the first season the library acts as a zone that allows for the battle preparations away from the bureaucratic and authoritarian interventions of the high school administration. The cage full of weapons and the books full of magic and historical knowledge provide the tools the Scooby Gang needs to combat the Hellmouth; nonetheless, no violence breaches the boundaries of the library until the end of the first season. In "Prophecy Girl," everyone but Buffy convenes in the library to figure out where the Hellmouth will open (as is prophesized) when zombies begin to converge on the library. The gang erects barriers in the library but, as a discursively and physically porous place (its public status; its swinging doors, skylight, and multiple, easy-to-reach windows), they cannot secure the space completely. As the many-headed and -tentacled demon erupts from the library floor, the gang realizes that the library is under siege because it sits right on top of the Hellmouth. So the place that before had acted mainly as sanctuary, as site for research and restoration, altered at the end of the season. The mechanisms of danger that had been there all along were laid bare.

"Prophecy Girl" further cements the library's newly visible status as site of danger by providing the first glimpse of the library's skylight; this panopticon view belongs to the Master as he stands on the roof, looking down through the skylight, surveying the library and its impending ruin while calling on the demons to come forth. He has a visual and spatial advantage over those in the library who can only see and block off the library in parts. They have no way of grasping the complete scene and so can only scramble to survive in the face of these multiple and diverse onslaughts by the enemies.

The library's role was foreshadowed narratively in several moments of library surveillance that go completely unperceived by the gang, from the vampire Darla who spies on Willow and Buffy to the invisible girl Marcie and her close watch on the Scooby Gang from the crawl space in the library ceiling. ("Angel"; "Out of Mind"). These acts of unperceived surveillance with their connotations of encroachment and violation reinforce the possibility of further incursion into the library's ostensibly safe space.

The library/Hellmouth coupling, with its fundamentally bispatial structure and its attendant binary concepts of safety vs. danger, information flow vs. control, and surveillance vs. privacy, demonstrates that undoing these binaries is nearly impossible. This library, *BtVS* suggests, is no sanctuary, no perfect and unchanging clean and well-lighted place that shelters the Gang as they absorb the information they need. Instead, it feeds them new challenges and threatens them occasionally. But those threats and that risk make new knowledges possible.

LEAVING THE HIGH SCHOOL LIBRARY

While the school library is unassuming (and, at a glance, has only paltry holdings), its power to act as a constitutive place and to be transformed in kind cannot be denied. In contrast, when Willow and Buffy enroll at UC Sunnydale in season four, one of the first things they do is go by the university library. As they step over the threshold they are both awestruck. Their reaction within the grand space echoes Jeremy Garrett's observation following Voltaire that "there has always been . . . something inherently terrifying about entering a large library" (Garrett 44). It's no wonder that the show's viewers never see that library again. Its architectural and informational greatness overwhelms its ability to act as a place that would create community or the conditions for collective knowledge. Because of that it can also never present matters of risk, of the nature and limits of community, or question how knowledge can and should be negotiated. In fact, the contrast between the university library, never seen again, and the Sunnydale high school library confirms the importance of first impressions and the need to build a library that "reveal[s] most efficaciously the organization scheme in a way the user will comprehend" (Garrett 60). However, *Buffy the Vampire Slayer* also urges us to reconsider the library's role as an information dump by emphasizing how the user's initial desires (like Buffy's for a textbook) are not always what they need (a book on vampires, a mission to slay, a gang of helpers). The organization of the Sunnydale library privileged community, common goals, and a quest for unconventional knowledges are only attainable through collective and physical searches. No Internet threshold, no Web gateway, no magnificent holdings could replace the act of convening at the table piled high with books.

The library's destruction at the end of the third season does not, then, suggest the demise of the library but, rather, its incredible power and importance ("Graduation Day Part 2"). Only there can the mayor-demon be eliminated, through the combination of mind and body, of strategy and fire power. The books' removal before the battle intimates that, eventually, the library will rise from the ashes. After all, it occupies a pivotal place in the battle between good and evil, between heaven and hell. The contradictions of human practice and desire form and mold the library.

NOTES

1. See Tonkin for an analysis of *BtVS* as "suburban noir" that contrasts "the relentless glare of the weather and the deep darkness and perpetual turbulence of the region's reputed moral climate," which provides another instance of appearance belied by reality (38).

2. Markus argues that the best architectural design demonstrates a "correspondence between epistemology, book classification and spatial organization" (177).

3. From the opening voiceover to all *BtVS* episodes.

REFERENCES

"Angel." *Buffy the Vampire Slayer*. WB. April 4, 1997.

"A Sense of Place: New Facilities and Renovations Emphasize Community." *American Libraries* 33.4 (2002): 45–59.

Borges, Jorge Luis. "La Biblioteca De Babel." *Ficciones*. 3rd ed. Mexico: Alianza, 1989. 89–99.

Crawford, Walt. "Library Space: The Next Frontier?" *Online* 23.2 (1999): 61–66.

Cullen, John. "Rupert Giles, the Professional-Image Slayer." *American Libraries* 31.5 (2000): 42.

Curry, Michael R. "Everyday Practices and Public Places." *Transforming Spaces: The Topological Turn in Technology Studies*. Technical University Darmstadt, Germany. March 22–24, 2002. Retrieved 10 June 2004 from http://www.geog.ucla.edu/~curry/.

"The Dark Age." *Buffy the Vampire Slayer*. WB. 10 Nov. 1997.

DeCandido, GraceAnne A. "Bibliographic Good vs. Evil." *American Libraries* 30.8 (1999): 44–47.

Demas, Sam, and Jeffrey A. Scherer. "Esprit De Place: Maintaining and Designing Library Buildings to Provide Transcendent Spaces." *American Libraries* 33.4 (2002): 65–68.

DiMattia, Susan. "Silence Is Olden." *American Libraries* 36.1 (2005): 48–51.

Fifarek, Aimee. "'Mind and Heart with Spirit Joined': The Buffyverse as an Information System." *Slayage* 3 (2001): 38 pars. Retrieved 5 June 2004 from http://www.slayage.tv.

Foucault, Michel. *Discipline and Punish: The Birth of the Prison*. 1977. Trans. Alan Sheridan. 2nd ed. New York: Vintage, 1995.

———. "Of Other Spaces." *Diacritics* 16.1 (1986): 22–27.

Garrett, Jeffrey. "The Legacy of the Baroque in Virtual Representations of Library Space." *Library Quarterly* 74.1 (2004): 42–62.

"Gingerbread." *Buffy the Vampire Slayer*. UPN. 12 Jan. 1999.

Gorman, Michael. *Our Enduring Values: Librarianship in the 21st Century*. Chicago: American Library Association, 2000.

"Graduation Day Part 2." *Buffy the Vampire Slayer*. UPN. 13 July 1999.

Harris, Kevin. "Your Third Place or Mine?" *Public Library Journal* 18.2 (2003): 26–29.

Howard, June. *Publishing the Family*. Durham: Duke University Press, 2001.

"I, Robot–You, Jane." *Buffy the Vampire Slayer*. WB. 28 April 1997.

Lefebvre, Henri. *The Production of Space*. Trans. Donald Nicholson-Smith. Oxford: Blackwell Press, 1995.

"Lie to Me." *Buffy the Vampire Slayer*. WB. 3 Nov. 1997.

Markus, Thomas A. *Buildings and Power: Freedom and Control in the Origin of Modern Building Types*. London: Routledge, 1993.

McNeilly, Kevin, Christina Sylka, and Susan R. Fisher. "Kiss the Librarian, but Close the Hellmouth: 'It's Like a Whole Big Sucking Thing.'" *Slayage* 2 (2001): 26 pars. Retrieved 4 June 2004 from http://www.slayage.tv.

Miller, Jessica Prata. "'The I in Team': Buffy and Feminist Ethics." *Buffy the Vampire Slayer and Philosophy: Fear and Trembling in Sunnydale*. Ed. James B. South. Chicago: Open Court, 2003: 35–48.

"Never Kill a Boy on the First Date." *Buffy the Vampire Slayer*. WB. 31 Mar. 1997.

Oldenburg, Ray. *The Great Good Place: Cafés, Coffee Shops, Community Centers, Beauty Parlors, General Stores, Bars, Hangouts, and How They Get You through the Day*. 2nd ed. New York: Marlowe, 1997.

"Out of Mind, out of Sight." *Buffy the Vampire Slayer*. WB. 19 May 1997.

"Prophecy Girl." *Buffy the Vampire Slayer*. WB. 2 June 1997.

Putnam, Robert D. and Lewis M. Feldstein. *Better Together: Restoring the American Community*. New York: Simon & Schuster, 2003.

Sayer, Karen. "'It Wasn't Our World Anymore. They Made It Theirs': Reading Space and Place." *Reading the Vampire Slayer: An Unofficial Critical Companion to Buffy and Angel*. Ed. Roz Kaveney. London: Tauris Parke, 2002. 98–119.

"Teacher's Pet." *Buffy the Vampire Slayer*. WB. 25 March 1997.

Tonkin, Boyd. "Entropy as Demon: Buffy in Southern California." *Reading the Vampire Slayer: An Unofficial Critical Companion to Buffy and Angel*. Ed. Roz Kaveny. London: Tauris Parke, 2002: 37–52.

Wandless, William. "Undead Letters: Searches and Researches in *Buffy the Vampire Slayer*." *Slayage* 1 (2001): 38 pars. Retrieved 4 June 2004 from http://www.slayage.tv.

Weber, Bruce. "Fewer Noses Stuck in Books in America, Survey Finds." *The New York Times*.
        Retrieved 8 July 2004 from nytimes.com.
Weise, Frieda. "Being There: The Library as Place." *Journal of the Medical Library Association*
        92.1 (2004): 6–13.
"Welcome to the Hellmouth." *Buffy the Vampire Slayer*. Dir. Charles Martin Smith. 10 Mar. 1997.
Westmoreland, Tracey Mendoza. "Maintaining Our Physical Spaces: Advocating the Library as a
        Sense of Place." *Texas Library Journal* 79.4 (2003): 138–42.
Wiegand, Wayne A. "Critiquing the Curriculum." *American Libraries* 36.1 (2005): 58–61.

Index

Academic libraries. *See* Libraries,
    Academic/Research
"Academic upbringing." *See* "Scholarly age"
African Americans
   and community, 80–81, 83
   and libraries, 79–99
Agency, 10
Alberti, Leon Battista, 210
Allayne-Jones, Alfred, 61
Anderson, Benedict, 12, 51
Antebellum America, 43
Appearential ordering, 119, 121
Architecture. *See* Libraries, design and layout
Areal differentiation, 5
Athenaeums, 42, 49, 55–56

Bennett College, 88, 97
Bertram, James, 61
Bibliothèque nationale de France, 213–15
   Controversia de nobilitate in, 213–15
   design, 214–15
   Rare Books Reserve Rooms, 214–15
Bookcases, 44–48, 51, 55, 57
Bookmobiles, 87, 89, 93
Books. *See* Libraries, books/collections
Bookstacks, 224–25, 227–29, 231
Bookstores, 110
Boston Athanaeum, 42–43, 54, 223–26
Boston Library Society, 52–54

Boston Public Library, 42–43, 55, 57
Bourdieu, Pierre, 12
British Army
   libraries as reform agent, 36–37
   literacy in, 29–30
   reform, 31
   social aspects, 32
   soldiers, 36–37
British Empire, 29–38
   governance of, 31
   literacy policies, 36–37
   military libraries, 30–31
Buffy the Vampire Slayer, role of library in,
    235–48
   as agent of community, 244–46
   book collection, 242–43
   contents, 242–43
   as cultural symbol, 239–41
   destruction of, 247–48
   and Foucauldian discipline, 247
   gothic tradition of, 237
   and sanctuary, 246–47
   and students, 244
   and surveillance, 246–47
   as Third Place, 244–45

Carnegie, Andrew, 61, 228
Carnegie Community Centre, Vancouver,
    71–74

Carnegie libraries, 228–30. *See also* Carnegie
    Negro Library ; Vancouver Carnegie
    Library
Carnegie Library, Vancouver. *See* Vancouver
    Carnegie Library
Carnegie Negro Library, Greensboro, NC,
    79–99
    collections, 86–87
    history, 84–88
    Library Board, 86
    membership, 89
Carson, Barbara, 41
Castells, Manuel, 12
Categorical knowledge, 120–21
Censorship, 63, 65
Central place theory, 5
Certeau, Michel de, 12, 102
Christaller, Walter, 5
Classification. *See* Information retrieval
Closed shelves, 47, 52–53, 227
Community
    and libraries, 79–99, 101, 105, 244–46
    as place, 12–13, 51, 80
Controversia de nobilitate, 209–15
    in Bibliothèque nationale de France,
        classifications of, 213–15
    classification and categorization of, 213–15
    and Montefeltro, Federico of, 213
Copyright, and digitized books, 195
Cotrugli, Benedetto, 210
Cromer, Lord, 31
Cultural symbols, libraries as, 61, 73, 80,
    209–12, 239–41

Dalhousie, Earl of, 32–33
De Certeau, Michel. *See* Certeau, Michel de
"Death of the Library" predictions, 164–65,
    175, 185, 191, 199, 204
Depth searching, 199–200
Descartes, René, 4
Digital libraries/text, 215
Disneyfication, 14
Douglas, R. W., 64–65
Dreyfus case, 194–95

Education and libraries. *See* Libraries,
    education/learning
Electronic resources. *See* Information
    retrieval ; Libraries, electronic
    resources
Elites, libraries of, 46–48, 53–55, 58, 209–10,
    223–28

Environmental determinism, 5
"Evolution of the library" thesis, 191,
    199–201, 204

Faculty
    "scholarly age," 173–74
    study carrels, 163–66
    use of academic/research libraries, 163–76,
        200
Fiction in libraries, 52, 222–23
Flogging, 36
Foucault, Michel, 237, 241, 246–47
Franklin, Benjamin, 41
Full text retrieval, 195–96

Garrison, Dee, 52
Gay/lesbian patrons and libraries,
    117–34
Gender, 33–35, 44–45, 54–58, 117–34, 225,
    228
Gibraltar Garrison Library, 34–35, 37
Giddens, Anthony, 12
Giles, Rupert (*Buffy the Vampire Slayer*),
    238–43
    and computers, 242
    as stereotype, 242
Great Depression and Vancouver Carnegie
    Library, 66–67
"Great Good Place," 50, 137
Greensboro (NC) Public Library, 79–99
Grier, Katherine, 49

Habermas, Jürgen, 15–18
Halifax Garrison Library, 31–34
Haraway, Donna, 12
Harvey, David, 7–8
High school libraries. *See Buffy the Vampire
    Slayer*
Home libraries. *See* Libraries, Private

Information retrieval
    browsing. *See* Libraries, and browsing
    and classified collections, 192–96, 203
    full text retrieval, weaknesses of for
        research, 195–96
    and Google, 201
    keyword searching, 195, 201–3
    Library of Congress Subject Headings,
        strengths of, 201–3
    and off-site storage, 192, 195
    online catalogs, 193–94, 201
Information seeking/behavior

faculty, 165–76, 200
in libraries, 149–51, 169–72, 184
public, 145–51
students, 180–86, 196–98

Keyword searching, 195, 201–3
Knitting group, 124–26

Landscape, 6, 138, 153
Lefebvre, Henry, 12
Lefroy, John Henry, 30, 37
Librarians, 148–50, 180–81
Libraries
    academic. *See* Libraries,
        Academic/Research
    and African Americans, 79–99
    bookcases, 44–48, 51, 55, 57
    bookmobiles, 87, 89, 93
    books/collections, 31, 33–37, 45, 52, 86–87,
        108–9, 112, 191–96, 209–19
        fiction, 52, 222–23
        as indicator of scholarly activity, 15th
            century, 211–12
        off-site storage of as poor substitute for
            research collections, 191–96
    bookstacks, 224–25, 227–29, 231
    branches, 81–99, 117–34
        Carnegie, 61–76, 79–99
    and browsing, 165, 169–72, 192–96,
        199–201, 203
    and class, 43–44, 47–48, 52–58, 210,
        230–33
    as commons, 117
    and community, 79–99, 101, 105,
        244–46
    as community centers, 90, 97, 203–4
    as cultural symbols, 61, 73, 80, 209–12,
        239–41
    design and layout, 44–45, 53, 124, 210–15,
        221–34
        rooms, 44, 45–48, 54–55, 56, 119,
            126–29, 211–13, 224–25, 227–29
        rooms for children, 229–30
    and education/learning, 42, 48, 56, 94,
        150–51, 173–76, 178, 180–81,
        191–92, 196–98, 200, 204
    electronic resources
        and copyright, 195
        and "death of library," 164–65, 175, 185,
            191, 199–204
        digital library paradigm, 215
        effects on libraries, 235–36

    effects on library space, 185
    "evolution of library" thesis, 191,
        199–201, 204
    and "scholarly age," 171
    and scholarship, 169–71, 201–3
    and elites, 46–48, 53–55, 58, 209–10,
        223–28
    and faculty, 163–76, 197, 199–200
    furnishings, 44–45, 46–47, 51–53, 55–57,
        86, 123, 210–12, 227–29
        bookcases, 44–48, 51, 55, 57
        bookstacks, 224–25, 227–29, 231
        bookstacks and classification, 199–202
        closed shelves, 47, 52–53, 227
        inadequate defenses of, 203–4
        open shelves, 52–53, 57, 222, 225,
            228–29, 231
    as information places, 149–51
    in homes. *See* Libraries, Private
    and information seeking, 149–51, 169–72,
        184–85
    and LGBQ patrons, 117–34
    as male spaces, 44–45, 54–58, 225
    mercantile, 42, 52, 56
    military, 29–38
    online catalogs, 193–94, 201
    as physical spaces, 142–45, 191–206
    as places, 10, 12, 80, 173–74, 236
    private. *See* Libraries, Private
    programs, 89, 93, 117–34
    public. *See* Libraries, Public
    and public sphere, 15–18, 102–3
    and reading, 29, 31, 33, 37, 173–74, 221–36
    rooms. *See* Libraries, design and layout
    as safe places, 90, 105–8, 112, 122, 246–47
    and segregation, 84–85, 87, 93
    and sexual identity, 105–8, 109–11
    and social capital, 117
    as social places, 37, 87–88, 90–91, 93,
        145–49, 180–86
    as storehouses/warehouses, 108–9, 111–12,
        192
    storytime, 123–24
    and students, 117–86, 196–201, 244
    user groups, 79–99, 101–15, 117–34,
        182–85, 196–98
        African Americans, 79–99
        faculty, 163–76, 197, 199–200
        LGBQ patrons, 117–34
        soldiers, 29–39
        students, 177–86, 196–201, 244
        women, 33–35, 54–58, 117–34, 225, 228

and women, 33–35, 54–58, 117–34, 225, 228
Libraries, Academic/Research
  and browsing, 165, 169, 170–72
  collections, 169–70, 172
  collections and "scholarly age," 171–74
  electronic resources, 169, 170–71
  and information seeking, 165–76
  as place, 164, 173–75, 183–85
  as quiet space, 165, 173–74, 183–85
  role/purpose of, 165, 175–76, 185–86
  as social space, 164, 183–85
  space, hierarchical divisions of, 184
  study carrels, 162, 165–66
  user groups, 163–76, 182–85, 196–98
Libraries, High School. *See Buffy the Vampire Slayer*
Libraries, Lighthouse, 192–94
  and Google search, 201–2
Libraries, Mercantile, 42, 52, 56
Libraries, Military, 29–38
  bylaws, 33, 35
  Gibraltar, 34–35, 37
  Halifax, 31–34
  India, 35–36
  Quebec, 34
  women's participation in, 33, 35
Libraries, Private, 42–43, 209–13
  book collections, 45, 210–13
  as elite spaces, 46–48, 53–55, 58, 209–10
Libraries, Public, 42, 61–74, 79–99, 101–15, 117–34, 222–23, 226–27
  bookmobiles, 87, 89, 93
  books/collections, 108–12, 147–51
  branches, 81–99, 117–34
  Carnegie, 61–76, 79–99
  Free access, 148–49
  Greensboro, North Carolina, 79–99
  and information seeking, 149–51
  programs, 89, 93, 117–34
  Seattle, Washington, 139–54
  storytime, 123–24
  user groups, 79–99, 101–15, 117–34
  Vancouver, British Columbia, 61–76
Libraries, Research. *See* Libraries, Academic/Research
Libraries, Social, 41–58, 223–26
Library Company of Philadelphia, 41, 43
Library of Congress Subject Headings, 201–3
Lighthouse libraries, 192–94, 201–2
Locale, 138, 153
Locke, John, 4

Loftland, Lynne, 118
Lyceums, 42

Machin, Edwin, 63–64
Mechanics Institutions, 33, 42
Mercantile libraries, 42, 52, 56
Military discipline, 36–37
Military libraries, 29–38
Montefeltro, Federico of
  book collection, 212–13
  studiolo, 211–12
Montemagno, Buonaccorso da, 209–11
Moorsom, William Scarth, 32–33

Napoleonic Wars, 29–30
Nobility and libraries, 210
Nobility, 15th century definitions of, 209–10

"Occupation of Carnegie," 66–67
Off-site storage, 191–96
Oldenburg, Ray, 50, 118. 137–38, 151–53
Open shelves, 52–53, 57, 222, 225, 228–29, 231

Parlors, Public, 48–50
  furnishings, 49
  as place, 49
Pattern books for houses, 44, 46, 48
People as agents, 10
Personal libraries. *See* Libraries, Private
Place
  affective elements, 7, 95, 138
  characteristics of, 135–36, 153
  community, 12–13, 51, 80
  and embodiment, 8–10
  habitation, 5
  landscape, 6, 138, 153
  locale, 138, 153
  pedagogic aspects, 178–79
  primary, 10
  rural, 11
  secondary, 10
  social relations of, 8–10
  socially constituted, 9–10, 101–2
  symbolic, 6
  Third, 50, 58, 118, 137–38, 151–53, 244–45
  Urban, 5, 10–11
Place attachment, 7, 95, 138
Pleasure reading, 29, 31, 33, 37, 173–74, 221–36
Public libraries. *See* Libraries, Public

Public space, 13–14, 49, 119–20
Public sphere
  and democracy, 15–18
  Disneyfication of, 14
  Habermasian notions of, 15–18
  and libraries, 15–18, 102–3
  and public space, 13
Principle of Least Effort, 193, 195–96, 198
Private/semi-private realms, 117

Quebec Garrison Library, 34

Ramsay, George. *See* Dalhousie, Earl of
Reading and libraries, 29, 31, 33, 37, 173–74,
  221–36
Realms, public and private, 118, 129
Recognition browsing, 199–207
Relationships, personal, 126–30
Remote storage, 191–96
Research libraries. *See* Libraries,
  Academic/Research
Robinson, Edgar S., 62, 66–67, 70
Rooms, Library. *See* Libraries, design and
  layout
*Rules and Catalogue of the Halifax Garrison
  Library*, 33–34

Safe places/sanctuary, 90, 105–8, 112, 122,
  246–47
Said, Edward, 12
"Scholarly age," 166–76
  and bookstacks, browsing, 171–72
  and electronic resources, 171
Scholarship and libraries, 163–76, 191–96,
  198–201
Scholarship and library as place, 173–74
Seattle Public Library, 139–53, 232
  architecture/design, 139, 142–43
  book spiral, 138–39, 232
  and education/learning, 150–51
  as information place, 149–51
  as physical space, 142–45
  as social place, 145–49
  as symbol, 142–43
Sennett, Richard, 12
Setting, 80
Shera, Jesse, 41–42
Social libraries. *See* Libraries, Social
Soldiers, 29–39
Space
  absolute, 4
  capitalist, 7–9

Cartesian, 4
cultural, 6–7, 9
Euclidean, 4
elite, 44–47, 53–55, 210
extensive, 4
feminist perspectives on, 8
humanist perspectives on, 9–10
Marxist perspectives on, 7–9
modernist, 10
pedagogic aspects, 178–79
physical setting, 5–6
postmodernist, 10–11
public, 13–14, 49, 119–20
relative, 4, 7
rural, 6, 11
social relations of, 8–10
socially constituted, 8–11, 101–2
Third, 50, 58, 118, 137–38, 151–53, 244–45
urban, 7–8, 11, 119–20
Spatial ordering, 120–21
Spatial practices, 101–2, 112
Stacks. *See* Bookstacks
Storage of collections. *See* Libraries,
  books/collections
Storytime, 123–24
Strangers, 119, 130
Students
  information behavior, 177–83, 196–200
  use of library space, 182–85, 196–98
Studiolos. *See* Montefeltro, Federico of,
  studiolo
Subscription libraries, British Army. *See*
  Libraries, Military

Third place or space. *See* Place, Third
Tobacco chewing, 63–64, 89

University campus as informing space,
  178–79

Valery, Paul, 194–95
Vancouver Art, Historical, and Scientific
  Society. *See* Vancouver Museum
Vancouver Carnegie Library, 61–74
  board, 64
  Carnegie Community Centre, 71–74
  censorship at, 63, 65
  as Central Library, 65
  as city museum, 70
  as civic space, 69
  early collections, 63
  Great Depression, 66–67

neighborhood, 70
"Occupation of Carnegie," 66–67
patrons' behavior, 63–64, 67
problems, 64–66, 68–69
as scholarly reference library, 64–65
as Vancouver Public Library Branch library, 71–73
World War II, 67–68
Vancouver City Council, 62–64, 66, 70–71
Vancouver City Librarians. *See* Douglas, R. W. ; Machin, Edwin ; Robinson, Edgar S.
Vancouver Museum, 63–64, 68

Vancouver Public Central Library (new), 68–70
Von Humboldt, Alexander, 5

Wealthy, libraries of, 43–44, 46–48, 52–58, 209–10, 223–28, 230–33
Women and libraries, 33–35, 54–58, 117–34, 225, 228
Women and work vs. leisure, 122–23, 130
World War II, 67–69

"Yankee Diaspora," 42

About the Editors and Contributors

KAREN ANTELL, head of Reference & Outreach Services at the University of Oklahoma Libraries, conducts research on public services in academic libraries. In 2006, she received the Oklahoma Library Association's "Outstanding New Librarian" award. In addition, she recently completed a three-year stint as "faculty in residence," living in a dormitory with 900 freshmen.

ADAM ARENSON is a PhD candidate in History at Yale University, where he is completing a dissertation titled "The Barometer at St. Louis: A Cultural History of Civil War and Reconstruction, 1848–1877," which includes an extended history of the St. Louis Mercantile Library's first 25 years. He has been the recipient of a Jacob K. Javits Fellowship and a St. Louis Mercantile Library Fellowship, and has published articles in the *Pacific Historical Review*, *California History* and *New York Folklore Journal*.

JOHN E. BUSCHMAN holds a BS in history and sociology and an MLS—both from Ball State University, and an MA in American studies from Saint Joseph's University. He has published two books: *Dismantling the Public Sphere: Situating and Sustaining Libraries in the Age of the New Public Philosophy* (Libraries Unlimited, 2003) and *Critical Approaches to Information Technology in Librarianship: Foundations and Applications* (Greenwood, 1993). He is co-editor of the journal *Progressive Librarian* and on the editorial board of *Library Philosophy and Practice*.

KIRSTEN CLEMENT won the gold medal in the MLIS program at Western in 2004. Following graduation, she led a study measuring the success of the Summer Reading Program at Hamilton Public Library before landing her current job of Educational Outreach and Teen Services Librarian at Brantford Public Library. She is a member of the Ontario Library Association and the Red Maple Reading Program Selection Committee and will be tutoring with the Southern Ontario Library Service Excel Program beginning in January 2007.

ANN CURRY is an associate professor, School of Library, Archival and Information Studies at The University of British Columbia, in Vancouver, Canada. Currently she is the Faculty of Arts representative to Graduate Council, and holds positions on the Faculty of Arts Library Advisory Committee and Library Appointments Committee. She is active nationally and internationally presenting papers at conferences and acting as a consultant for library building projects and for libraries dealing with intellectual freedom issues.

PHILLIP M. EDWARDS is a fourth-year doctoral candidate at the University of Washington Information School. He received an MS in information (2003) from the University of Michigan School of Information, and his research interests lie in the areas of open access publishing, institutional repository development, and management of library services. He also holds a BS in chemistry and a minor in mathematics (2001) from the University at Buffalo.

DEBRA ENGEL is director of Public Services and associate professor of bibliography at the University of Oklahoma Libraries. She conducts research concerning public services issues including librarian recruitment, web site development topics, and the use of library space by students and faculty. She serves as a past-president of the Oklahoma Library Association. She is listed on the 1999 Freedom to Read Foundation Honor Roll.

ADRIANA ESTILL is an assistant professor of English and American studies at Carleton College in Northfield, Minnesota.

KAREN E. FISHER is an associate professor in the Information School of the University of Washington, and chair of the MLIS program. Her latest books include *Theories of Information Behavior* (2005) and *How Libraries and Librarians Help* (2005). She won the 2005 Shera Award for Distinguished Published Research, the 1999 ALISE Research Award, and the 1995 ALISE Jane Hannigan Award. She is a member of several editorial boards as well as the Permanent Program Committee of the Information Seeking in Context (ISIC) Conference series, and was the 2004–2005 chair of ASIST SIG USE. Her doctorate is from the University of Western Ontario, and she was a post-doctorate fellow at the University of Michigan.

LISA M. GIVEN is an associate professor in the School of Library and Information Studies (Faculty of Education) and an associate adjunct professor in humanities computing (Faculty of Arts) at the University of Alberta. In 2002 she won the ALISE Methodology Paper Award for "Data Preparation Using the Principles of Knowledge Organization: A Guiding Model for Quantitative, Qualitative and Textual Research Methodologies" (co-author, Dr. Hope A. Olson; subsequently published in *Library & Information Science Research*). She is also a scientist of the International Institute for Qualitative Methodology, president of the Canadian Association for Information Science, associate editor for the *International Journal of Qualitative Methods* and review editor for the *Canadian Journal of Information and Library Science* and serves on the editorial boards of *Library & Information Science Research* and *The Reference Librarian*.

JULIA A. HERSBERGER, PhD, MLS, received her PhD in information science from Indiana University. Currently she is an associate professor in the Department of Library and Information Studies at the University of North Carolina at Greensboro. Her areas of research interests focus on social networks as information networks and the everyday life information seeking of socially marginalized populations.

GLORIA J. LECKIE holds an MLIS and an MA and PhD in geography. She has worked for over a decade as a librarian, primarily in cataloging positions. Currently, she is associate professor and associate dean of the Faculty of Information and Media Studies, University of Western Ontario, London, Ontario, Canada. In addition to her interest in library as place, her other research areas include information seeking behavior, online catalog use, information literacy in higher education, and academic librarianship.

JENS-ERIK MAI is vice dean and associate professor in the Faculty of Information Studies, University of Toronto. His research focuses on domain-centered approaches to organization and representation of knowledge—he is particularly interested in understanding how people use information in their workplaces and how information could best be organized and represented to support their work. He teaches courses on indexing, classification, design of controlled vocabularies, and the theoretical foundation of information science.

BONNIE MAK is postdoctoral fellow of the InterPARES Project (International Research on Permanent Authentic Records in Electronic Systems) at The University of British Columbia. Her doctoral thesis, "(re)Defining the Page for a Digital World" (2004), has garnered prizes from the American Library Association and the University of Notre Dame. Currently she serves on the Committee for Electronic Resources of the Medieval Academy of America.

THOMAS MANN has been a reference librarian in the Main Reading Room of the Library of Congress for twenty-five years. He received his PhD from Loyola University of Chicago and his MLS from Louisiana State University. A former private investigator, he is the author of *The Oxford Guide to Library Research* (3rd ed.; 2005) and *Library Research Models* (1993), as well as numerous articles in professional library journals and on the AFSCME 2910 web site (www.guild2910.org).

LYNNE (E.F.) MCKECHNIE is an associate professor in FIMS and the Beverly Cleary Professor (Visiting) in children's literature and libraries at the Information School at the University of Washington. She teaches in the area of literature and library services for children. She is also editor of the *Canadian Journal of Information & Library Science*.

PAMELA J. MCKENZIE is an associate professor in the Faculty of Information and Media Studies, The University of Western Ontario. Her research focuses on the ways that information needs, seeking, and use are collaboratively constructed by individuals in local settings. Her current research seeks to understand the information work of unpaid caregivers and of the professionals who serve them.

ADAM L. MURRAY, MLIS, is currently the head of acquisitions at Murray State University. He received his undergraduate degree from the University of North Carolina at Wilmington, and his MLIS from the University of North Carolina at Greensboro. This is his third collaboration with Julia Hersberger, with whom he has researched the information needs of stigmatized populations.

ELENA M. PRIGODA is a recent graduate from the MLIS program at the University of Western Ontario. As an undergraduate in zoology she published on the varying meanings attributed to specific zoological terminology. Currently she is conducting an evaluation of the effectiveness of informatics education for medical undergraduates and is leading a pilot project on the use of instant messaging in reference service. She holds a full-time appointment as an Instruction & Liaison Librarian at the Gerstein Science Information Centre, University of Toronto Libraries.

PAULETTE ROTHBAUER is a member of the Faculty of Information Studies at University of Toronto. She has a PhD in LIS from the Faculty of Information & Media Studies at the University of Western Ontario. Her thesis, "Finding and Creating Possibility: Reading in the Lives of Lesbian, Bisexual and Queer Young Women" was recognized with the 2005 Eugene Garfield/ALISE Doctoral Dissertation award. She is co-author of the recent publication, *Reading Matters: What the Research Reveals about Reading, Libraries, and Community* (Libraries Unlimited, 2006).

MATTHEW L. SAXTON is an assistant professor in the University of Washington Information School. His primary research interest is in question-answering behavior, intermediation, and the evaluation of information services. His book, *Understanding Reference Transactions*, used hierarchical linear modeling to investigate the factors that contribute to success in responding to reference questions in public libraries. He received the 1997 Methodology Award from the Association of Library and Information Science Educators. He earned a PhD in Library and Information Science from the University of California, Los Angeles.

LOU SUA, MLIS, formerly served as branch manager of the Vance H. Chavis Lifelong Learning Branch Library in the Greensboro Public Library System. The Chavis Branch is the newer iteration of the Carnegie Negro Library. Currently she is the media specialist at Peck Elementary School in Greensboro and is working on a PhD in the Department of Educational Leadership and Cultural Foundations at the University of North Carolina at Greensboro. She obtained her MLIS degree from the Department of Library and Information Studies also at UNCG.

RONALD TETREAULT is professor of English at Dalhousie University in Halifax, Nova Scotia, Canada. He is the author of *The Poetry of Life: Shelley and Literary Form* (1987) and co-editor of *Lyrical Ballads: An Electronic Scholarly Edition* (2003). An interest in rare books and textual transmission has taken him through digital media back to the history of print culture. His current research focuses on the growth of circulating and subscription libraries from 1815 to 1848 and their role in the dissemination of British literature.

ABIGAIL VAN SLYCK holds the Dayton Chair in art history at Connecticut College, where she also directs the architectural studies program. Having earned a PhD in architecture at the University of California at Berkeley, she has published extensively on the history of library architecture, including *Free to All: Carnegie Libraries and American Culture, 1890–1920* (1995). Her most recent book is *A Manufactured Wilderness: Summer Camps and the Shaping of American Youth, 1890–1960* (2006). For the Lyman Allyn Art Museum, she served as guest curator for "Commerce and Culture: Architecture and Society on New London's State Street," an exhibition that received awards of merit from the Connecticut Humanities Council, the Connecticut League of History Organizations, and the American Association for State and Local History.